Representing Scotland in Literature, Popular Culture and Iconography

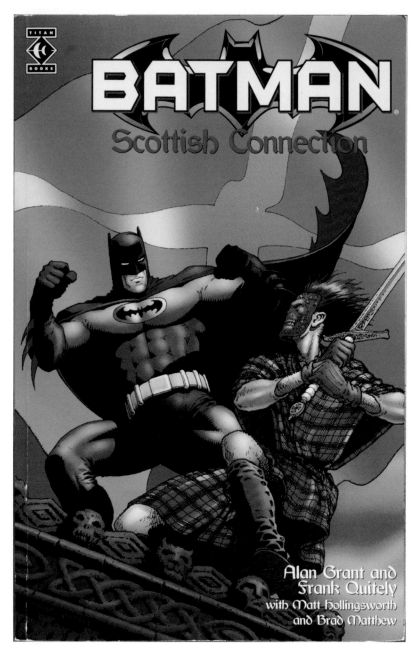

Representing Scotland in Literature, Popular Culture and Iconography

The Masks of the Modern Nation

Alan Riach

First published 2005 by
PALGRAVE MACMILLAN
Houndmills, Basingstoke, Hampshire RG21 6XS and
175 Fifth Avenue, New York, N.Y. 10010
Companies and representatives throughout the world

PALGRAVE MACMILLAN is the global academic imprint of the Palgrave Macmillan division of St. Martin's Press, LLC and of Palgrave Macmillan Ltd. Macmillan® is a registered trademark in the United States, United Kingdom and other countries. Palgrave is a registered trademark in the European Union and other countries.

ISBN 1–4039–4591–8 hardback

This book is printed on paper suitable for recycling and made from fully managed and sustained forest sources.

A catalogue record for this book is available from the British Library.

Library of Congress Cataloging-in-Publication Data
Riach, Alan, 1957–
    Representing Scotland in literature, popular culture and iconography : the masks of the modern nation / Alan Riach.
        p.   cm.
    Includes bibliographical references and index.
    ISBN 1–4039–4591–8
    1. Scottish literature—History and criticism.   2. National characteristics, Scottish, in literature.   3. Nationalism and literature—Scotland.   4. Popular culture—Scotland.   5. Scotland—In literature.   6. Scotland—In mass media.   7. Scotland—In art.   I. Title.

PR8518.R53 2004
820.9'32411—dc22

2004054897

10   9   8   7   6   5   4   3   2   1
14   13   12   11   10   09   08   07   06   05

Printed and bound in Great Britain by
Antony Rowe Ltd, Chippenham and Eastbourne

For Rae

Contents

List of Illustrations

Frontispiece: Frank Quitely (artist) and Matt Hollingsworth and Brad Matthew (Computer Colorists), *Batman: Scottish Connection* (front cover) © 1998 DC Comics

Acknowledgements

Some of the work gathered in this book appeared in earlier forms in various journals, in the form of conference papers, in discussions with individuals and in classes at universities in New Zealand, Scotland and elsewhere. I am grateful to the editors of the following periodicals: *Studies in Scottish Literature* (South Carolina, USA), *Scotia Pacific* (New Zealand), *Children's Literature in Education* (New York) and the *Scottish Literary Journal*; and to Dr John Jowett and Professor Russell Jackson of the Shakespeare Institute, Stratford-upon-Avon, for inviting me to deliver the paper on Shakespeare and Scotland at the heart of professional Shakespeare scholarship in 2002. A revised version of it was delivered at the University of Helsinki in 2004 and I am grateful to colleagues there for their invitation and comment.

An earlier version of the chapter 'Nobody's Children' appeared in *Studies in Scottish Fiction: 1945 to the Present*, ed. Susanne Hagemann (1996); and some parts of 'The International Brigade: Scotland and the Modern Movement' first appeared in my 'Introduction' to *Contemporary Scottish Studies*, ed. Hugh MacDiarmid (1996); parts of Chapter 6 dealing with Wilson Harris appeared in 'The Scottish Element in *Black Marsden*', in *Wilson Harris: The Uncompromising Imagination*, ed. Hena Maes-Jelinek (1991).

The library staff who have helped me with this book were exemplary and I am grateful to many individuals who have made the following institutions shine: the Scottish Music Information Library (Glasgow); the Scottish Poetry Library (Edinburgh); the Mitchell Library (Glasgow); Glasgow University Library; the National Library of Scotland (Edinburgh); Edinburgh University Library; the University of Waikato Library, Hamilton, New Zealand; the National Library of New Zealand, Wellington. And the institutions where I discussed some of the ideas in this book were professionally welcoming to the wandering scholarship the book pulls together, far apart as they are, from the University of Waikato (New Zealand) and the National University of Samoa, Western Samoa, to the Free University of Amsterdam and the University of Glasgow.

Finally, there are individuals, scholars, friends and family without whom the book would never have been delivered. Among many, I must especially thank Marshall Walker, Edwin Morgan, Jan Pilditch, Douglas Gifford, John Caughie, James Achison, Bruce King, Brian Davies; I owe particular debts to Angus Calder, Alexander Broadie, John Purser and the reader for Palgrave Macmillan, who offered a number of very shrewd comments and helpful suggestions, and to my parents Captain and Mrs J.A. Riach, and my wife Rae and the family my wife comes from. The opportunity to occupy more than one world seems more possible now than ever before, but it comes at a cost. This book is partial repayment and I hope its dedication acknowledges this freely.

I expect at least nine-tenths of today's crop – an estimate from past averages – to embarrass me tomorrow, and I know that a still higher percentage will not survive my 'better judgement' for as long as a month. Whereas the relatively weatherable leftovers are largely concerned with matters of negligible consequence, moreover, the loudest howlers ('Beethoven lacks melody'; 'Falstaff is corrupted by Wagnerism'), following the bad-penny principle, are impossible to lose. Then why bother, when silence can keep me from being wrong and foolish? Because the mistakes and embarrassments do not count compared to even a single minor accident of truth, provisional and hypothetical as it would have to be, that could occur.

– *Igor Stravinsky*, Themes and Conclusions

Preface: The Representation of the People

It neither was the words nor yet the tune ...
It was the singing.
It was the human sweetness in that yellow,
the unpredicted voices of our kind.

– Iain Crichton Smith, 1992

This is a book about cultural change and continuities, underpinned by the sense that because of a particular national history, the cultural production of Scotland has been weighted gravitationally towards a democratic idea of what 'the popular' – and what people – might be.

This might be described in these terms: There is general tendency in Scotland to accept specialisms as open to serious approach, rather than closed off by the hermetic jargon of the specialists themselves and other more physical exclusiveness. Aspects of this tendency can be found in 'Common Sense' philosophy and are rooted in the contradictions and complementarities of the Enlightenment and the Romantic era in Scottish culture. Their working-out and further developments in the generalist principles of Scotland's tertiary education in the nineteenth century are elaborated in George Davie's seminal book, *The Democratic Intellect* (1961). It's worth noting the significance of the title Davie gave to the sequel, about Scottish universities in the twentieth century – *The Crisis of the Democratic Intellect* (1986), in which he considers the increasing pressure to move away from the generalist, democratic base.[1] This general cultural tendency connects all specialisms with a social world of egalitarian possibility.

While this generalisation might be described as mythic it also reflects a deep idealism that might pull gravitationally towards attitudes reflected in cultural production in a variety of ways. Myth, desire and actuality are never entirely several. Hugh MacDiarmid sketches the implications lightly and clearly:

> I never set een on a lad or a lass
> But I wonder gin he or she
> Wi' a word or a deed 'll suddenly dae
> An' impossibility.[2]

But there is another side to this manger-faith, typical of a crude, reductive irony, such as the once-popular Scots saying, 'I kent his faither' (implying, 'I knew the boy's father and he amounted to nothing, so I can assure you that the child won't amount to anything either'); or, as Alexander Scott puts it in his two-line poem 'Scotch Equality':

Kaa the feet frae
Thon big bastard.[3]

The tendency to democratic ideals rests on a crucial respect for education as a birthright and a sympathy with the common human needs and the unpredictable potential any individual has. This sense is what rescues Iain Crichton Smith's poem, 'Two Girls Singing' from which my epigraph is taken, from merely offering thankful recognition of familiar 'voices of our kind'. The voices he hears are not only recognisably akin to his – and by non-exclusive extension, our own – but also 'unpredicted'. Their surprise is a distinction as important as their affinity. That is what the poem challenges us to feel kinship with: a kind of unpredictability.

The political context in which these poems are written and on which they comment is continual. It involves daily and pragmatic politics as well as speculation about potential and the enactment of unpredicted possibility. Its tension is in the conflict or balance between, on the one hand, a recognised need for change – sometimes radical change, in social, material and psychological terms – and, on the other hand, the desire to preserve and foster continuities through comprehension and regeneration.

Crucially, this requires popular understanding being geared towards an immediate recognition of certain symbols or cultural icons which offer the comfort of stability and the reassurance of conservative continuities across time and especially through times of political upheaval. These icons can serve more than one political purpose, from reactionary conservatism to progressive futurism, and Scotland is peculiarly rich in them.

The Nigerian writer Ben Okri once described a visit to Scotland in terms which might lead one to wonder how profitably his own nightmarish visions in the short stories of *Incidents at the Shrine*, in his novel *The Famished Road* and elsewhere might be read through lenses made in Scotland. In a 'Diary' column for the British periodical *New Statesman* in 1986, Okri described a visit to Scotland in these terms:

It is another country. The air is sharper. The hills, stark in their solidity, sheer out in the lights. It is a country in which history breathes from the landscapes. My first impression of Edinburgh was of staircases which seemed to have been carved on boulders and cobbled streets which reminded me of secret courtyards in Paris and the South of France. It is a city of the imagination in which dwelled another city of frustrated yearnings. It is impossible to miss the contrast between the architecture of the castles, magnificent and incantatory, and the strange restrained air of the people. I couldn't perceive the connection between the spirits of those who built the castles and those who reside in the city...It is the only city I know where the old resides so solidly in the new, where the music of the place blasts out its ancient lore amid the living spaces of the inhabitants.

Okri concluded that while culture, 'during a time of political impotence, can become kitsch, it can also function as continual declaration and resistance'.[4]

Okri's volume of short stories, *Stars of the New Curfew* (1988) opens with an epigraph by Christopher Okigbo which resonates as powerfully in Scotland as in Nigeria:

> We carry in our worlds that flourish
> our worlds that have failed[5]

This truth might apply to popular culture and mass media productions as well as to more specialised art forms, and the energy it describes is perhaps the deepest resource of all the arts. Those 'frustrated yearnings' Ben Okri notes are motivational forces in all art, across media, geography and time, just as Okri's visions of social squalor and human degradation, whether in post-Civil War Nigeria or the Britain of the 1980s, where a ruthless Conservative government oversaw urban and industrial collapse, might be considered as imaginative cousins of the fictions of Alasdair Gray and James Kelman, which came to prominence in the same period. Okri's understanding that while culture in a period of political impotence might become kitsch, it can also function as resistance is crucial, and we shall return to it.

Kitsch may be an advantage but it is also a liability. The advantage is that there are instant and reliable icons and codes of recognition, both within the country and internationally. Teaching Scottish literature in New Zealand, as I did for fourteen years, students' answers to the question, 'What do you think of when you think of Scotland?', were always dependable: tartan, haggis, whisky, heather, wild mountain scenery and bad weather. Robbie Burns, Billy Connolly and the television series *Taggart* would come up regularly. There was comfort and humour in the familiarity of these answers but there was also a sense that such stereotypical images and icons were constricting. They can severely limit understanding. Yet they might be approached in certain ways and contextualised with purpose. This need not deny the pleasure they afford, but it should help us to remember that by itself, pleasure can serve any political principle.

The representation of Scotland in popular terms has its own pleasures and tediums. Much of it derives ultimately from the literary representation of the country in popular versions of Burns – the 'ploughman poet' as he was described by Henry Mackenzie – and Scott, whose writings helped activate the spectacle of Scotland as landscape. To consider this leads from literary production to popular reception and international accommodation of it, and to the reconfiguring or refashioning of literary work in other forms – painting and music (the landscapes of Horatio McCulloch or the orchestral or operatic works of Hamish MacCunn and the tone poems of William Wallace and John Blackwood McEwen, for example). Since the 1950s, many of the iconic representations of Scotland have been conveyed through the technologies of other media: postcards, audio recordings, radio, television and film. *Representing Scotland* is predominantly a book of literary study, but in following a chronological trajectory, we cannot but remark on the technological changes which have made storytelling possible in different ways.

Part I begins by discussing the terms, if not defining them: masks, popular culture, iconography, modernity and nationality. I want to use these terms to approach my subjects, not to extrapolate floating theories, and the central focus of the book is on literary texts. There are chapters specifically on canonical works such as Walter Scott's *The Heart of Midlothian* and Robert Louis Stevenson's *Treasure Island*. But there is a larger context for these close studies.

The opening thesis is that the foundations of modern Scottish literature are to be found in the changes that happen in the period between the work of Burns and that of Scott, and that these changes are crystallised in understanding what the word 'popular' means from the late eighteenth to the early nineteenth centuries.

Burns's songs, satires and poems were popular among farmers' labourers, illiterate people, men and women; they were also popular with the highly educated literati, first in Edinburgh, where Burns was lionised, caricatured and almost smothered by the Establishment, and then internationally. They were – and continue to be – memorised and carried in the minds and on the voices of people who quote or recite them or, most importantly, sing them for pleasure, for themselves, among company and to others. Something changes, however, between the act of singing for one's own pleasure, alone or in the shared pleasure of company, and the performance of a song which is addressed and projected to other listeners. A different focus concentrates and directs particular effort. There is a transition between Burns's works as popular property and the value of the printed versions of them. Such differences continue to co-exist. People still sing the songs while first printings of the Kilmarnock edition are auctioned and locked up.

After Burns's death, the increasingly popular appeal among the print-reading public was shifting from long narrative poems to the novel. The burning trajectory of Byron goes down beneath the galvanising accumulations of prose heaped up by Walter Scott. Scott's novels, while they redefine genre expectations and deepen narrative structures that remain foundational, are a vast attempt to accommodate everything their author could detail. Their effort is towards immense inclusiveness, both in narrative accommodation and in the amassment of antiquarian detail. And yet it is clear that the deep structures are often easily described and memorably simple. They activate familiar conventions. Let me offer a few examples.

There is the convention of doubled heroes. Scott's are familiarly passive/active, Hanoverian/Jacobite, politically futurist/politically doomed, practical/romantic and so on; but once activated, the convention evolves. Later examples after Scott range from Long John Silver and Jim Hawkins to Sherlock Holmes and Doctor Watson. The prototype may have been Don Quixote and Sancho Panza but Scott's elaborations were crucial.

Then there is the convention of panoramic landscapes, inviting spectacle, ownership, land-speculation, property, tourism, subjection of native populations and the privileging of class over clan. This convention travels in cultural terms from novel to film. Could John Ford's Monument Valley landscapes be read as an interpretation of the relationship between people and landscape that derives specifically from Scott? Scott's forests, precipices and waterfalls become Ford's desert plains and high escarpments, dwarfing people and their cultural differences with their geological scale. (We shall consider the relation between Scott and the western genre in Chapter 8.)

Scotland also makes its particular contribution to the universal convention of the journey, hurried yet often pedestrian, like the long march of Waverley or Jeanie Deans's southward trek to the seat of earthly authority in London. This convention has its dynamic legacies through David Balfour and Alan Breck Stewart in Stevenson's *Kidnapped* to Richard Hannay in John Buchan's *The Thirty-Nine Steps*, to Ian Fleming's James Bond's international secret missions, and the endless number of films predicated on the breathless spectacle of the chase. (The most perfectly balanced example is the film version of Fleming's *On Her Majesty's Secret Service*, where Bond spends the first half of the movie tracking down his arch-enemy Blofeld, then the second half running away from him.) Of course, the degree of self-consciousness and irony we might discern in these later representations is variable.

The structures may be clear – and universal enough not to be limited to a specifically Scottish source – but the popular international readership for Scott was phenomenal and the influence of his activation of these cultural conventions remains incalculable. More than that, however, his accumulating *ouevre* continued throughout his life in an attempt not only to honourably discharge commercial debt but also to bring into his world of fiction the broadest possible spectrum of human beings his culture would allow him to contemplate and treat. For generations of young readers, in the late nineteenth and early twentieth centuries, Scott's comprehensive understanding of humanity was considered parallel with Shakespeare's – and when big, broadly sweeping novels were more attractive than knottily plotted, linguistically voracious, chunkily laid-out narrative plays, Scott was often preferable. Of course, critical as well as social conventions have changed that, and there is more than fashion involved in these changes.

At the axis of the era of Burns and Scott were the French and American Revolutions. The relation of the English Romantic poets to the revolution in Europe has been studied in depth, but much remains to be understood about those Scots writers who, through upbringing, society and recent history, were brought into a different relationship with these moments of radical social change, with all their democratic ideals and bloody realities. The shift in the weight of meaning in the word 'popular' through the crisis of 1789 is axial. This book will only indicate a little of that. What I would like to highlight here, though, is the critical importance of the conflicts, contradictions and tensions in this era and its consequences for modern Scottish literature. (Space does not permit me to do more than note that there are significant parallels and contrasts with the devlopment of Irish literature over the same period, although much more work has been done with Irish than with Scottish literature.)

The importance of this shift in the idea of the 'popular' can be seen in the ways some of the icons and characteristic aspects of Scotland – Scotland's masks – have been deployed, developed and transformed through the nineteenth and twentieth centuries. Therefore the book tells a chronological story, but it slips from one location to another, from one genre to another, and from writing intended for a mass readership to more esoteric work of specialist interest which nevertheless clearly bears out the characteristic aspect of human commonality and 'the democratic intellect'. It is concerned with works of Scottish literature and Scottish cultural production both in their own right and in their inter-action with non-Scottish works.

Before we begin that, however, it is important to go back to an earlier moment, the first crucial moment in the creation of modern Scotland and modern Britain: 1603.

This is a convenient date but of course its convenience may be misleading: the Reformation in Scotland, especially from the 1560s, began to establish principles of egalitarianism which underpinned the development of Renaissance individualism and might be connected further back to the ideals of representative authority signalled in the Declaration of Arbroath in 1320. Yet 1603 is a pivotal year in any description of the development of modernity.

Shakespeare's centrality and quality in literary history seem crucially dependent on three concurrent dynamics: the centrality of London as city and economic crux, the function and action of the theatre in that city, and the radical transition from the late medieval to the early modern world, a transition marked by the end of the Elizabethan and the beginning of the Jacobean age, literally the death of Elizabeth I and the accession of James VI as James I to the rather abruptly united kingdom or, more precisely, kingdoms. (It is worth noting that in *King Lear*, 'the division of the kingdom' in the Folio text is 'the division of the kingdoms' in the Quarto.) The effects these three things had on Shakespeare's writing range from banal intentionality, as *Macbeth* is pitched as flattery and (most importantly) legitimation, to subtle enquiry, for example, into the question of what Britain is, in *Cymbeline*. The accession of James also permits Shakespeare to explore tragedy to its fullest extent in public. Would Queen Elizabeth have allowed the great tragedies such public provenance?

An opening chapter on 'Shakespeare and Scotland' begins with a consideration of Shakespeare's representation of Scots characters in the history plays; it then notes how 'The Scottish Play' – which, because of its disregard for the internal dynamics of Scottish national history and commitment to its own moment, may be more accurately termed 'The English Play' – is central in the tragedies' depiction of human potential at its worst; but it is most concerned with the late plays. How is Shakespeare's re-visioning of the matter of Britain in *Cymbeline* intended to resolve national conflicts within the newly united kingdom? And more intimately perhaps, in *The Tempest*, if Prospero recovers imperial authority and asserts dynastic succession as the central arbiter of power and justice in terms of his own position as head of family and state, what of that other gauge of the limits of human identity in which Prospero is centred, between Caliban and Ariel? Caliban is on the extremest edge of servility and Ariel on the furthest limit before freedom, one inseparable from nativity and earth, the other always urging towards flight and sky, one surly and rebellious, the other complicit and collaborative with Prospero's central authority. As we shall see, Willy Maley has suggested that Caliban and Ariel are representations of, respectively, Ireland and Scotland. As caricatures they may well have been increasingly recognisable as what they represented became distorted and established for later generations than Shakespeare's. I think one problem Shakespeare's play poses now is how far we can trust the centralising structure of the relationships between Prospero, Ariel and Caliban. How far must we acquiesce to the centrality of Prospero's authority? The chapter concludes by looking at a number of twentieth-century poems, most famously Rilke's 'The Spirit Ariel' but then also poems by Norman MacCaig and Edwin Morgan, which address this problem and resolve it in more fully human terms, beyond the reach of caricature.

Having suggested the ways in which the terms of iconographic representation of Scots (and Irish) national types are foreshadowed in Shakespeare's plays, we can discuss the foundational texts of modern Scottish literature in the era of Enlightenment and Romanticism with this 'long perspective' in mind. Conventional chronology separates these movements in sequence, but the Scottish example tells a more complex story, exemplified in the multiple contradictions between James Macpherson, David Hume, Robert Fergusson, Samuel Johnson, Henry Mackenzie, Robert Burns and Walter Scott.

Part I of the book, then, is an exploration of the historical forces that helped give rise to modern Scottish literature and the complex arguments that lie within it. Part II follows a more conventional form, beginning with a case-study of Scott's great novel *The Heart of Midlothian*, centred on the strange exclusiveness which haunts the comprehensive vision of this romantic-individualist man of enlightenment. This is the story of The Whistler, who is finally sent by Scott to the wilds of America, a piece of 'surplus population' like Mary Shelley's Frankenstein's monster, with whom he is associated.

Perhaps the most exceptional canonical author in the mainstream tradition is Robert Louis Stevenson: unmistakably Scottish yet coloured and flamboyant by Francophile flair, and given to international voyaging, across America and into the Pacific. My chapter on Stevenson focuses on *Treasure Island* as a text whose responsibility to childhood is seen in its subversive, pleasurable enactment of adult recognition and stability coming through the child's sense of appetite, movement and quickness. The understanding it offers is deeper than fixed or static images allow: Long John Silver is slippery, quick-silvery, attractive but murderous, and Jim is a wee boy who has to grow up. Imperial certainties and childhood's prerogative to remake the world, to make it new, are in a wonderfully packed conflict of energies in *Treasure Island*. The resolutions affect our sense of what children's literature has been and might be, and of what 'adult literature' must not forget and should never abandon or maroon.

Children's literature as a genre is a crucial axis at the end of the nineteenth century as so much Scottish (and American) writing seems appropriate to it: Stevenson, but also Melville, Scott, Fenimore Cooper, R.M. Ballantyne, J.M. Barrie and Andrew Lang. The close relation of Scottish and American literature at this point seems partly to do with the assumption of adult adjudication by the authority of English literature and English literary judgement (Prospero's books once again). I would like to suggest a way to bridge the distance between the pre-World War I era of late British imperialism and the post-colonial era after the Second World War, from Conan Doyle's *The Lost World* of 1912 to Amos Tutuola's *The Palm-Wine Drinkard* of 1952, a stunning little book quickly recognised as a herald of new writing in indigenous adaptations of the English language from formerly colonised countries. Dylan Thomas and Hugh MacDiarmid both leapt to praise it in the 1950s.

Conan Doyle's book emerges from a world demonstrably racist, sexist and imperialist. He was in 1912 very much the grand old man of empire whose benevolence grew strongly out of imperial history. What redeems his writing from pathological imperialist absolutism or from being merely symptomatic of imperialist presumption is a quality of vision and a recognition of imaginative continuity which, I will argue, links him with Tutuola and 'post-colonial' writers. Through a habitation of the exotic-imaginary worlds of childhood and dream we might invigorate our sense of what is possible in reality. Doyle is masterful in this exercise of the imaginary and Tutuola pushes us forward with it, into the later twentieth century, where this capacity for regeneration and continuity is increasingly desperately needed. The fiction of Wilson Harris and especially his Scottish novel *Black Marsden* suggests the ways in which the Scottish imagination and a post-imperial world of multiple and seemingly discordant identities can be co-ordinated.

Part III begins by returning to Scotland in the wake of the First World War with the writers, artists and intellectuals who began to work coherently towards a political and cultural revival and reassertion of Scotland in the international theatre of the arts. They arrived from the theatre of war and wilfully entered a cultural arena in which matters of value had to be sifted from the establishment's sanctioned sentimentalism and jingoism.

The attempt had been begun in the 1890s and early twentieth century, with writers such as Stevenson, John Davidson and James Thomson addressing Scotland's darker aspects seriously. A cultural revival had been announced by Patrick Geddes in terms of a 'Scottish Renascence' [*sic*]. In music and painting as well as literature, important work was redressing the easy clichés. The benevolent ministrations of the Kailyard writers – Ian Maclaren and S.R. Crockett – were confronted by the vicious commercialism of small-town Scotland depicted in John Macdougall Hay's *Gillespie* and George Douglas Brown's *The House with the Green Shutters*. In the latter, the merciful God who benignly presides over small-town Scotland in J.M. Barrie's Thrums or Maclaren's Drumtochty, is confronted by John Gourlay's dying widow, handing back her ticket: 'Mrs Gourlay raised her arms, like a gaunt sibyl, and spoke to her Maker quietly, as if He were a man before her in the room. "Ruin and murder," she said slowly, "and madness; and death at my nipple like a child! When will Ye be satisfied?"'[6]

The work of painters, composers, artists of various kinds was also pushing deeply towards new forms of expression. However, it was not until after the First World War that the attempt to create an artistic Renaissance in Scottish literature, music and art developed effectively in a coherent and politically dynamic way. Pre-eminently active in this campaign was Christopher Murray Grieve, journalist, polemicist and poet, whose writing as Hugh MacDiarmid became notorious by the 1930s. In the 1920s, his attack on the establishment heralded this Scottish Renaissance, an activation of national cultural awareness – what he called a 'propaganda of ideas'. It was an attempt to demolish the weight of convention suffocating creativity in the adoration of Burns, political obsequy to outmoded Anglocentrism and moral piety. His association with the popular novelist Compton Mackenzie, the painters and sculptors William McCance and William Johnstone, and the composers F.G. Scott and Ronald Stevenson suggests the marshalling of energy across all the arts. From the first, it involved pragmatic politics. Liberationist and radical in intent, he was, in Norman MacCaig's words, 'a torchlight procession of one' – creating an army of pseudonyms, many of whom fell for the cause.

It is attractive to see MacDiarmid as unique, but in the longer view of this book, I would like to emphasise that his work draws on important initiatives of the late nineteenth century, in painting and music as well as literature, and how in its openness to all forms of cultural expression, it points forward to the increasing diversity of technological opportunities for cultural production available in the twenty-first century. Moreover, in an increasingly international (or 'globalised') context, Scotland's masks are made not only by exiles from the country, but also by visitors to the country, bringing fresh vision and new perspectives. The chapter on Scotland and the Modern Movement therefore focuses on the significant internationalism the Scottish Renaissance emphasised and discusses a number of international writers: exiles, travellers and visitors.

In 1964, in the Kinross and West Perthshire constituency, MacDiarmid fought against the then Prime Minister, Sir Alec Douglas Home, in the general election. Douglas Home, Conservative, was returned with 16,659 votes. MacDiarmid, Communist, got 127. Douglas Home was then taken to court on the grounds that the election was invalid since broadcasting time on radio and television had not been shared equally between the big parties and the smaller ones. MacDiarmid gave his opinion that if he had been allowed to broadcast and put the Communist case he would have secured more votes. He lost the case, but the essential question of the extent to which public broadcasting media were 'keyed to the requirements of the Establishment' and 'deliberately intended to hamper the activities and prospects of minor parties' remains. In his petition, MacDiarmid accused Douglas Home of '"corrupt and illegal practices" under the Representation of the People Act, 1949'.[7]

In consequence of this, the variety of technological languages available after the Second World War might be seen coherently or, at least, interconnectedly. *Representing Scotland* comes forward to a conclusion with studies of generically popular forms charting the post-war American influence and the ways native writers have 'colonised in reverse' assumptions of cultural superiority with increasing confidence and wit. In Bud Neill's cartoon comic strip 'Lobey Dosser' serialised in the Glasgow *Evening Times* in the 1940s and 1950s, the conventions of contemporary cowboy movies are transmuted into the social mores and habits of a West of Scotland community with hilarious consequences. (The Lobey Dosser statue was erected in Glasgow by public subscription on 1 May 1992 in memory of Neill, and remains the only known two-legged equestrian statue in the world.) Neill's example is singular, but the James Bond story running from the 1950s, 1960s and 1970s through to the twenty-first century is an international phenomenon, in which the Scottish identity of the hero is quintessentially important in the 1960s. The comic-books or 'graphic novels' serialised as *The Bogey Man* in the 1990s thoroughly revise American models from the native perspective. Their premise is an immediately sympathetic recognition of the mental derangement of Francis Forbes Clunie, who escapes from an asylum near Glasgow convinced that he is in fact a series of characters played by Humphrey Bogart in films of the 1940s and 1950s. Everyone who has seen a Hollywood film will recognise the attractiveness of the proposition of identifying with the hero and structuring the world imaginatively from given premises supplied by American certainties. Alan Grant, the author of *The Bogey Man*, exploits the pleasures of the milieux, but subversively redresses assumptions of cultural authority implicit in previous examples of them.

A similar story of cultural reappropriation can be seen in other media. In cinema and television, depictions of Scotland appear in different guises – Jacobite romance, urban cityscape, the documentary tradition – all embodying the counterpoint, dialogue or conflict between realism and the exotic imaginary: from Clydeside shipbuilders to *Brigadoon*, from *The Cheviot, the Stag and the Black, Black Oil* to *Edge of Darkness*, from *Braveheart* to *Trainspotting*. The iconography of comic books is brought into focus again with visits made to Scotland by the secret agent Nick Fury and two of the West's most popular superheroes, Spider-Man in 1990 and Batman in 1997 and 1998.

The cultural energies that animate the masks of Scotland are vividly palpable in the post-war world. In a nation whose statehood has become imaginable again for the first time in 300 years, this book is intended to remind ourselves that what is wanted is an economy that allows us to sustain those energies and give forms to their animation, and to help ourselves speak more clearly in what Wilson Harris calls 'a theatre of infinity'.[8]

The concluding discussion brings us back to questions about change and the canon, language and voice, continuities, cultural colonisation and forms of resistance, closing with a consideration of visual imagery in a series of depictions of Scottish figures – from Sir Edwin Landseer's *The Monarch of the Glen* to Peter Howson's *Heroic Dosser*, a defiant symbol of individual self-determination in the viciously antisocial world of Thatcherite homelessness. But the argument follows through to question whether, from the kitsch of Victorian tartanry to contemporary manifestations of the same iconography, the seeds of insight and ideological disruption might be found even within worlds that seem utterly foreclosed.

Notes

1. George Davie, *The Democratic Intellect* (Edinburgh University Press, 1961); *The Crisis of the Democratic Intellect* (Edinburgh: Polygon, 1986).
2. Hugh MacDiarmid, *Complete Poems*, 2 vols, eds Michael Grieve and W.R. Aitken (Manchester: Carcanet Press,1993–1994), Vol. 1, p. 258.
3. Alexander Scott, 'Scotched', in *The Collected Poems*, ed. David S. Robb (Edinburgh: The Mercat Press, 1994), pp. 229–233 (p. 230).
4. Ben Okri, 'Diary', *New Statesman*, Vol. 112, No. 2889 (8 August 1986), p. 16.

5. Ben Okri, *Stars of the New Curfew* (Harmondsworth: Penguin Books, 1988), p. vii. The source is Christopher Okigbo, 'Lament of the Silent Sisters', III, in *Labyrinths with Path of Thunder* (London: Heinemann, 1977), p. 41.

6. George Douglas Brown, *The House with the Green Shutters*, ed. Dorothy Porter (Harmondsworth: Penguin Books, 1985), p. 234 (Chapter xxvi).

7. Hugh MacDiarmid, 'My Election Contest', *Selected Prose*, ed. Alan Riach (Manchester: Carcanet, 1992), pp. 239–253.

8. Wilson Harris, *Black Marsden: A Tabula Rasa Comedy* (London: Faber & Faber, 1972).

Part I
The World of Things Undone

The world of things undone has far more matter
than this one...

                           – Edwin Morgan, *Virtual and Other Realities*

Part 4
The World of Things Undone

1

Introduction: The Terms of the Question

Because English is the international language of modernisation, the mask is also the modern world.

– T.J. Cribb[1]

Not despite the kitsch to which it is drawn is Mahler's music great, but because its construction unties the tongue of kitsch, unfetters the longing that is merely exploited by the commerce that the kitsch serves.

– Theodor W. Adorno[2]

Masks

The ancient Greek word for mask – *prosopon* – was the normal word for face or appearance or countenance, especially with emphasis on the features and the eyes: the *prosopon* revealed the identity of an individual in his or her relation to others. In her introduction to Colin Teevan's translation of Euripedes's *Bacchai*, Edith Hall insists that the word had none of the modern connotations of 'concealment or dissimulation' but indicated the *representation* of relations.

It is this sense of the word I hope to evoke by my title. I do not intend to suggest that various forms of Scottish cultural production conceal an essential, irreducible national identity, but rather that they present themselves as ways and forms in which relations are expressed and revealed, and that these change in history and through the creative use of different technologies. Masks may represent dissimulation or distortion but even while doing so they are in active dialogue and engagement. Edith Hall notes: 'In Greek myth and ritual the mask signifies change – it marks boundaries between one condition and another.' The mask of Dionysus constantly plays with disguises and transformations of the self, for Dionysus is the most protean and dangerous of the gods, erupting into public life 'a realm of being totally alien to the everyday world'. Euripedes's play and the god himself finally prove that 'human perceptions of reality are fundamentally unreliable and that the truth can sometimes be better discovered through the illusion available in the theatre than by strict empirical inspection of the observable world'. Dionysus 'subverts binary thinking, inverts all hierarchies and confounds all reason'.[3]

The texts we are going to look at might be read as completely separate instances, in studies centred on their author, period, genre or subjects. But I want to try to offer a more comprehensive approach by considering them each as aspects of Scottish self-representation: Scotland's masks. The theatrical and dramatic component here is paramount and paradoxical. It is paramount because masks (or social functions and roles, designated positions of authority) encourage us to be engaged, not to be silent, quiescent or passive, but to take part in a context of dynamic inter-relationships. It is paradoxical because, rich as Scotland's theatrical history is, after *Ane Satyre of the Thrie Estaits*, it is relatively weak in great plays: drama is the least developed of Scotland's literary genres. The primary reason for this was James VI's removal to London in 1603. There was no social basis for theatre until the eighteenth century. But there is another consideration: to risk a generalisation, the opposition to theatres enacted by church authorities involved a co-option of the function of theatre by the church itself. For generations, the regular public meeting-place for the dispersal of interpretation and opinion about social as well as religious matters, was the church. The pulpit presented a solo-performer, spotlit by God, and congregations enjoined vigorous debate following the regular sermons.

To suggest the theatricality of church conventions like this throws into hard light the development of two strands of secular theatre which, by the early twentieth century, stood distant from the church and from each other: that of the commercial music hall and that of politically overt drama. There is a vital overlap between them, but the three strands of moral force, racy entertainment and political commitment seemed cripplingly separated from each other until the 1970s, when the 7:84 Theatre Company re-united them in their touring production of *The Cheviot, the Stag and the Black, Black Oil*.

It's worth pausing on the separation of the elements that held sway in the nineteenth century. An excellent case-study would be the novel *Macleod of Dare*[4] by William Black (1841–1898), where the last of Lady Macleod's six sons, the titular hero, falls in love with a London actress. The whole novel unfolds the weary saga of their relationship, a sequence of prevarications, nervousnesses and vanities on her part, and yearnings, beseechments and finally black resolution on his. In the melodramatic ending, Macleod kidnaps his beloved and takes her to sea in suicidal passion. The last of the Macleods of Dare takes the actress Gerty down with him and their incompatibilities are resolved only in death. The novel hints at possible sentimental happy endings and takes a grand guignol delight in crushing them. It would warrant close study for its representation of a nineteenth-century independent woman, a Highland laird, and their respective inadequacies. The central contrast between them sets metropolitan duplicity, the comforts of the city and theatricality, against the austerities of neo-feudal Mull. The rigid structures of family and social loyalty in Scotland are in conflict with the dangerous flexibilities of the life of the theatre in London.

In *The Marquis of Lossie* (1877), a minor novel and the sequel to *Malcolm*, by the author of *Phantastes*, George MacDonald (1824–1905), there is a key scene that might be studied in the same context.[5] In Chapter 15, 'A Difference', the hero, Malcolm, decides to play a jape on his friend, Blue Peter. Malcolm 'knew well the prejudices of the greater portion of the Scots people against every possible form of artistic, most of all, dramatic, representation. He knew, therefore, also, that Peter would never be persuaded to go with him to the theatre: to invite him would be like asking him to call upon Beelzebub.' Yet finding that Shakespeare's *The Tempest* is playing in a theatre nearby, Malcolm guides his friend towards Drury Lane at the appropriate moment. Peter's comment is voluntary: 'This'll be ane o' them Lon'on kirks, I'm thinkin'?'

Peter assumes that there must be many 'guid fowk' in London to come in such numbers to church on a Saturday night and commends the way of taking up a collection which sees the theatregoers paying before entering the theatre, as 'I hae h'ard o' the plate bein' robbit in a muckle toon afore noo.' Peter is 'a little staggered at sight of the decorations', fears he might be in a Catholic establishment but reasons that Westminster is heavily decorated too, so even if episcopal, it is still likely to be a Protestant church. Peter is silently attentive through the opening of the play, identifying storm, shore and cave not as Shakespearian fiction but as a depiction of his native place. He seems to assume a personal application for whatever sermon is to follow. Only with the entrance of Ariel is the spell broken: 'With a look in which doubt wrestled with horror', Blue Peter turns to Malcolm and asks, 'it's no a play-hoose, this?' and when Malcolm nods, Peter groans and leaves.

Malcolm catches up with him and explains why he should take a different view from the majority of his countrymen: 'I hae h'ard in a kirk in ae ten meenutes jist a sicht o' what maun ha'e been sair displeasin' to the he'rt o' the maister o' 's a'; but that nicht [in the theatre] I saw nae ill and h'ard nae ill … The play-hoose is whaur ye gang to see what comes o' things 'at ye canna follow oot in ordinar' life.'

But Peter is not persuaded. Offended that his friend should have tricked him into a 'hoose o' iniquity' he resolves to leave London altogether. Malcolm complains that he did not even stay 'to see the thing out' but his remonstration assumes moral height with recourse to an English idiom – he abandons Scots vernacular speech. Peter's rejection at this point equates a common language with fair play, and Malcolm has departed from both: 'There ye are at yer English again! an' misgugglin' Scriptur' wi' 't! an' a' this upo' Setterday nicht – maist the Sawbath day! Weel, I ha'e aye heard 'at

Lon'on was an awfu' place, but I little thoucht the verra air o 't wad sae sune turn an honest laad like Ma'colm MacPhail intill a scoffer...I'm thinkin' it'll be aboot time for me to be gauin' hame.'
The conflict is unresolved. The two friends are reconciled later in the novel, and even by the end of the chapter, they part 'in mutual, though, with such men, it could not be more than superficial estrangement'. However, Malcolm's description of the value of the theatre and caution about the dangers of blind acceptance of church pronouncement remain unanswered. Despite MacDonald's description of Malcolm's 'Celtic' love of 'show', the understanding of what theatres and plays can do is soundly empirical, as is the complaint that Peter did not wait to see the whole thing through or give himself a fair opportunity to evaluate its worth. It is as if MacDonald himself leaves these questions in the air, an indictment unsettling the securities normally associated with the wisdom of the old friend and leaving Malcolm's intelligence increasingly lonely and alienated, thrown upon its own resources in the foreign city. The place of theatre in Scottish literary and social traditions is pointedly called into question here.

So is the place of the church. One further illustration, from the autobiography of the composer Sir Alexander Campbell Mackenzie, *A Musician's Narrative*.[6] Recollecting his family and friends from childhood in Edinburgh in the 1850s, Mackenzie writes,

> Keen musicians and busy men, the surreptitious pleasures of ensemble playing could only be indulged in on Sunday mornings during church hours in some friendly back drawing room. Such desecrations of the Sabbath being liable to be visited by the rigour of the law, the ire of landladies and neighbours, the fearful joy of quartet playing had frequently to be snatched in our house. On one occasion a sharp-eared policeman interrupted the harmony. 'But this is sacred music,' said my father, showing him a quartet by Haydn. Whether this undeniable fact, or the half-crown and a dram convinced the departing constable, remained purely a matter of conjecture.

For Mackenzie, whose finest works include the ravishing operatic oratorio *The Rose of Sharon* and the adaptation of Dickens's comic, poignant Christmas story 'The Cricket on the Hearth' (with its adult concerns with marital fidelity and sexual jealousy sharply expressed through a mask of pantomime playfulness), literature primarily meant Scott, Smollett and Dumas.[7] Mackenzie's love of dramatic flair and theatrical magic is wonderfully suggested:

> My first introduction to the region known as 'Behind' took place on an occasion when, in a fright at the sudden appearance of a strange animal cautiously creeping down a narrow staircase with a huge tail tucked under its arm, I timidly squeezed against the wall to let it pass.

'Don't be afraid; I'm only the cat!' a kindly voice assured me.
He who has forgotten his first pantomime gets no sympathy from me.[8]

But the social context for this richness of temperament and insight is unresolved in literary and theatrical terms. Scottish critical writing has been slow to comprehend and celebrate the relation between pantomime and adult understanding, or theatre and church.

In 1922, MacDiarmid noted that 'Scottish literature, like all other literatures, has been *written* almost exclusively by blasphemers, immoralists, dipsomaniacs, and madmen, but, unlike most other literatures, has been *written about* almost exclusively by ministers.'[9] The effect, MacDiarmid claimed, was critical response of the most platitudinous, banal and dulling kind, for example: ' "as a novelist, Robert Louis Stevenson had the art of rendering his writings interesting" and "his faculty of description was fairly good" '.[10] MacDiarmid wanted a more radical interpretative criticism to be developed in the 1920s. By the late twentieth century, it had arrived. The culture had radically altered.

The playwright Peter Arnott has made various helpful comments about this.[11] Born in 1962, Arnott recollects his childhood as initially influenced by cinema:

I'd be taken to every new Bond movie – apparently I saw *Dr No* when I was six months old. Most of my memories of childhood are media memories – the *Thunderbirds* and the Beatles are what are really vivid...
There was a disused quarry near the house where we'd play and everything I'd do was based on television series – on doing them, being the characters. But the games always had a storytelling element to them – I used to tell stories, using my friends as the characters, right up to an embarrassingly late age, and usually very violent.

At the University of Cambridge, Arnott recalls, 'it was acting which was a big influence: going into an environment in which theatre was so much more naturally part of the culture than in Scotland...'.

Arnott's experience may be representative of a generation in which mass screen media came to dominate popular cultural discourse, but the link to theatrical traditions is singularly important, both as it foreshadows Arnott's own development as a playwright and as it reflects on Scottish theatrical history. In the early 1980s, this was crystallised in social terms both in national and class-based conflict. Arnott returned to Glasgow in March 1984, the month the Miners' Strike started, and wrote *White Rose*, a play 'about people having to cope practically with the situation they were in and finding the resources of invention to deal with it...'. 'White Rose' was the name given to Lily Litvak, the famous Russian fighter pilot at the siege of Stalingrad during the Second World War: there was nothing *literally* descriptive of the Thatcher-governed United Kingdom in the play. Yet few original plays of the period address the necessity of finding ways to survive the destruction of socially inherited ways of life so forcefully.

The prospect for cultural production and political change in Scotland in the 1980s and 1990s seemed packed with a positive potential comparable to that of the 1920s or even to that of the foundational period of modern Scotland, in the late eighteenth and early nineteenth centuries. Whether or to what extent that potential can be realised continues to depend partly on our understanding of the masks Scotland has worn since its reinvention from the late medieval into the early modern world. This book will study a small selection of them.

Popular culture and modern Scotland

'Form is never more than an extension of content', Charles Olson wrote memorably in his influential essay of 1950, 'Projective Verse'.[12] But is it always and in any genre 'never more than'...? It may be more true of verse but it's surely difficult to maintain when one considers the limitations of content dictated by generic forms like the television police procedural serial, the children's novel or the popular comic book – the Batman or Spider-Man series, for instance.

The American poet Stephen Rodefer once remarked: 'The modern battlefield is dense with signals. Most of them will be decoys / to fool the other side.'[13] We are familiar with a world in which selectivity is at a premium. If the selection of texts I have made in this book is intended to represent certain aspects of the evolution of Scottish cultural production, then I should emphasise here that *Representing Scotland* is not and could not be comprehensive. Many major authors, important movements and shifts in social preference will be passed over in silence or mentioned only in passing. Among those most glaring will be the rise to prominence of writing by women, though my comments on Janice Galloway and A.L. Kennedy in the Conclusion might be read in a context of acknowledged resurgence in writing by women, about the experiences of women, which is a significant development in Scottish literature, especially after the 1960s, with precedents and traditions embodied in the work of Susan Ferrier, Margaret Oliphant, Catherine Carswell, Willa Muir, Jessie Kesson or Naomi Mitchison, for example; their writing has waited a long time for critical assessment and revaluation. Similarly, there is little attention paid in this book to literature in Gaelic or Gaelic popular culture, although I make full acknowledgement of the complexity of Scotland's linguistic fabric as far as I understand it. There is little but an acknowledgement of the increasing use of libraries in the nineteenth century, and those Victorian 'favourites' (novelists popularly borrowed from libraries), the popular urban fiction published serially in newspapers and recovered through research by William Donaldson in the 1980s; and there is only brief reference to the work of the folk revival fostered and encouraged by scholarly collectors and archivists such as Alan Lomax and Hamish Henderson. Many of these areas have their own specialists but I regret not having been able to include critical consideration of more neglected forms of cultural production which I believe are undervalued or under-discussed, such as radio drama, where the work of Iain Crichton Smith, Stewart Conn and John Purser would warrant discussion; or more generally on Scottish theatre or popular Scottish television programmes such as *Dr Finlay's Casebook* or *The White Heather Club*; or the significant overlap between the idioms of concert music and popular music embodied in Edward McGuire's work, for example in his opera for children and adults, *Peter Pan*; or in his compositions for orchestra and his performances with the group The Whistlebinkies; or phenomena of Scottish popular music from Andy Stewart through Kenneth McKellar and Moira Anderson to The Corries; or 'Celtic' music; or rock bands from Deacon Blue to Alex Harvey. I have said nothing about the major tradition of translation in Scottish literature, from Gavin Douglas through Sir Thomas Urquhart to Hugh MacDiarmid, Edwin Morgan and Liz Lochhead, and how this tradition has addressed the question of popular appeal by virtue not only of its representing work from a variety of languages, cultures and periods, but by doing so for as wide a readership or audience as possible, according to the technologies of the translators' times. And there are also forms of popular culture and mass media phenomena with which this book has nothing to do, such as architecture, cooking, church history or 'sport'.

However, what I will say in this book is sufficiently rich and varied. To help structure it, my organisation is simple but strong. There are two key contextualising moments in Scottish history: the Union of the Crowns in 1603 and the Union of the Parliaments in 1707. The first is Shakespeare's time. It was once remarked, in a university English department, that Shakespeare was the real torso, the centre of English studies – everything else mere limbs and appendages. The metaphor is flippant but the centrality of Shakespeare to the critical *ouevre* of, for example, Harold Bloom demonstrates a more serious truth about the way the pivotal position he occupies is understood and reproduced in the Anglo-American critical establishment. It would be rash to deny it, like the fatuous (but spunky) exclamation of the hyper-enthused playgoer after a performance of John Home's *Douglas* in 1756, who rose to his feet in the theatre to call out, 'Whaur's yer Wullie Shakespeare noo?'

Following 1707 and the Jacobite risings of 1715 and 1745, from the critical turn between Enlightenment and Romanticism, at the hinge of the eighteenth and nineteenth centuries, in the overlap of Burns and Scott, English literature began to dominate Scottish literature as a measure of value just as the predominant language of written expression – English – dominated vernacular and local idiomatic forms of language – Scots. Scots was current and vital in a great deal of fiction and verse published in newspapers in the late nineteenth century, particularly in Aberdeenshire and north-east Scotland, but this work was specifically for local consumption as the language and idiom of a particular place, where Scots remained vital and current predominantly in speech.

There is an abrasion between popular work – stories, songs and poems – that is essentially oral, memorised, sung or recited and popular work – long narrative poems and novels – that is printed and intended for a mass international readership. There is also an elision, in the sense that both bodies of work – respectively, that of Burns and that of Scott – are 'popular', concerned with people, with ways of engaging in a popular culture that differ according to their own expertise and inclination, and according to the technologies of production and distribution available to them. The significance of the printing press in the stories of each of their lives was vital. Burns's life hinged upon the publication of the Kilmarnock edition. Scott's life and work was changed by the fortunes of his financial relations with his publishers. But the effect of the culture of print and book-reading should not blind us to the extent to which both were concerned with popular culture of a decidedly more ephemeral kind. The ballads and songs Burns knew, collected, revised and published, and those edited by Scott for publication as the *Minstrelsy of the Scottish Border*, belonged to a culture that was both oral *and* literary. Research in Scott's library at his home at Abbotsford began to recognise in the early twenty-first century just how significant is Scott's vast collection of chapbooks, suggesting that Scott's interest in the popular printed works of his time was also extensive.[14] This is more than the antiquarian interest of the comfortably established writer. It represents, rather, an artist's active grappling with the terms, traditions and expressions of popular imaginative experience. Scott's chapbooks fall into many categories – historical, supernatural and so on. But the sheer quantity of them is daunting, defies neatness and signals Scott's appreciation of the ways in which popular culture found expression in his time. Scott's appetite for popular culture overwhelms any attitude of elitist disdain he might have been expected to display and runs against the exclusive cultural pretensions of the social class with which he was keen to associate. In this sense he may be described as a pioneer of what we now term 'popular culture'.

The narrative of Scott's novels is English, the dialogue of many of his characters is Scots, reflecting both a literary and a political hierarchy. One consequence of this was that in the late nineteenth and twentieth centuries, as master narratives fragmented and gave way in importance to philology and linguistics, Scott – who had been thought of as equally important as Shakespeare – was eclipsed by the playwright in academic, and then popular, attention.

If one takes 1603 to signify the dawn of modernity, it also marks the beginning of the diminishment of Scotland's political authority. After

1603, Scotland's political autonomy, linguistic registers and social structures could no longer be assumed. They vary according to condition, location and moment in relation to the changing meaning of 'Britain' or 'the United Kingdom'. To recognise this is not to endorse mere pluralism and assert the value of locality and moment according to relative conditions, but to understand a quality of stress or strain in a national cultural dynamic that remains unresolved. In Scotland, in different ways from England or Ireland, feudal, clan and capitalist economics evolve and co-exist in strained, intermingling structures. Whether or not a completely devolved or indeed independent parliament would offer resolution remains debatable, but in the 1920s, it was towards that end that Hugh MacDiarmid began working for a literary and political endorsement of autonomous nationality.

In 1922, in the first editorial of the first edition of the journal which launched what is now called the modern Scottish Literary Renaissance, *The Scottish Chapbook* (Vol. 1, No. 1, August 1922), MacDiarmid wrote this:

> A young Edinburgh artist interested me greatly not long ago by asking me to 'visualize a typical Scotsman'. When I assured him that I had this mythical personage securely established in my mind's eye, he turned to a blackboard and rapidy sketched a Glasgow 'keelie', a Polish pitman from Lanarkshire, a Dundee Irishman, an anarchist orator of a kind frequently seen at the Mound in Edinburgh on Sunday nights, a Perthshire farmer, a Hebridean islander, and a Berwickshire bondager. I had to admit that in my wanderings I had met people precisely similar. 'These,' the artist remarked, 'are only a first selection of the varieties of the *genus homo* in contemporary Scotland. They serve, however, to show that the Window in Thrums [or, small-town Scotland and parochial mentality] gives an obsolete outlook on Scottish life.'[15]

MacDiarmid's insistence on the variety of different kinds of person, the impossibility of assuming a common or generic type or stereotype, seems a salutary and resonant rejection of the lure of the idea of racial uniformity. Scotland's masks are various and innumerable. But then he goes on: 'The artist proceeded to make subtle strokes here and there. The result was that each of these acutely differentiated faces acquired a peculiar unplaceable resemblance – an elusive likeness that had in each case a faintly ennobling air.'

This is intended to emphasise the possible awakening of national identity. The word 'ennobling' leaves no doubt that MacDiarmid thinks it is a good idea. But far from being an abstract, ahistorical, universal idea, it has a particular application in time: 'A like task confronts Scottish writers today. I believe that forces are now discernible in Scottish life and literature which will have a similar unifying and uplifting effect.'

This is a key moment in the crucial identification of literature and politics, and it reaches through Scottish literature in terms of language and social expressiveness, from Burns and Scott, through Stevenson and MacDiarmid, to James Kelman and Irvine Welsh. MacDiarmid's push was to create a comprehensive understanding of Scotland's cultural production, to go back to before the Enlightenment, to before the Unions of 1707 and 1603, beyond the Sixteenth-Century Renaissance, to deeper roots. This might be made clear in another way.

Alexander Nasmyth's painting, 'Edinburgh from Princes Street', depicts a bright, bustling city, full of progressive commercial activity and prospects. It is a painting about draining away the past and building for the future. The view is from the north-west of the city, looking south-east, but almost everything in the picture is coming towards you, riding, walking, under construction, promising to become more than it already is. The fresh-fronted facade of the New Town smiles on the left, Princes street – Edinburgh's main street for fashionable and expensive shopping – and all the prosperous people moving along it, in carriages or on foot, fashionable and well-dressed, charges out of the horizon and into the foreground. On the right, the Royal Institution – later the Royal Scottish Academy – is being built, the classical columns going up to proclaim the antiquity of the pedigree of new Edinburgh's quality. In the

Illustration 1   Alexander Nasmyth, 'Edinburgh from Princes Street with the Royal Institution under Construction' 1825 (National Galleries of Scotland)

middle-distance, the Nor' Loch is being drained to make way for the railway: the Industrial Revolution is coming and the trains with it, and with them, Waverley Station at the end of the line, another monument to Walter Scott. But as the painting slopes uphill to the horizon, the Old Town is visible as a misty, receding, far-away place, and the Castle – surely Edinburgh's most distinctive landmark – is placed beyond the scope of the canvas, literally outside the frame. The painting was completed in 1825. It tells us that the ancient, pre-Union, walled city capital belongs in the past. The present and future is being celebrated. The painting is wonderfully confident, positive, clever and purposeful. It might even be predicting its own longevity in that the Royal Institution, under construction in the painting, was the predecessor of the building that now stands adjacent to it, the National Gallery of Scotland (the Royal Scottish Academy), whose foundation stone was laid in 1850 by Prince Albert and which was opened to the public in 1859. Both were designed by William Henry Playfair (1790–1857). Nasmyth's painting came to be exhibited in the latter. So the art gallery under construction in the painting came to be its own sheltering location. The prosperity and progressiveness the painting celebrates also holds forth the promise of its own preservation.

Illustration 2 William Crozier, 'Edinburgh from Salisbury Crags' 1927 (National Galleries of Scotland)

Compare it with a painting of a hundred years later, William Crozier's 'Edinburgh from Salisbury Crags'. This dates from 1927, so it is centrally located in the decade of the Scottish Renaissance. Crozier's painting looks from a position diagonally opposite to Nasmyth, from south-east of the city looking north-west. As you look over the roofs from Salisbury Crags, it is as if what is depicted is not receding so much as rising and turning back to meet you. You look over the roofs of the Old Town and the Castle rises above, looking west but also strangely looking over its shoulder back at you as well. This is a painting about the present impact and immediate relevance of the past. Curiously, it is full of houses but there are no people prominently visible. One imagines a population – not only the people in Nasmyth's painting: shoppers, artisan builders, investors, engineers, professionals and commercial classes – but residents, working people, people who inhabited these buildings, this piece of territory, in histories other than the present, where the very economic structure was different. It is a reminder that the way people are changes in history.

It is painted in a manner which is not Cubist but is certainly aware of Cubism. Crozier has surely been looking at paintings by Cézanne. In other words, he is choosing to paint the Old Town of Edinburgh using emphatically modern techniques. The colours are too dark to evoke a sentimental 'golden glow' – the lines are hard, the tones are not soft – but there is an inviting demonstration of curiosity about the maze-like design of the structures. The affinities with the work of, for example, F.G. Scott in music and MacDiarmid in poetry should be clear. Both Scott in songs and MacDiarmid in poems, in the 1920s, catch an idiom of pre-Enlightenment vernacular liveliness, linked to ballad metres, the Scots language, qualities of tenderness and eerie, unearthly effects of light and shadow. Similarly, Crozier is indicating a way back behind the Industrial Revolution, behind Romanticism and behind the Enlightenment, to a Scotland that existed before the Union of the Parliaments and before the Union of the Crowns. It is anti-nostalgic, however. It does not propose a return to the past but rather a deepened occupation of the present and future.

These paintings highlight a contrast that takes place within a fabric woven of national traditions. People are being represented in different ways. The direct and immediate *correlations* between social organisation, hierarchy and morality, painting, music, language, speech and literary art is unmistakeably vital in Scottish cultural production. The categories are less tightly kept – the incisive penetration of perception can create pleasurable illumination across disciplines, genres and expectations. The central importance of the language of written texts and the speech of characters is much greater in Scottish literature than in English – much more important in Burns, Scott, Hogg, Galt, Stevenson, Lewis Grassic Gibbon, Neil Gunn and Irvine Welsh, than in Jane Austen, George Eliot, Martin Amis or Anita Brookner.

The argument might be extended to consider how applicable the observation is to American literature. The opening note, 'Explanatory' by 'The Author' of *Huckleberry Finn* (1885) seems an almost forgotten assertion of linguistic variety in the American grain.

> In this book a number of dialects are used, to wit: the Missouri Negro dialect; the extremest form of the backwoods South-Western dialect; the ordinary 'Pike-County' dialect; and four modified versions of this last. The shadings have not been done in a haphazard fashion, or by guess-work; but painstakingly, and with the trustworthy guidance and support of personal familiarity with these several forms of speech.
> I make this explanation for the reason that without it many readers would suppose that all these characters were trying to talk alike and not succeeding.[16]

However, twentieth-century American literature generally takes less notice of the country's various forms of vernacular speech and uses a more uniformly idiomatic American English.

In the end, what remains is a question of excluding or diminishing the possible variety of languages and forms. By this I mean to suggest that the languages people use and the artistic forms by which painters, composers, poets and novelists express themselves may be considered together as masks in a context of commercial exchange. And this question calls up matters of time and space, literally – how much time people will spend watching, listening to or reading this material, and how much space can be taken up by it, on the shelves of shops and in homes? The question that always haunts the affirmative aspect of popularising anything is, at the expense of what? At what cost is such space occupied? What is not being said here? Art might assume an exceptional status in this context but it is always vulnerable to the work of mundane politics and commercial prioritisation. James Kelman's impassioned attacks on commercial priorities keep reminding us that all writers are forced to accept a context of suppression and censorship, particularly in terms of media discourse, such as film-writing, radio, television drama and journalism, and popular genre fiction. As Kelman has argued, 'Poetry and prose fiction are the only free artforms at present.'[17] This paradox might be put in another way: because poetry – or in Kelman's case, prose fiction – 'makes nothing happen', it is the only literary form free to address the things that really matter. Kelman adds a rider to this: 'at present' – to remind us that there is no reason to assume such conditions will continue without interference. Indeed, when his own essays were reviewed, critics who thought he was being hypersensitive about editorial interference seemed perfectly blind to the larger context which Kelman was aggressively pushing against – a context of pervasive editorial exclusiveness. Kelman seems to be in accord with John Pilger, who opens his book *The New Rulers of the World* by saying, with regard to the 'war on terrorism' advocated by American and British politicians in 2001–2002: 'The most potent weapon in this "war" is pseudo-information, different only in form from that Orwell described [in *Nineteen-Eighty-Four*], consigning to oblivion unacceptable truths and historical sense. Dissent is permissible within "consensual" boundaries, reinforcing the illusion that information and speech are "free".'[18]

At the heart of this danger is the understanding that any working democracy needs educated and informed people, and that education and information need training, creativity and art. In Scotland, education has traditionally been considered a birthright rather than the privilege of a more prosperous class. Despite the limited success of libraries and publishers such as Everyman and Penguin Classics in making world literature accessible and affordable, the overwhelming condition of post-Second World War artistic distribution in the West is not the priority of education but commercial viability. The relationship between what is available for public consumption and what should be made available because of non-commercial priorities becomes increasingly vexed. What remains popularly available – on the airwaves, on screens in homes and cinemas, in advertising imagery, in newspapers and magazines, in conversations between people – is informed by such priorities.

It is this upon which Hugh MacDiarmid is pouring vitriol in his poem 'Glasgow'. Talking of the composer F.G. Scott, he notes that others, 'whose jobs impinge on music' would try to keep Scott's compositions from being broadcast in order to keep their own, less-important work, in circulation. Then he notes this essential distinction between 'popular' as, on the one hand, work that is made available to people or work that is accepted by the greatest number of people and, on the other hand, work that is intrinsically *about* people and essentially *for* people, in touch with reality, attentive to the spirit of people and intended *to help people to live*. It is impossible to think that this composer could be 'popular' in Glasgow, MacDiarmid says, meaning that he could not be 'sold cheap'. Yet his work is essentially of the people –

> Scott popular? – Scott whose work is *di essenze popolare?*
> This popular not meaning plebeian or poor in content,
> But *sano, schietto, realistico,*
> *e religiosamente attinente al profundo spirito della razza?*
> Scott popular – in Glasgow?
>
> What a place for bat-folding![19]

The poet George Bruce, F.G. Scott's nephew by marriage, sums the thing up clearly. Remembering Scott's judgement on Vaughan Williams – 'That man knows nothing about folk song!' – Bruce commented,

I understood that remark. I could accept that remark. Because – the distinction is this, and it's a very important distinction. MacDiarmid... Francis George Scott... They were part of the reality of Border life. They knew – not only the history, but the *sensation* that just over the Border was an enemy, and an enemy by this time in terms of sensibility, in terms of what I might call *detachment* from population. In a curious way, Francis George Scott and MacDiarmid were *popular* – but I don't mean well-liked, I mean *of the people*. They grew out of this situation – robust, earthy people. But in music, and this is the thing, F.G. had an idiom which related to that particular concept. You get the reality in the ironies... This to me is the point of beginning, the point of true beginning.'[20]

States of fantasy/dream states

In her book, *States of Fantasy* (1996), Jacqueline Rose helpfully reminds us of the important distinction Freud draws between fantasies and dreams. In his earliest correspondence with Wilhelm Fleiss in the 1890s, Rose notes, Freud suggested that dreams travel back from perception to the unconscious, 'disintegrating and reordering themselves as they go' but by contrast, Freud described fantasies as 'always progressive'. Fantasy 'is always heading for the world it appears to have left behind'. Crucially, this is linked by Freud to another 'presentiment' – 'the source of morality': 'the question of how subjects tie themselves ethically to each other and enter a socially viable world'.[21]

In the light of Benedict Anderson's work on nations and nationalism in *Imagined Communities* and Homi Bahba's elaborations and theoretical considerations in *The Location of Culture*, it is worth emphasising how closely Freud associated the moral and fantasy components in the structuring of social organisation and their concomitant aspect: guilt. Freud's notion of 'guilt for crimes not committed, unconscious wishes, troubled identifications which... formed the basis, the emotive binding, of social groups' is certainly arguable, as Rose develops her discussion with reference to Palestine, Israel and Zionism. However, the central perception of ambivalence or contradictory dynamics is closely relevant to our discussion in terms of Scotland's cultural representations: 'there is no way of understanding political identities and destinies without letting fantasy into the frame'. And her cautionary note is salutary: 'If fantasy can be grounds for license and pleasure (the popular meaning is not of course completely out), it can just as well surface as fierce blockading protectiveness, walls up all around our inner and outer, psychic and historical, selves. Political passion might take on the colours of resistence... but there is no guarantee that it will travel that way. In fact in psychoanalytic language, resistence as a concept is far closer to defensiveness than to freedom; you resist when you don't want to budge.'[22]

Rose is right to warn us that to some, 'the concepts of state and fantasy are more or less antagonists, back to back, facing in opposite directions towards public and private worlds'. But remember the Freudian distinction between fantasy and dream: fantasy is progressive – it 'always contains a historical reference in so far as it involves, alongside the attempt to arrest the present, a journey through the past'. That journey is not a disintegration as happens in dreams but an essential component of regeneration. This is not to suggest that the public world is characterised by regeneration and progress, but rather that if fantasy and private worlds seem antagonistic to public and state realities, progress and regeneration depend on an interpenetration of these two seemingly opposed concepts, however difficult that might be at times.

Consider the alteration of implication in the title of two editions of an anthology of Scottish poetry by twenty-five writers 'all under forty' when the first edition appeared in 1994: *Dream State: The New Scottish Poets*, edited by Daniel O'Rourke. The book's title is ambiguous in these terms: it could signify 'dream' as dissolution, failure, guilt, disintegrated reality; but it also suggests a fantasy collectively held, an imaginary community, yet attached to reality through history and unexplored potential – a possible future. It was taken from the title of a poem by Stuart A. Paterson, which begins: 'a country so awake that / dreaming is for the sleepless...'. This is 'a huge country / of undiscovered tastes // to fill the thoughts of small heads / put to bed before their world grew...'. The poem ends:

> ...you'd maybe
> catch the dream state long before
> it woke to morning's red sky
>
> laid along the contours of
> a massive upset dustbin
> someone ransacked while we slept.

When the anthology was first published in 1994, the political context of the United Kingdom drew the implication of the two-word title gravitationally towards being interpreted as adjective and noun. The 'new generation of Scottish poets' – unacknowledged legislators – inhabited and preserved a 'dream state'. As imaginative writers, the exercise of the imagination they presented was refreshingly drawing upon and inhabiting a world of universal truth (the child dropping into sleep in Paterson's poem could be any child, anywhere). Yet there was usually a specific Scottish reference: Scotland itself was the 'Dream State'. The idea of a national psychology was evoked.

When *Dream State: The New Scottish Poets Second Edition* appeared in 2002, after the Scottish Parliament had been resumed in 1999, after the popular vote in the referendum of 1997, in favour of devolution and in favour of the devolved parliament having 'tax-varying powers', the implication of the title seemed to have changed. It seemed to signify an urgently commanding *verb* and noun. It was now possible to imagine statehood as something that might happen in actuality. It was as if the second word of the title were implicitly italicised and as if an invisible exclamation mark followed it. (The editor's name had changed too, from 'Daniel' to 'Donny' – as if the more English formality had given way to a more self-confident Scottish colloquial informality.) In Freudian terms, this was not merely 'dream' anymore, it was much more emphatically progressive 'fantasy' – an imaginable reality, a more proximate possibility. The world inhabited by the second edition had been increasingly affected by the desire behind Alasdair Gray's famous commandment or secular prayer, which his readers found printed concealed beneath the dustjackets on the hardcovers of his books: 'Work as if you were living in the early days of a better nation.'[23]

To consider Scotland in these terms is to perceive immediately the dangers and the values of what I will call icons. The popular iconography of the nation has been unmistakeable, internationally bankable and unusually stable for a long time. Through major changes in social economy, iconic images of Scottishness have been persistently and widely maintained.

The foundational descriptions for this process of iconographic establishment in literary and painterly idioms are to be found in the works of Walter Scott, and the defining moment in terms of social fashion is normally located in Scott's stage-management of the visit to Edinburgh of King George IV in August 1822. There are various accounts, but still the most readable is by John Prebble, *The King's Jaunt*.[24] As is well-known, this was the first visit of a reigning monarch to Scotland for almost two centuries and more crucially, the first visit of a British monarch to Scotland after the Jacobite Rising of 1745, the slaughter at Culloden in 1746 and the vicious reprisals that followed. If it is ever difficult to see past the shortbread-box image of Bonnie Prince Charlie glowing in reds and golds and sounding tinnily hollow, it is worth remembering that during the Jacobite march on London the value of the British pound dropped to sixpence. The Jacobites were an intensely serious threat to the British economy, even more delicate since the state of Britain had been so recently formed. The situation when put alongside fluctuations in the economy in the wake of the terrorist attacks on America in 2001 and the extremities of violence – both physical and in long-term caricatures of the otherness of the Highlanders – is perhaps more understandable.

George IV visited Edinburgh not long after the Highlands had begun to be subjected to a rigorous programme of clearances and the Sutherland factor Patrick Sellar had been acquitted in Inverness of the accusation of causing injury or forced eviction by burning or murder; it was not long after Andrew

Hardie and John Baird, two Glasgow weavers, were hanged for treason after the Radical Rising of 1820; not long after Mary Shelley published *Frankenstein* and Scott had sent his own representative of surplus population, the violent rebel the Whistler, into the forbidden zone of exclusion from enlightenment accommodation in *The Heart of Midlothian*. The King's visit, with Scott pulling the wires and designing the backdrop, was self-consciously intended to reinstate a legitimate popular celebration of pageantry and to affirm the public presence of colour and costume in Scotland's capital city, while deeply asserting a British accommodation of Scottish identity. From the mid-eighteenth century to the early nineteenth century, the icons of Highland dress, tartan, bagpipes, the Gaelic language – had become symbols. But, characteristically in cultures of oppression, they had become symbols of themselves. Once the thing is made illegal, it becomes a sign for its own actuality as well as its legal status. The very sound of the pipes still carries this meaning.

As Angus Calder has argued, however, if Scott and George IV secured the hooks from which generations of people have deigned to hang their Scottishness, the moment needs to be seen not only in terms of its effect on its immediate past but also in terms of its characteristic position in the approaching nineteenth century:

> the tartanry and frolics of 1822 are less significant as a facade masking the dispossession of Highland Gaels than as an episode in the transition from the Dundas-Melville era of aristocratic management to the New Scotland of Liberalism and manufacturers. They typified the ideological means by which a Union of practical convenience became a Union of irrational love and fears, sublimated in militarism, tartanry, royalism and, eventually, imperialism.[25]

While massive industrialisation drew the majority of the nation's population to the central belt and especially Glasgow in the nineteenth century, a general currency of images associated with the Highlands became internationally familiar and assumed. As late as the 1950s the critic David Daiches was telling students in America that if they had imagined their 'granny's Hieland hame' then it was high time they thought about its plumbing.[26] The 'wee hoose amang the heather' was removed from the squalor of slums not primarily by economics or geography but by a stretch of imagination, a lapse from the progressivism of 'fantasy' to the unreality and impotence of 'dream' in the terms we have just discussed.

In the 1990s, something radical happened to ways in which it was possible to imagine a redeployment of the arsenal of clichés of Scottish iconography. This can be illustrated by two consecutive events. The political commentator Tom Nairn once made a pronouncement of exasperated anger that became increasingly familiar through the 1980s: 'Scotland will be free when the last minister is strangled by the last copy of *The Sunday Post*.'[27] In other words, the Protestant Church and the mass-media representation of Scotland in the pious conservative tabloid press, such as that for which Dundee's publishing firm of D.C. Thomson became notorious, have such a debilitating effect on the full expression of the national culture that only by destroying them might liberation be begun. The phrase was adopted as a cover-image then made available as a poster by the magazine *Radical Scotland* in 1983 and came to stand as an oppositional and resistant icon in the 1980s. But in the 1990s, things changed.

A glance at the books that began to be published in the late 1980s and in increasing numbers through the 1990s shows clearly the extent of intellectual revaluation that was going on across the arts. The fruits of massive academic research were gathered in reappraisals of Scotland's literature, art and music, providing confident and panoramic views of territory that had been approached too tentatively, apologetically and only partially mapped.

In the 1980s but especially through the 1990s, scholarly works offering critical reassessment of Scottish cultural history altered the ways in which Scotland's cultural production might be understood. There had been important precedents: T.F. Henderson's *Scottish Vernacular Literature* in 1910 and J.H. Miller's *A Literary History of Scotland* (1903). Most influentially, in 1919, G. Gregory Smith's *Scottish Literature: Character and Influence*, offered the idea of contrariness as a fundamental Scottish characteristic and gave C.M. Grieve/ Hugh MacDiarmid fuel in the 1920s to assert both the value of Scottish literary traditions and the valuelessness of 'Tradition' as a governing principle. These two contradictory assertions are encapsulated in the two famous slogans MacDiarmid published in the 1920s: 'Not Burns – Dunbar!' and the one which appeared on the front cover of the first issue of his periodical, *The Scottish Chapbook*, in 1922: 'Not Traditions – Precedents.'[28]

One might paraphrase the implications of the first slogan thus:

Forget the vast quantity of superficial attention spuriously expended on Burns, and forget the iconographic, black-hole centrality Burns occupies in the Scottish literary pantheon, go back further, beyond the Unions of 1707 and 1603 to an earlier period altogether, when Scotland was an independent country, and rediscover, or recover, the value of older Scottish poetry in the context of much longer, and implicitly richer and unsuspectedly complex traditions of Scottish poetry, literature and the arts, because Scotland had these Great Traditions but they need to be uncovered and their value reassessed – what stands in the way of that is the opposition.

And one might paraphrase the second slogan like this:

Abandon any sense of 'Tradition' completely, when or if it becomes constricting or defined by uniformity or stultifying continuity and especially if it acts as a constraint on creativity – what is needed is not 'Tradition' but 'Precedents' – by which one might assume anything that might be put to creative use, from wherever in the world one might find it, models not to be imitated but used as points of departure for new creative work in a world the past could not have predicted.

These slogans are evidently contradictory but they are effectively complementary. They indicate necessary work in two fields which often overlap but are distinct: that of the critic or literary critical historian and that of the poet or literary artist or artist of whatever kind. MacDiarmid's push was for both self-conscious, comprehensive critical understanding of a national cultural potential and for intuitive, artful creative production independent of the responsibilities of categorical knowledge.

The plurality of voices MacDiarmid encouraged was at the heart of the nationalist movement he endorsed. It was most deeply opposed (perhaps to some extent unknowingly) in 1936, by Edwin Muir, in his book *Scott and Scotland*. Central to the *geist* of Scottish literature of the 1920s and 1930s was the gravitational pull of Scotland in opposition (often voiced, almost always implied) to Anglocentrism. However, in *Scott and Scotland*, Muir denied the viability of autonomous Scottish traditions in the modern world, comparing Scottish and Irish literatures and arguing that the international provenance of the latter was due to its medium: the English language. His conclusion was that 'Scotland can only develop a national literature by writing in English.'[29]

To MacDiarmid, this was brutal acquiescence in English cultural supremacy and a betrayal of all he had achieved and hoped to do: it was a strangling of literary possibility and an obsequious surrender to foreign authority. MacDiarmid spurned Muir's friendship and alliance, and scorned his conclusions. In both the introduction and contents of his 1940 *Golden Treasury of Scottish Poetry* (which included poems in Scots and English and translated from Gaelic and Latin but carried nothing by Muir), MacDiarmid demonstrated a fantastically plural linguistic and cultural identity as opposed to Muir's monoglot proposition. The appearance of new, major, modern Gaelic poetry in the 1940s confirmed MacDiarmid's hopes. Maurice Lindsay's anthology of Scottish Renaissance poets published by Faber & Faber in 1945 marked a watershed in reaching a broad critical readership and in 1947, Lindsay wrote *A Pocket Guide to Scottish Culture* (in 52 pages) which was followed in 1951 by Sydney Goodsir Smith's 40-page *A Short Introduction to Scottish Literature*. Both these slim pamphlets offered attempts to introduce Scotland's cultural and literary production briefly, comprehensively, coherently and enthusiastically. Heavier scholarly work followed: in 1958, Kurt Wittig's *The Scottish Tradition in Literature* and in 1964, Duncan Glen's *Hugh MacDiarmid and the Scottish Renaissance*.

However, the scene changed most in the 1980s and 1990s with such seminal work as Roderick Watson's *The Literature of Scotland* in 1984, the four-volume *History of Scottish Literature* (1986–1987) edited by Cairns Craig, Duncan Macmillan's *Scottish Art 1460–1990*, John Purser's *Scotland's Music* (1992), Marshall Walker's *Scottish Literature since 1707* (1996), *A History of Scottish Women's Writing* edited by Douglas Gifford and Dorothy McMillan (1997), Cairns Craig's *The Modern Scottish Novel* (1999), Duncan Petrie's *Screening Scotland* (2000) and the 2002 publication of the 1269-page *Scottish Literature in English and Scots* edited by Douglas Gifford, Sarah Dunnigan and Alan MacGillivray. In the same period, other kinds of reappraisal were taking place. For example, Tom Leonard was rediscovering forgotten poets of the nineteenth century whom he published in the anthology *Radical Renfrew* (1990) and the *Collected Works* of Hugh MacDiarmid began to be edited and published in a multi-volume edition from 1992 through to the twenty-first century.

Years after his death, MacDiarmid was winning his battle. He had fought for the development of a multi-valent, multi-vocal literature and a culture whose coherence could be conferred by an identifiable but non-prescriptive national identity, and which could be evaluated in an international context. In many respects this has happened. A Scotland of multiple voices and aspects, a nation whose plurality of masks is a defining characteristic, would be a benign interpretation of the nation's evolved cultural condition. However, if the value of artistic work depends to unconscious degrees on history (the moment), personality (the character and approach of the artist) and substance (language, form, the specific gravity of any work), then endless pluralism and superficial differences might signify no more than an increasing tendency towards a bland and undifferentiated, globalised uniformity.

Nevertheless, the extent of the change in the 1990s was positive and progressive. It can be illustrated in another way, linking back to Tom Nairn's pessimistic pronouncement. In 1996, the first of a series of republications of D.C. Thomson comic strips appeared as a large-format hardback book in time for the Christmas market: *The Broons and Oor Wullie, 1936–1996 (60 Years in The Sunday Post)*. The sub-title, presumably unconsciously, is inescapably reminiscent of Scott's *Waverley* – '*Tis Sixty Years Since* – suggesting that six decades on, one might begin to appreciate the whole saga historically, in a more disengaged, rational, analytic way, whether that saga is the Jacobite rising in Scott's novel or the long lives of the Brown family (the Broons) and their near-neighbour, a boy named William (Wullie). These cartoon pages from *The Sunday Post* had been part of the national imagination since before the Second World War. Living in a perpetual, benign urban landscape (but close enough to the rural world and the Highlands to permit regular excursions), the Broon family ('Scotland's happy family that makes every family happy') and Wullie had been published in annual soft-bound volumes before, but this was the first time that a full, representative selection of their adventures had appeared, packaged for a generation old enough to have grown up with them. The effect went beyond the planning of a merely commercial ploy. The book announced that these cartoon phenomena were historical facts, that their currency belonged to its era. Wullie is an 'everyboy' figure of comfortingly predictable appetite and mischief, a domesticated Jim Hawkins. No unpredictable foreign voyages for him, though. Almost every strip sees him set off from his favoured place – his seat on an upturned metal bucket in the garden of his parents' home – and return to it at the end. The slogan – 'Oor Wullie', Your Wullie, A'abody's Wullie – that is, 'Our William' – he is one of 'our' family – 'one of your family – in fact he belongs to and represents everybody' – if it enacts the vocabulary of identification and kinship, structures itself against an undefined, unspoken otherness. Generations of readers are assured that there cannot be much wrong with the world if, by the bottom of the page, Wullie gets back safely to his bucket.

Oor Wullie and *The Broons* were written in the context of a reactionary ideology of 'popular' conservatism (not only deliberately constructed as persuasive but also fondly thought of). Their vernacular street idiom is cognate with a social order which is reaffirmed. Play is normally recreational in this world: it endorses that order. The relations in the Broon family or Wullie's relation to figures of authority are all fixed and reliable. Yet at the same time, play might engender its subversion. In the first issue of the children's comic, *The Beano*, published in 1938, a character named Lord Marmaduke of Bunkerton made his debut. Becoming better known as Lord Snooty, it was clear that he would rather be playing with his pals from Ash Can Alley than with the snobbish types who visited him at the castle. Like *Oor Wullie* and *The Broons*, *Lord Snooty* was created and drawn by Dudley Dexter Watkins, an Englishman whose career was spent working for D.C. Thomson and *The Sunday Post*. Lord Snooty's world was directly connected with contemporary politics. The adventures of Lord Snooty and his pals – Hairpin Huggins, Happy Hutton, Skinny Lizzie and Gertie the Goat – included an encounter with Hitler and the German Army during the Second World War, special war-time stories created by the artist Sam Fair caricatured the enemy as 'Winken & Blinken' and 'Musso the Wop', and a long-running rivalry with The Gasworks Gang. Helping the war effort by dumping old comics in salvage bins was to ensure high prices would be paid for them as collectors' items fifty years later. The engagement with contemporary class structures and the war clearly illustrates the intentional use of the comics as propaganda, but the surreal aspects of the story (the proximity of an aristocracy and gasworks slum-dwellers united in an eagerness to play) and the strip's linguistic liveliness (even when put to the use of caricature and racist stereotyping) suggest that a more elusive and anarchic humour glimmers through even the most conservative messages.

The retrospective selection of *The Broons and Oor Wullie* published in 1996 was a commercial success. Printed in a relatively small run, it sold out and became a collector's item itself. It was followed by a further series of annuals collecting strips from the war years, the 1950s and 'The Swinging Sixties'.[30]

The repackaging worked, but it also brought about the possibility of reviewing the parochialism and circumscriptions of mass-media representations of Scots people such as those promulgated by *The Sunday Post*. They were no longer irresistible, unexamined components of the national culture; their iconic status could be described historically. It might cease to be dominant as an unquestioned presence and begin to be seen in a more variable context in which priorities and values could be strategically rearranged.

A final example. When I first went to work in New Zealand in 1986, the Head of the Maori Studies Department at the University of Waikato told me that he had once attended the Edinburgh Military Tattoo at the Edinburgh International Festival, and he could not understand how any Scot, looking at such a wonderful display of national cultural identity, could feel anything but immense pride. I was thinking of Hugh MacDiarmid's comment in 1978, that the Edinburgh Military Tattoo was a disgraceful spectacle perpetrated by an army of occupation upon a nation of sheep.[31] But the man from Maori Studies was right too. Ben Okri's comments on the possible value of kitsch made me keep his words in mind. The dialogue I imagined between MacDiarmid's condemnation of exploitation and Okri's recognition of the subversive value of kitsch is going to haunt this book.

Iconography, pop charts, old songs and new

Scottish icons were widely celebrated in the late 1990s, both in literary and broader cultural terms. It is arguable whether this was brought about simply by a commercial decision based on journalistic judgement or whim, or by a desire to reassess national values in the wake of the 1997 referendum and at the approach of the millennium – or a reciprocal arrangement of both. Some examples are worth considering seriously for a moment, however. In *The Herald* of Monday 5 October 1998, Alexander Linklater announced the result of a readers' poll on the best Scottish novel. Over 5000 votes were received for over 500 novels. The clear favourite turned out to be a trilogy, Lewis Grassic Gibbon's *A Scots Quair*, but the list of the top twenty is worth looking at:

1. *A Scots Quair*, Lewis Grassic Gibbon
2. *Kidnapped*, Robert Louis Stevenson
3. *The Private Memoirs and Confessions of a Justified Sinner*, James Hogg
4. *Lanark*, Alasdair Gray
5. *Treasure Island*, Robert Louis Stevenson
6. *Trainspotting*, Irvine Welsh
7. *The Silver Darlings*, Neil Gunn
8. *The Prime of Miss Jean Brodie*, Muriel Spark
9. *Dr Jekyll and Mr Hyde*, Robert Louis Stevenson
10. *The Thirty-Nine Steps*, John Buchan

11. *The Cone Gatherers*, Robin Jenkins
12. *Old Mortality*, Walter Scott
13. *The House with the Green Shutters*, George Douglas Brown
14. *The Heart of Midlothian*, Walter Scott
15. *The Wasp Factory*, Iain Banks
16. *The Crow Road*, Iain Banks
17. *Morvern Callar*, Alan Warner
18. *Swing Hammer Swing*, Jeff Torrington
19. *The Trick is to Keep Breathing*, Janice Galloway
20. *The New Road*, Neil Munro

Commenting on this list, Douglas Gifford said that it was what you might expect 'from a country in a transition of education about its culture... If you'd asked the question 20 years ago it would have been only the likes of *Kidnapped* or – no harm to him – Nigel Tranter. And if you did it 20 years from now you'd get another set of different results, because of the way Scots keep changing the way they think about themselves.' The observation highlights not only the quantity of novels contemporary with the survey, but also nineteenth-century novels still popular with a late twentieth century reading public re-evaluating them.

On Saturday 18 December 1999, the tabloid *Daily Record* published the results of a poll conducted by *Who's Who in Scotland*, which asked 1600 'establishment figures' to pick 'the greatest Scots of the Millennium and of the 20th Century'. The icons were predictable in the top three 'Scots of the Millennium': Robert Burns, William Wallace and Robert the Bruce; perhaps less so in the 'Scots of the Century', where Alexander Fleming, John Logie Baird and Hugh MacDiarmid topped the list. It would be unwise to make too much of this, but it seems notable that in the top fifteen of both lists there was only one woman – The Queen Mother, and that in the top 20 of the best-novels list above, there are only two women – Muriel Spark (whose decision to live away from Scotland for most of her career is well-known) and Janice Galloway, whose first novel is about a woman moving in and out of hospitalisation, cripplingly sensitive to the dominant masculinity of Scotland's normative society. Also, of course, there is the matter that the poets Burns and MacDiarmid had been placed so highly. The *Record*'s Editorial noted of the lists, 'The nation can be proud' but it might have been more appropriate to suggest that the nation might be curious. Reporting on the same poll on Saturday, 18 December 1999, *The Herald*'s Rosemary Fee remarked that Burns's iconic status had been affirmed despite the fact that 'More than half of Scots do not know the words to his most famous song'. Nevertheless, the global familiarity of 'Auld Lang Syne' and 'My Love is like a red, red rose' needs no emphasis. The declaration of love that will last till the mountains are washed to the sea is surely Burns-derived in George Gershwin's refreshingly self-conscious, snappy lyrics for 'Love is Here to Stay' from the 1938 film, *The Goldwyn Follies* and published after Gershwin's death in 1937:

> it's very clear our love is here to stay;
> not for a year but ever and a day.
> the radio and the telephone and the movies that we know
> may be just passing fancies, and in time may go.
> but oh, my dear, our love is here to stay;
> together we're going a long, long way.
> in time the rockies may crumble,
> gibralter may tumble,
> they're only made of clay,
> but our love is here to stay.

Burns's influence and effect is potently visible if we consider a moment at the reopening of the Scottish parliament in Edinburgh on 1 July 1999. As reported by David Luhnow in the *New Zealand Herald* via Reuters:

> The royal family was subjected to an embarrassing moment during the opening of Scotland's new Parliament, enduring an emotional rendition of a song that mocks royalty.
>
> As the Queen, the Duke of Edinburgh and Prince Charles sat stony-faced in front of the 129-member body, Scottish folk-singer Sheena Wellington performed 18th-century poet Robert Burns's socialist anthem *A Man's a Man For A' That*.
>
> The song, which marked the highlight of the opening ceremony and was chosen by organisers instead of Britain's national anthem, God Save the Queen, hails the nobility of honest poverty and pokes fun at the titles and trapping of nobility.

Pointing out that the song praises 'men of independent minds' the article concluded that to members of Britain's nobility, it was a slap in the face to the royal family. The Earl of Lauderdale was quoted as saying, 'By choosing this song and rejecting the national anthem, they are flaunting a sort of separatism in a Parliament which is supposed to preserve the United Kingdom.' Yet it would surely have been surprising if a reassembled Scottish Parliament had chosen to sing an anthem in which the 'missing verse' (the third verse) is so notoriously anti-Scottish:

> God grant that Marshal Wade,
> By thy almighty aid,
> May victory bring,
> May he sedition hush,

> And like a torrent rush,
> Rebellious Scots to crush,
> God save the Queen![32]

The report delivered in the *New Zealand Herald* squared exactly with Robert McNeil's article on page 3 of *The Scotsman* of 2 July. This began by quoting the Queen: 'It is a moment, rare in the life of any nation, when we step across the threshold of a new constitutional age.' Describing the ceremony in the assembly Hall on the Mound in Edinburgh, McNeil described Sheena Wellington looking directly at the Queen, smiling, and singing Burns's words relegating any strutting lord to the status of a common fool, even if 'hundreds worship at his word' while a man of independent mind would look and laugh at all that. Scotland's first minister, Donald Dewar, drew attention to the words of the song emphatically: at its heart, he said, lay a characteristically Scottish conviction 'that honesty and simple dignity are priceless virtues, not imparted by rank or birth or privilege...'.

My point in dwelling on these events is to establish, quickly and lightly I hope, something scholarship often neglects: the immediate relation between literary and political practice, the possibility of art's pragmatic effects. The *Fanfare for the Scottish Parliament* opening the procession was commissioned from the composer James MacMillan. This was a long way from any simplistic populism or clichéd representation of musical Scottishness: MacMillan's music, while it has achieved widespread recognition and is held in high critical esteem, is not only lyrical and compelling but also challenging and intellectually tough. And Burns's song was not the only verse contribution at the centre of the political moment of July 1999. One of the last poems written by Iain Crichton Smith before his death was commissioned to be read as a secular blessing on the Parliament's reopening. Its title, 'The Beginning of a New Song', refers to the judgement passed in 1707 by the Chancellor, the Earl of Seafield: 'There's the end of an auld sang.' (The implication is, perhaps, not only that the arguments which had run furiously around the idea of union had, finally, been brought to closure but also that the parliament itself was a kind of song.) Again, while Crichton Smith is held in great affection by many readers of his stories and novels as well as his poems, his verse is a far distance from popular rhyme or sensationalist doggerel. The distinction of these acts of political moment was that they managed to strike an appropriate and exact balance between the seriousness of the occasion, its significance in Scotland's history, and the democratic openness to experience which it seemed to mark and celebrate. Crichton Smith's poem is a simple wish for such balance in representation through moving words, bringing together possible ways of representing Scots internationally and to each other, in Gaelic, Scots and English. It is a poem about language:

> Let our three voiced country
> Sing in a new world

joining the other rivers without dogma,
But with friendliness to all around her.

> Let her new river shine on a day
> That is fresh and glittering and contemporary;
> Let it be true to itself and to its origins
> inventive, original, philosophical,
> its institutions mirror its beauty:
> Then without shame we can esteem ourselves.[33]

The sentiment is more dramatically evoked in the lines from Smith's poem 'Two Girls Singing' which are quoted as an epigraph to the Preface. But this is a declaration of hope intended to affirm value in a plurality of voices – different languages finding ways to communicate. It praises the vitality made possible by voices which are not only 'of our kind' (which means, not only Scottish but in touch with humanity) and are also 'unpredicted'. These qualities are firm and signal deep difference in literary as well as political terms between Scotland and England.

Hugh MacDiarmid's popular influence, like Burns's, had special relevance at the time of the reopening of the Scottish Parliament. On a television programme broadcast on BBC 1 on 12 May 1999 (2.05–3.25pm), *The Scottish Parliament – The First Day*, a reporter asked a question of Alex Salmond, the leader of the Scottish National Party, and got a curiously literary reply:

Brian Taylor: Finally, on a slightly more romantic note, Mr Salmond, you and your colleagues wearing the Jacobite rose there, a reminder of an older Scotland perhaps?
Alex Salmond: Well, it's actually the MacDiarmid rose. I mean this is the eh... not quite the Jacobite rose, this is the little white rose of Scotland that smells sharp and sweet and breaks the heart. Now, no hearts broken today but I think a nice symbol for Scotland's day.
Brian Taylor: But you were using it to make something of a point, perhaps, about a reminder of the loyalties that you said you were expressing rather than taking the oath to the Queen which, of course, is obliged by law.
Alex Salmond: Well, I mean I set out our position and the fundamental sovereignty of Scotland belongs to the people of Scotland. There's no disrespect intended to the Queen, none was taken I'm sure. The oath was taken but our loyalty is to Scotland and the Scottish people. I think the rose of Scotland symbolises that.[34]

It is clear how the journalistic clichés are being rejected and redeployed here: Salmond is spurning the 'romantic' or 'older Scotland' imagery of 'dream' – failure, dissolution, lost causes, Bonnie Prince Charlie and ineffectuality, and offering instead an invocation of a poem with immediate emotional appeal, MacDiarmid's 'The Little White Rose' published in the volume *Stony Limits and Other Poems* in 1934. The appeal is sentimental (it advocates

exclusive preference for singular national identity) but entirely appropriate
to the political party in question. It is effective, being both well-known and
reliably emotive. But it is, in context, a surprise – in Iain Crichton Smith's
term, 'unpredicted'. And it leads on to a reference to the sovereignty of
Scotland as something belonging to the nation's people rather than to
the monarch, a conviction at the heart of Scottish constitutional discourse
since the Declaration of Arbroath in 1320. It is noted in the appellation of
the crown belonging not to the land but to the people (not Mary Queen of
Scotland but Mary Queen of Scots). The poem itself, as if to confirm its own
unpredicted provenance, was widely available in 2001, printed on the
laminated label attached to the potted white roses on sale at Garden
Centres. On a Stewart tartan border, a photograph of the rose is topped with
the words: 'The Jacobite Rose – Rosa Alba Maxima' and captioned, 'White
Rose of Scotland':

> The Rose of all the world is not for me
> I want for my part
> Only the little white Rose of Scotland
> That smells sharp and sweet
> And breaks the Heart

Centred on the lower third of the card, with its own capitalisation and no
punctuation, the poem is reproduced without reference to Hugh MacDiarmid.
It has achieved the fame of anonymity, another icon.[35]

  This is one reason for my epigraph from Adorno. It should draw our
attention to something else we often forget. Popular art – mass media, Garden
Centre flower labels, the post-Second World War advance of saturation
advertising with its strafing commercialism, the elaboration of prevalent
systems of disinformation, the massive distractions of neon and glitz, the
material production of 'kitsch' – is, clearly, a commercial exploitation. But
within it there is a longing. No matter how embarrassing an example we
might take – television advertisement, logo-stained clothing, breakfast food-
stuffs – the crudest demonstrations of that longing require reading.

  Understanding of that longing can be made possible by art, where the
not-completely conscious, the intuitive and quick, operate along with organisation and consciously formed structures, the things that artists make. To
paraphrase Adorno, one of the major reasons why Mahler's music is great is
not *in despite of* the kitsch to which it is attracted, the melodrama, the whole
range of what we mean by 'sound-effects' – but because *the construction* of
Mahler's music allows us to understand the language of kitsch. It is crucially
performative, utilising masks and descriptive gestures of all kinds, yet it is also
profoundly informed by an intuitive feel for Austro-Hungarian folk-echoes,
the rhythms and phrases of the Alps. He helps us to live in a world recognisably modern and contemporary precisely because of the saturation levels
this language has reached. Mahler's art – and that of others – allows us to see

into the real human desire that is represented in clichés, caricatures and conventional pieties, which is summed up in kitsch and merely exploited by the commerce it serves. The work of art can expose this, it can decry it, satirise it or celebrate it but it begins with a recognition of affinity between itself as a document of common humanity and the kitsch it sees into. The artist might envy the commercial success of kitsch or work within its dictated parameters. Many do. But whatever form expression takes or is given, the practice of it is based on this recognition of desire or longing. This recognition can be found not only in art but also in critical discussion – such as Adorno's study of Mahler.

Such recognition arises through conscious perception of the unnaturalness of language in art and through a trust in the desire it may represent. T.J. Cribb, in an essay on the Nigerian novelist Ben Okri, notes that 'although the English used is perfectly standard, the way it is used is not; it is calqued on a quite different set of cultural and syntactic relations. In some situations Standard English itself is subtly altered. Usually it remains superficially standard, but is made to respond to unfamiliar lines of force, like a mask occupied by a new spirit.'[36] Cribb's point is crucial to the linguistic situation in which many of the Scottish texts we will be looking at are located. This is partly because of the history of relations between the three languages Scottish literature is written in (as emphasised by Iain Crichton Smith in the poem for the resumed parliament): Gaelic, Scots and English. Modern Scottish Gaelic is connected back to old Irish Gaelic and to written forms in *The Book of the Dean of Lismore* (compiled between 1512 and 1526) and older Irish manuscripts, but the history of the Gaelic language is predominantly oral, written Gaelic literature achieving high distinction in the eighteenth century. Scots was both an oral and, simultaneously, a written idiom with major literary distinction from at least the fourteenth century on. In the nineteenth century, English begins to supersede Scots and, in a sense, to eclipse Gaelic writing altogether. As a primary idiom for writing, English dominates. Not until Lewis Grassic Gibbon in the 1930s does the narrative idiom mix in the 'speak of the place' (the vocabulary of spoken Scots), the 'song of the earth' (rhythms and intonations of Scots vernacular sound-structures) and English. But in almost every case, the English language itself, as Cribb says, 'is subtly altered'. The standard it observes becomes changed and the extent of the art involved reflects the subtle craft of that change. Cribb continues in the sentence I have used as my first epigraph: 'Because English is the international language of modernisation, the mask is also the modern world.'

It is time to consider some of Scotland's masks from the transitional moment when that modernity began.

2
Shakespeare and Scotland

The linguistic energy of London at the start of the seventeenth century was Shakespeare's medium. The clash and mix of forms and sounds within it was vitalising. The centrality of the theatre for Shakespeare's work gave focus to that energy, partly because of the dynamics of the city and the political transition in that city from the medieval to the early modern world – that is, on the death of Elizabeth I and the accession of James VI. The energies that quicken in Shakespeare's life do so at the moment when they lapse in the courtly tradition of Scottish literature, when James rides south.

The Anglocentralising in all these aspects is neat, compared to the arguable transition in Scotland from medieval to Renaissance eras. In a European context, it is more possible to see the Renaissance in Scotland beginning in the reign of James IV – the music of Robert Carver, the poetry of William Dunbar, Robert Henryson and Gavin Douglas, all seem much closer to a Renaissance world than to a Chaucerian one. Curiously, in some respects Dunbar's language seems more akin to that of the Gawain poet than Chaucer's. It is leaner, with more tension, muscle, bite and signature. Vernacular energies occupy courtly formalities. The relegation of Dunbar, Henryson and Douglas to the position of 'Scottish Chaucerians' that was effected for generations does not recognise this. It took as renewingly caustic an eye as Ezra Pound's to suggest that they were less late medieval and more early Renaissance. If Renaissance is strictly understood as rebirth, and the rebirth of this Renaissance is understood to lie in the rediscovery and redeployment of Greek and Roman sources, then Henryson and Douglas are surely much closer to Shakespeare than to Chaucer. The pathos in their work – in the figure of Henryson's Cresseid, for example – leads away from religious consolation and points towards humanist tragedy. At the end of *The Testament*, Cresseid cannot be promised salvation in a good European Catholic empyrean as she is a Pagan; Henryson leaves no doubt about his sympathy but the suggestion that her punishment of suffering has not been sufficient for her redemption leaves the alternative of a materialist sense of human tragedy.

These are preliminary divagations. Our attention here will be partly on Shakespeare's writing as it speaks out of these energies of London, theatre and political transition, and partly on a kind of politically reciprocal force with which to return to modern Scottish literature. The work of some modern Scottish writers has definite things to say about the Shakespearian legacy, and I will return to them later. In this chapter, I would like to do four things:

1. Rehearse briefly the representation of two exemplary Scottish characters from the repertoire of Shakespeare's histories.
2. Consider two aspects of Shakespeare's representation of nation and state in the late plays, *Cymbeline* and *The Tempest*.
3. Touch on the pragmatics of political topicality in what might be called the English play.
4. Cite a few examples of modern Scottish poets returning to or reinventing Shakespeare from the northern side of the border.

Two of Shakespeare's Scots

The most familiar example of Shakespeare's representation of national identity is in *Henry V*, Act III, Scene ii, when the Welsh captain Fluellen refers to the Irish Captain Macmorris's 'Nation' and gets a blast of angry questions in response: '. . . my Nation? What ish my Nation? Ish a Villaine, and a Bastard, and a Knave, and a Rascal'. The reply, Declan Kiberd points out, carefully indicates a declaration of loyalty to the British crown, despite the identification of the speaker with Irish national culture. Macmorris's name discloses that he is 'a descendant of the Norman settlers of the Fitzmaurice clan, some of whom changed their surnames to the Gaelic prefix "Mac"'. Macmorris's anger signals a 'painful awareness that a figure of such hybrid status will forever be suspect in English eyes'. For Kiberd, Shakespeare's Macmorris presents 'those traits of garrulity, pugnacity and a rather unfocused ethnic pride' which would come to typify the stage Irishman, along with the vaguely condescending air that he should be so anxious about national identity.[1]

It is worth considering Shakespeare's presentation of the Scots Captain Jamy in the same play for a moment. Like 'Macmorris', the word 'Jamy' is also a curious signal. Does the familiar use of a first name suggest a greater fondness for the Scotsman's loyalty, that it is more easily acknowledged? or, as a diminutive form, does it suggest a patronising aspect? He is introduced by Fluellen as 'a marvelous falerous gentleman, that is certain, and of great expedition [readiness, eagerness or forwardness] and knowledge in th' aunchient wars . . . he will maintain his argument as well as any military man in the world in the disciplines of the pristine wars of the Romans'. That is, he is brave, ready with argument and packed with knowledge of old wars and classic strategies. There is already an air of caricature about this, as there is in the Welsh Fluellen's respect for him and the accent in which it is delivered. And it is the accent – the voice – that marks Jamy as soon as he appears: 'I say gud day...' where 'I say' is already a 'discourse marker' signifying superfluous rhetoric and 'gud' is clearly designating a Scots inflection. The word and Jamy's repetitive insistences are hammered out in his next speech, responding to both Fluellen and Macmorris: 'It sall be very gud, gud feith, gud captens bath, and I sall quit [answer] you with gud leve, as I may pick occasion. That sall I, mary.' When Macmorris tells him that this is not the time for talking but for action ('there is throats to be cut'), Jamy responds quickly: 'By the mess, ere theise eyes of mine take themselves to slomber, I'll do gud service, or I'll lig i' th' grund for it! Ay or go to death! And I'll pay't as valorously as I may, that sall I suerly do, that is the breff and the long. Mary, I wad full fain heard some question 'tween you tway.' (ll.76–121)

Here the explanations, repetitions (to lie in the ground *or* to go to death is lavish), and inversions ('that sall I suerly do') – all amount to a caricature of reflexive rhetoric. This is a character whose language is full of verbal device, but the devices are self-evident, overdone, not actively persuasive or insidious, but overt, visible, and as such, perhaps, rather self-indulgent and inept. Jamy says that he would have wished to listen to 'some question' between Fluellen and Macmorris and indeed he gets it, for this is the moment at which the 'what is my nation?' speech commences. The scene itself ends twenty lines later with acknowledgement of 'the disciplines of war': these dictate closure of the present 'question', yet the scene has told us all that we need to know about the contradictory condescension and sympathy with which Shakespeare presents these characters.

Fluellen, Macmorris and Jamy are much more characters in their place and time in Henry's army than caricatures which the exaggerations of later centuries and other genres or different media will foster. But it is worth pausing to ask whether or how or to what extent if at all Shakespeare's Jamy and Macmorris foreshadow the representations of Ariel and Caliban in Aimé Césaire's 1969 version of *The Tempest*.[2] It may be that Césaire's play relies on paradigms intrinsic to *The Tempest*, yet there are seeming echoes. In Act 2, Scene 1, of Césaire's version, Caliban and Ariel are together. Ariel muses, 'I know you don't think much of me, but after all we are brothers... in suffering and slavery. Brothers in hope as well. We both want our freedom, only our methods vary.' But when he rebukes Caliban for his oppositional defiance – 'What use your struggle?' he is rebuked in turn by Caliban's austere response: 'What good has your obedience done you, you Uncle Tom....' The first word Caliban utters on stage is the Swahili for freedom, Uhuru. By contrast, Prospero is monoglot. He cannot engage in dialogue; he can only dictate. But Caliban is transgressive; he journeys back and forth between languages. Prospero uses language to close down consciousness; Caliban opens it out. Ariel is a mulatto slave, Caliban is a black slave and a new character is introduced, Eshu, a black demi-god. Eshu is the Yoruba god of boundaries between worlds. He arrives unannounced. Caliban says early in Act 3, 'I am subject to a tyrant, a sorcerer by his cunning hath cheated me of the island.' (The Shakespearian precedent suggesting the intellectual–supernatural hinterland of *The Tempest* is Sycorax, of course, but where Sycorax remains an implicit, potent force in that hinterland, Eshu is very much an active presence in Césaire's version.)

In Act 3, Scene 5, when Prospero sets Ariel free, Ariel looks forward to being 'the thrush / perched on an agave stalk that hurls / its mocking cry to the too-patient labourer: / "Black toiler! Black toiler!" '. A stage-direction notes that he speaks as if drunk, and Prospero exclaims as he ends, 'What an unsettling agenda!' and advises him to 'Fly! Before I change my mind!' However, it is Caliban who tells Prospero, when the Magus suggests that they have been living together for ten years and should continue to live in peace, that he is 'not interested in peace. I'm interested in being free.' And it is Caliban's song which can be heard, '*above the sound of the surf and the mewing of birds*' as the play ends: 'LIBERTY, OH-AY! LIBERTY!'

The disputatious Scot prefigured in Jamy, naïvely expecting fair exchange of opinion rather than a war of persuasion and coercion, becomes a more familiar trope through the eighteenth and nineteenth centuries. The point to emphasise here, however, is that language defines and delimits identity for these characters – Césaire's Caliban as well as Shakespeare's – in a special way: it is more extremely evident for them than it is for others.

There is one other pre-eminent example of the Scot in Shakespeare's history plays: Douglas in *Henry IV*, part one. Jamy and the Douglas have similar characteristics, but the political context in *Henry IV* is more complex and the matters of loyalty and nationality are suggested with greater subtlety and curiosity. When Hotspur, Worcester and Douglas come on stage in Act IV, Scene i, the play is already moving towards the climactic battle in which Douglas will figure colourfully. In Hotspur, Douglas is matched by faster rhetoric and quicker, more slippery intention:

> Well said, my noble Scot. If speaking truth
> In this fine age were not thought flattery,
> Such attribution should the Douglas have
> As not a soldier of this season's stamp
> Should go so general current through the world.
> By God, I cannot flatter, I do defy [despise]
> The tongues of soothers [flatterers]! But a braver place
> In my heart's love hath no man than yourself.
> Nay, task me to my word; approve me, Lord.

Douglas's response is an acknowledgement, but held in:

> Thou art the king of honour.
> No man so potent breathes upon the ground
> But I will beard [confront] him.

It is another declaration of loyalty, this time to the leader who will oppose the English King. Hotspur declares that it is possible to make a 'push against a kingdom' then 'o'erturn it topsy-turvy down' and Douglas affirms: 'There is not such a word/Spoke of in Scotland as this term of fear.' Douglas ends the scene in apocalyptic mode (though his ultimate survival is perhaps a denial of Hotspur's apocalyptic view). Hotspur calls his forces to arms: 'Domesday is near. Die all, die merrily' and Douglas seems to assert a supernatural assurance in his own ability: 'Talk not of dying. I am out of fear / Of death or death's hand for this one half-year.' He is eager for the fight, disgusted at the caution before battle counselled by Worcester, and bristling with lust for it when the engagement approaches: 'I have thrown / A brave defiance in King Henry's teeth' he boasts in Act V, Scene ii. However, on the battlefield of Shrewsbury, Douglas is confounded by the counterfeit King: Walter Blunt in disguise. Douglas rises to rhetorical flourish, haughty disdain and self-confident proclamation as he squares up to Blunt. Yet as he speaks the words, the audience is surely aware that he is fooling himself. Blunt is part of a ruse to protect the King, who, Hotspur tells us 'hath many marching in his hosts': his disguise takes Douglas in and Douglas falls for it further through the flourish of his own rhetoric:

Blunt: What is thy name, that in battle thus thou crossest me?
   What honour dost thou seek upon my head?
Douglas: Know then my name is Douglas,
   And I do haunt thee in the battle thus
   Because some tell me that thou are a king.
Blunt: They tell thee true.

They fight; Douglas kills Blunt; Hotspur enters and tells Douglas he recognises the corpse as Blunt, not the King; Douglas is disgusted, sets out to 'kill all his coats' (all those disguised as the King): 'I'll murder all his wardrobe, piece by piece / Until I meet the King.'

This is impressive, fanatic and extreme, but it is also comic and absurd. Douglas is brave, strong, a warrior, but he is outclassed by Hotspur and outmanoeuvred by the King. When he encounters the King his language rises to even greater flamboyance but the comic component – clearly implied by the opening question – is ambiguous. It makes his fanaticism even wilder than before and a far less reasonable thing than the commitment that underlies Hotspur's wiliness. The Yoruba God Eshu is perhaps not far away.

Douglas: Another king? They grow like Hydra's heads.
      I am the Douglas, fatal to all those
      That wear those colours on them. What art thou
      That counterfeits the colours of a king?
King: The King himself, who, Douglas, grieves at heart
      So many of his shadows thou hast met,
      And not the very king...

Here the momentary compassion for others reminds us of the gulf between
the king with his care for his subjects and the rebel whose sole aim is murder. They fight, and as Douglas is about to win, the Prince intervenes. It is
a moment of great effect:

Douglas: I fear thou art another counterfeit;
      And yet in faith, thou bearest thee like a king:
      But mine I am sure thou art, whoe'er thou be.
      And thus I win thee.
They fight, the king being in danger – enter the Prince of Wales.
Prince: Hold up thy hand, vile Scot, or thou art like
      Never to hold it up again.

They fight, and *'Douglas flieth'*. The implication appears to be that despite
assertive claims of fixed identity ('I am the Douglas') the Prince is the 'truer'
man.

Douglas makes one further appearance on stage. When Falstaff enters to
urge Prince Hal to victory, Douglas re-enters and engages Falstaff. When
Falstaff *'falls down as if he were dead'*, Douglas takes off again, leaving Hal to
kill Hotspur. Prince Hal and the King have won the day.

What of the Douglas?

His fate is delivered in the closing lines of the play, and it is characteristic:
the Prince describes how 'the noble Scot, Lord Douglas' when he saw the
day turned and Hotspur dead, fled with his men, but, falling, was captured.
Hal requests the King to be allowed to 'dispose of him'. The King replies,
'With all my heart.' And Hal directs that he should be delivered up 'to his
pleasure, ransomless and free'.

      His valours shown upon our crests today
      Have taught us how to cherish such high deeds,
      Even in the bosom of our adversaries.

In other words, he gets off Scot-free.

The characterisation of Douglas: belligerent, proud, strong, skilled, suscep-
tible, yet resilient and elusive, is perhaps as prophetic as that of Jamy in *Henry V*.
Although it is important to see how freshly and dramatically sharp they

are in Shakespeare's plays, the point need not be laboured that they are also both characterisations which subsequent representations of Scots in fiction, theatre and film have sometimes exaggerated into caricature and cliché. As with Fluellen, Macmorris and Jamy, Hotspur and Douglas are defined by their language as well as by the narrative trajectory of their characters, and their roles are circumscribed by their capacity for language and understanding. If Hal carries the day, it is not only because of martial prowess, youth and speed, but because, as he claims to Poins (Act II, Scene iv, ll.17–19): 'I am so good a proficient in one quarter of an hour that I can drink with any tinker in his own language during my life.' Douglas is an Elizabethan representation of a Scot; in the tragedies and late plays, the question of national identity becomes more complex.

Late plays

At the other end of the Shakespeare canon, in *Cymbeline* and *The Tempest*, a writing life away from the history plays, I would like to begin to consider Shakespeare's imagination working in terms of national identity in less-specific, more-general terms. Once again, however, the proleptic quality is significant. Perhaps the clearest assertion of this is in Mary Floyd-Wilson's essay, 'Delving to the root: *Cymbeline*, Scotland and the English race'. She makes an excellent case for *Cymbeline* representing the accommodative imperial politics and authority of Britishness and suggests succinctly the lasting significance of this:

> Generated by the ethnological tensions of the early seventeenth century, *Cymbeline* spins out an English historical fantasy in which the Scots submit to Anglo-British rule and the English emerge as a race unaffected by Britain's early history of mingled genealogies and military defeats. *Cymbeline*'s allusions to the competing claims in English and Scottish histories might be aligned with the current efforts in British historiography to represent Britain in non-Anglocentric terms. However...the play also responds to a strain of contemporary pressures within early modern historiography that gave rise to modern Anglo-centricism: the antiquarians' embrace of England's Anglo-Saxon ancestry. In other words, the traditionally Anglo-centric bent of British history was shaped in part by early modern England's investment in ethnic distinctions. While union advocates may have relied on the assimilative effect of depicting Britain's future as a revival of its past, those historians attesting to English-Saxon roots aimed to extricate the English people from a history of Briton savagery, Roman domination, and Scottish kinship...Shakespeare's *Cymbeline* romanticizes the nascent historiographical impulses toward English exceptionalism that the new British history now aims to redress.[3]

Colin MacCabe has also discussed two of the ways in which *Cymbeline* raises questions about national, familial and sexual identity. In his essay, 'The Voice of Esau' – and it is worth noting that MacCabe's enquiry into this aspect of Shakespeare is refracted through the specific focus of his essay, James Joyce's Stephen Dedalus in the library in *Ulysses* – he says that the play 'turns around the question of lawful inheritance and the passage from father to son. The question is interwoven with the identity of the nation, or, to be more precise, of Britain. It is the change from England to Britain that makes *Cymbeline* so important a re-statement of the themes of the earlier history plays.' Shakespeare brings together in the play themes which offer a strange configuration of ideas about identity, sexuality, nation and race. This 'nation' is emphatically Britain, not England (meaning, in the first instance, pre-Saxon England and Wales). 'The word *Britain* and its cognates occur no less than 47 times in *Cymbeline*, a startling fact when one realises that in no other play, except for the similarly late *Henry VIII*, does it occur more than once.' Neither *England* nor *English* occurs once in the play. There is, says MacCabe, 'evident cause in the changed status of the realm after the accession of James VI of Scotland to the throne of England'. Indeed, although Cymbeline is set in southern Britain, some of the plot is spliced in from Holinshed's *The Description and Historie of Scotland* (1587).[4]

Unlike *Henry V*, where language and reality are disrupted, in *Cymbeline* they are in direct relation. Belarius says in Act III, Scene iii, 'this story / The world may read in me. My body's marked / With Roman swords...'. And the narrative, quoting Holinshed, includes Scotland in its configuration of nation and language in the idea of 'Britons'. The play is full of demands and urgings that characters should speak, or strive to speak, which are frustrated when no sounds or noises issue, but which are resolved when, through speaking, language confers identity, place and relation. Muteness is fore-shadowed; the speechlessness of 'others' who have no 'voice of their own' – is in the making. Through the consideration of constraints in language and speech, confirmation and, indeed, celebration of them is possible in the play, in a context of inclusive nationality, or in MacCabe's words, 'national totalisation which, ignoring the actual political division within the British Isles and Europe, produces an imaginary unity which embraces in peace everyone from the Druid priests to the Roman Emperor'.

The trouble is, this transparent language of national unity is pellucidly English, unclotted by velar fricatives, glottal stops or vernacular idioms, let alone the other languages within the realm. From the perspective of what it excludes, the peace it confers is a desert. It prefigures Aimé Césaire's monoglot Prospero, foreclosing dialogue through the assertion of his own authoritative ignorance of other languages. For MacCabe, this 'peace' was what James Joyce was to spend his life writing *against*, using as one of his three best weapons that skill which sets all speech at naught: not only cunning and exile, but also, silence. The play ends by asserting an imperial resolution which joins Celts to English and English to Rome:

> Publish we this peace
> To all our subjects. Set we forward; let
> A Roman and a British ensign wave
> Friendly together. So through Lud's Town march,
> And in the temple of great Jupiter
> Our peace we'll ratify, seal it with feasts.
> Set on there! Never a war did cease,
> Ere bloody hands were washed, with such a peace.

What does 'Rome' signify here? Presumably, it stands for an imperium centred elsewhere, not 'here' in Celtdom, and so, ironically, if read from Scotland, it might signify England. For MacCabe, Joyce's opposition to this is clear. For Hugh MacDiarmid there was another factor: the language, idiom and speech called Scots, which might offer much deeper and unexplored resources not only in its vocabulary and tonal expressiveness but also in its position as a 'double tongue' – neither quickly identifiable as a self-defined 'language' nor reducible to a mere 'dialect' of 'English'. It lives between categories and dialogue, works with both oral and written pronouncement, clogs itself with earth and gives itself to air. Eshu is nearby again. This crucial position prompts consideration of the last play I want to talk about here: *The Tempest*.

Before we go there, however, I would like to give an example of MacDiarmid's use of Scots, because it clearly connects with the disruptive energies in language which the inclusive peace at the end of *Cymbeline* cannot accommodate. These lines come from *To Circumjack Cencrastus* (1932) and are relevant here for the way they bring together the problematic nature of Scots – written and spoken – in a context of social and economic power, along with a sense of the Caliban-like spirit of unreconstructed opposition to the authority of that power. MacDiarmid or his persona seems to be a junior clerk in an office, bitterly resentful of his boss:

> Curse his new hoose, his business, his cigar,
> His wireless set, and motor car
> Alsatian, gauntlet gloves, plus fours and wife,
> – A'thing included in his life;
> And, abune a', his herty laughter,
> And – if he has yin – his hereafter.[5]

MacDiarmid observes bitterly that the will to ignorance and the line of least resistance which is typical of his boss 'ruins life' as much as disease might ruin what people are physically capable of. He curses everything that makes him 'pretend or feel / That life as maist folk hae't is real' or that he should waste his time on 'silly sociabilities' or anything that will distract him from his art. And then, suddenly, he curses his own language, and the speed with which he turns from outward condemnation of his boss to internalised agonising about language and thought is astonishing:

> Curse on my dooble life and dooble tongue,
> – Guid Scots wi' English a' hamstrung –
>
> *Speakin' o' Scotland in English words*
> *As it were Beethoven chirpt by birds;*
> *Or as if a board school teacher*
> *Tried to teach Rimbaud and Nietzsche.*

The sudden vulgarities of rhyme belie the subtlety of mind and quickness of movement. The verse moves more swiftly than could be suggested by the frustrations it describes, as if the muddy weight of the language were electrified and sent flying, an Ariel movement with Caliban's voice, or a Caliban with Prospero's self-consciousness. However closely we might describe the verse, the point is that not only the speaker's position of power in relation to his boss is analogous to Caliban's to Prospero, but that this relation is embodied in the language, in the relation of Scots to English. (In the early 1930s, vernacular Scots would certainly more frequently have been the speech of employees and English that of employers but the political significance of voice would remain crucial in Scottish writing, especially in the work of Tom Leonard, which we will come to in the conclusion.)

In MacDiarmid's 1926 poem, *A Drunk Man Looks at the Thistle*, the blasted heaths of a Lear-like tragic universe of human potential running to waste and destruction seems close, evoked partly by the landscape of wasteland and weed that surrounds the poem's speaker, partly by the ballad-like rhythms of the verse and partly by the intensity of the Scots language. By contrast, the next major extended poetic sequence in modern Scottish literature explicitly addressing the matter of Scotland, Edwin Morgan's *Sonnets from Scotland* of 1984, not only adopted the sonnet form (though not the Shakespearian sonnet rhyme-scheme) but also used a relatively standard English. In contrast to MacDiarmid, Morgan creates a more mobile, figurative, populated landscape of potentially magical, shapeshifting, alternative realities, a history of Scotland in terms of what happened that is less familiar, and of what might yet be. The world of *A Midsummer Night's Dream*, in its ethos of happy possibility and celebration, seems closer to Morgan's affirmation of multi-faceted nationality. Yet the ballad-stanzas of so much of *A Drunk Man* keep it close to song, whereas the careful structures of Morgan's sonnets evoke a tradition of print and books.[6]

Some of these dichotomies might be more fully explored now, in *The Tempest*. Prospero mediates. The doubleness is figured in Caliban and Ariel, his slaves and servants, animal and spirit, one scaly, resentful, hating, self-pitying, brutish, heavy; the other svelte, cheeky, clean, asexual, always on the point of becoming a movement in the air, like a song, nimble, light. Yet perhaps their key characteristic is that they are both emergent figures, always on the point of becoming something else. Their strength is that they are not fixed; their definition remains elusive.

I should acknowledge here Willy Maley's suggestion that Caliban and Ariel are analogous to Ireland and Scotland respectively. (This is complicated, but not invalidated, by parallels between Prospero and James.) In his essay, ' "Another Britain"?: Bacon's *Certain Considerations Touching the Plantation in Ireland* (1609)', Maley writes this:

> Scotland is the third term that gets lost in 'Anglo-Irish,' the hyphen, hymen, suspension, or ligature that binds three nations under one heading, the third lobe of a trefoil, recalling a contemporary vision: 'And some I see / That two-fold balls and treble sceptres carry' (*Macbeth* IV, i, 119–120). For Bacon, like Banquo, the future comes in twos and threes. Can Scotland be inserted into a seamless English narrative, or an uninterrupted discourse on Ireland? Only by an act of violence. Revisionist Irish history has not reinscribed Scotland. It remains within an 'Anglo-Irish' problematic. Cultural Materialism, Irish Revisionism, and the New Historicism all seem content to leave the binary opposition intact. Yet the exclusion of Scotland from discussions of Ireland matters. It is the matter of Britain, the matter of the British Problem, the problem of identity and difference in a multi-nation state. How did Scotland and Ireland come to play Ariel and Caliban to England's Prospero?[7]

It is a provocative question. The answer begins in what is seeded in Shake-speare's play, and the question of what matters in it is partly answered by reinterpretive poems by two Scots looking back on Shakespeare's characters in the late twentieth century. We will come to them in a moment.

Caliban's ancestry and Prospero's succession to his mother's power in his authority over both Caliban and Ariel, is explained to Ariel in Act I, Scene ii. Prospero reminds Ariel that he had been imprisoned in 'a cloven pine', a victim of Sycorax, where he remained for twelve years, abandoned after the witch's death. At that time, there were only two inhabitants of the island, Ariel and Caliban (whom Prospero describes as 'A freckled whelp, hagborn'). Ariel's response to Prospero here is of gratitude – he thanks him for freeing him from the tree – and obedience: indeed, he is eager to please when he hears Prospero's promise that he will 'discharge' the spirit once his bidding has been done.

The contrast with Caliban is vivid. Prospero calls forth his 'slave, who never / Yields us kind answer'. He is greeted with curses, sullen resentment, anger and rebelliousness. Césaire's Caliban is already implicit. Rights of possession and personal appetite combine with a suppressed pathos: 'I must eat my dinner' Caliban tells us, then adds, 'This island's mine by Sycorax my mother, / Which thou taks't from me. When thou cams't first . . . then I loved thee / And showed thee all the qualities of the isle . . . .' The sexual threat Caliban represents is quickly delineated: he would have raped Miranda and 'peopled else / This isle with Calibans' if Prospero had not stopped him. He is unrepentant. To Prospero he is an 'Abhorred slave': the villainy seems as much in his desire to miscegenate and populate the island with hybrid offspring as in his intended violence upon Miranda.

Of course, around 1603, at the time of the Union of the Crowns, there was fear that the English might be overrun by Scots and it is arguable that the threat of similar violent miscegenation was associated with this idea. A familiar reference can be noted in *Eastward Ho!* the cynical, urbane London comedy collaboration by Ben Jonson, John Marston and George Chapman, written early in 1605. 'Chapman and Jonson were thrown into prison (Marston escaped) for commenting adversely on the purchase of knighthoods, authorised by James, and on the influx of Scots following James to England in 1603.'[8] In Act III, Scene iii, imagining a new life in Virginia, Scapethrift asks if it is a pleasant country, and Seagull tells him it is:

> you shall live freely there, without serjeants, or courtiers, or lawyers, or intelligencers, only a few industrious Scots perhaps, who indeed are dispersed over the face of the whole earth. But as for them, there are no greater friends to Englishmen and England, when they are out in the world, than they are. And for my part, I would a hundred thousand of 'em were there, for we are all one countrymen now, ye know; and we should find ten times more comfort of them there than we do here.[9]

The irony is thick. Particularly so, considering Jonson's connections with Scotland (reputedly he came of a Scots family and visited the country, as recorded in memorable conversations with William Drummond of Hawthornden).

In *The Tempest*, Ariel and Caliban seem opposite forces yet they are emphatically connected: both prisoners, both slaves, both held in service first to Sycorax then to Prospero. Both are obedient; both are subversive. The pattern of relationships that emerges in the opening scenes of the play suggests a radically different scenario from that of the all-inclusive unity of a British identity in *Cymbeline*. Further, Prospero not only mediates but also demonstrates that his own identity is every bit as much the puppet, the fictional creation of the author, as are his daughter and his slaves. And the explicit theatricality of these scenes insists that the stage conventions are understood as part of the construction of their characters.

The mediator is not omnipresent, nor all-powerful, and neither is his author. Negotiations, in language and desires, are happening continually.

Divisions, polarities, splitting and reconfigurations of loyalty and preference are constantly unfolding. They seem magical, inexplicable, to the perception of strangers coming upon them for the first time. When Ferdinand hears Ariel's song, 'Come unto these yellow sands...' he is left wondering: 'Where should this music be? I' th' air or th' earth?' The question opens up the dichotomy: the music is in the air all right (it must be, to enter by sound), yet it is also in the earth, for it also enters by physical contact, with the earth, and with the sea, as Ferdinand remembers how it 'crept by me upon the waters...' as he wept for his drowned father. (Maybe this is one of the sweetest and most poignant evocations of the relation between personal, familial and local identity, even though – or especially because – the 'local' is strange here, multisensory and bewildering.)

Of course, Ariel is luring Ferdinand into Prospero's plan, seducing him into further lamenting his father's supposed death. In Act III, Scene ii, Caliban is performing a similar trick on Stephano:

Caliban: Art thou afeard?
Stephano: No monster, not I.
Caliban: Be not afeard, the isle is full of noises,
          Sounds and sweet airs that give delight and hurt not.

Within moments, however, Caliban has evoked a music of 'a thousand twangling instruments' and 'voices / That, if I then had waked after long sleep, / Will make me sleep again': a world of comforting sleep and dreams, where, Stephano recognises, music might be had 'for nothing'. Caliban agrees, but this will only happen, he says, 'When Prospero is destroyed.'

The destruction of Prospero in the context of the play would not only signify the disintegration of plot in the banal sense, it would also confer defined identity on Caliban and Ariel. Their liberation, in that sense, would be another kind of imprisonment: a fixed, fulfilled identity for each of them in which the mediation and negotiations between them ceased to be possible. Of course, in the banal sense, it does not happen. But in another sense, is not this exactly what does happen at the end of the play, as, one after another, resolutions are arrived at and characters find their partners or their fate? The three climactic farewells of Caliban, Ariel and Prospero are not only representational of characters in a story but explicit and overt representations of *theatrical* characters whose representatives – literally, the actors – are about to leave the stage.

Caliban is sent back to Prospero's cell with Prospero's comment on him: 'He is as disproportionate in his manner / As in his shape.' Prospero sends him away with the promise that he will be freed, but the last words reflect back upon the ugliness Caliban has embodied: 'As you look / To have my pardon, trim it handsomely.' Caliban promises to do so and 'be wise hereafter, / And seek for grace'.

Ariel's liberation is, fittingly, quicker and less clogged with language. It is a brief aside: he is charged to keep calm seas and fair winds for the royal fleet, but having done that, Prospero is finished with him: 'Then to the elements / Be free, and fare thou well!' The cast exits, leaving Prospero alone for his famous epilogue: 'Now my charms are all o'erthrown / And what strength I have's mine own / Which is most faint.' He is now addressing the audience directly, as the Duke once again, and not the magician: 'Now I want [lack] / spirits to enforce, and to enchant....' He begs release not only from the island in the story but also from the stage in every actual performance, a release that is given by the applause of the audience: 'As you from crimes would pardoned be, / Let your indulgence set me free.'

At exactly this moment, in the parenthesis of silence that exists between the dying away of the music of these spoken words and beginning of the audience's 'indulgence', Rainer Maria Rilke sets his poem, 'The Spirit Ariel (After reading Shakespeare's *Tempest*)'. It is the moment in which Ariel might be imagined, 'incomprehensibly / far-scattered fragrance, making the invisible / at last complete'. And Prospero is

> Smiling, to think you'd been
> on nodding terms with that, such great acquaintance
> so soon familiar. Perhaps weeping, too,
> when you remember how it loved you and
> would yet be going, always both at once.[10]

Prospero becomes the second person singular, and thus, an autobiographical persona, the poet speaking to himself, as well as the reader, while Ariel is this elusive thing that 'loved you and / would yet be going, always both at once'.

But then Rilke adds a further seven lines, literally in parenthesis, and effects a radical change of tone in the poem, from near-rhapsody to cold observation:

> (And there I left it? Now he terrifies me,
> this man who's duke again. – The way he draws
> the wire into his head, and hangs himself
> beside the other puppets, and henceforth
> begs mercy of the play!... What epilogue
> of achieved mastery! Putting off, standing there
> with only one's own strength: 'which is most faint'.)

'The Spirit Ariel' dates from early 1913 and catches exactly that sense at the end of the play, that Prospero, as well as Caliban and Ariel, is no more than words in air embodied in that puppet-man, the actor.

The emergent identities are freed at the moment of their release from the stage. If Caliban stays with the earth, the island, or the island earth, and if

Ariel is freed to the elements, Prospero, equally, finds himself 'mine own' and no more. As Shakespeare's masks are taken off, the actors leave to put on their own.

Rilke's poem helps define a moment of realisation about identities and transition, fixed securities and movement and literary form. It alerts us sharply to the metaphor working between actual theatre and imaginary narrative. Perhaps one reason why 'this man who's duke again' is terrifying is because that resumption of identity fixes and secures him: the plot no longer unfolds. Prospero, in the story, might live on as the Duke, but in the play, he returns himself to the wire, waiting to be taken down again.

Macbeth, or, the English play

Literalism should prompt caution. In 1921, Lilian Winstanley claimed in *"Hamlet" and the Scottish Succession*[11] that in *Hamlet*, Denmark is Scotland and Hamlet is both Essex and James VI and I. This seems extravagant, but as Stuart Kurland comments, 'despite the advent of the "New Historicism", many critics remain uneasy about topicality in Shakespeare . . . Critics interested in Shakespearian topicality must attempt to reconstruct . . . the "local" dimensions of the plays in ways that will inform, rather than determine (or supplant), interpretation'.[12] If literalism and specific correspondences such as those asserted by Lilian Winstanley seem unlikely, nevertheless, as Kurland observes, 'the politics of *Hamlet*' do require a sense of 'the context of the uneasiness surrounding the late Elizabethan succession question'.[13] Kurland himself attempts this in reading *Pericles* as a play in which the behaviour of the King is recognisable.[14] For Kurland, Pericles's 'casual attitude towards rule' seems to reflect 'the progresses and hunting trips that marked the residence of King James I in England' when *Pericles* was being written, around 1606–1608.[15] He continues: 'For the first audience of *Pericles*, aware of King James' apparent unwillingness to place the demands of government before his personal desires, the example of Marina might have offered a more compelling model of rule.'[16] (Timon or Lear might have been better examples.)

Moving between the extremes of Winstanley's brassy assertions and Kurland's cautious speculations, the general points I want to make about Shakespeare and Scotland are perhaps quite simple.

In Douglas and Jamy, Shakespeare presents Scottish characters whose idiosyncrasies suggest images and aspects that helped generate iconographies and caricatures that have been drawn out and exaggerated in later representations.

Deep among the tragedies, centrally in Shakespeare's career, explicitly designed as a welcome (several years on) to James the VI and I, *Macbeth* achieves three complimentary acts: in the canon of tragedy, no play offers us more of the representation of our worst potentialities; in the canon of adaptation, no play so thoroughly distorts the historical account for subsequent imagination (Macbeth, by historical records, was a very long way from the character in the play); and in the context of its own history, no play is more explicit in its overt design: to flatter James by reassuring him of the moral rightness and political justice of his own ascendancy. This is the meaning of the 'show of eight kings and Banquo' in Act IV, Scene i, where the 'last [King] enters with a glass [a mirror] in his hand' – a 'show' which immediately prompts Macbeth's lines: 'Thou art too like the spirit of Banquo. Down! / Thy crown does sear mine eyelids.'

The assumption of a court performance is reasonable. It is possible to imagine these lines in at least one production of the play being addressed directly to this last King, James himself, whose actual face may have been caught, reflected in the mirror, so that Macbeth is heard literally talking into the future. Macbeth's vision – even through closed eyes – is burned into him by the insight that his own rule must be severed, and Banquo's successors resume the royal line whose incarnation in James VI and I prompted the writing of the play itself.

Having established the characteristics in the history plays and extended the boundaries past breaking in the great tragedies, the atmosphere and direction in the late plays attempt reconciliation, harmonisation, and a reunifying coherence of spirit and presence. The ruptures and discordances in *The Winter's Tale* and *Pericles* are incipiently tragic but the tragic potential dissolves; in *Cymbeline* that dissolution of possible ruin and devastation is carried further and a rising sense of wholeness, resolved unity and pleasurable conjoinment is asserted and maintained through the wishful, mythical term 'Britishness'. But in *The Tempest*, in crucial ways, the tensions and differences are bodied forth once more, explicitly and dramatically in the isolated groups of particular characters with their own political motives and structures of design, in the lovers and the relationships of love beween a young man and a young woman and between grown-up children and their fathers, and finally, most mythopoeically, in Caliban and Ariel. The association of Caliban with the word cannibal and by extension native or simply earlier inhabitants of colonised lands, is familiar. Yet he does draw upon some of those aspects of character in Douglas, Jamy (and indeed Macbeth – a mixture of pathetic helplessness and vicious intention).

So is Caliban Scottish? The question reverses Willy Maley's one-to-one allegorical linking but begs another: if he might be, then what of Ariel? And now that the questions are opening complexities, what of Prospero?

Scotland's Shakespeare

The title of Norman MacCaig's 1983 volume, *A World of Difference*, already foreshadows the divided and re-united identity represented in his poem 'Go away, Ariel'.[17] In the first six lines, Ariel is rejected with gestural vulgarity:

described as 'heartless', 'musical' and 'supersonic', he is told to 'zip round the world / or curl up in a cowslip's bell'. The question, 'does everyone prefer Caliban to you, / as I do?' hangs in the air unanswered, for if Ariel is being told to leave, it is his presence that is such a pest. Ariel's obstinate, annoying attention keeps the tension and irony in the poem unresolved, so that when line 6 expresses MacCaig's preference, the poem will go on to enact the desired thing: 'I'd rather be visited by Caliban.'

Caliban has arrived by line 7, the beginning of the third stanza. The first sentence brings them all together: the poet's persona, Caliban and the circling Ariel (to whom the poem is addressed, after all). 'As I am, I am. I chat with him...' MacCaig recognises himself more clearly in him, 'spilling out of an armchair / scaly on the carpet'. MacCaig tells us he is teaching Caliban how to smoke, a consolation when he weeps self-pityingly about his unattainable love for Miranda and 'goes on about his mother'. The vulgar command of the last stanza reminds us, however, of Ariel's presence: 'Leave us / to have a good cry – to stare at each other / with recognition and loathing.'

MacCaig sees himself in Caliban as they talk and smoke together; but the ironic form of the poem suggests a simultaneous affinity with Ariel. Spirit and matter, air and earth, music and selflessness ('Heartless') in ethereal movement, and the sense of living physically in a bodily world are held together. The grumble and moan in the poem is also a celebration of that connectedness. MacCaig's poetry of this period enacts this connectedness memorably. In the first poem of the same book, 'Helpless collector', he describes the awkward position of being the recipient of gifts that might please or be hateful, but when the ugly 'crooked mask' is placed behind the beautiful, translucent, 'delicate jar' its image 'moves to the front'.[18] The last poem entitled 'Journeys' in *The Equal Skies*, the volume that immediately preceded *A World of Difference*, begins by asserting that 'Travelling's fine', according to stars, waves, wind and trees in the wind; there are 'always receding headlands'. But there are other, 'bad journeys' to 'a bitter place' that remains unreachable:

> I lean towards it,
> tugging to get there, and thank God
> I'm clogged with the world. It grips me,
> I hold it.[19]

'Journeys' occupies a tragic sense of irrecoverable loss; devastation is nearby in its vocabulary of temporal balance. But 'Go away, Ariel' is comic, an evocation of preference for being 'clogged with the world' that is itself masterly in its lightness and deftness of touch.

The sense of being 'clogged with the world' is there too in Edwin Morgan's sound-poem 'Caliban Falls Asleep in the Isle Full of Noises', which dates from 1979.[20] But Morgan's poem does not state preference. It subtly evokes both the matter of the cloggy world and the transcendent spirit in it, as Caliban himself nods down to sleep and dream, and the noises change from monstrous belchings and thunderous bodily expressions to the sounds of upwardly directed birdsong. The poem is made up of words made up of letters which evoke sounds but offer no immediate grammatical or narrative meaning. The sounds enact associations. The first line seems to begin with forest mudpools and clumsy syllables, then, after an oblique, there is the echo of Caliban's chant from *The Tempest*: ''Ban, 'Ban, Ca – Caliban / Has a new master. Get a new man!' (Act II, Scene ii, ll.192–193). Morgan's poem begins:

> grobravara hollaglob / ban ban cacaliban
> thargarbonder skeelohera / ban ban cacaliban
> twing fang kong-pan-lang / ban ban cacaliban
> stegzerbogzer stravavoorian / ban ban cacaliban
> grawk blag bololozzin / ban ban cacaliban
> stritch fretch bredzerbroz / bab ban cacaliban

As the poem progresses, the 'noises' of the isle seem more or less identifiable; heavy-sounding mammalian grunts and semi-Russian ('stravavoorian') or semi-Chinese ('twing fang kong-pan-lang') transmute into the repeated 'squawk' of a parrot (returning eleven times), the 'roar' of a lion or tiger (coming ten times), the 'caw' of a crow or vulture (also ten times) and the 'cheep' of a little bird. This word is repeated eleven times in eleven lines, then breaks off, then returns two more times, to end the poem: 'cheep / cheep'. Meanwhile, on the other side of the oblique, on the right of the page, Caliban's line is repeated and shortened down to 'ban ban caliban' then 'ban ban caban' then 'ban ban ban' until in the sixteenth line only the word 'ban' remains, as if the noises continue past the moment at which Caliban drifts off to sleep. As he slumbers, beside him, we still hear the squawking, roaring, the sardonic 'caw' or chirruping 'cheep'. The poem's comic playfulness makes a serious point: the slumber of beasts concurs with the birdsongs of spirits. If reason has its nightmares, monsters might give birth to angels, or, to paraphrase Nietzsche, no carnival without cruelty, but chaos brings forth dancing stars. The poem celebrates the 'clogged' realities of material and bodily life, but it moves towards air and dream, and the freedoms they suggest are tender.

Morgan's 1997 volume, *Virtual and Other Realities* is divided into five sections: three separate commissioned poem-sequences open the book. Each one is a virtuoso piece: a descriptive journey of sperm and egg towards the moment of conception (as effective as it is unlikely); a bestiary of Scotland (including wolf, eagle, deer and female midges like a hostile cloud of Lady Macbeths out for blood); a celebration of Burns from unexpected perspectives; and then the title-sequence itself. The fifth and final section of the book is a single poem of thirteen lines, climactic, affirmative and ending the book in exclamation: this is 'Ariel Freed'.[21] (It is worth correlating Morgan's Ariel with Maley's notion of Ariel as Scottish, though as we have seen, Caliban is also familiar to Morgan's imagination.)

It warrants close attention. Isolated, the poem speaks in cool, elated tones, opening in release and exhilaration, an upward lift from darkness into night sky: 'I lifted my wings at midnight.' Suddenly we are already in flight and the second and third lines allow us the pleasure of fondly looking back while rising further: 'Moonlit pines, empty paths, / broochlike lagoons dwindled below me.' The exotic-sounding 'lagoons' are 'broochlike': badges, 'memories of earth', to use a phrase which entitles another of Morgan's poem-sequences.[22] The familiar Scots 'pines', the neutral 'paths' and the 'lagoons' crystallise in the fleeting moment of the lines. Their images 'dwindle' while the word suggests, perhaps, 'kindle': sparkling, bright. We see *with* Ariel, become Ariel, at the same time as we are imagining Ariel flying, becoming both an intimate of our imagination and also increasingly distant. It is reminiscent, too, of the opening of Morgan's poem 'Jack London in Heaven': 'Part the clouds, let me look down. / Oh God that earth.'[23] But where Morgan's Jack London wants it all again – the sun hitting Frisco, the brisk day on the Bay – Ariel is joyous in his soaring departure: 'Oh I was electric: my wingtips / winked like stars through the real stars.'

This is elation. In the assonance and alliteration crossing and connecting the lines, from 'wingtips' to 'winked like' the shimmer of repeated sound prepares us for the simile, the flashing wingtips 'like stars' but surrounded by 'the real stars': metaphor and actuality interweave. Note how the word 'the', prosily, quietly, slows down the rhythm in that line, emphasising the 'reality' of the stars – without that word they would be much more 'imagined' – the word de-rhapsodises them. Imagination penetrates the real and the real returns through imaginary things. The quickness of it here should not blind us to the centrality of this commitment in Morgan's work. In *A.D. A Trilogy of Plays on the Life of Christ*, Morgan's Jesus miraculously cancels out the morbidity of mortality with an assertion that keeps the real and the imagined wedded: 'In the midst of life I find myself in art / In the midst of art I find myself in life.'[24]

There are two more sentences in 'Ariel Freed'. The first moves forward fluently and quickly into an encompassing sense of the ocean surrounding the movement of the figure in it, and others in it too:

> Cold, brisk, tingling that journey,
> voyage more than journey, the night
> had waves, pressures I had to breast
> thrust aside, I had a figurehead or
> perhaps I was a figurehead with
> dolphins of the darkness as companions.

The correction is crucial: 'voyage more than journey'. Why? The word 'journey' suggests strongly a point of origin and a point of ending, a terminus. But a 'voyage' might evoke more purely the movement, the travelling itself, voyaging. The word occurs most famously in Morgan's 'A Home in Space' from *Star Gate: Science Fiction Poems* (1979). 'A Home in Space' describes an intrepid band of astronauts who cut off their connections with 'the earth base' and launch themselves 'outwards – / outwards in an impeccable trajectory' in order 'to keep a – / a voyaging generation voyaging':

> and as far –
> as far as there could be a home in space –
> space that needs time and time that needs life.[25]

It is *movement* as well as *identity*. 'Ariel Freed' most fully expresses that 'outwards' 'trajectory' and, while it affirms the needs of space and time, suggests that the human need to reach beyond the earth-bound pull of gravity is no less essential and in this instance, both urgent and unhurried. The gravitational authority of Prospero (or the earth base) has been dissolved. In this, perhaps the most remarkable feature of 'Ariel Freed' is that it has the wisdom and poise of age: it preserves the spirit of youth and yet – the description is, I hope, praise – it is an old man's poem: Morgan was 77 years old when it was published. The reversals that fill the poem's last sentence turn repeated negatives into a positive exclamation of endless flight and fine resolution, and shiver with delight in the expression of them: the voyaging continues – 'Only to have no shore, no landfall, / no runway, no eyrie, no goal and no fall!'

The momentary panic at the discovery that there is no harbour to moor by at the end of this voyage gives way to recognition and joy: there is no 'runway' to swoop down from flight to land on, there is no 'eyrie' to rest in, arriving at the topmost branches of a tree, no 'goal' that would define fulfilment and closure, and, finally and most surprisingly perhaps, there is 'no fall' – no reason to fear an end or collapse to earth again. It is the Pelagian heresy in its cheekiest and most ungraspable expression. The poem's movement is defined by a trust in art and life combined, a desire for form and a liberation from constraint, brought together in exemplary action. The poem is an evocation of endless possibility, but directed, flexing, articulate and specific. This represents not mere pluralism but the multiplicity of possible expression co-ordinated in a common purpose, and recognised. Morgan's words catch, and let fly, that spirit.

MacCaig and Morgan, following Rilke and MacDiarmid, propose a resolution to the division of identities Shakespeare sets out in *The Tempest*. Recognition of the multi-facetedness of human character effects a kind of reconciliation. It is not simply that the plays enact drama through representing difference between characters and the poems represent a lyrical, multi-faceted unity. Through these self-evident distinctions of genre an evolution of forms of self-definition might be observed. The authority of Prospero, the air and earth of Ariel and Caliban, are masks any actor might inhabit. The Scottish poets, subtly, by implication and quiet suggestion, reinterpret the Shakespearian legacy and break into a new time, new affinities and new aspiration towards self-determination. That resolution in Scottish writing in the 1980s and 1990s and early twenty-first century came after two crucial periods of revolutionary cultural change: 1890–1928, especially the Scottish Literary Renaissance of the 1920s, and 1760–1814, the period to which we must now turn, moving forward from the foundations of modernity in 1603 to the foundational texts of modern Scottish literature.

3
Foundational Texts of Modern Scottish Literature

The foundational texts of modern Scottish literature are laid down in the half-century between *Ossian* and *Waverley*, in the overlap between the Enlightenment and the Romantic era, in the transition from Burns's world to that of Scott. As Shakespeare remains foundational to modern English literature, so Burns and Scott remain foundational to modern Scottish literature, despite MacDiarmid's 1920s command, 'Not Burns – Dunbar!'

The Scottish Renaissance of the 1920s, as we noted when we looked at William Crozier's painting 'Edinburgh from Salisbury Crags', sought to look beyond the unions of 1707 and 1603 to an earlier Scotland and to establish a longer perspective as the way in which the modern world might be best approached and inhabited. This was concurrent with Mac-Diarmid's contradictory, complementary arguments of the period, as we also discussed in Chapter 1. Yet despite MacDiarmid's slogans and the revitalising dynamics of the 1920s, Burns and Scott and their era exert continuing and various forms of influence. This chapter is intended to sketch certain key elements in the transition from Burns's time to Scott's and to note their influence extending through later distortions, variations, exaggerations and caricatures.

The foundational texts of modern Scottish literature, from 1760 to 1814, and the key moments in the transition from late classical to early romantic periods, may be noted in this brief chronological table. The era of the assertion of American independence in 1776 and the French Revolution in 1789 was the one time before the first two decades of the twentieth century when it was possible for the western imagination to conceive comprehensively the possibility of a new social order.[1] These are the dates along with some of the texts and events concurrent with them:

1760: James Macpherson, *Fragments of Ancient Poetry Collected in the Highlands of Scotland and Translated from the Gaelic or Erse Language*
1763: Hugh Blair, *Dissertation on the Poems of Ossian*

1764: Thomas Reid, *An Inquiry into the Human Mind* (the great work of the Scottish school of common sense philosophy)

1767: Adam Ferguson, *An Essay on the History of Civil Society*

1768: James Cook, son of a Scottish father who moved south after the Jacobite rising, charts the coasts of New Zealand and Western Australia

1771: *Encyclopedia Britannica* (essentially the major Scottish enterprise of categorising and codifying an imperium of knowledge in the English language); Henry Mackenzie, *The Man of Feeling*; Tobias Smollett, *Humphrey Clinker*

1773: Boswell and Johnson tour the Highlands and Western Isles; Fergusson, *Poems*

1776: American Declaration of Independence; Adam Smith, *The Wealth of Nations*

1786: Burns, *Poems* (Kilmarnock Edition)

1787: Burns and Johnson, *Scots Musical Museum*

1789: French Revolution and Storming of the Bastille; Blake, *Songs of Innocence*

1791: Burns, 'Tam o' Shanter'

1791–1792: Thomas Paine, *The Rights of Man*

1798: Wordsworth and Coleridge, *Lyrical Ballads*

1800: Wordsworth and Coleridge, 2nd edn of *Lyrical Ballads*, with 'Preface'

1802–1803: Scott, *Minstrelsy of the Scottish Border*

1804: Beethoven, *Eroica*; Napoleon crowned Emperor

1805: Scott, *Lay of the Last Minstrel*; Mungo Park in Africa

1812: Byron, *Childe Harold's Pilgrimage*, Cantos I–II

1814: Highland Clearances begin; Byron, *The Corsair*; Scott, *Waverley*.

The Enlightenment and its discontents

David Hume had already started to write God out of the universe in the *Treatise of Human Nature* in 1739–1740, and through the 1740s and 1750s he set scepticism forth as a philosophical principle, settling his own subjective, meticulously reasoned argument as an exemplary measure of judgement. If the key tenets of the Enlightenment included the exercise of autonomous reasoning and the speaking of one's mind in relative safety, then the seeds of Romantic individualism are already here: dare to know, think for yourself. And yet, Hume's was an intensely social sensibility. The attractions of comfort and the requirements of balance necessitated by the gravitational pull of civilised society were essential to his world. These are what delimit it, finally. If the very word 'Enlightenment' engages the ideal of making clear a movement from darkness to light, what of the foundations, the roots in that darkness awaiting rediscovery, portending rebirth? As Adrian Poole has written,

Everyone would like to be able to look back with the equanimity attributed to David Hume on the brink of his classically enlightened passing. Or would they? Hume is said to have rebuffed the well-meaning efforts of his friends to take an optimistic view of his chances of recovery. Their hopes, he said, were groundless: 'I have done every thing of consequence which I ever meant to do, and I could at no time expect to leave my relations and friends in a better situation than that in which I am now likely to leave them; I, therefore, have all reason to die contented.'

Poole's comment here is that

One would hesitate in practice to disturb such an enviable state of self-satisfaction. Yet as one reads this, one cannot help wanting to. Do we not want to take the part of the world that Hume is leaving without regrets, the world in which we are left behind – is it worth so little? What – 'done every thing of consequence'? Nothing undone, done amiss, still to do? No one and nothing to feel the pain of parting from? A contentment that depends entirely on 'reason'?

One might qualify this. Hume did not claim to have done everything 'of consequence' but everything of consequence that he had intended to do – a more modest claim and one which might well lead to contentment and serenity rather than anything like complacent self-satisfaction. Moreover, he could reasonably feel the pain of parting from others who would mourn him but he could not reasonably claim to feel it for himself since he believed his own identity would be annihilated. And yet, Poole is surely right to register the temptation to go to the other extreme and shout back at Hume with Dylan Thomas,

> Do not go gentle into that good night,
> Old age should burn and rave at close of day;
> Rage, rage against the dying of the light.

Poole recognises 'different kinds of truth in the rage for which Thomas yearns and the tranquillity which Hume expresses'. (There is an irony in the fact that Hume, radically progressive in thought, subscribed so fully to the instruction in medieval treatises *de artibus moriendi*, of the art of dying well.) It is not entirely comforting when, in *King Lear*, we hear the Doctor assure Cordelia that Lear's 'great rage...is kill'd in him' (IV.vii.78–79). 'There is a satisfaction in finding that this is not the last word about Lear, that the vigour of his "rage" revives to help him kill the man who hangs Cordelia.'[2]

Hume had no children: this was one of the things that he congratulated himself on not needing to worry about....'He has no children,' says Macduff of the man who has robbed him of his most precious possessions. Tragedy asks some difficult questions about our belongings, what and whom we most fear and desire to give up and cling on to. Not all tragedies are 'about' children and parents, but all tragedy draws on the models of belonging provided by our experience of family relations, the ones which tax most severely our powers of choice and reason.[3]

Tragedy is where Hume's world of the Enlightenment betrays its limitations. Achieved reason will always run the risks of complacency and the dangers of equanimity. This is to generalise and it would be wrong not to offer particular qualifications to balance the broad judgement. Hume never ceased in his attempts to undermine religion but at the same time he recognised the unlikelihood of ever achieving success. People will always hoodwink themselves or be hoodwinked by others in this matter. He dedicated himself to a task in which he thought he would fail. Both in the pathos of his own effort and in the very real dangers he risked in publishing what he did, it would be wrong to underestimate Hume's courage, determination and intellectual integrity. Equanimity and complacency are nowhere in sight as Book I of the *Treatise on Human Nature* draws to a close. The tone is of fear and anguish: Hume was a tormented spirit at this point. And yet, the Enlightenment does not dwell in this: its dynamic always pushes upwards, towards the light, resistant to the pull of darkness, the pathos of the irrecoverable, the human fact of tragedy.

Michael Long is succinct about this: 'That small group of literate gentlemen, who lived in cities in north-west Europe but were attached so firmly to their own cultures as to think of themselves as constituting The World, failed with Shakespearian tragedy in ways which are significant and representative.' Reading their work, it is always worth imagining the experience of those of their contemporaries who were not literate, who did not live in the cities of North Europe, who knew their world only through their own experience of it. Is it not fair to say that their experience, though perhaps more difficult for us to know, is no less valid? If illiterate, can it be literary? Burns's poems and songs say so. And, in a different way, so do some of Scott's novels.

Long cites Nahum Tate's alteration of the ending of *King Lear* as the most famous example of 'a culture's innocence of any need to contemplate, and inwardly accommodate, those forces in life which are volatile beyond all human control'. The complaint against Shakespeare's neglect of 'poetic justice' was made by Dr Johnson and many others, but if tragedy is about things that are painful, poetic justice is no more than an idealised and sentimentalised celebration of the morally ordered human world. The neo-classic answer to the radical incomprehension which is the Enlightenment's response to the pleasure of tragedy, is given by Hume, and as Long says, it

derives from a mentality which has no way of allowing that the contemplation of the uncontrollably destructive in life might be something in which a civilized mind would willingly engage. Hume therefore must reduce the impact of tragedy, modulate its passion into sentiment and its despair into elegy, and claim it as the function of 'art' thus to present what is difficult in life in a form suited to the undisturbed entertainment of civilized men.

Long's conclusion is crucial:

> The failure is catastrophic. There is an entire dimension missing from the moral thought of both Johnson and Hume. The sceptic and the religious moralist, though otherwise entirely hostile to one another, are here joined as eighteenth-century men by what, in sum, amounts to a shared conviction – the conviction that the relationship of the ordered to the wild is that the former supervenes upon the latter in a way which is unambiguously gratifying. In the end it is always that conviction, so opposed to the Shakespearian under-view, which makes it impossible for a neo-classic mind to get very far with the tragic vision of this gothic or barbarian poet.[4]

This conviction, characteristic as it is of the eighteenth century, is what connects Burns and Scott in a deeply contradictory way.

Similarly, the gulf between Hume's thinking and Gaelic poetry contemporary with the Jacobite rising was not entirely unbridged in the national culture, but it was deep. Hume was at the centre of the burgeoning Enlightenment; the Gaelic world spoke to that world through stylised hyperbole, tailored for a particular readership, precisely in the manner Long describes – through a tonal palette of sentiment and elegy, in the versions of *Ossian* produced by James Macpherson. Writing and speech in vernacular Scots and Enlightened English were in contest for a viable way to articulate human experience. But whose experience? Where does one locate the wild in this world? Robert Fergusson set a precedent Burns would recognise, honour and take further, but where Fergusson positioned himself in opposition to the vapid pieties of the Edinburgh literati, Burns played to them. He used masks more deftly. The wildness of Fergusson was unrepeatable. Where it is found in Scott – in Madge Wildfire, for example, or flashing intermittently and fatally in *The Bride of Lammermoor* – the narrative that accommodates it cannot allow it a centrally dominant position. However, its containment in Scott's great narratives is not a cancellation. The tragic aspect of *Waverley*, the pathos of absurdity in *Redgauntlet*, the Beckett-like solitudes of *The Bride of Lammermoor* (his most haunting novel, piercingly recreated in Donizetti's operatic version) and the David Lynch-like quasi-surrealism of some aspects of his humour, all speak of an understanding of the wild and a courageous attempt to accommodate it and commemorate it within ordered narrative.

But perhaps the very genre of narrative prose creates a security of delimitation by which such wildness might be described and defined, whereas the language of poetry represents or embodies it in itself, even when the tension between form and expressive content is at its fiercest and most flamboyant. (Consider the formal religious and social, as well as poetic, structures, by virtue of which the language of Dunbar achieves its greatest energetic expressivity.) We shall examine one example of this tension between what cannot be fully accommodated by Scott's narrative prose but that is nevertheless recognised, when we look at *The Heart of Midlothian.*

Two songs

The establishment always moves quickly to accommodate innovation. Normally, initial exclusion is followed by readjustment, inclusion and then dismissal: the radical challenge becomes accepted as convention, defused and made subject to fashion. The differences between two songs clearly show the contrasts and continuities of the period.

> Now westlin winds and slaught'ring guns
>   Bring Autumn's pleasant weather;
> The moorcock springs on whirring wings,
>   Amang the blooming heather:
> Now waving grain, wide o'er the plain,
>   Delights the weary farmer;
> And the moon shines bright, when I rove at night,
>   To muse upon my charmer.
>
> The partridge loves the fruitful fells,
>   The plover loves the mountains;
> The woodcock haunts the lonely dells,
>   The soaring hern the fountains:
> Thro' lofty groves the cushat roves,
>   The path of man to shun it;
> The hazel bush o'erhangs the thrush,
>   The spreading thorn the linnet.
>
> Thus ev'ry kind their pleasure find,
>   The savage and the tender;
> Some social join and leagues combine,
>   Some solitary wander:
> Avaunt, away, the cruel sway!
>   Tyrannic man's dominion;
> The sportsman's joy, the murd'ring cry,
>   The flutt'ring, gory pinion!
>
> But, Peggy dear, the evening's clear,
>   Thick flies the skimming swallow;

The sky is blue, the fields in view,
    All fading green and yellow:
Come let us stray our gladsome way,
    And view the charms of Nature;
The rustling corn, the fruited thorn,
    And ev'ry happy creature.

We'll gently walk, and sweetly talk,
    Till the silent moon shine clearly;
I'll grasp thy waist, and, fondly prest,
    Swear how I love thee dearly;
Not vernal show'rs to budding flow'rs,
    Not Autumn to the farmer,
So dear can be as thou to me,
    My fair, my lovely charmer!

Burns's 'Song, composed in August' ('Now westlin winds') is a very early work; Kinsley considers it likely that it was the second song Burns composed but it brings together a number of key themes in Burns's work and is deeply representative in various ways. It is a love poem, self-consciously located in the tradition of masculine love poetry, but here the male ego and the woman the poet is trying to charm by his song seem subordinate as the song begins. And it begins as a description of the outdoor world of fields and farms, and wilderness (uncultivated, wild land overrun by the national flower, the heather – the rhyme with weather combines wildness and blossom in a paradox, for this is an August evening and the weather is far from wild – it is 'pleasant'). As August portends Autumn and the hunters' guns will surely come, the poet is pausing to sing praise in the present moment ('Now...') – praise of both the farmers' ordered world of 'waving grain' and full harvest, and nature's abundant bird-life in the countryside. The birds of moor, valleys, mountains, lonely glens, waterways and hill-forests are all named and celebrated in their ordered location: 'Thus ev'ry kind their pleasure find, / The savage and the tender', Burns assures us, bringing the wild into an ordered accommodation. Social organisation or solitariness is their free choice, an option nature offers; but mankind's dominion is 'Tyrannic' – murderous, sporting, flag-fluttering and gory. This is enlightened romanticism, or a Romantic Enlightenment at work.

The poet, therefore, sides with nature and wilderness, but nature and wilderness represent harmony, orderliness and balanced organisation. Human intervention is the unwelcome, unreasonable threat of wasteful destruction and loss. At this point, Burns pulls back from violence, addresses his lover, reminds her and himself of the loveliness of this particular, transient evening, the skimming swallows, blue skies and yellow fields. The gentle walk he coaxes her into will be moonlit and as fondly and dearly enjoyed as rain to budding flowers or as harvest-time to the farmer (the two images are barely suggestions of the sequence of germination and procreation, given with dexterous quickness and lightness of touch) and the final words give all the charm to the young woman the poem itself is intended to encourage into keen participation.

An explanation like this may lay the verses bare but it cannot reduce the wonderful construction of balances enacted every time we listen to them. They are beautifully rendered by Dick Gaughan on the CD *Handful of Earth* after which, who but the most cold-blooded could resist?[5] Despite the longeurs of the foregoing analysis, this is surely a poem to memorise and sing. Its points of reference and the situation it evokes are easily imagined and evidently an actual component of lived experience. The element of fantasy in any love poem does not depend here on imaginary locations, stage-sets or dramatic paraphernalia. The tropes of the natural world, farming, seasons and birds of field and hill all contextualise the sexual relation at the heart of the song's story and purpose. Identification with the poet is invited by the song's form. It seems to be implying the idea that nothing could be more reasonable than this. It is an act of seduction. Pleasurable in itself, the consequences may breach moral rectitude and physically determine the parameters of life to come. But, for the length of the song, cast care to one side and be seduced. Rather than drugged acquiescence, it invites active, willing participation. It beckons with the promise not of resignation, but of cheerful resolution in the face of the inevitable things of life. Now consider this: 'Jock of Hazeldean'

> 'Why weep ye by the tide, ladie?
> Why weep ye by the tide?
> I'll wed ye to my youngest son,
> And ye sall be his bride.
> And ye sall be his bride, ladie,
> Sae comely to be seen' –
> > But aye she loot the tears down fa'
> > For Jock of Hazeldean.
>
> 'Now let this wilfu' grief be done,
> And dry that cheek so pale;
> Young Frank is chief of Errington
> And lord of Langley-dale;
> His step is first in peacefu' ha',
> His sword in battle keen' –
> > But aye she loot the tears down fa'
> > For Jock of Hazeldean.
>
> 'A chain of gold ye sall not lack,
> Nor braid to bind your hair;

Nor mettled hound nor managed hawk,
Nor palfrey fresh and fair;
And you, the foremost o' them a'
Shall ride our forest queen' –
     But aye she loot the tears down fa'
     For Jock of Hazeldean.

The kirk was decked at morning-tide,
The tapers glimmered fair;
The priest and bridegroom wait the bride,
And dame and knight are there.
They sought her baith by bower and ha';
The ladie was not seen.
     She's oer the border and awa'
     Wi' Jock of Hazeldean.

This presents a different account of experience: spectacular, formulaic, happy and clearly structured as a narrative. The contrasts with Burns's song are evident. 'Jock of Hazeldean' (or, when sung, more colloquially, 'Jock o' Hazeldean') begins dramatically as a voice asks a question to which listeners require an answer: '"Why weep ye by the tide, ladie?"' The question might imply our identification with the sympathetic questioner, but then the questioner is revealed to be the patriarchal authority against whom the 'ladie' is about to declare her choice. The assumption of generosity in the singer's promise – '"I'll wed ye to my youngest son"' – is mockingly powerful and, if uncomprehending, a little repulsive too. The lady's continuing tears register longing for Jock o' Hazeldean – the familiarity of the name and the note of location might suggest a farmer's worker, a much poorer man than the landowner's son. It is the landowner, the patriarch, who continues, not without apparent sympathy or compassion, advising the woman to give up her 'wilful' grief and count her potential good fortune: his son has property, dances well in peacetime and fights bravely in war, the lady will have riches and fashionable gear. The trappings of property are described as if to tempt her. Above all, she is promised her place, 'foremost o' them a''. The slip here from the list of gold, braid, hound, hawk and palfrey to 'you' suggests how comprehensively the patriarch sees his potential daughter-in-law as further, 'foremost' property, another acquisition to be 'managed'. But she continues to cry, yearning for Jock o' Hazeldean.

One might infer the hint of a subterranean narrative here: could it be that her familiarity with Jock has been more intimate than is ever said, and that her tears are prompted by care for the likely consequences? But that would be over-reading. The surface narrative is brightly enamelled and free of any darker suggestion. The dramatic shift and heightened tension follow a for-mulaic structure in the final verse, as the church is described, the wedding prepared for and all the participants waiting and ready. The candles burning down suggest not only the flickeringly-lit scene but the moral judgement underlying the tale: that because time is so fleeting, the heart must be followed in matters of love. The lady – who remains unnamed throughout the song – has disappeared, and in the last two lines of the song the singer assures us in climactic, happy relief, that she has escaped over the border – literally, but also metaphorically, out of the jurisdiction and domain of this patriarch and his sons – with Jock o' Hazeldean.

It is a happy ending and a pleasing story, wonderfully delivered once again by Dick Gaughan on *No More Forever* or in a beautifully evocative version sung by Jo Miller on *The Whistlebinkies 5*.[6] The contrasts with Burns's song make very clear a general shift in popular sensibility which Burns and Scott respectively were addressing and which comes through most evidently on a larger scale in terms of the chosen generic forms of their writing. Burns's song is essentially inward, designed to be reproduced in memory and voice; its purpose is to draw the listener in, to seduce the lover, to involve the listener irresistibly. By contrast, Scott's song is a spectator's sport, it invites the imagination to construct a setting of castle, kirk, land and border, sexual relations and property, natural justice and patriarchal law, and to savour, from a safe distance, the pleasure of the heightening suspense. It is a ballad, after all. The refrain increases tension and the release of the climactic escape is as deft an image of sexual fulfilment as Burns's closing evocation of vernal showers and Autumn harvests. Burns's poems and songs appeal to a popular participation that reaches into desires and impulses and reaffirms them – dangerously sometimes, for no matter how ordered the creatures of the wilderness are in 'Now Westlin Winds', there is a wilder, non-human world they represent as well, and Burns is always aware of it. It is what animates 'Tam o' Shanter' and what makes that poem a gloriously irreverent song of praise to common intoxication and human sexuality while it evokes the proximity of the price that might be paid for them. With Scott, the pleasure of hearing the song, of following the story visually, of imaginative dramatic reconstruction, is more vicarious.

What these two songs provide, I think, is a concise way of suggesting a much larger shift in the sense of address at the centre of popular cultural production in Scotland in the late eighteenth and early nineteenth centuries. It is not simply that Burns was attached to a world where oral culture was a predominant medium and Scott stands at the beginning of the print-bred culture of long narrative poems and novels which he helped to develop for an international readership. Such a distinction would be simplistic. The overlaps are too complex. The continuities – Burns's reading and regard for the literate critics and judges of his work, Scott's immersion in oral culture and fascination with popular print-culture such as chapbooks and printed ballads – are too important to allow us to suggest any such distinction was absolute. It is rather that the human comprehension of non-human wildness, excluded from the Enlightenment imagination, must find different ways to express itself. The image of Burns's benevolent patriarch in 'The Cottar's Saturday Night' tends towards the nineteenth-century image of Bible-revering Caledonian sternness. The image of Scott's comprehensive, all-encompassing imagination discovers in itself an imperial predisposition to rise above and oversee a global dominion. These images found a kind of unconscious and anxious expression in one of the most famous pictures of the late nineteenth century.

George Washington Wilson's photograph of John Brown, Queen Victoria and the gamekeeper John Grant was taken in 1863. The figure of John Grant was cut out and it became the only published '*carte de visite*' of the two figures together, selling 13,000 copies in its first year of issue alone. The archetype was established and reproduced in innumerable cartoons satirising Victorian upper-class flirtation with the Highlands. As Malcolm MacLean and Christopher Carrell have noted, the Highlands, at the height of the land agitation for reform, were also at the height of fashion.[7] The image sets out a relationship between icons, one standing for Scotland narrowly defined, instantly recognisable not only in the posture, the hands braced on the lapels with an air of pulpit authority, the dour face and gloomy brows and set of cheeks and mouth, but also in the costume, the kilt and outlandish sporran, the legs a little apart with the heavy shoes set slightly angled – not military, then, but ready for action nonetheless – standing four-square on the ground beside

Illustration 3 George Washington Wilson, 'John Brown, Queen Victoria and John Grant' 1863 (Aberdeen City Art Gallery)

and below the mounted monarch, looking perhaps a little troubled by the knowledge of his duty, that he may be relied upon to do as authority – God, Queen and Empire – directs, to do as he is told, and die if need be. The uncontrollable wildness of tragedy has been driven out beyond the borders of this image, but it will erupt in time. In the late nineteenth century, imperial expansion was concurrent with popular imagery of Scotland instantly recognisable in an international arena. But in the twentieth century, to writers and artists such as MacDiarmid in the 1920s, the ultimate consequence of imperialism was world war.

Ploughed under by kailyard sentimentalism in the late nineteenth century the uncontrollable energy of tragedy resurfaces from the 1890s to the 1920s in the excessive violences of *Gillespie* and *The House with the Green Shutters*, and in MacDiarmid's early lyrics and *A Drunk Man Looks at the Thistle*, where absurd, quasi-surrealist, dream-visions never allow their comic potential to surrender the sense that tragic waste is essential to the human experience. When, in lines 27–28 of the latter poem, MacDiarmid advises that 'ony man s'ud wish / To dree the goat's weird tae as weel's the sheep's' (any human being should wish to suffer the fate of the goat – the damned – as well as that of the sheep – the saved) he is reclaiming the tragic for Scottish literature. The connection back to Fergusson, or at least to James Hogg, should be evident.

It is a willing acceptance of the sinner's fate, human potential at its worst, as well as that of the saved, humanity at its best, that MacDiarmid insists on. Where only the pious seem to populate the fiction of Ian Maclaren and everyone in the worlds of J. Macdougall Hay and George Douglas Brown seems damned, MacDiarmid's insistence on the range of possibility comes as an antidote to exclusive extremism.

Fergusson, Johnson and Mackenzie

In the *Life of Johnson*, Boswell recollects a moment in 1773 when he offered to teach Johnson how to understand the Scots of Allan Ramsay's popular play, *The Gentle Shepherd*. '"No, Sir, (said he,) I won't learn it. You shall retain your superiority by my not knowing it."' Boswell speculates:

> This brought on a question whether one man is lessened by another's acquiring an equal degree of knowledge with him. Johnson asserted the affirmative. I maintained that the position might be true in those kinds of knowledge which produce wisdom, power, and force, so as to enable one man to have the government of others; but that a man is not in any degree lessened by others knowing as well as he what ends in mere pleasure: – 'eating fine fruits, drinking delicious wines, reading exquisite poetry.'[8]

Scots poetry may be exquisite but Johnson will remain ignorant of it and since his arbitration of knowledge is a force in itself, he may have lost the argument with Boswell but he has certainly indicated the way the English language in its normative authority relegated Scots to beyond the pale. Johnson's position stands mid-way between Shakespeare's Prospero and Aimé Césaire's. Hypersensitive to what was portended, Robert Fergusson writes an address 'To Dr Samuel Johnson: Food for a New Edition of his Dictionary':

> Great Pedagogue! whose literarian lore,
> With syllable on syllable conjoined,
> To transmutate and varify, hast learned
> The whole revolving scientific names
> That in the alphabetic columns lie,
> Far from the knowledge of mortalic shapes:
> As we, who never can peroculate
> The miracles by thee miraculized,
> The Muse, silential, with mouth apert,
> Would give vibration to stagnatic tongue,
> And loud encomiate thy puissant name,
> Eulogiated from the green decline
> Of Thames's bank to Scoticanian shores,
> Where Lochlomondian liquids undulize.[9]

Fergusson's sarcastic wordplay escalates both exuberant comic flamboyance and unrelenting satire. He chastises Edinburgh for not extending a fitting welcome to 'him whose potent Lexiphanian style / Words can prolongate' and cries out a welcome on behalf of 'hills and valleys' – a wilder Scotland – 'where emerging oats / From earth assuage our pauperty...'. Then he asks Johnson whether he should not 'let lignarian chalice, swelled with oats, / Thy orifice approach' and if he has 'applied / The kilt aerian to your Anglian thighs, / And with renunciation assignized / Your briches in Londona to be worn?'

> It cannot be: – You may as well desire
> An alderman leave plumpuddenian store,
> And scratch the tegument from pottage dish,
> As bid thy countrymen, and thee, conjoined,
> Forsake stomachic joys. Then hie you home,
> And be a malcontent, that naked hinds,
> On lentiles fed, could make your kingdom quake,
> And tremulate Old England libertized!

Fergusson was astute to perceive the imposition that the linguistic authority of 'Dictionary Johnson' was to exert over his own native tongue.

Indeed, it was already there. A similar gulf opens up between Fergusson and Henry Mackenzie's *Man of Feeling*. The title of the poem Fergusson wrote in response to it, 'The Sow of Feeling', says enough: these two texts provide an object lesson in how far two contemporary writers can be from each other in one nation's capital city. Their dates suggest one aspect of their relationship. Mackenzie (1745–1831), five years Fergusson's senior, far more advantaged in Edinburgh society, exposes a hypersensitive underbelly to the poet's sharp and energetic wit. Fergusson (1750–1774) does not hold back. Burns's response to both of them registers the accommodative nature of his own vision. It is well-known that to Burns, Fergusson was a 'brother Bard' – an 'elder brother' in misfortune and the Muse. Burns recognised the vigour and dash of Fergusson's language and the revolutionary irreverence of his democratic stance. But Burns was equally attracted to *The Man of Feeling*. The book brought tears to his eyes as he read Mackenzie's impassioned protests at injustice in human society, the conflict at the heart of empire-building. Burns responded at once to the Mackenzie who wrote: 'You tell me of immense territories subject to the English: I cannot think of their possessions without being led to inquire by what right they possess them. . . . Could you tell me of some conqueror giving peace and happiness to the conquered?'[10]

Mackenzie's sensibility was fired with a sense of social indignation. The politics of imperialism and colonisation were hateful to his refined moral sense, and Burns concurred. That Mackenzie was complicit in the linguistic imperialism of the literati is what Fergusson's poem so eloquently exposes. It begins:

> Malignant planets! do ye still combine
> Against this wayward, dreary life of mine?
> Has pitiless Oppression – cruel case!
> Gained sole possession of the human race?
> By cruel hands has every virtue bled,
> And Innocence from men to vultures fled?[11]

Fergusson's attitude and tone are clear the moment the reader recognises that the sow is speaking. He is a young spark making cheeky fun of a famous older writer. He is sprightly, quick and clever but at the core he is Swiftian in steadiness and intensity. Written not in vernacular Scots but in precisely poised English, the language itself effects a satiric alienation from guttarals and fricatives, as if the imperial authority of English were implicitly understood to be supplanting or overwhelming native forms of speech. (The point is as apt in terms of Scots as it is of Gaelic and its long-term application has been international in the establishment of the centrality of the English language in our approaches to literature. American, Australian or New Zealand writing in English remains more approachable to an international readership in English than writing translated from native American Indian, Australian Aboriginal or Maori languages – or, until recently, Gaelic.)

> Thrice happy, had I lived in Jewish time,
> When swallowing pork or pig was deemed a crime;
> My husband long had blessed my longing arms,
> Long, long had known love's sympathetic charms!
> My children too, – a little suckling race,
> With all their father growing in their face,
> From their prolific dam had ne'er been torn,
> Nor to the bloody stalls of butchers borne.

This is more ferocious than Burns. Fergusson's sow cries out, 'I'll weep, till sorrow shall my eye-lids drain, / A tender husband and a brother slain!' and her author is clearly alienating Mackenzie's exaggerated gestures of excessive emotional sympathy. In his own poetry, Burns attempts a closer counterpoint. In a higher register, carefully tuned for the ears of Mackenzie and the literati, he refers to Fergusson's 'Auld Reekie' as 'Edina – Scotia's darling seat!' but he also writes songs, satire and 'sclatrie' (bad-tempered, scathing verse, sometimes obscene) memorised and loved by illiterate people. It is the immediate legacy of such counterpoint – a kind of multi-vocal propensity, the ability to use different registers and, indeed, voices – that Hugh MacDiarmid revived in the 1920s. The alternative, a uniformity of stilted Anglocentric diction, he opposed.

In 1786, Burns decides against emigration to Jamaica and publishes the Kilmarnock edition of his *Poems*. There are 612 copies printed on 31 July, 350 promised to subscribers. Three weeks later only thirteen copies are left. Burns is to be lionised as a poet of direct utterance and immediacy. Scott, remembering meeting him as a wee boy, refers famously to the immediate, piercing strength of his eye. Indeed, Burns sets himself up as self-determined, in 'Epistle to J. L*****k an old Scotch Bard', when he calls for 'ae spark o' Nature's fire, / That's a' the learning I desire' and in the next poem, 'To the Same' declares roundly, '*I, Rob, am here.*' In 'The Vision' he is 'A *rustic Bard*' but in 'Epistle to a Young Friend' he advises:

> Ay free, aff han', your story tell,
> When wi' a bosom crony;
> But still keep something to yoursel
> Ye scarcely tell to ony.[12]

The Kilmarnock edition contains thirty-six items; more than half of them take the form of letters or addresses, speeches intended to be heard or read by people other than the book-buying public and some in the voices of other characters, some of them animals. They are, in other words, masks.[13] No one is more adept at the use of linguistic costume:

> From scenes like these, old Scotia's grandeur springs,
> That makes her lov'd at home, rever'd abroad:

> Princes and lords are but the breath of kings,
>   'An honest man's the noblest work of God...'[14]

The 'scenes' just described in 'The Cottar's Saturday Night' are of the family gathered around the patriarch reading the word of God from the Bible. The pious homiletic evening prayer inspires an exclamation which endorses moral correctness and idealises rustic poverty. This is the other side of democratic republicanism so dangerous in revolutionary Europe. The questions of how deep is the sincerity and how untroubled the assertion linger with the ambiguous depiction of Britain, not Scotland, as a single 'isle' united and protected by a virtuous peasant population, in the last line of this stanza (it recollects the notorious song for the Dumfries volunteers, 'Does haughty Gaul invasion threat...' and, to be generous, confirms that Burns's love of Scotland and the Scots language did not entail a rejection of England or English):

> O Scotia! my dear, my native soil!
>   For whom my warmest wish to heaven is sent!
> Long may thy hardy sons of *rustic toil*,
>   Be blest with health and peace and sweet content!
> And O may Heaven their simple lives prevent
>   From *Luxury's* contagion, weak and vile!
> Then howe'er *crowns* and *coronets* be rent,
>   A virtuous *Populace* may rise the while,
> And stand a wall of fire around their much-lov'd Isle.[15]

The following year another Mason wrote an opera in its own way marking the end of aristocratic authority and delivering a verdict of social justice radically new in its own right, in Mozart's *Don Giovanni* of 1787. The opera is uniquely poised between a world of symbols and a world of realist psychology. Actions and consequences are singularly described in a moment of transition in interpretation, from classically balanced structures to unpredictable, unrepeatable effects and outcomes. Of course, the libretto is by Da Ponte so Mozart does not control the language of the opera, but he does contribute musically to its psychology. When the Commendatore thrusts Giovanni into Hell, it is one aristocrat achieving justice over another. While it would be dubious to attribute explicit sentiments in his operas to Mozart himself, the first audience for *Don Giovanni* would undoubtedly have seen some connection with the revolutionary sentiments abroad at the time.

In 1789 the French Revolution and William Blake's *Songs of Innocence* began their intersecting courses through western ways of imagining social justice and human potential. Idealism and innocence confronted the Reign of Terror in 1793–1794 and a new sense of what popular culture might be started to shape itself. In 1802 Walter Scott published his collection of ballads, some retouched for genteel readers, the *Border Minstrelsy*, and in 1805 he produces his own version, *The Lay of the Last Minstrel*:

> The way was long, the wind was cold,
> The Minstrel was infirm and old
> His withered cheek and tresses gray
> Seemed to have known a better day
> The harp, his sole remaining joy
> Was carried by an orphan boy.
> The last of all the bards was he
> Who sung of Border chivalry
> For welladay! Their date was fled
> His tuneful brethren all were dead
> And he, neglected and oppressed,
> Wished to be with them and at rest...[16]

Scott's minstrel is the last of his kind and in this he preserves an emblem of national identity through withered infirmity and age, into an era where a former reality has the appearance of a fabrication. Yet the preservation of the past, while it reminds us of Ben Okri's observation quoted earlier, also insists that it refers to a reality that might be reactivated, that might not be lost in fiction. The Minstrel represents an older aristocracy than that which had gone under in 1789. He is, in a sense, Ossian after the Fianna, the last of the clan, conveying and prophesying an image and a stance that were, partly as a direct result of Scott's success as a novelist and mythologist, to become very familiar in time to come.[17]

Three traditions

The question of the disparity between the period's separate traditions, some-times clashing in the national fabric, is clarified by David Daiches. For Daiches, there were three major traditions in eighteenth-century Scottish literature.[18] The Lowland Scots tradition that flourished in the poetry of William Dunbar, Robert Henryson and Gavin Douglas in the fifteenth and sixteenth centuries, had been revived by Allan Ramsay and Robert Fergusson, in the seventeenth and eighteenth centuries, and came to fruition with Burns, both as poet and as song-collector.

But there was also the ancient Gaelic tradition which represented a different Scotland, with the poetry of Rob Donn, Alexander Macdonald, Duncan Ban MacIntyre and William Ross. In 1756 Jerome Stern drew attention to this tradition with his publication of the first translations of Gaelic poetry ever printed in Scotland, in the *Scots Magazine*. Although there are exceptions (for example, Dugald Buchanan wrote in both English and Gaelic), generally the Highland and Lowland poetic traditions did not cross-fertilise. The lifetimes of the Gaelic poets named above overlapped those of Fergusson, Burns and Hogg but they never met and were never familiar with each other's work.

Finally there was the eighteenth-century tradition of Edinburgh literati, the Enlightenment philosophers, academics and novelists who were to foster an Anglocentric style. To them, irreverently robust demotic poetry was vulgar, bodily, unlettered, often associated with dissipation and drink (though, of course, Boswell and Hume were hardly averse to drink and the legal subculture was sodden with it: consider Henry Dundas). At best it could be quaint and curious. As for the Gaelic world, the literati shuffled it off towards the realm of antiquarian curiosity. It became acceptable only, and only to some, in the garb stitched up by James Macpherson. Macpherson represented the acceptable face of Gaeldom. His versions of Highland poetry were arguably the first evidences of Gaelic ways of saying things, in rhythms and techniques, in English (for example, in the preference of metaphor over simile). They deserve credit for the revolutionary introduction of these forms of address, especially because they were tuned not to a local but to an international, educated, and above all, contemporary readership, which needed neither roots in contemporary Highland society nor in the vernacular Lowland tradition.

Daiches reminds us that these three strands of Scottish tradition never really came together, although the prevailing Anglocentrism of the interpreting language – English – has favoured the literati's view of Burns as a heaven-taught ploughman and Macpherson's version of heroic Gaeldom. Modern scholarship has begun to investigate deeper connections and complexities but Daiches's general point holds good. When Burns went to Edinburgh in what Robert Chalmers called 'the interregnum between Hume and Scott', one of his earliest champions was a Dr Thomas Blacklock, well-known as poet, critic and musician. Blacklock enthused about Burns, but when he 'and other Scotch gentlemen' published in 1760 a 'collection of original poems' they gave to the world a set of verses which even as careful a critic as Daiches himself described as 'unrelieved in its badness'. Such lines as these, from 'A Drinking Song', are ample proof:

> With roses and with myrtle crown'd,
> I triumph; let the glass go round.
> Jovial Bacchus, ever gay,
> Come, and crown the happy day...

Yet the English language itself can be altered, for example, into an American vernacular idiom in the poetry of William Carlos Williams, or in Norman MacCaig's poems, where the high idiom of Enlightenment philosophy is adapted to immediately accessible Scottish tones – English with a wry, innately Scottish accentual edge. This is a matter of tone and inflection, rather than vocabulary or grammatical structure. No distinctively English regional tone of voice could suggest the wry humour working in the integration of the logical meaning or 'statements' and the linguistic poise and irony in MacCaig's poems. Marshall Walker has suggested how close MacCaig is to Hume's 'secular and materialist insistence on subjective imagination as an organ of limited cognition' in the poem, 'An ordinary day': 'I took my mind a walk / or my mind took me a walk – / whichever was the truth of it.'[19] As MacCaig strolls on, he notices the difference words make in the description of things: 'The light glittered on the water / or the water glimmered in the light.' As cormorants with their wings spread look as if they are trying to stop traffic that is not there, ducks move in ways shaped by the water they move upon, and flowers give volition to bees, an unexceptional observation starts to shimmer with silvery strangeness: 'my mind observed to me, / or I to it, how ordinary / extraordinary things are or // how extraordinary ordinary / things are, like the nature of the mind / and the process of observing'.[20]

The process of observing, the act of cognition, the shift between the cut of perception and the warmth of comprehension, is as central to MacCaig's work as it was to that of the Enlightenment. Equally, the Gaelic tradition of praise-poems is represented by MacCaig with characteristic access of wit and imagistic accuracy. 'Praise of a collie', 'Praise of a boat', 'Praise of a thorn bush' (he calls it 'an encyclopedia of angles'), 'Praise of a road' or 'Praise of a man' betrays no simplistic banalities of utterance but balances keenly between directness of emotional intent and subtlety of descriptive and celebrative power.[21] If it might be argued that the adoption of 'English' in Scotland cannot be described as simply 'linguistic imperialism' since it was Scots who set up the standards for what came to be literary English, then nevertheless, it is the contradictoriness of these dynamics that remains foundational.

Yet, if the three traditions specified by Daiches may be understood in the twenty-first century as interrelated, nevertheless, the exclusivity of each from the other continues to affect their legacy. In *Landscape and Memory*, Simon Schama draws attention to the way in which artists frequently repainted and reinvigorated their landscapes by appealing to the developing Romantic imagination, overpainting classical scenes of pastoral tranquillity with lowering mountains and overgrowths of untended flora, to emphasise the ruggedness and wildness of Scotland. For example, Paul Sandby did exactly this with his 1747 painting 'View in Strathtay' in the 1780 version of the same work.[22] There is no denying the overlap or continuity, but equally, there is no denying the difference.

The foundational texts in the tradition of modern Scottish literature were fashioned in this era of complex transition from Enlightenment to Romanticism: the key works were by 'Ossian' Macpherson, Johnson and Boswell, David Hume, Adam Smith, Adam Ferguson, Allan Ramsay, Robert Fergusson, Robert

Burns and Walter Scott. The nexus of concerns centred in these works brings together matters of language and landscape, civilisation and barbarism, sobriety and intoxication – the word itself suggests the proximity of inspiration and drunkenness – purity of diction and rebarbative language, intellect and feeling. These concerns are foundational in modern Scottish culture and underlie most of what I have to say in this book.

The foundations are, in the late eighteenth and early nineteenth centuries, set down in a period of conflict and contradiction, the era of the encyclopedias and dictionaries, the categorisation and codification of knowledge and language, a period which, for all its embrace and collective appetite to accommodate – corpulent Johnson and *le bon David* – was nevertheless an age of exclusivity. It was after all the age of slavery and foundational in this respect too. Hume's racism may be understandable in its era but it was also the judgement of 'rational man'. For the first time, in the turn from the eighteenth to the nineteenth century, Scotland was beginning to define what would be the country's surplus population.

In the absence of a self-determined nation, there are four major qualities in Scotland's cultural character in this foundational era: the transition and overlap between oral and written culture; the divisions between the three literary traditions within Scotland; the changing dynamics of Scotland's relationship with England, both politically and linguistically, at the beginning of the century of Empire; and the sense of the rapidly expanding world stage, the international arena in which Scotland's self-expression – Scotland's masks – might find wider dialogue.

That wider dialogue might help, in time, in the discovery of ways to reapproach the question of self-determination, to come back at the unfinished business of 'home'. The distances across which such individual artistic self-expression sought to find forms is the subject of Part Two of *Representing Scotland*.

Part II

Lost Worlds and Distant Drums

O sea...
　　　You first made me know
That the puny agitations
Of my heart were only momentary motions
In yours; that there lay at the base
Of my life your terrifying law: to be as various
As vast, yet fixed in place...
　　　– Eugenio Montale, from 'Mediterranean', trans. Edwin Morgan

Yet this albeit restricted [Athenian] democracy had features not only unique in its own day, but in advance of those advocated for democracy in nineteenth-century Britain. And it contained two ideal principles which have not lost their force in two and a half thousand years: *democracy is daily dialogue*, and *true democracy lies in the equality and equal power of all parties to that dialogue*.
　　　– Tom Leonard, *Radical Renfrew: Poetry from the French Revolution to the First World War*

4
Walter Scott and the Whistler: Tragedy and the Enlightenment Imagination

The Heart of Midlothian is generally considered Scott's most approachable novel. David Daiches tells us that 'most critics consider [it to be] the best of Scott's works'.[1] In his short but influential 1965 study, it is the only novel to which Thomas Crawford devotes an entire chapter, and in his 1982 revision of the same book, Crawford preserves the emphasis, citing the 'extended critical debate' to which the novel has been subjected by Robin Mayhead, Dorothy van Ghent, Joan Pittock and David Craig.[2] In Scottish Literature since 1707, Marshall Walker tellingly chooses The Heart of Midlothian above any other of Scott's works for extended consideration before addressing the question of Scott's fluctuating appeal as a novelist 'then and now'.[3] When Ludovic Kennedy enquired in 1969, he found that the Edinburgh City Library's nine copies of the work were all out. The librarian estimated that there were between 180 and 200 borrowings of the book each year.[4] So in terms of critical acclaim and popular appeal, The Heart of Midlothian is central. One reason for this is its crucial position in Scott's career, not only chronologically and nor because its principle character, the 'common cow-feeder's daughter', Jeanie Deans, embodies an ideal of Romantic individualism as a heroine from 'the common people', but also because of its balance of thematic, personal and social concerns and compulsions. (It is worth noting that Jeanie is only one 'Romantic' ideal: she is a long way from Childe Harold or other, more aristocratic forms of the Byronic hero. In The Heart of Midlothian, Robertson or Staunton is quasi-Byronic in this sense.)

The two most influential accounts of Scott's career are those of Georg Lukács in The Historical Novel, and David Daiches's essay, 'Scott's Achievement as a Novelist'.[5] For Lukács, the 'tapestry' or 'tushery' novels of a past of knighthood, feudalism, courtliness, chivalry and majestic nature are no less significant than those set in Scotland. They are all engaged in the initiation of a new genre and a newly invented vision of the past. For Daiches, it is the first nine novels of the *Waverley* series plus one, *Redgauntlet*, written a little later (and all set in Scotland), which are important in the tradition of the genre of the novel.

Since these accounts were published, however, another overview of Scott's work has been elaborated by Graham McMaster, who contrasts the first of the series and the later Scottish novel like this: '*Waverley* ... bids a regretful farewell to the past and looks forwards with a jaunty optimism to the future. . . . *Redgauntlet* imagines a world in which the past is even more unavailable, but the future questionable.' Scott's focus in the later novel is much more 'the societal basis of personal identity, and the limits imposed by society upon autonomous action and feeling'.[6]

The Heart of Midlothian is exactly mid-way in this structure. It keeps the optimism, strengths and hope of the earlier novels, but it also involves darker, more unanswerable questions and stories that refuse progressive resolutions. The most poignant, brilliantly etched and suggestive of these is the Whistler's story. In the overall context of the novel, it has often been forgotten, or else it has attracted hostile criticism. Before we begin to discuss it, though, we should have some sense of the grand design and intensely related personal and social dilemmas which the novel sets forth.

The Heart of Midlothian was written in 1818, but it is set in 1737. Scotland, having united her kingdom with England in 1603, had removed her parliament to Westminster in 1707. There had been civil unrest: riots and protests were widespread. The country now had national identity but no independent political authority. This is not to say that there was not rich political life in Scotland: it was certainly delegated, and the Third Duke of Argyll, for example, had massive political authority over internal Scottish matters. In other words, Scotland could run its own affairs so long as it did not get too uppity and indulge in uprisings. Nevertheless, when grave injustice happened, the highest court of supreme earthly appeal was in London. Scott's novel describes a dangerous time. The events are carefully located in this period of civil unrest, after the Jacobite rising of 1715 and not long before that of 1745. The Porteous Riots, with which the novel begins, were in effect the Edinburgh mob's protest against the Union of 1707 and, both as novelist and as historian, Scott catches the mood in Chapter 4: 'the hitherto silent expectation of the people became changed into that deep and agitating murmur, which is sent forth by the ocean before the tempest begins to howl'.[7]

The outlaws (robbers, gypsies, highwaymen, smugglers) who populate the novel are part of this great ocean, but it is the respectable individual Jeanie Deans who is at its centre. The central event of the novel's plot depends entirely upon her heroic walk, from Edinburgh to London, to plead for an intercession to save her sister Effie from execution as punishment for the crime of child murder. (At this time, the inability to present a child was considered proof that it had been murdered, and Effie does not know what has become of her son.) Queen Caroline's merciful sympathy is given and the pardon arrives. Jeanie's heroism is celebrated and the letter of the law is upheld.

But the questions the narrative proposes remain questions, resolved by the plot but unresolved in society. In the novel's happy resolution, luck is in the service of justice, but the sense that that might somehow misfire is never entirely absent, and sustains a tension in the narrative. In this it resembles the Shakespearian comedy of *Twelfth Night*: ultimately celebrative, a comic release of festive energy in which malevolent aspects are banished, it is nevertheless a world in which tragedy, mistakes, bad timing and missing correspondences are always, and always felt to be, imminent. The conventions of realism Scott is obliged to observe as a novelist may seem ponderous by comparison, but they should not obscure the artifice with which his story is contrived – an artifice at least as dramatically tense as that of *Twelfth Night*.

This structure of personal and social themes is evident in the careful balance of extreme emotions and steadfast convictions which are held and revealed in an unfolding pattern by the main characters: the sisters, Effie and Jeanie, both daughters of the staunch Presbyterian Kirk elder David Deans, a man whose paternal authority and religious humility combine in a stern yet sympathetic portrait. His character is beautifully brought out in the opera *Jeanie Deans* by Hamish MacCunn, in which his aria on discovering Effie's alleged crime is a masterly expression of grief, compassion, rage, defeat and sustained dignity.[8]

Effie, whose rebellious nature has led her to consummate her affair with the outlaw Robertson and give birth to the child whose disappearance prompts the charge against her of child murder, is a free spirit whose trust in justice and the law is held despite temptation. When the prison is stormed by the Edinburgh mob, her lover, the outlaw Robertson, urges her to take the opportunity to escape. She refuses. Jeanie, however, is the pivotal figure who will not compromise herself (even by lying to save her sister) and instead sets out to London to seek intercession. (For the sake of quickly clarifying the plot, Robertson is later revealed as the nobleman Sir George Staunton, and marries Effie, who becomes Lady Staunton, and we will come back to them later.)

Around these characters whose story forms the central plot, a number of other more colourful, melodramatic and highly spiced figures come and go, from the grand old Laird of Dumbiedykes (whose death-bed scene in Chapter 8 is richly comic) to the fresh Tabasco ferocity of Madge Wildfire, whose cruelty and heavy hints of prophecy interleave the world of reason and law with that of chaos, nature and demonic energy. It is Madge who has carried Effie's baby away and precipitated the action which moves the plot of the novel along. Her primary actions are dark: before the novel begins, she had been seduced by Staunton and lost her own child, so that her abduction of Effie's baby provides the basic motivation of the novel's core-plot and is a frightening reminder of the persistence of the past's capacity to affect the present.

Yet it is in the structure of the book as a whole that Scott's artifice, and the extent to which his characters and their social world are interdependent, can best be understood.

The novel was published in four volumes, conventionally enough for the period, and much criticism has been made of Scott's writing to fill out the obligation of the fourth volume. (He was paid by the word.) But the book is much more clearly divided not into four, but into three parts:

Part 1, Chapters 1–7, is introductory, a panorama of Edinburgh describing the events surrounding the Porteous riots.

Part 2, Chapters 8–46, is Jeanie Deans's story: she is the main focus of our attention as she comes to terms with the family predicament, makes her picaresque journey, returns with the pardon and saves her sister.

Part 3, Chapters 47–52, is a balance to the introductory chapters, and counterpoints the civic unrest depicted there against the domestic happiness achieved by Jeanie and the man she marries, Reuben Butler (whose character is that of the 'passive hero' formerly centre-stage in Scott's fiction). But this final section also contains the story of the Whistler.

This last section has often been criticised. Crawford says it works on a 'lower level' because Scott is less interested in the peasantry than in the paternalist landlord class.[9] Frequently the Whistler's story itself has been dismissed. Daiches approves the pastoral ending and following him, Marshall Walker endorses John Buchan's view that the domestic chapters are justified: 'he wanted to show Scottish life passing into a mellower phase in which old unhappy things were forgotten.... The figures, who have danced so wildly at the bidding of fate, should find reward in a gentle, bright, leisurely old age. Even so Tolstoy rounded off his *War and Peace*.' But this evaluation is at the expense of the Whistler's story: Buchan's judgement is right, Walker says, despite 'Scott's undesirable interest in money' *and* 'the perfunctory melodrama of George Staunton's death at the hand of his and Effie Deans's son'.[10]

The episode has been problematic from the book's first publication. The 1818 notice in the *British Review* describes it in detail before dismissing it as 'trash':

> As an instrument of vengeance upon the heads of his guilty parents, the youth, for whose supposed death when an infant, Euphemia Deans had been sentenced as a murderer, is brought upon the stage in the character of a smuggler ... on the Highland border, and has the part assigned to him of shooting his father, in a random fire of musketing. This event, so

unnatural and unexpected, is another atonement made to the stinted
morality of the tale...

...[I]f he [Scott] had not been compelled by his mercantile engagement to spin out the thread of his story, with or without materials, so
as...to secure the *fourth* thousand pounds, he would have scorned to
introduce any part of the trash...[11]

In the *Quarterly Review* in 1821, there is a greater interest in Scott's assiduous
attention to the sheer number of stories involved in the novel, and an
amused caution at the resulting work foisted upon the reader: 'instead of
floating down the united stream of events, we are forced separately to
ascend each of its tributary branches, like Humboldt examining the bifurca-
tions of the Oroonoko...'. Nevertheless, 'we are not sure...that it might
not have been politic in the author to suppress almost all his fourth
volume'.[12]

For Crawford, in both 1965 and 1982, the Whistler episode is also merely
'perfunctory melodrama'. But Crawford also notes that the Whistler 'seems
to belong to a work with a different subject and a different tone' and Scott's
attitude to him is first, sympathy, then, disapproval.[13] Crawford's observation
of that conflict of feeling is acute. It is too schematic to say, as James Kerr
does, that 'The motive behind Staunton's career is to debunk an ideology
that poses a threat to the form of social order in which Scott believes.' The
novel delivers a punishment the British government could not, killing off
the leader of the Porteous riot. 'While Effie and Staunton succeed in evading
the force of the law, they cannot escape the pattern of fatality that seems to
determine the form of Scott's historical romances.'[14]

But this misses a crucial component of Scott's novel: his sympathy. It is
certainly there for Effie through the whole course of her life; it is there for
Staunton, otherwise Robertson, the charming (but always slightly anxious)
rogue who has ruined Madge Wildfire but whose devotion to Effie is constant,
and whose criminality is always on the point of being redeemed by both his
aristocratic birthright and his incipient nobility of purpose. And it is there
most importantly for the Whistler himself.

His appearance, in Chapter 50, to Lady Staunton (Effie) and her guide,
David, occurs as they are on an excursion to visit a waterfall in the hills. The
grand scene reveals itself after a five-mile walk, and to get the best view they
have to climb around a precipice, 'clinging like sea-birds to the face of the
rock'.[15] David Richards has noted the importance of this setting: 'The
landscape, and the precipice in particular, is an apt historical symbol for
Scott's dynamic historical presentation of Highland culture since the Highlanders fell, were pushed or jumped to destruction. Precipices abound in
Scott's novels.'[16] Effie – Lady Staunton – is about to slip and cries out; she is
held by the 14-year-old guide – she screams with terror, and,

> To her amazement, the scream was answered by a whistle from above, of a tone so clear and shrill, that it was heard even amid the noise of the waterfall.
>
> In this moment of terror and perplexity, a human face, black, and having grizzled hair hanging down over the forehead and cheeks, and mixing with mustaches and a beard of the same colour, and as much matted and tangled, looked down on them from a broken part of the rock above.
>
> 'It is the Enemy!' said the boy...

' "No, no," ' exclaims Lady Staunton, ' "it is a man – For God's sake, my friend, help us!" '

But:

> The face glared at them, but made no answer; in a second or two afterwards, another, that of a young lad, appeared beside the first, equally swart and begrimed, but having tangled black hair, descending in elf locks, which gave an air of wildness and ferocity to the whole expression of the countenance...though she [Lady Staunton] observed the lips of the younger being whom she supplicated more as he spoke in reply, not a word reached her ear.[17]

The poignancy of this encounter in the melodramatic context is carefully layered. The first dark figure, the adult, is silent, stares on the unfortunates without moving to help or even appearing to recognise their predicament. He is unresponsive, and his seeming indifference to their fate (neither sympathy nor cruelty is registered in his posture, looking 'down on them'), as well as his wild appearance, prompts the guide to identify him as the Devil – 'The Enemy!'

But then the Whistler appears, a young lad who resembles the first wild man in dress and physique, but is immediately responsive to the cry for help from the woman neither of them can yet know is his mother. His words come forth inaudible to her. For her, at this moment, he is mute.[18]

'A moment afterwards it appeared he had not mistaken the nature of her supplication.... The younger apparition disappeared, and immediately after lowered a ladder of twisted osiers....'[19] She ascends the ladder; her guide (her nephew, in fact, therefore the Whistler's cousin) follows, and they find themselves 'surrounded on every side by precipices' – in an unknown recess confronted by their rescuers. The tall old man, now lying down, looks on them with 'lazy and listless apathy' but the Whistler is described as

> a tall, lathy, young savage; his dress a tattered plaid and philabeg, no shoes, no stockings, no hat or bonnet, the place of the last being supplied by his hair, twisted and matted like the *glibbe* of the ancient wild Irish, and, like theirs, forming a natural thickset, stout enough to bear off the

cut of a sword. Yet the eyes of the lad were keen and sparkling; his gesture free and noble, like that of all savages. He took little notice of David Butler, but gazed with wonder on Lady Staunton, as a being different probably in dress, and superior in beauty, to any thing he had ever beheld.[20]

He helps them up a further ladder and out to the way back to the safety of the Manse.

How far the Whistler stands from 'Lady Staunton' is poignantly emphasised, but that distance works both ways. It is also a register of how far she is from him, or, to elaborate, it is a signal of the distance between the world of landed society and order to which Effie has been promoted and which Scott himself belonged to and was determined to keep, and the world of 'all savages' to which the Whistler is consigned. The Whistler's tragedy cannot be accommodated by Scott's world. His life must be passed elsewhere.

Chapter 52 begins with the encounter which leaves Sir George Staunton a 'bloody corpse' and the Whistler in captivity in a hay-filled barn. When Jeanie Deans visits this 'born imp of Satan' she tries 'in vain to trace the likeness of either of his very handsome parents. Yet how could she refuse compassion to a creature so young and wretched, – so much more wretched than even he himself could be aware of, since the murder he had too probably committed with his own hand, but in which he at any rate participated, was in fact a parricide.'[21]

She gives him food and asks him what his intention would be if he were to escape the sentence of death '"Join wi' Rob Roy…"' he replies. Overcome with compassion, Jeanie frees him. He instantly sets the place on fire and makes his bid for liberty. Later enquiries reveal he escaped to a ship whose captain transported him to America where he was sold 'as a slave, or indented servant, to a Virginian planter, far up the country. When these tidings reached Butler [Jeanie's husband], he sent over to America a sufficient sum to redeem the lad from slavery, with instructions that measures should be taken for improving his mind, restraining his evil propensities, and encouraging whatever good might appear in his character. But this aid came too late.'[22]

What follows, Scott's 1995 biographer John Sutherland describes as 'volumes of romance compressed into two sentences'[23]:

> The young man had headed a conspiracy in which his inhuman master was put to death, and had then fled to the next tribe of wild Indians. He was never more heard of; and it may therefore be presumed that he lived and died after the manner of that savage people, with whom his previous habits had well fitted him to associate.[24]

Placed only a page or so from the end of the novel, the resonance of these lines is emphatic and enduring.

Scott was of course an enormously productive writer, but there is surprisingly little reference to America in his work. Other than Major Bridgenorth's memories of New England life in *Peveril of the Peak*, America figures largely by analogy. The generalised analogy between Scottish Highlanders and Native American Indians, symbolising romantic barbarism as opposed to the civilised Hanoverian world, has been widely noted and received ample comment. In Alexander Welsh's study *The Hero of the Waverley Novels*, for example, the dedicatory epistle to *Ivanhoe* is quoted, in which the recent government of the north of Scotland (that is, the Highlands) is likened to a state 'nearly as simple and patriarchal as those of our good allies the Mohawks and the Iroquois'.[25] Also, Welsh says, 'Rob Roy [with whom the Whistler had hoped to find refuge], shares his symbolic stature with that of an Indian...'.[26] The 1829 introduction to *Rob Roy* notes that the hero's character, which blends 'the wild virtues, the subtle policy, and unrestrained licence of the American Indian, was flourishing in Scotland during the Augustan age of Queen Anne and George I'.[27] The proximity of Rob Roy's savage world to that of the court in London is more than geographical, however. As the Whistler's story makes painfully clear, there are ties of family that cross the boundaries of cultural, political and economic identity. In *Rob Roy* this is made emphatically important as the Highland rogue and the Lowland merchant Bailie Nicol Jarvie (his companion, counterpoint and clever foil, comic, but never ridiculous) are in fact full cousins.

In a general sense Scott is simply drawing upon the conventional imagery of Rousseau's 'noble savage' to endorse ideas of romantic heroism, foreshadowing the outsider as Byronic devil and building on the idea of epic atavism, as described by James Macpherson in *Ossian* in the 1760s with specific reference to the Scottish Highlands (though we should note that Scott despised *Ossian* as a thin and poor example of proto-romanticism). Of course, Scott is also drawing on an aspect of Milton's Satan, the first of the great 'Romantic Sinners'. But the specific identification of 'the other' as a being excluded from civilised European society is pre-eminent in John Locke's *Two Treatises of Government* of 1690, where Locke says that 'in the beginning all the world was America' and 'America...is still a Pattern of the First Ages in Asia and Europe.'[28]

Perhaps this sense of the 'First Ages' represented in America could be embodied in an iconography of savagery from various other parts of the world. To Dr Johnson, visiting the Highlands of Scotland in 1773, the inhabitants and their country seemed as remote to Lowlanders as those 'of Borneo or Sumatra', and Scott also likens the Highlander to 'oriental mountaineers' or 'reconstructed Afghani tribesmen'. In 'The Culloden Papers' Scott says that Highlanders were considered as 'complete barbarians; and the mass of the people cared no more about them than the merchants of New York about the Indians who dwell beyond the Alleghany mountains'. This identification of a remote and alien being is, as David Richards puts it, intended 'not simply to satisfy a desire to understand other cultures, but to articulate an alternative social world for a European readership to occupy imaginatively'.[29]

The problem is that while this may be true of the world described by Johnson and Boswell, or the world invented by James Macpherson, or the world of *Rob Roy* in Scott's great fiction, it is not true of the Whistler's story. The tradition of 'Romantic Sinners' is a form of accommodation; the Whistler's story is one of exclusion. It is too short, brutish and nasty for an enlightened imagination to occupy fully or for any length of time, and the 'savage people' the Whistler joins are beyond the scope of even Scott's most generous sympathy. The Whistler has crossed over from a world of savagery which might be seen to endorse theories of progressive civilisation to a world of savagery and tragedy the Enlightenment mind could not accommodate. Unlike Highland society in *Waverley*, for example, which Scott clearly shows giving way to the developing mercantile economy of the recently united kingdom, the society in which the Whistler survives does not pass away into the new. It is pushed west, relocated, exists elsewhere, independent of British law altogether. The Whistler is another kind of prototype: damned but defiant. And we will return to this iconic image in the conclusion to the book.

In *The Ignoble Savage*, her study of 'American Literary Racism' between 1790 and 1890, Louise K. Barnett draws attention to the fact that although Scott was immensely popular in the United States and demonstrably inspired American writers, 'Neither Scott's chivalric spectacle nor his stratified society could be reproduced' in America. 'The political conflicts of English [*sic*] history – Jacobite and Hanoverian, Cavalier and Puritan – had to be replaced by the struggle of opposing colonial groups: English versus other nationalities of settlers each with supporting Indians, or by the stark racial and cultural confrontation of Whites and Indians.'[30] The frontier romance, in Barnett's view, by concluding with the union of the white American couple and the death or defeat of Indians, conveyed the insistence upon a new national identity. In such general terms, one might argue that Scott's work is analogous. As his major biographer Edgar Johnson says, 'Scott's great theme was always the struggle between the dying and the emerging...'[31] and in David Richards's words, 'Taken as a body of material, the Highland novels portray a process of repression of dissident ethnicities which borders on genocide.'[32]

It *borders* on genocide because Scott is always making as well as unmaking the reality and dream of Highland life. As Richards correctly stresses, Scott is both a novelist and an antiquarian: his work is a delivery into the realm of explicit articulation of 'the "unconscious" schemes of folklore'.[33] This allows and encourages a kind of survival through forms of codification and regulation that might lead to suppression. Again, this recollects the point made by Ben Okri when he visited Scotland in 1986, quoted in the Preface, 'while culture, during a time of political impotence, can become kitsch, it can also function as continual declaration and resistance'.[34] But in this reading, Scott might be seen to hold a creatively ambivalent position, as his recording or 'making' of the dream can be recaptured as resistence to its suppression. The other side of charm is repulsion and if the Whistler is repulsive rather than charming to his contemporaries and immediate family, that too brings about a memorability, just as Long John Silver holds a stronger position in his creator's affections than Captain Smollett, as we shall see in the next chapter.

I began by referring to the shift in Scott's work, from an optimistic, rational, classical temper in which the concerns of judgement, balance and order are predominant and which the attractions of glamour effectively endorse, to a temper more given to darkness, dream and symbol. If the 'modern' always arrives at the expense of the 'savage' this expense seems to be higher in Scott's later work. The Whistler's story points forward to *Redgauntlet* but it is more disturbing than anything in the later novel, and this, perhaps, is the deepest reason why it has been found 'unsatisfactory' in the context of *The Heart of Midlothian* as a whole.

Scott is frequently seen as 'a man of the Scottish Enlightenment, who believed in progress, rationality, moderation, reconciliation'.[35] 'Here, then, is the basic Scott: the realist, the sceptic, the Augustan man of letters, the British patriot of the Age of Reason.'[36] Scott's was the first country house in Scotland to be illuminated by gas. A true progressive, he installed gas at Abbotsford and became the first chairman of the Oil Gas Company. He welcomed the advent of steam transport and was interested in the development of a railway for moving coal and lime.

But the other side of this is not simply the lover of the past, the assiduous collector of innumerable mementoes and trinkets from Scotland's history, the High Tory patriot whose national sympathies were always to be contained by Unionism. These are both aspects of a man of reason. There is another Scott, to be found in the nightmares of *The Bride of Lammermoor* and *Redgauntlet*, and in the Whistler's story.

The title of the novel, *The Heart of Midlothian*, was the name given to the Old Tolbooth, the prison where Effie was incarcerated, Edinburgh's version of the Bastille, which was torn down the year before the novel was written. Its massive door was presented to Scott, who had it set into a wall at Abbotsford, where it can still be seen. That Scott considered the prison door worth preserving like this says something about the symbolic importance he attached to it. To recall the title of Goya's famous etching, 'The Sleep of Reason Produces Monsters': nightmares lie behind that door.

The world of the Enlightenment from which Scott emerged, no matter how much equanimity and accommodation it possessed, was also exclusive. As Archie Turnbull has shown, the role played by the ideas and ideals of the Scottish Enlightenment in the birth and development of the United States is

Illustration 4 Goya, 'The Sleep of Reason Produces Monsters' 1797–1798 (Glasgow University Library Special Collections)

enormously significant: in literal terms (the teachers of three – possibly four – of the first five Presidents of the United States were all Scots from an Enlightenment background, and acknowledged by their pupils as mentors) and in broader philosophical terms (the elective monarchy described in the Declaration of Arbroath clearly foreshadows the recognition of the value of life, liberty and the rights of people enshrined in the Declaration of Independence 450 years later).[37] But to Scotland and America alike, there were people to whom the words could not apply.

In March 1818, a few months before *The Heart of Midlothian* was completed and published (in late July or early August), Scott wrote a review for Blackwood's *Edinburgh Magazine*.[38] The review was of a novel Scott later declared to be his favourite work of fiction, and, given the paucity of references to America in Scott's work, it is worth noting for a curious slip of detail, and a curious association of identity. The review begins by emphasising the shifting scenes and 'stupendous drama' of the 'real events of the world' in recent years – the Napoleonic era – 'so rapid and so various' – that have seen the career of 'a private adventurer' rise 'to the greatest of European thrones' and end 'an exile, in a remote speck of an island, some thousands of miles from the scene of his triumphs'. This reflects upon Scott's judgement of the novel under review: 'The very extravagance of the present production will now, therefore, be, perhaps, in its favour, since the events which have actually passed before our eyes have made the atmosphere of miracles that in which we most readily breathe.'

Scott describes the story of a monster who, like the Whistler, is literally 'surplus population'.[39] Gradually, he learns how to speak and to hear music from a blind man who plays beautifully on a guitar, airs 'sweet and mournful', before being discovered, forced to flee and confront his maker with the question he must ask himself: 'I had never yet seen a being resembling me ... What was I?'[40]

The monster, Scott says, 'makes himself to be' 'a very amiable personage ... one day on his rambles, lighting on a portmanteau, which contained The Sorrows of Werter, a volume of Plutarch, and Milton's Paradise lost, – he becomes quite an adept in German sentiment, ancient heroism, and Satanic sturdiness'. This literary imagination clearly appeals to Scott, and his sympathy for the monster is evident as he describes how, thus 'qualified', he introduces himself to the blind man's family, who react predictably. Scott's description continues: 'He flies to the woods, furious with rage, and disappointed affection; and, finding on his return that the cottagers had forsaken the place, scared by his portentous visit, he amuses himself in his rage with setting it on fire, and then sets out in search of his creator.'[41]

The monster's recognition of his own estrangement, difference and exclusion from human beings is worth quoting for the affinities with the Whistler it may have suggested in Scott's imagination. Reading Goethe, the monster says, 'I found myself similar, yet at the same time strangely unlike the beings concerning whom I read, and to whose conversation I was a listener... "The path of my departure was free;" [an apt quotation from P.B. Shelley's "On Mutability" which had already been quoted in the novel, in Vol. 2, Chapter 2, p. 64] and there was none to lament my annihilation. My person was hideous, and my stature gigantic: what did this mean? Who was I? What was I? Whence did I come? What was my destination? These questions continually recurred, but I was unable to solve them.'[42] Milton offers him recognition of his affinity with Adam, like whom, he says, he 'was created apparently united by no link to any other being in existence...'. But it is Satan he considers 'the fitter emblem of my condition...'.[43]

The novel, of course, was *Frankenstein* and the curious association of identity between the monster and the Whistler is signalled by a tiny slip in Scott's review. In Vol. 2, Chapter 9 of Mary Shelley's novel, the monster promises that if Frankenstein creates a mate for him, then ' "neither you nor any other human being shall ever see us again: I will go to the vast wilds of south America..." '.[44] Scott paraphrases the passage: the monster 'concludes with devouring vengeance against Frankenstein and all his race, if he does not agree to one request, to create a female companion for him like himself, with whom he proposes to retire to the wilds of North America, and never again to come into contact with man'.[45]

The *Frankenstein* review was written at almost exactly the same time that Scott was about to write the Whistler away into the wilderness of North America, not to be seen again. The change from Shelley's 'south America' to Scott's 'North America' might be a slip suggesting Scott's unconscious recognition of affinity between the two unaccommodated figures. Both of these outsiders, it seems, were, in the words with which Mary Shelley famously brought her novel to an end, to be 'borne away by the waves, and lost in darkness and distance'.[46]

5
Treasure Island and Time: Childhood, Quickness and Robert Louis Stevenson

The space in between

Treasure Island opens by drawing attention to the gulf that has been crossed between the experiences to be described in the book, the writing of the book and the reading of it. Part I, Chapter I, 'The Old Sea-Dog at the "Admiral Benbow" ', begins, magnificently, thus:

> Squire Trelawney, Dr Livesey, and the rest of these gentlemen having asked me to write down the whole particulars about Treasure Island, from the beginning to the end, keeping nothing back but the bearings of the island, and that only because there is still treasure not yet lifted, I take up my pen in the year of grace 17–, and go back to the time when my father kept the 'Admiral Benbow' inn, and the brown old seaman, with the sabre-cut, first took up his lodging under our roof.[1]

One long sentence, this opening paragraph begins with an adult, legal terminology. The very titles (*Squire* Trelawney, *Dr* Livesey) signify the adult, professional status of these characters and their company among *gentle*men. The sentence proceeds: '...having asked me to write down the whole particulars about Treasure Island, from the beginning to the end, keeping nothing back but...'. The geographical, measurable bearings of the island are withheld, kept away from our attention to facilitate the passage of our imagination; but one is assured that there *are* definite co-ordinates: '...keeping nothing back but the bearings of the island, and that only because there is still treasure not yet lifted, I take up my pen in the year of grace 17–, and go back...' – And now the sentence carries us across a 'space in between' as the exact (fictional) year of writing is not specified, and the present, adult world (which is the fictional world of the adult Jim Hawkins, but also the actual world for any reader taking up the book) moves away from us into vagueness as we are taken back to an immediate and intense evocation of 'the brown old seaman, with the sabre cut' lodging in the Admiral Benbow inn.

Stevenson's negotiation of the worlds of adult reason and childhood immediacy is itself speedy as well as careful, immediate and intense as well as reasoned and crafty. What is foreknown by the narrator subsides into implicit promise as the second paragraph takes us into the details of his past. You can hear the creaking hand-barrow and smell the salt in the portrait of Billy Bones:

> I remember him as if it were yesterday, as he came plodding to the inn door, his sea-chest following behind him in a hand-barrow; a tall, strong, heavy, nut-brown man; his tarry pigtail falling over the shoulders of his soiled blue coat; his hands ragged and scarred, with black, broken nails; and the sabre-cut across one cheek, a dirty, livid white.

Stevenson has moved us very quickly from the framing terminology to the vividly evocative details of the characters and the promise of action and story. A similar speed is evident in the voyage of the *Hispaniola* in Chapter X. Returning to the rational and legalistic style of the adult Jim Hawkins, the narrator tells us that he does not propose to spend much time describing the details of the voyage, but will simply give the reader the most important facts regarding what happened in its course. Consequently, there is very little sense of a long journey by sea. It takes only a few pages to set off from the bustling port and arrive at the island, and those pages describe incidents on board, rather than any sense of the ship's long passage. Departure is precipitous:

> But soon the anchor was short up; soon it was hanging dripping at the bows; soon the sails began to draw, and the land and shipping to flit by on either side; and before I could lie down to snatch an hour of slumber the *Hispaniola* had begun her voyage to the Isle of Treasure.
>
> I am not going to relate that voyage in detail. It was fairly prosperous. The ship proved to be a good ship, the crew were capable seamen, and the captain thoroughly understood his business. But before we came the length of Treasure Island, two or three things had happened which require to be known.

What is especially curious about this transmission is the temporary restitution of adult terminology tangible in the language of Jim Hawkins's narrative. Stevenson stops recording or evoking the experiences of the characters and removes them from one site to another. He moves them across a different 'space in between' – the space between two points on a chart, or more exactly, from a point upon a map (offering the security of land) to a point upon a chart (suggesting the impreciseness of ocean) – with the minimum of fuss; and he is perfectly open about his procedure. He spells it out for us.

What happens in the transit is of some moment, of course. Mr Arrow is discovered to have 'no command among the men' – an adult incapable of adult authority, 'useless as an officer', who mysteriously procures a supply of alcohol, and drinking himself senseless, goes overboard one dark night. Long John Silver takes centre-stage now, and he and his parrot are a colourful foil to the disgruntlement of Squire Trelawney and Captain Smollett. Then in Chapter XI, 'What I Heard in the Apple Barrel', we have young Jim's first sense of Silver's duplicity and potential murderousness. Jim is about to be discovered in the barrel when the mutineers are diverted by sight of Treasure Island and a cry of 'Land ho!'

This swift passage from port to island demonstrates all the tensions between vision and experience which the book will exploit and explore. The obscurity which covers the exact date of the events and the exact location of the island is in contrast to the evocative imagery in the reference to the sabre-scar, or any of the immediate and tangible experiences vividly described as they happen to young Jim. Yet this obscurity or elision performs the most important function. The 'dirty, livid white' scar on Billy Bones's cheek is itself the ugly sign of an earlier experience, and thus prefigures the clusters of vivid images which fill the story, each of which refers us to earlier events than those the story deals with, and each of which continues to haunt the memory. They reach through the wilful vagueness surrounding their location. The central melodrama takes place in a timeless, anarchist state, an island where laws do not apply, where almost anything is possible, because in this state, actions, while informed by past events, are not controlled by them. The tale is framed by and written out of a condition of social and political stability, where social rules are observed. But within the frame, the rules are subject only to the capacities of the narrators themselves.

In *The Case of Peter Pan or the Impossibility of Children's Fiction*, Jacqueline Rose argues that 'Children's Fiction is impossible':

> not in the sense that it cannot be written (that would be nonsense), but in that it hangs on an impossibility, one which it rarely ventures to speak. This is the impossible relation between adult and child. Children's fiction is clearly about that relation, but it has the remarkable characteristic of being about something which it hardly ever talks of. Children's fiction sets up a world in which the adult comes first (author, maker, giver) and the child comes after (reader, product, receiver), but where neither of them enter the space in between.[2]

'There is', she declares, 'in one sense, no body of literature which rests so openly on an acknowledged difference, a rupture almost, between writer and addressee.'[3]

While clearly provocative, Rose's language is woolly. Does the repeated word 'about' in the third sentence of the paragraph quoted mean 'emerging from and surrounding' or 'surrounding and enquiring into'? The ambiguity itself is suggestive. For Rose, the 'acknowledged difference' creates the 'space in between' adult and child, author and reader, giver and receiver. The 'space in between' is a slippery and ambiguous phrase: she describes it as 'a rupture, almost' – suggesting not a space but an internal act – but it is also a period of time, and a passage through time, which can be described (as in a traditional *bildungsroman*) or elided. It is like an irreparable tear because the adult cannot literally return to the 'space' by becoming a child again in order to pass through it, and the child crosses the 'space' once and once only, to become an adult. Any relation to the 'space' therefore recognises its uniqueness. Yet if the phrase 'Children's Literature' generically refers to such a 'space' surely readers of whatever age or legal status may return to an imaginary space in the act of reading, a space in which imagination moves back and forth across and between the realms of fantasy and reason?

This sense of difference or rupture is particularly relevant to *Treasure Island*. It is a paradigm of 'Children's Fiction' even more revealing than the text Jacqueline Rose focuses on, J.M. Barrie's *Peter Pan*. The similarities between the texts need not be detailed here, but the fact that both present a world where childhood is a privileged status is surely related to the fact that both authors were expatriate Scots, and this premise underlies what I have to say here. The legacy of Scotland was also inherited by R.M. Ballantyne, of course, and although Jacqueline Rose notes that there are similarities between Ballantyne, Barrie and Stevenson,[4] she gives little weight to the common factor of national identity and makes no connection between this legacy and the 'impossibility' of their vocation as writers. Themes to do with dissociated sensibility and the rupture between writer and addressee may be profitably discussed in abstract theoretical terms or under the generic rubric of 'Children's Fiction', but they acquire another sort of specific weight if we bear in mind the relation between the traumatic history of Scotland and the legacy inherited by Barrie and Stevenson before him. As Angus Calder has written, 'Culture is a superstructure upon geography rather than on an economic base.'[5] The cultural geography of childhood haunted both men and continues to haunt their writing.

Narrators, humble and otherwise

There are three narrators in *Treasure Island*: as well as Dr Livesey and the adult Jim Hawkins there is Jim as a boy. Each stands in a different relation to time. Dr Livesey is completely of the adult world, without recourse to childhood's quicknesses and luck. The adult Jim, by contrast, has clearly come *out of* his own childhood and therefore is an emphatic reminder that adult and child cannot be independent, autonomous entities. But it is the young Jim Hawkins whose quick imagination animates the tale in a way the adults cannot. Indeed, the adult and the childhood worlds reciprocate each other's attention. For example, the climax of Part III, the end of the first section of Jim Hawkins's narrative, sees the fighting begun, and young Jim running for his life towards the besieged stockade. Chapter XV closes with the portentous image of security and law beleaguered: 'The cannon-shot was followed, after a considerable interval, by a volley of small arms. Another pause, and then, not a quarter of a mile in front of me, I beheld the Union Jack flutter in the air above a wood.' When the narration resumes in Chapter XVI, which begins Part IV, it is taken up by the doctor, who, like the other adults, has structured his perceptions on enforcible divisions whose security depends upon their being maintained. (The stockade itself is a physical and symbolic example.) When he tells us 'I was not new to violent death – I have served his Royal Highness the Duke of Cumberland' he is making a reference few adult Scottish readers (and perhaps generations of children as well) could fail to pick up, to the military commander whose bloody reprisals among the Highlanders after the massacre at Culloden made him notorious. The adult world of real history, conquest and suppression, threatens to overwhelm Jim's childish world of action and movement. Jim wants it to do so, of course: he is running towards it. It will offer shelter, security, protection, safety and stability. But such offers will come only with certain conditions.

The witness and comical chorus throughout is Silver's parrot Cap'n Flint, whose name links back to a piratical past. It is two hundred years old, according to Long John in Chapter X, for 'they lives for ever mostly; and if anybody's seen more wickedness, it must be the devil himself'. 'I calls my parrot Cap'n Flint', Silver tells Jim, 'after the famous buccaneer – here's Cap'n Flint predicting success to our v'yage. Wasn't you, cap'n?' To which the bird replies with its unknowing cry for commercial reward, 'Pieces of eight! pieces of eight! pieces of eight!'

Landscapes of the imagination

Treasure Island is pre-eminently about a landscape of the imagination, a world where birds can speak and living things can live forever, where language signifies much more than it says. It is a foreign land, a subject very much the provenance of post-Union Scottish writing. Scottish writers are frequently writers for whom their own land has become foreign in a specific sense. After 1603 and 1707, the project of the British Empire led to many of Scotland's writers travelling abroad. This literally meant that the land of their childhood became far-away, never to be returned to. It was certainly Stevenson's own experience.

Stevenson wrote *Treasure Island* in Scotland, before he left the country of his birth for exile. But one might argue that in post-Union Scotland national identity can be fully inhabited only in childhood, because with adult recognition of political structures, Scotland's status within the United Kingdom relegates the idea of an autonomous national identity to the realm of fantasy. The anthology of Scottish poetry we noted in the Introduction is making this point by its title, *Dream State*.[6] Such a 'dream state' is more securely and safely located in the past than thought of as something worth struggling for in the future, although, as we noted when we looked at the two editions of the book, events do bring change.

It is not only physical exile from the geography that is important here; it is also the banishment of national identity from the political and, ultimately, the spiritual life of the exile. It becomes something that can only be perceived as a lack. This is what Stevenson foresaw intuitively as a faculty shared between children's fiction and Scottish literature, particularly of the late-Victorian period and the early twentieth century. It is as much an aspect of George MacDonald as of S.R. Crockett, Kenneth Grahame as of Norman Douglas, of John Buchan as of George Douglas Brown, of Conan Doyle as of J.M. Barrie. All of these writers bear witness to a peculiarly ambiguous relation between imperial authority and the aspirations of childhood. All of them came from a Scotland closed off from national autonomy in their imagination. None of them endorsed nationalist or republican politics. All were brilliantly successful creators of literary fantasy.

Treasure Island was Stevenson's first novel, completed in 1881, serialised, and then published as a book in 1883. In 1888, he and his wife were to charter a yacht and cruise the South Pacific in search of a home which might be congenial to his health. In a literal geographic sense, the place of his childhood was distant. But in an economic and social sense too, the adult world of law and government was constructed by co-ordinates drawn from imperial certainties rather than national traditions. The two worlds were mutually incommunicative. One could contain the other: the empire could contain Scotland, by suppression and obfuscation, just as Stevenson's opening, adult terminology contains the boyhood memory of the man with the scar – but they cannot talk to each other. There is an obscuring 'space in between' them. And this time, Jacqueline Rose's phrase seems perfectly apt. It is always, in this scenario, looked at from the point of view of the adult the child has become or the empire the nation is part of – and such a perspective necessarily emphasises the idea that it is a one-way journey.

Yet for Stevenson, writing itself makes possible another entry, a way back to imagine different possibilities, a range of possible journeys. A dichotomy is set up in *Treasure Island* between realism (which proposes a commercial and socially respectable world) and fantasy (which proposes a world that is both adventurous and sordid), between self-justified good reason which orders and explains, and clear vision of incomprehensible experience which generates further adventures and elaborations. This in turn produces a set of ambivalent possibilities. What appears to be good may in fact be evil, the apparently innocent traveller abroad may in fact be rapacious, out for booty or conquest. Any 'space in between' fixed points is not only a site of transmission but also a place for transformation.

The full ambiguity of the phrase can be savoured here. The 'space in between' is not only between places but also between times. If the worlds of adult and child are demarcated by adult rules and laws, the child's dynamic by its nature enacts a subversion of such rules. This is fun, but also dangerous. The security of identity is mutable between fixed moments, and therefore such moments offer reassurance while they threaten oppression. Scotland is a crucial repository of these fixed and altering forces, for it exists as a named fiction, an unreal fact. A nation without statehood is the condition of childhood, and children, like Scots, are both the victims and the perpetrators of empire. Like Jim, they run towards imperial certainty even as they subvert it. Thus reading *Treasure Island* as 'Children's Literature' should prompt us to read it also as 'Scottish Literature': such a reading must take into account the relation of nation to empire and of protean form to statehood.

Luck and the law

Stevenson's fictional story-world is lucky. It is not simply that there are coincidences in the plot; rather, it is a world of luck, a world which has luck as its essence. In this sense, both Jim and Long John Silver are lucky: they both inhabit this world and play by the rules of luck more successfully than anyone else. They are attracting opposites in age and experience, but united by loneliness and idiosyncrasy. Jim is, in a sense, an orphan; Long John is an *isolato*. If Long John is duplicitous and murderous, he is also a victim; if Jim starts off innocent of crime, by the end of the book he will have become a fine judge of character and a killer of men. Such violent dualities counterpoint each other throughout *Treasure Island*. Long John himself is a pirate and a man of action, but he is also married and crippled with a wooden leg, and rather than a first mate or a captain, he is professionally employed below deck as a cook (the book was originally to be entitled *The Sea-Cook*). Such a role gives him an extra depth of significance, feeding the crew as he feeds the imagination of the boy in the story. When Long John tells Jim tales of high adventure 'with a great deal of spirit and the most perfect truth' he is eloquent, seductive, threatening and alluring as Othello is to Desdemona. It is Silver's command of language and his self-control which orders his charm and channels his greed. It is this which marks his maturity. It is an evolved form of the same command and control which Jim will inherit from him, and put to work in the civil world he comes to inhabit.

Perhaps the most important duality is social. Long John belongs to an earlier social world than the one Jim Hawkins grows up to inhabit. The island with its treasure (still there to draw upon, as Stevenson reminds us in that opening sentence), belongs to the past, the world before the Jacobite uprising of 1745, the slaughter of Culloden in 1746, the suppression of Highland culture and the political transformation of Scotland which followed. This is the meaning of the specified century, unspecified year in the '17–' of the opening sentence. The world of Squire Trelawney, Dr Livesey and the adult Jim Hawkins comes after all that. They are civilised people, and their civilisation is British.

These matters underlie *Treasure Island*. In the book's narration and multiple narrators, switching from the adult Jim to the youthful Jim, then to the narrative of the adult Dr Livesey and then back to Jim, we are witness to a range of interpretive strategies. We witness different kinds of experience, different kinds of judgement, different kinds of sense. Just before Jim climbs into the apple-barrel, at the end of Chapter X, Cap'n Flint the parrot screams 'Stand by to go about' – forewarning us that everything is about to turn, Silver will be revealed to be ruthless, cold-hearted, self-serving and unremittingly adult. Stevenson's language registers a clarity of vision by ruthlessly deleting all the overload of speculation and abstraction of adult thinking. Young Jim's vision depends literally upon his size, his speed and his ability to avoid or simply dodge the obscurities or ambiguities that live in the space 'between'. The book records his acquaintance with them – not in a chronological way, as in a *bildungsroman*, but as a testament to their perpetual imposition. As youth is counterposed to adulthood, so singleness of identity is counterposed to multiple identities (and deceit), laws (and social structures), politics (and national identities) and sexuality and family (and their ambivalences). Luck is counterposed to morality and mortality: luck is a means of realising potential, morality is the inevitable definition of it, and mortality alters and fixes the shape of one's career – luck turns to destiny. The adult Jim's financial status is unquestionable. But the vitality of the book lies in its refusal to endorse the adult values of empire and statehood unequivocally. (Just as the moral ending of Burns's 'Tam o' Shanter' is hopelessly and deliberately doomed by the sheer subversive energy inhabiting the poem.) Luck stays in Stevenson's writing because he himself always stays part child: quizzical, unconfirmed, Tusitala, the story-spinner.

This aspect of Stevenson was irrepressible. In 'A Fable, *The Persons of the Tale*' he extracted two of the puppets – Silver and Captain Smollett – out of *Treasure Island* and supplied them with *ex cathedra* dialogue explicitly in the space between, 'After the 32nd chapter...' (the Fable begins) and before '...the author was just then beginning to write the words: CHAPTER XXXIII' (as the Fable ends). Silver salutes the Captain and points out that they are ' "off dooty now; and I can't see no call to keep up the morality business" '. The Captain replies: ' "You're a damned rogue, my man...." '

'Come, come, Cap'n...There's no call to be angry with me in earnest. I'm on'y a chara'ter in a sea story. I don't really exist...But I'm the villain of this tale, I am; and speaking as one seafaring man to another, what I want to know is, what's the odds?'

'Were you never taught your catechism?' said the Captain. 'Don't you know there's such a thing as an Author?'

'Such a thing as a Author?' returned John, derisively. 'And who better'n me? And the p'int is, if the Author made you, he made Long John, and he made Hands, and Pew, and George Merry – not that George is up to much, for he's little more'n a name; and he made Flint, what there is of him; and he made this here mutiny, you keep such a work about; and he had Tom Redruth shot; and – well, if that's a Author, give me Pew!'

'Don't you believe in a future state?' said Smollett. 'Do you think there's nothing but the present story-paper?'

'I don't rightly know for that', said Silver; 'and I don't see what it's got to do with it anyway. What I know is this: if there is sich a thing as a Author, I'm his favourite chara'ter. He does me fathoms better'n he does you – fathoms, he does. And he likes doing me. He keeps me on deck mostly all the time, crutch and all; and he leaves you measling in the hold, where nobody can't see you, nor wants to, you may lay to that! If there is a Author, by thunder, but he's on my side, and you may lay to it!'[7]

Language and time

This alerts us to the difference between seeing or reading something for the first time, and seeing or reading (or re-reading) the same thing again. The overlay of primary or primal experience with repeated readings of it in various kinds of circumstance is especially important in Stevenson's writing. Our fondness for particular readings seems unusually relevant to Stevenson, whether we are thinking of *Kidnapped* or *Travels with a Donkey in the Cevennes*, or *Dr Jekyll and Mr Hyde*. The spontaneity of visual experience is registered again and again in *Treasure Island* – think of young Jim's first sight of the man with the scar or the clarity with which he sees the corpse of Israel Hands lying on sand under the transparent water, with the fishes swimming above him, at the beginning of Chapter XXVII. Landscapes of the imagination change in time. Arguably, in a pre-television, pre-cinema world, the visual element could reside in words differently, giving words their own dimensionality. This is what Louis MacNeice is referring to in his 1952 poem, 'To posterity':

> When books have all seized up like the books in graveyards
> And reading and even speaking have been replaced
> By other, less difficult, media, we wonder if you
> Will find in flowers and fruit the same colour and taste
> They held for us for whom they were framed in words...[8]

Adherents of Jacques Lacan might insist that the unconscious is structured as a language, yet seeing comes before words, as John Berger reminds us: 'The child looks and recognizes before it can speak.'[9] But, one should note, it hears before it is born and it can smell things before it can see them. How, then, does Stevenson convey this experience to us, freshly, in language? He does so precisely by using the vagueness of the 'space in between' the vision (or the sensory apprehension) and the articulation of it. As we have seen, this is shown in the speed with which Stevenson's language moves. Narrative prose cannot depict experience spontaneously as it happens, nor can it retrospectively control it in an absolute sense. Peculiarly sensitive to this, Stevenson's writing unfolds its experiences in a self-conscious method, as if the writing itself could not foretell the events which follow upon each other in it. Nothing appears as an inevitable consequence, but every act is lucky or unlucky depending *retrospectively* on one's position and status. The train of events is logical only with hindsight, and this is a security we are vouchsafed as readers. It returns, of course, with the frame and we are offered reassurances at various points. But, while the story is happening, it is a security which the characters *in* the story lack. Indeed their lack of that security is what makes their actions exciting. Meanwhile as we read the book, the comfort of knowing that the storyteller is still with us, a familiar, avuncular presence, is constant and unstressed. Thus John Berger continues:

> It is seeing which establishes our place in the surrounding world; we explain that world with words, but words can never undo the fact that we are surrounded by it. The relation between what we see and what we know is never settled.[10]

One method of attempting to 'settle' that relation is by using language to appropriate experience, rather than to enact it. We touched on this point in Chapter 3, discussing the ways in which the genre of narrative prose is distinct from that of poetry: the former may more easefully *accommodate* the unpredicted wildness of lived experience while the latter may more immediately *embody* it. A literary use of language to dramatise and enact the experience of characters in the most immediate way possible is most evidently exemplified in Shakespeare; by contrast, language used to appropriate and secure experience is the traditional procedure of the great Victorian novels, where the respective identities of reader, author and the panoply of characters are all (more or less) secure in a defined hierarchy. Any reader might identify with Hamlet or with Maggie Tulliver; but there are innumerable ways to produce a play, whereas the great Victorian novels, to a greater or lesser degree, are finished productions in themselves: they are pre-eminently settled forms, full of pondered weight and security.

Exceptions abound, and of course, the dissolution of certainty is characteristic of the late nineteenth century. Even in *The Mill on the Floss* (1860), there are passages where George Eliot's writing seems much more fluid and unreliable, when she moves into morally ambiguous areas. For example, towards the end of Chapter XIII, 'Borne Along by the Tide', when Maggie and Stephen have gone 'out too far' with their boat, the writing itself seems much less certain about where it is taking us:

> Behind all the delicious visions of these last hours, which had flowed over her like a soft stream, and made her entirely passive, there was the dim consciousness that the condition was a transient one, and that the morrow must bring back the old life of struggle – that there were thoughts which would presently avenge themselves for this oblivion. But now nothing was distinct to her: she was being lulled to sleep with that soft stream still flowing over her, with those delicious visions melting and fading like the wondrous aërial land of the west.[11]

And indeed, in the next chapter, 'Waking', Maggie refuses the option of marriage to Stephen as she knows it would be a forced solution to their social predicament:

> It is not the force that ought to rule us – this that we feel for each other; it would rend me away from all that my past life has made dear and holy to me. I can't set out on a fresh life, and forget that: I must go back to it, and cling to it, else I shall feel as if there were nothing firm beneath my feet.

The secure sense of what is at stake described by this passage has been evoked in the previous chapter by a tangible yet uncertain quality in George Eliot's writing itself. The vivid sense of the *adult*'s discovery of 'nothing firm' beneath the feet is particularly telling, since *The Mill on the Floss* is one of the finest depictions of childhood in English literature (that of Maggie and Tom Tulliver) and the passage quoted here is of course consequent upon that earlier depiction. However, George Eliot was imbued with the spirit of Scottish and German philosophy: the limits of knowledge rather than the certainty of knowledge was the crucial issue for her. It was arguably the most radical achievement of her writing to push the insight and enquiry into this issue beyond the securities vouchsafed by *Middlemarch* (1871–1872) and into the world of uncertainties and unresolvable tensions represented in her last novel, *Daniel Deronda* (1876), which begins in a social structure as defined and apparently integrated as Jane Austen's but ends with individuals as isolated and lonely as they are in Beckett.

Twenty-one years after *The Mill on the Floss* and five years after *Deronda*, Stevenson's writing in *Treasure Island* often and characteristically slips *past* the great Victorian securities, sliding into a much more ambiguous and *unsettling* world of alteration and becoming. His greatest work focuses on the condition of a man whose identity is loosened from the securities of social form and finds only horror in an uncontrollable access to the energies of youth. For Henry Jekyll there is no becoming, there is only a world of increasing unsettlement and spiralling demise. But *Dr Jekyll and Mr Hyde* (1886) is a work for adults; in Stevenson's work for children, the same question arises in a different formulation. Physically, to feel nothing firm beneath one's feet may be more quickly exhilarating for a nimble, running child than for an adult fully weighted and sensitive to the impersonal pull of gravity. Yet although his adventures are exhilarating, for most of *Treasure Island* Jim is uncomfortable. His adventurousness is a means of surviving in an 'unsettled' condition and his excitements are tainted with proximate dangers.

The word 'unsettled' is doubly pertinent if one considers the meaning of settlement in the colonial world. A colonial settlement is an investment of authority, an imposition from abroad or in hierarchical terms, from 'above'. Stylistically, Stevenson's writing itself sometimes seems to attempt to avoid the imposition of such authority. Arguably, in *Treasure Island* he uses a technique of narration which insists that even such authority is constructed. It might be authoritative and unquestionable, but it is clearly something made, and therefore threatened by proximate unmaking: there is a kind of instability in the law itself. To come to the 'lawful state' may involve the acknowledgement of 'difference' and 'rupture' and an unrepeatable movement through a 'space in between' – yet even as it seems to subscribe to it, Stevenson's writing is working against this conclusion. It is as if the 'space in between' is a constant presence, always carried with us. *Treasure Island* ends in the security of an adult world, but that world is haunted by its own past. The last paragraph runs thus:

> The bar silver and the arms still lie, for all that I know, where Flint buried them; and certainly they shall lie there for me. Oxen and wain-ropes would not bring me back again to that accursed island; and the worst dreams that ever I have are when I hear the surf booming about its coasts, or start upright in bed, with the sharp voice of Captain Flint still ringing in my ears: 'Pieces of eight! pieces of eight!'

For young Jim Hawkins, adventure signifies travel and luckily moving on, and is opposed to colonisation and conquest, settlement and residence. Perhaps it was this aspect of Stevenson's writing which led Brecht to mistake him for an American writer. There is a similar urge to light out for the territories in Huckleberry Finn. But unlike Huck, Jim Hawkins grows up.

To that adult Jim Hawkins, the childhood world, like Long John Silver himself, has 'gone clean out of my life'. They are both banished to the world beyond obscurity: there are no co-ordinates to chart a voyage of return; there is no date to refer to in history books. Youth is thus equated with dream-world or nightmare, but in an inverted sense, for the memory of Treasure Island becomes for Jim what it has become for generations of Stevenson's readers: a nightmare full of horrors that can be remembered *affectionately.*

They can be remembered affectionately (like the scar on Billy Bones's cheek) only because, despite the obscurity which surrounds them, they are securely located, locked in isolation and irrecoverably *past.* But their *memory* can be and continues to be revisited, within the covers of the actual book, and this forms a cycle of security that might only be disrupted by a different configuration of childhood's geography.

Such a configuration might reconstitute the geography of childhood as one from which the adult has neither banished himself or herself, nor been sent from into endless exile. Rather, it would bring a sustenance and nourishment of adulthood, rather than a fixed, framed counterpoint and contrast to it. Many vested interests keep the channels between child and adult closed. The palisade still stands. But the horrific truth told by the story of *Dr Jekyll and Mr Hyde* is that they are both a single man, suffering the fate of the damned as they strive to illuminate the grace of the saved. And similarly, Silver and Jim see themselves in each other, which is why *Treasure Island* has so much to say to adult readers even now.[12]

6

In Pursuit of Lost Worlds: Arthur Conan Doyle, Amos Tutuola and Wilson Harris

Scottish by birth, Irish by descent, British by self-determination, Sir Arthur Conan Doyle was one of the grand old men of Empire. His dates, 1859–1930, when we put them alongside Stevenson's, 1850–1894, may remind us how young Stevenson was when he died, how prophetic Stevenson's writing was of modernity, and how easy it is to see Doyle firmly rooted in the imperial world from which he came. However, the magic of his writing will not be confined to history. The Sherlock Holmes stories are legitimately works of Scottish literature not only because they were written by a Scotsman, not only because their hero was based on a Scottish doctor Doyle knew, but also because the London they depict is in many respects modelled on Edinburgh, a much more walkable city. And they are perennially popular. Stevenson himself enjoyed them keenly, writing to Doyle from Samoa on 5 April 1893:

> I hope you will allow me to offer you my compliments on your very ingenious and very interesting adventures of Sherlock Holmes. That is a class of literature that I like when I have the toothache. As a matter of fact, it was a pleurisy I was enjoying when I took the volume up; and it will interest you as a medical man to know that the cure was for the moment effectual. Only the one thing troubles me: can this be my old friend Joe Bell?[1]

Stevenson's recognition of their mutual acquaintance Joseph Bell, upon whom Doyle modelled Holmes's skills of deduction, signals an affectionate regard for the younger writer and a friendly, companionable sense of their shared Edinburgh youth. The full extent of Stevenson's influence on Doyle has yet to be explored but Prince Florizel in *New Arabian Nights* (1878) surely prefigures a long line of independently licensed heroes operating between the law and criminality, from Holmes through Richard Hannay to The Saint and James Bond. Moreover, Stevenson's dark London in *Jekyll and Hyde* (1885) foreshadows Doyle's London in the Holmes stories both in its moral murk and its resemblance to Edinburgh.

Yet Stevenson seems prophetic of twentieth-century writing and Doyle seems to belong in the Victorian world, partly through his reliance upon the formulae of Victorian melodrama, partly because of his repeatedly drawing upon the outposts of Empire to provide villains and villainous motives (sometimes accompanied by snake, ape or mongoose). Nevertheless, in this chapter I would like to suggest that Doyle's imagination bridges forward also, towards the work of writers apparently vastly different in ethos, style and historical moment. Doyle, I shall argue, points forward to 'post-colonial' writers such as the Nigerian Amos Tutola (1920–1997) and the West Indian/ Black British Wilson Harris (b.1921), by virtue of imaginative insight and a capacity to engage with fantasy which need not be confined to categories of 'Children's Literature' or 'literature that I like when I have the toothache'. This capacity to engage with fantasy, as we saw in the last chapter, may form an essential part of adult experience, and to read Doyle, Tutuola and Harris in this way, might begin to explore that experience in terms of Scottish literature in a novel light, moving between and connecting the broadly popular and the intensely esoteric in fruitful forms of interpretation. More especially, the imperial world and the post-colonial context seem essentially opposed to each other, yet the literary imagination is a bridge connecting them and it is this to which my selection of the three writers discussed in the present chapter is intended to allow us to cross.

I would like to begin with an aspect of Doyle's writing that seems even more removed from the Scottish environment than the Holmes stories and to think about it in an international context. *The Lost World* works within the established tradition of fantasy, where the exotic or unpredictable location is taken as a context. The possibility of transformation is the dangerous promise of this context, and in this respect too, Doyle points forward to the post-imperial world.

The crisis of the modern

In a poem published in 1926, Hugh MacDiarmid imagines the spirit of God inhabiting a world of sea and light like a giant serpent, flickering its coils in the heights of space and encompassing his personal life as a tide might swallow a sea:

> I feel like a star on a starry nicht
> A'e note in a symphony,
> And ken that the serpent is movin' still,
> A movement that a' thing shares,

> Yet it seems as tho' it twines in a nicht
> When God neither kens nor cares.[2]

In other words, the spirit of God might be glimpsed, felt, imagined like this, but God himself is absent. MacDiarmid speculates that a cry sent out from 'the hert o' a man / When it feels the twist in its quick' might, just possibly, call God back to his work again, but in this poem, the lonely reaches of space and night are solely occupied by the poet's questing energies: the poem ends with no divine security permitted.

It is helpful to begin this chapter with MacDiarmid in the 1920s because a poem like 'Sea-Serpent' is central to the major changes of the Modern Movement on either side of which stand the three authors I am concerned with here. Also, I want to foreshadow the internationalism at the heart of the Scottish Literary Renaissance of the 1920s, which will be the focus of the next chapter. I intend to go ten years back from MacDiarmid to talk about work by Conan Doyle, and then thirty and fifty years forward respectively, to Amos Tutuola and to Wilson Harris. But reference to MacDiarmid and the spiritual universe he inhabited allows me to introduce what I am going to say now by evoking the Modern Movement. It was, essentially, a cultural crisis which emerged from Doyle's world and which, in some respects, made the worlds of Tutuola and Harris possible.

Into the forest primaeval

But we can set off now from an earlier point of departure, into the Amazonian forest with Arthur Conan Doyle's intrepid adventurers. Every time we do so, the visual impression is vivid. Chapter 8 of *The Lost World* is set on the threshold of entry to the plateau and is entitled 'The Outlying Pickets of the New World'.[3] The visual impression Doyle had of the place is vivid. Michael Swan, in his 1958 account of his visit to the interior of (what was then) British Guyana, *The Marches of El Dorado*, tells us that Mount Roraima, a flat-topped mountain of some 9000 feet, where Brazil, Venezuela and British Guyana meet, haunted Doyle:

> At the beginning of the century Roraima caught the interest of the scientific world. There had been a dispute for some years in the learned journals; supposing, thousands of years ago, the earth had thrown up by volcanic eruption a large area of earth, so that it was isolated from its surroundings by impassable precipices? What would happen to its flora and fauna? One school denied the possibility of suspended development... The other believed that life in this static environment would be unique. A search was made for places with the required conditions, and expeditions set out for Roraima to study the ecology of its slope and summit. Conan Doyle's novel was a dramatization of this pursuit of lost worlds.[4]

Once again, as we noted with the imagery of landscape in Walter Scott's fiction, the precipices, escarpments and dense forests suggest a symbology of steep cultural changes, the past preserved in suspended forms, whether literally suspended in the high space of the plateau or cliff-top or in evolutionary terms, with reference to languages and cultures or monstrous, prehistoric forms of life. Does the Whistler's face looking down over the edge of the cliff towards Lady Staunton in Chapter 50 of *The Heart of Midlothian* not seem to foreshadow that of the homunculus that startles the narrator, the reporter Ed Malone, when he climbs a giant tree to reach a look-out position and gazing round through the branches, is suddenly confronted as if in a mirror, by this:

> It was a human face – or at least it was far more human than any monkey's that I have ever seen. It was long, whitish, and blotched with pimples, the nose flattened, and the lower jaw projecting, with a bristle of coarse whiskers round the chin. The eyes, which were under thick and heavy brows, were bestial and ferocious, and as it opened its mouth to snarl what sounded like a curse at me I observed that it had curved, sharp canine teeth. For an instant I read hatred and menace in the evil eyes. Then, quick as a flash, came an expression of overpowering fear. There was a crash of broken boughs as it dived wildly down into the tangle of green. I caught a glimpse of a hairy body like that of a reddish pig, and then it was gone amid a swirl of leaves and branches.[5]

In contrast to the visual impact of Roraima, however, and as that passage demonstrates, Doyle's text is emphatically literary. Malone *reads* hatred and menace in the eyes of the ape-man. The artifice of Doyle's writing is highlighted with self-conscious deliberation. The book's individual chapters take the form of 'despatches home'. He opens Chapter 8 by drawing attention to the great distance between the position of the writer and that of his readers 'at home'.[6] Malone gets ahead of himself in his excitement.

> Our friends at home may well rejoice with us, for we are at our goal, and up to a point, at least, we have shown that the statement of Professor Challenger can be verified...I must hark back, however, and continue my narrative from where I dropped it. We are sending home one of our local Indians who is injured, and I am committing this letter to his charge, with considerable doubts in my mind as to whether it will ever come to hand.

Then the narrative doubles back to describe the expedition from the point where the previous chapter ended: 'When I last wrote we were about to leave the Indian village where we had been deposited by the *Esmeralda*.' The verisimilitude claimed by this careful attention to the pedantic realities of writing the expedition in the form of 'letters home' counterpoints the increasingly fantastic visions that will be related. This narrative form itself is an important organisation of narrative time. It is analogous to the structure of Lewis Grassic Gibbon's *Sunset Song*, where each new section of the book begins with the principal character returning to the location in which the previous section closed, after a period of time has elapsed. Both Gibbon's and Doyle's narrative create an effect of heightened tension: the reader is assured of the final location from which the narrator (in Doyle) or the main character (in Gibbon) is writing or remembering, but what happened between the close of the previous section or chapter and the opening of the next is unknown and unpredictable. The opening of Chapter 8 displays a range of Doyle's stylistic and narrative modes in a variety of tones and scenarios: melodramatic, comic, and above all, wondrous, in the imaginative fantasy of the forest itself.

The melodramatic is found in the episode Malone relates next:

> I have spoken of our English-speaking half-breed, Gomez – a fine worker and a willing fellow, but afflicted, I fancy, with the vice of curiosity, which is common enough among such men. On the last evening he seems to have hid himself near the hut in which we were discussing our plans, and, being observed by our huge negro Zambo, who is as faithful as a dog and has the hatred which all his race bear to the half-breeds, he was dragged out and carried into our presence.

Once Zambo disarms the belligerent Gomez, they are 'compelled to shake hands... there is every hope that all shall be well'.

The unqualified caricature and racism evident here is a function of the security of category and hierarchical division upon which the whole expedition is predicated – both in the sense of the specific professions of the adventurers themselves and their complementary forms of expertise, and also in the sense that their trip to the plateau is intended to revise and redefine the secure categories and hierarchies of their contemporaries' paleontological and scientific understanding of the world. Revision of this kind might alter the securities by which such racist priorities are defined. The massive volcanic upheaval that created the plateau is an eruption into the stability of scientific knowledge.

This is what keeps the two professors in the novel in comic conflict with each other. Challenger is always, as his name tells us, on the edge of advancing knowledge by disrupting previous certainties. His sceptical colleague, Summerlee, is more determined to stay in the relaxed and temperate shelter of untroubled accommodation, as *his* name suggests. Malone writes it up as comedy.

Last night Challenger said that he never cared to walk upon the Thames Embankment and look up the river, as it was always sad to see one's own eventual goal. He is convinced, of course, that he is destined for Westminster Abbey. Summerlee retorted, however, with a sour smile, by saying that he understood that Millbank Prison had been pulled down. Challenger's conceit is too colossal to allow him to be really annoyed. He only smiled in his beard and repeated 'Really! Really!' in the pitying tone one would use to a child. Indeed, they are children both...[7]

Malone's observation, however, cannot fully persuade us. It is always Challenger, bearded, conceited, short-tempered and colossal, who is intrinsically more appealing to our childish sense of anticipation and desire. I will come back to this point.

As Malone describes the journey upriver he orders things in careful sequence, explicitly using the categories and classifications of the scientists. The river itself is described by its affluents, sometimes transparent, sometimes whitish and opaque, indicating vegetable decay or clayey soil. Then the primaeval forest, unforgettably mysterious and cathedral-like, with 'Gothic upward curves' coalescing into a 'matted roof of verdure' above them as they walk noiselessly upon 'the thick, soft carpet of decaying vegetation' while 'the hush fell upon our souls which comes upon us in the twilight of the Abbey...'.

Alone, I should have been ignorant of the names of these giant growths, but our men of science pointed out the cedars, the great silk cotton trees, and the redwood trees, with all that profusion of various plants... Vivid orchids and wonderful colored lichens smouldered upon swarthy tree-trunks, and where a wandering shaft of light fell full upon the golden allemanda, the scarlet star-clusters of the tacsonia or the rich deep blue of ipomaea the effect was as a dream of fairyland.[8]

The animal world is sensed far overhead, the 'multitudinous world of snake and...howler monkeys' and parakeets breaking into shrill chatter. Then finally, beyond their immediate world, indications of other forms of *human* life are felt:

On the third day out we were aware of a singular deep throbbing in the air, rhythmic and solemn, coming and going fitfully throughout the morning...
  'What is it, then?' I asked.
  'Drums,' said Lord John, carelessly...
  'Yes, sir...' said Gomez, the half-breed. 'Wild Indians...watch us every mile of the way; kill us if they can.'

'How can they watch us?' I asked, gazing into the dark, motionless void.

The half-breed shrugged his broad shoulders.

Malone's partial understanding powerfully conveys a sense of wonder because it uses specialist terminology to emphasise the link between the scientific world and 'dreams of fairyland'. In the analytic description of the river, the cathedral-like forest and its inhabitants (the animal kingdom and the threatening human presence signified by the 'deep throbbing' drums), scientific names are always tokens of a kind of authenticity and civilisation in a world of pagan dream and primordial wonder.

A different world

Hodder and Stoughton published *The Lost World* in 1912. Forty years later, Faber & Faber published Amos Tutuola's *The Palm-Wine Drinkard*. Between them there was the impact of two world wars, the Russian revolution, the Easter Rising in Ireland in 1916 and the growing number of national and anti-imperial movements and the developments that were to lead to colonial independence in Africa and elsewhere. Doyle comes out of the nineteenth century; Tutuola stands at the beginning of the late twentieth century. But before we go on, I would like to quote the opening of his first book:

I was a palm-wine drinkard since I was a boy of ten years of age. I had no other work more than to drink palm-wine in my life. In those days we did not know other money, except COWRIES, so that everything was very cheap, and my father was the richest man in our town.

My father got eight children and I was the eldest among them, all of the rest were hard workers, but I myself was an expert palm-wine drinkard. I was drinking palm-wine from morning till night and from night till morning. By that time I could not drink ordinary water at all except palm-wine.

But when my father noticed that I could not do any work more than to drink, he engaged an expert palm-wine tapster for me; he had no other work more than to tap palm-wine every day.

So my father gave me a palm-tree farm which was nine miles square and it contained 560,000 palm-trees, and this palm-wine tapster was tapping one hundred and fifty kegs of palm-wine every morning, but before 2 o'clock p.m., I would have drunk all of it; after that he would go and tap another 75 kegs in the evening which I would be drinking till morning. So my friends were uncountable by that time and they were drinking palm-wine with me from morning till a late hour in the night. But when my palm-wine tapster completed the period of 15 years that he was tapping the palm-wine for me, then my father died suddenly, and when it was the 6th month after my father had died, the tapster went to the palm-tree farm on a Sunday evening to tap palm-wine for me. When he reached the farm, he climbed one of the tallest palm-trees in the farm to tap palm-wine but as he was tapping on, he fell down unexpectedly and died at the foot of the palm-tree as a result of injuries. As I was waiting for him to bring the palm-wine, when I saw that he did not return in time, because he was not keeping me long like that before, then I called two of my friends to accompany me to the farm. When we reached the farm, we began to look at every palm-tree, after a while we found him under the palm-tree, where he fell down and died.[9]

At this point, the drinkard and his two friends bury the poor tapster and return to town. Next day he has no palm-wine left and finds that his friends shun him. Though their fickleness is never explicitly judged, the moral implication regarding their priorities, and those of the drinkard in entertaining them, is clear. The drinkard tries another tapster who fails to provide sufficient quantities of palm-wine; he tries drinking water – but that is no good. So then the moment comes when he realises what he must do, and he embarks upon his own quest:

When I saw that there was no palm-wine for me again, and nobody could tap it for me, then I thought within myself that old people were saying that the whole people who had died in this world, did not go to heaven directly, but they were living in one place somewhere in this world. So that I said that I could find out where my palm-wine tapster who had died was.

One fine morning, I took all my native juju and also my father's juju with me and I left my father's hometown to find out whereabouts was my tapster who had died.[10]

Contrasts between Doyle and Tutuola are clear enough. My purpose here, rather than emphasise the contrasts, is to draw attention to the imaginative connections between them.

Fantasies and facts

The similarities are, first of all, generic. Both are first-person narratives working within the established tradition of fantasy. Travel to and in an exotic location is a familiar component of romance fiction but the genre of fantasy (which overlaps or coincides sometimes with science fiction) takes the exotic or unpredictable location as its context.

In this respect the first-person of each narrative tells what is clearly intended as an autobiographical story, but each voice fulfils a different role.

Malone, in *The Lost World*, is constructed as an acceptable fictive voice, reliable, accountable, sober, balanced and carefully judging, in an increasingly unbelievable world. Tutuola's drinkard is unreliable, unaccountable, rarely sober (and only under sufferance). He is always slightly off-balance and, at least in these opening pages, he does not judge.

What connects these two texts most closely is also what marks the most severe distinction between them. This is the idea of transformation itself. It is enacted every time we read or re-read these books (and it is worth noting that, like Stevenson's *Treasure Island* and *Kidnapped*, they have been frequently re-read).

In Doyle, transformation is always seen as a possible threat. This is why the categories and classifications offer such security and are so constantly required. Challenger braces them, shocks the securities, but he reasserts them too. Summerlee relies upon them. Each professor, Malone says, has 'a brain which has put him in the front rank of his scientific age'. But even more revealing is how necessary the classifications are to Malone: if he is the spokesman for the type Doyle once said he imagined himself to be – 'the man in the street' – then he shows no plebian scepticism about the value of scientific knowledge.[11]

It is, after all, one way of coping with the palpable absence of spiritual assurance characteristic of the modern age, and felt even more keenly by MacDiarmid in the poem I quoted at the beginning of this chapter. Doyle's most famous creation, of course, is God-like, benign, insightful, infinitely reliable, a materialist scientist who works in mysterious ways. In Doyle's own life, where science failed to offer answers, he immersed himself in the occult.

There *is* factual information in Tutuola. We learn that the drinkard started drinking at ten and his tapster was employed for fifteen years before his untimely death. So at the age of 25, the drinkard loses his father suddenly, and six months later, equally suddenly, his tapster. The numbers he gives us seem strangely definite and reliable. The palm-tree farm held 560,000 trees and the tapster produced 150 kegs every morning. These numerical details seem to assure us of reliable fact inside the fantasy of the narrative. But the major difference from Doyle's writing is that the fantasy provides the context for them. The drinkard does not intrude upon the exotic world as Malone, Challenger and Doyle's other expeditionaries do on theirs. The drinkard is already in it. In Tutuola's world, transformation is a natural and continual practice. Component parts shift their ground, categories change without being assessed, realities alter and the unreliable nature of the world is not perceived as a threat to be feared and avoided ('The drums! The drums!') but as difficulty to be encountered, problems to be engaged.

The movement of each narrative is fired by a relationship between logic and intoxication. In Doyle's case, scientific sobriety and categorical knowledge are fuelled, in Challenger's character, by appetite and curiosity. In Tutuola's case, the drinkard's unreliability leads to a similar state of renewable appetite and a curiosity for what will help sustain its replenishment. Both forms of curiosity lead to different kinds of wonder and adventure. In Doyle's story, the wonder of discovery and the adventure of the expedition into the unknown is sustained by the narrative device of Malone's letters. The further the expedition moves into the lost world, the more it seems impossible that they will get any messages back out, let alone be rescued or escape themselves. In Tutuola's story, the drinkard's adventures follow an unpredictable episodic course, leading from one scene and its consequences to another without any immediately apparent retrospective plan. Tutuola has no recourse to Doyle's dovetailed doubling-back narrative line. And the ending of *The Palm-Wine Drinkard* refuses closure in a very different way from that of *The Lost World*.

The Lost World ends with the promise of a return journey to the plateau: the prospect of adventure renewed. *The Palm-Wine Drinkard* seems to end with the line (and the italics are Tutuola's), 'That was *how* the story of the palm-wine drinkard and his dead tapster *went*.'

Having followed the drinkard's adventures through Death's house and the underworld of skulls, where he finds his wife, to Wraith-Island, to the great white tree, the home of Faithful-Mother, and to Red-Town, and at last to the Deads' Town itself, we might have been content for the story to end there. But Tutuola carries on for seven more pages, describing a Famine brought about by a conflict between Land and Heaven, and how the drinkard managed to feed the world with a magic egg. When people start fighting, the egg is smashed and when he repairs it, it only produces whips. Finally, the rain falls for three months and there is no famine again. There the book ends. Natural harmony is restored, but without the sense of foreordained closure affirmed by the handshake Lord John Roxton offers to Ed Malone at the end of *The Lost World*.

Initiation, childhood and new worlds

I do not want to conclude with the idea that the gulf separating Doyle and Tutuola is unbridgeable, or that Doyle's *Lost World* is inaccessible because of the historical events that followed its publication. The racist and imperialist aspects of his writing are clear enough. Curiosity, for example, when it belongs to the 'half-breed' Gomez, is no more than 'a vice' but if Gomez suffered from 'the vice of curiosity', what did the two professors have? The idea expressed by Conan Doyle's 1943 biographer Hesketh Pearson, that 'since then we have discovered that nothing sub-human, pre-human or preter-human could possibly surpass in horror the primitive doings of ordinary humanity', cautions us against glib approval of the generosity of Doyle's imaginative sympathy.[12]

I said I would return to Challenger's childish sense of anticipation. It is this that keeps him fresh. And it is this, I think, which might prompt reflection on the relation between the texts and how we might best understand them both. As Adam Phillips says, it is the 'capacity for transformation, for the imaginative and often bizarre refashioning of everyday experience' which is the child's 'unerring, ineluctable talent'.[13] It is the child who makes something of his own or her own from whatever he or she might find, as we have seen in our study of *Treasure Island*. 'Children are fervent in their looking forward to things....' In *The Beast in the Nursery*, Phillips reminds us that instead of the Freudian death instinct which attends the surfeit of appetite, we should never lose sight of the child's renewing curiosity. 'If growing up did not mean growing out of things but growing into them again and again, our good life stories would have to change their shape. We would be accountable in quite different ways.'[14]

The childishness so apparent in Challenger and the drinkard is shared and equally ambivalent, for just as Challenger's expedition is motivated by his own engagement and curiosity, so, too, by the end of Tutuola's novel, the drinkard's blissful ignorance is overcome by a more deeply engaged knowledge about himself and humanity. There is, as Paul Edwards has demonstrated, 'a shaping imagination at work here of a more complex kind than is usually associated with this tale'.[15] The opposed worlds of, on the one hand, dance, music, farm, garden, harmony and accommodation, and on the other, nightmare, scapegoat, bondage, pain, confusion, apocalypse and famine, are worlds the drinkard moves through in a journey of knowledge and propitiation, so that his people might ultimately be saved.

Perhaps it has been too easy to see Doyle's work as merely the provenance of children, or of those of doggedly child-like mind, just as it has seemed to some appropriate to criticise Tutuola for attractive disingenuousness. We should remember that it was not for its naïveté but for its youthfulness (or childishness, perhaps) that *The Palm-Wine Drinkard* was welcomed by Dylan Thomas in 1952 in *The Observer*, as 'the brief, thronged, grisly and bewitching story, or series of stories, written in *young English*'.[16] Three years later the book was saluted by Hugh MacDiarmid in his poem *In Memoriam James Joyce*: 'Amos Tutuola, the Yoruba writer, / Who has begun the structure of new African Literature....'[17] The youth and originality of Tutuola is suggested in Doyle's latter-day imperial adventures, too, precisely because, either through their penetration of the jungle and crossing to the plateau or their descent to the Deads' Town, they both have access to what Arthur Hugh Clough once called 'The buried world below'.[18]

It is precisely this buried world, this sense of childish curiosity, wonder and renewing appetite which is invited by the obtrusion of the volcanic plateau upon which the lost world is sustained. Doyle's great perception was to recognise in the plateau of Roraima a metaphor by which the adult could encounter the child once again. The adventurers sustain their youth, even as they grow up. In a strangely similar paradox, the drinkard does the same. All cross the bridge over 'the space between'.

When the drinkard sets out on his expedition, in the passage I quoted earlier, he takes with him not only all his own 'native juju' but also that of his father: 'and I left my father's hometown to find out whereabouts was my tapster who had died'.

It is a moment curiously reminiscent of one of the great opening sentences in Scottish literature, when, on 'a certain morning early in the month of June, the year of grace 1751', the young David Balfour says that he 'took the key for the last time out of the door of my father's house'.[19]

There is tenderness towards initiation. To place Stevenson beside Tutuola in this way is to mark a community of identity in the human story. To place

Illustration 5 Harry Rountree, 'The Journey across the Tree Bridge' from *The Lost World* in *The Strand Magazine*, June 1912, p. 619 (Mary Evans Picture Library)

Conan Doyle beside Tutuola in this way is to propose an affinity between late imperial and post-colonial worlds across historical change, in defiance of the gravities that pull them apart. And this is to suggest that a map might be sketched in which literature could be located by virtue of these co-ordinates. To place Stevenson's *Kidnapped* beside *The Lost World* in this way invites a sympathetically renewing sense of what being an adult means.

The imaginative quest story crosses over boundaries of culture, language and time. It remains something intrinsic to the human attempt to make sense of the world we inhabit. Similarites as well as discontinuities that relate across imperialist and post-colonial contexts have been suggested here in ways which, I hope, begin to articulate the questions that remain to be asked: questions about the urgent and pressurised voice of MacDiarmid's speaker with whom this chapter began, whose passionate, visionary 'prayer' for God to recover his lost energy and re-energise his human creation is located at a crucial point between the different scenarios of accommodation, exploration and initiation in Doyle and Tutuola.

'blown across seas and landscapes...'

When we turn to the work of Wilson Harris, the dynamics of writing themselves have been altered in the post-imperial context. Harris was born in British Guyana in 1921, of mixed ancestry (Amerindian, African, and European – including Scots). He studied and became qualified in land surveying in 1939, leading many expeditions into the heart of the rain forests of the interior, and eventually becoming the Senior Surveyor for Projects for the Government of British Guyana. The plateau of Roraima was familiar territory to him before he came to Britain in 1959 and settled with his wife just north of London.

His novel *Black Marsden* (1972) is actually set in Scotland, but interweaves memory and presence, absence and actuality, so that a deliberate uncertainty, a volatile attentiveness, is maintained, not simply in the narrative but in a more complex way, in the quality of the writing itself. In *Black Marsden*, the curious association between Scotland and South America is indicated in the first paragraph. The book begins with one of the great opening sentences (fit to put alongside those of *Kidnapped* or James Hogg's *The Brownie of Bodsbeck*): 'I came upon him in a corner of the ruined Dunfermline Abbey of Fife like a curious frozen bundle that may have been blown across seas and landscapes to lodge here at my feet.'[20]

The 'doubled-up' figure on the ground turns out to be Black Marsden. But before the reader discovers this, the narrator explains a little about himself, recalling journeys he had made through Scotland, to the abbey of Culross and the Firth of Forth, all of which seem in his memory 'sunken into a transparent film or subaqueous world':

The ancient palaces and corridors I visited were an extraordinary and naive cradle of kings woven nevertheless into complex, sometimes implacable legend. This combination of naive and complex features was true of kings whether in pre-Columbian America or pre-Renaissance Scotland or Europe.[21]

Harris elaborated on this in discussion: 'There are many Europes. There's the Europe we know now and underneath that there is the Europe of the Renaissance and underneath that again there is the Europe of the Middle Ages. There is the Europe in which Mary Queen of Scots and John Knox were contemporaries... And Scotland in a way may be a microcosm of them all, more so than England perhaps. You have a whole theatre in Scotland, don't you?'[22]

The first paragraph of *Black Marsden* brings this point home forcibly, as having suggested a mysterious, evocative connection between pre-Columbian America and pre-Renaissance Scotland; it concludes with wilful twentieth-century bathos: 'The idea obsessed me and I found myself at liberty to trace its contours around the globe since winning a fortune from the Football Pools.' The narrator's name is blatantly symbolic: Clive Goodrich. When his eyes meet Marsden's, he feels 'an uncanny twist or stab from within myself as if I *knew* him though I had not seen him before'.[23]

So far, the scenario will be familiar to many readers of Scottish literature. A man, financially independent, benevolent but naïve, is to be tested in some way by an unforeseen encounter with a mysterious and possibly malevolent stranger. Inevitably, the stranger will have something devilish about him; he may be acting as a hellish emissary, or indeed he might actually be the devil himself. Readers of James Hogg's *The Private Memoirs and Confessions of a Justified Sinner* (1824) or John Herdman's modern version, *Pagan's Pilgrimage* (1978), will have certain expectations about this kind of tale. In certain respects they will not be disappointed. Marsden evokes dream-characters who haunt and hurt the vulnerable Goodrich: Jennifer Gorgon, Knife and Harp. Their existence in the novel depends on a conspiracy between the mischievous (and potentially murderous) intent, on Marsden's part, and the generosity and good will of Goodrich, his host. As long as Goodrich entertains Marsden and his creatures, so long does his imagination become infected with motives and desires he can neither comprehend nor cure.

In places, *Black Marsden* is unexpectedly comic. Goodrich's housekeeper, Mrs Glenwearie, is summed up as 'a woman with a heart of gold' and this phrase is used self-consciously, in a way that seems ironic: it is so patently a cliché. And yet it is not reductive: Mrs Glenwearie plays a stalwart, resourceful role. She is of that family of benevolent Scottish matriarchs which includes Sherlock Holmes's Mrs Hudson, Ma Cleghorn in Lewis Grassic Gibbon's *Grey Granite*, Dr Finlay's Janet, James Bond's Mae, Ma Broon

in *The Sunday Post*'s 'The Broons' and the Mrs Girvan who is presented in
a brilliant vignette in Troy Kennedy Martin's *Edge of Darkness* (we will
encounter her in Chapter 12). Mrs Glenwearie is an archetypal character like
these, but she is possessed of some surprising idiosyncrasies which show
how the bridge might be crossed with comic unpredictability. Prompted by
Marsden's plans to stage a dramatic production, she informs Goodrich that
she once acted herself, in her younger days, performing the role of Grace
Darling (a figure of Victorian melodrama, the heroic lighthouse-keeper's
daughter who rescued the crew of a foundering ship). To Goodrich, and to
the reader familiar with the type of character Mrs Glenwearie is, this is
unsurprising. But, she adds, she also played Haile Selassie in a church play:

> 'Haile Selassie?' Goodrich was astounded. He stared at Mrs. Glenwearie,
> trying vainly to imagine the transformation.
>   'It was a long while back,' she told him. 'And then I remember my
> mother being very proud when I was chosen to read Tam O' Shanter at
> a Burns Supper.'[24]

Grace Darling, Haile Selassie and Tam o' Shanter each occupy Mrs Glenwearie
for a few moments, moving into and out from her personality with an easy
fluency, through which she still retains her indomitable balance. This
unlikely combination of presences or anthology of masks surprises the
reader as much as Goodrich.

In *Black Marsden*, the opacities and oblique elisions of narrative and the
clotted, twisting syntax and structures of the language itself suggest an
understanding of complex historical depth which, in Harris's vision, is
wedded to geographical scope, so that the traditional Western unitary
understandings of place, time, character and linear progress are upset. The
field is tilted.

Deep in the novel, one of the ambivalent characters, Knife, takes Goodrich
on a dream-like journey into the mythical north, towards a town called
'Namless'. The absent 'e' at the heart of the town's name is an absurd
symbol for (among other things) the absence to be felt in the very name of
Scotland, the stateless nation, whose people cannot escape their national
legacy. This is a liability as well as a privilege. Knife explains to Goodrich
that 'Namless' is the name of the whole territory as well as the town itself. It
is particular and local but also universal. In return, Goodrich explains that
Namless was his birthplace, referring ambiguously to his father, an American
engineer, who died when he was one year old, and his stepfather, who disappeared in Brazil when Goodrich was five. This explanation creates further
ambiguities, however. It remains uncertain just *where* Namless is (Scotland?
South America?). The journey 'is articulated upon an Edinburgh stage'
Harris comments above – but we read about it through the medium of
Goodrich's diary. All these uncertainties fog the chance of any naturalist or

realist sense of concrete particularity in a linear narrative, but the clusters of images and recognitions with which Harris confronts us are immediate and vivid. Passing deserted villages, cleared townships, Knife remarks, 'There was an uprising...Crushed at a blow.' Then there follows this remarkable passage:

> Now all of a sudden, as if with a wave of a wand, Goodrich was struck by a fantastic assembly of features – to which he already possessed a prelude on the rickety road or ribbon of sea across which Knife drove – features which may have been plucked from the loneliest reaches of the Highlands of Scotland like transplanted snow from the Cairn Gorms to the Cordillera Real in the Bolivian-Peruvian Andes which reach to Lake Titicaca on one hand, but on the other descend phenomenally to the Amazon basin. Such a spectre in which blister turns to cool, ice beckons to fire, snow to rainforest was a family tree of contrasting elements.
>
> As far as eye could see it may have been carved or erected as a vast nameless cradle by a refugee chorus of mankind dispersed from Pole to Pole, who celebrated within this mosaic overlapping features of their original heartlands: *When the bough breaks, the cradle will fall.*
>
> Or it may have been borrowed from diverse peoples and inhabitants (stretching back into pre-Columbian mists of time) who had been shepherded out of sight in order to create a theatre of infinity.[25]

This is a kind of religious invocation, a profound consolation derived from a sense of the global dispersal of races and cultures. The Caribbean provides a microcosmic example of that global theatre, and so does Scotland. By interweaving images of both, Harris suggests a vivid cultural affinity and a sense beyond that of the whole human community.

Judgement is delivered upon Marsden and his associates at the end of the novel, when Goodrich makes what seems to be his final choice. But it should be noted that Harris's next novel, *Companions of the Day and Night* (1975), is introduced by Goodrich as extracts from voluminous papers and diaries sent to him by Black Marsden. So perhaps the old devil is still in the wings somewhere, waiting to make another appearance.

It is appropriate that he should not completely disappear. The problem he embodies is at the heart of a psychic reality which Scotland (and Ireland) and the Caribbean share. In *Black Skin White Masks*, Frantz Fanon refers to the 'wrestling contradiction of a white mind in a black body', and one might consider this colonial Janus-effect in Scottish terms.[26] To do so would help explain the affinity Harris found in Scotland and it would also help us to consider Scotland in a global and comparative way. Fanon's phrase is clearly similar to the notorious formulation applied to Scots by different generations of modern cultural theorists in linguistic terms, most famously by Edwin Muir in the 1930s: that Scots are a people who feel in one language and think or intellectualise or write in another. Leaving aside the questions that are begged in this formulation (about Scottish Gaelic writing, for example, or the legitimacy of acquired or 'artificial' languages for public expression, or the necessity of artifice in literary forms), and allowing for its simplification of complex matters, it is demonstrably true that the contradictions of linguistic and cultural identity are part of the social and imaginative fabric of Scotland in a very different way from England. They are intricately knotted to the country's peculiar national history and they were the principal condition of the current of intellectual life in twentieth-century Scottish literature, most intensely felt in the 1936 conflict between Edwin Muir and Hugh MacDiarmid, as we noted in Chapter 1.

In both Scotland and the Caribbean, the diversity that is present in the complex identity of each necessarily confers an understanding of difference, of otherness as part and parcel of the self. This is a perception highly developed by individual writers and artists in or in connection with Scotland throughout the twentieth century, as a direct development of the national/international dialogue set up so emphatically in the Scottish Renaissance and so distinctive in the modernist era. We shall explore this more thoroughly in the next chapter. But there is a more intimate aspect to this understanding of difference also.

It lies at the heart of Hugh MacDiarmid's famous lyric 'O Wha's the Bride' in *A Drunk Man Looks at the Thistle* (1926). Contemplating the union of male and female which produces an individual human being of either sex, MacDiarmid is confronting one of the most essential mysteries of otherness in the human vocabulary. The suppressed female surfaces in MacDiarmid's poetry to subvert the rules of unitary identity sanctioned by patriarchal society. A similar process is at work in Lewis Grassic Gibbon's characterisations of women in his fiction – not only Chris Guthrie, but also Thea Mayven, Gay Hunter, Rachel Gault and others. Caribbean writers such as E.K. Brathwaite, Jean Rhys and Wilson Harris himself have also pursued these questions. The emphasis given to circularity (rather than on towering, male, vertical structures of power) and the concern Harris shows for what he calls 'enabling space': these are repudiations of Western patriarchal systems. In the words of Michael Gilkes, Harris seems to possess that rare quality that Coleridge thought characteristic of a great mind: androgynous thinking.[27] A variety of images of 'felicitous space' recur in his work as his 'inner-space' journey proceeds: cave, womb, shell, cradle, egg, room, boat. The journey is always towards amnesis, a 'recovery' or 're-membering' of broken history, broken community, the broken relationship between man and woman and it helps generate a peculiar energy and resourcefulness.

This resourcefulness is to be found in *Black Marsden* in the ways in which the experience of Scotland complements the experience of South America, to build into a vision of human possibility. When Goodrich goes on one of his favourite walks through the city of Edinburgh, he takes great delight in the open sky, which appears to knit itself into everything: brick, green tree, the everchanging mirror of water and space.

> Was it, Goodrich wondered, because of that texture of sky that Edinburgh was regarded as a masculine city? Was it that open sky which accentuated the verticality of every spire or monument raised by man or nature?
>
> He made his way now along Silverknowes Road back to the water's edge and dawdled along the foreshore to Cramond. The blue, green waves curled into animated frescoes of memory that seemed to reach towards Harp's horizons and lakes across the Atlantic: to reach also further south into the South Americas – South American savannahs pasted upon the globe like an abstract realm within fiery longitudes.
>
> He recalled the sky-line of Edinburgh which he had seen for the first time, he believed, from the vicinity of the disused quarry of Craigleith. It had been a clear day like this and upon the slate of time one could see spires, the hunched back of Arthur's Seat and the Castle.
>
> He recalled also a view of the Lawnmarket from the roof of St Giles Cathedral and the rock ridge with its pattern of the Old Town accentuated against the sea of the sky.
>
> All these vistas seemed to curl and uncurl now into ebbing and flowing waves or tides. The sea of the sky reached everywhere, spires and rocks seemed equally fraught with energies that shot upwards but witnessed to an inherent spatial design, geology of psyche.[28]

As an illustration of the feminisation of a masculine landscape, this passage could bear close reading. The 'geology of psyche' seems to encompass the masculine spires. Verticality is located in a sea of 'ebbing and flowing waves and tides'. This evokes William Crozier's Edinburgh, much more than Alexander Nasmyth's. As an instance of the Scottish element in Wilson Harris, it is a typical mix of familiar landscape and distinct sensibility. It is pleasurable, as well as salutary, to experience that landscape becoming defamiliarised through that sensibility, and at the same time to witness that sensibility becoming familiar through association with that landscape. It is in touch with, not excluded from, the Edinburgh of Arthur Conan Doyle, Professor Challenger and Sherlock Holmes, and it promises an international provenance for it, in the words of the epigraph to this part, from Eugenio Montale via Edwin Morgan, 'to be as various / As vast, yet fixed in place' or, as Harris himself puts it, to create 'a theatre of infinity'.

In it, Doyle's world and those of Tutuola and Harris are connected, from imperial to post-imperial writing contexts. The acts of initiation we spoke of above require tenderness and an intuitive imagination and both these qualities develop in relation with their subjects. Doyle's writerly mind is related in this way to Tutuola's picaresque imagination (which is connected to eighteenth-century motives in narrative and political evolution as well as traditional storytelling) and to Harris's encompassing yet open, enabling, interpenetrative vision of what occupies space in his 'theatre'. This 'theatre of infinity' is the modern world, and how Scotland comes to inhabit it, and what might yet be done in it, is the subject of the next part of this book.

Part III
The Theatre of Infinity

If there is ocht in Scotland that's worth ha'en
There is nae distance to which it's unattached
                    – Hugh MacDiarmid, *To Circumjack Cencrastus*

Part III

The Theatre of Infinity

7

The International Brigade: Modernism and the Scottish Renaissance

In praise of Ivan Sanderson

In 1943, in *Lucky Poet*, Hugh MacDiarmid wrote of 'the young scientist and artist, Mr Ivan T. Sanderson, author of those fine books, *Animal Treasure* and *Caribbean Treasure*', who ranked, according to MacDiarmid, 'as one of the greatest Scottish writers, and personalities, to-day'. With reference to *Caribbean Treasure*, MacDiarmid continued, although it

> deals with a scientific expedition to Trinidad, Haiti, Surinam, and Curacoa, I feel that he is really writing all the time about his native Edinburgh, and that when he describes a grison (a kind of weasel) as 'circumambulating an obstacle by pouring round it, like a train', whence he mistook it at first for a snake, or writes of a cave in which he flashed his torch on a circle of land-crabs who 'dropped their tall periscopic eyes, and waved their huge pincers in front of them – a few blew bubbles that hissed and squeaked in the silence', or tells us of the three-fingered sloth, the absurdity of its subhuman face only less absurd than its three blunt, stumpy, insensitive paws, or of the pigmy ant-eater whose eyes on capture filled with tears, though if you were sentimental enough to be taken in by that, it produced its highly effective armament, 'claws as dense, tough, and sharp as a gaff', he is not describing the strange fauna he found round the Saramanca, Coppename, Surinam, and Parva rivers, but giving masterly word-pictures of many of the types of citizens of his native Edinburgh to-day, and wish that he would come back to Scotland here and continue his work, along lines not unlike the 'Mass Observation' activities of Tom Harris[s]on and Charles Madge and their colleagues.[1]

From MacDiarmid's description we can characterise Ivan T. Sanderson as a perfect example of a particular kind of Scottish writer. He belongs to a particular constellation of Scottish writers whose work has been produced furth of Scotland and deals with themes, ideas or characters not overtly

Scottish in themselves. Despite this, the work of such writers and others in different but related constellations constitutes a set of traditions that lies behind the internationalism of the Modern Movement in Scotland. These traditions have historical depth, but they also continue to provide an international context for the study of anything homegrown. The inescapable development of this international context is one of the most essential characteristics of the twentieth century and it informs every sense of what 'the popular' might be in the twenty-first.

In this chapter I would like to do two things: first, offer a brief account of the movement in which this began to be recognised as vital, the Scottish Renaissance of the 1920s. This cultural movement was portended in the 1890s and work associated with it continued to be produced well into the 1930 but it was in the 1920s that its main protagonists set out to regenerate, artistically and politically, a vision of nationality that might be presented on a global stage.

Secondly, I want to locate that movement and that national vision in an international context and to sketch some of its long-term effects, from the 1920s back, in terms of a long history of Scottish writers and artists moving around the world, sometimes returning to Scotland, sometimes not, and then from the 1920s on, listing a number of writers whose work bears upon Scotland from oblique or singular angles of approach.

This is not only to locate MacDiarmid alongside Pound, Eliot and Yeats in the international context of the Modern Movement. Such internationalism is normally bound by a conservatively Anglo-American imperium. Rather, I would like to come at the whole phenomenon of cultural appraisal from a different angle and try to endorse perspectives that amount to a more effectively comprehensive way of seeing the world.

Necessarily, then, the second part of this chapter will be a compilation of encounters. The artists we meet there might be refreshingly unfamiliar or seen in unusual company, but the tesserae of their works might build into a mosaic of different identities and forms, and perhaps, by considering their many differences patiently, we might begin to approach a coherence of enquiry into, and recognition of, the meanings of home and abroad.

After all, the central tenet of the Modern Movement was exile. This resulted in a renewal of linguistic energy in its greatest writers and artists. The equivalent aspect of the Scottish Renaissance was a fresh alignment between the sense of being earthed to native soil and an international context for it. This distinguishes the Scottish Renaissance – or Scottish Modernism – from that of Ireland, England or the United States in the same period, and partly this depends upon the centrality of Scots as a language and a spoken idiom represented in writing to the period's literature. The sense of native loyalty that is aligned with this language is very different from the cosmopolitan provenance of English which appeals so strongly to a city-centred view of modernism. Bartók is as critical to this understanding as Joyce.

If my approach here runs the risk of making everything that follows the Scottish Renaissance seem like an expression or articulation of that movement's principles, it should be acknowledged that the principles I discern were of their era and many later writers and artists adopted different conceptions of their relation to the nation than those espoused by the movement's most voluminous theorist, Hugh MacDiarmid. Yet I do wish to emphasise that those principles were intended to encourage expressivity in a multiplicity of forms, not to foreclose or constrain nationality in uniformity. Perhaps this has the effect of making the aspiring experimental diversities of the late nineteenth century and further back seem like vitalising pretexts for the work of the 1920s and also of endorsing continuities from the 1920s to the present, rather than emphasising the disruptions and differences between individuals and generations. I would not wish to underestimate the differences but I do think the overall patterns of relationship can be addressed in a more enabling and invigorating way than has been common. I would not attempt to describe a parallel with those ways of viewing Irish literature which find it to be no more than the fragmentary reflections of Joyce's 'cracked looking glass of a servant'. Rather, I wish to evaluate MacDiarmid's best hopes for how Scottish literature and art might be constructively appreciated, alongside the practice of reading some of those neglected or undervalued artists and their work.

Modernism and the Scottish Renaissance

One might sketch the character of the Modern Movement by saying it began in the 1890s, in fin-de-siècle Europe, heralded by Robert Louis Stevenson and Oscar Wilde. Stevenson's dark, psychotic stories, his bohemianism and Francophilia, his internationalism, travelling to France, and then across America and into the Pacific, and finally his sense of strangeness in language, the poise of his work, are all prophetic of tendencies in the major writers of the Modern Movement. Wilde's Irish identity, like Stevenson's Scottish one, lies under the flashing surfaces of wit and Anglophone internationalism, but it is unmistakeable. Wilde's deeply subversive ironies, cutting cleverness and radical challenge to Victorian sexuality and the vicious censoriousness of polite society also prophesied revolutionary art.

There are paradigmatic examples of that art. The furore caused by Picasso's *Les Demoiselles d'Avignon* (1907) was less because it depicted hard-edged prostitutes with faces like African masks and had more to do with its rejection of the traditional pleasures of the contemplation of paintings. These women stared straight out at the viewer, implicitly asking the question, 'Who's looking?' Equally aggressive and forward, equally attached to the use of dark rhythms and imagery, Stravinsky's *The Rite of Spring* (1915) also, famously, caused violent controversy when first performed. In literature, when James Joyce, T.S. Eliot and Ezra Pound confronted a reading public with radically new kinds of prose fiction and poetry, they defined tendencies that had been developing throughout the previous century. Traditional Victorian hierarchies of authority had already been breaking down through the era of Darwin, Marx, Freud and Nietzsche. We are now familiar enough with the idea that the secure positions of author, readers, fictional characters, all flew apart after the First World War, and in 1922, the *annus mirabilis* of the movement, Joyce's *Ulysses* and Eliot's *The Waste Land* changed what writing could be forever.

If we date the Modern Movement roughly from the 1890s to the 1930s or early 1940s, and say that after 1945 a different ethos prevailed, we can legitimately call the new era 'postmodernist', and characterise it too. After Hiroshima and Nagasaki, a sense of radical egalitarianism went along with increasing plurality of media and different forms of artistic expression. In all the arts – architecture as much as poetry – a developing reliance on quickness, superficiality and variety seemed typical. The rise to dominance of America as an arbiter of cultural authority in the post-war era might be registered in the burgeoning accomplishments of American poets – the Beat movement rising through the 1950s and breaking out internationally through the immensely influential anthology *The New American Poetry* in 1960. Allen Ginsberg, Robert Creeley, Charles Olson and Edward Dorn became critically important at the same time as new writing from hitherto colonised countries began to revitalise prose fiction. Novels from Africa by Chinua Achebe and Wole Soyinka, poetry and fiction from the West Indies by Derek Walcott and Wilson Harris, new literatures in India, Canada, Australia and New Zealand: all were redefining the possibilities of English on a global stage.

Every crisis in art is a crisis of form. The Modern Movement changed artistic forms and postmodernism inherited and exaggerated their diversity. In Marshall Walker's words, 'Poems look different after Pound.'[2] The central propositions of the new forms might be named: political self-consciousness; the value of the physical human body; the fragmentation of narratives; attachment to the ancient past; concern with Eastern, African and Oriental cultures and forms; the defamiliarisation of language; and increasingly through the twentieth century, a generalising sense of irony, quotation and egalitarianism; and a move from Joycean disinterestedness to the silent and sinister context of multi-national franchises, where the healthy, political corrective of pluralism might become an apparently endless, saturating superficiality throughout diverse media and its unreliable languages. It is worth recollecting Stephen Rodefer's memorable lines which have already been quoted in the Introduction: 'The modern battlefield is dense with signals. Most of them will be decoys / to fool the other side.'[3]

How can we describe what was happening in Scotland in these terms? The 'Scottish Renaissance' is the term now applied to the literary and cultural regeneration of Scotland initiated by Hugh MacDiarmid (C.M. Grieve) in the 1920s. More precisely, the term might be located in what happened between the first appearance of MacDiarmid's lyric poetry in Scots in 1922 and the publication of a series of controversial and iconoclastic essays by C.M. Grieve, 'Contemporary Scottish Studies', in *The Scottish Educational Journal* from 1925 to 1927. Grieve/MacDiarmid, as poet, critic and cultural revolutionary, effected an assault upon the intellectual and emotional conventions of his era. He took hold of the pillars of the Scottish literary, cultural and political establishment and did the job of Samson. As Tom Normand says, 'The commitment to an independent Scottish nation was, in this period, predicated upon a belief in the viability and validity of an authentic Scottish culture, the recovery of which might be fulfilled only through the restoration of a national status in the form of self-government.'[4]

The effort of national regeneration meant an attempt to recover national traditions, and MacDiarmid's early lyrics and long poem *A Drunk Man Looks at the Thistle* are deeply sustained by the metre and rhythm of the ballad tradition. In this, their prosody is apparently conservative. Both for Mac-Diarmid and his contemporaries such as William Soutar, the example of Pound composing 'in the sequence of the musical phrase, not in the sequence of a metronome' was not one to be followed blindly.[5] Pound's radical poetics influenced a later generation of Scottish poets, but, as we saw in the Introduction when we looked at the paintings by Nasmyth and Crozier, in the 1920s there was a deliberate attempt to draw from the country's past, from pre-Enlightment, pre-Union times. This was more important than Poundian poetics. Indeed, when Soutar submitted some poems to Pound in 1928, the American wrote back advising Soutar to read and learn more from the French: 'I know nothing about Scotland. England is sunk in mental sloth and filth (i.e. dead matter)....I mean HAVE you ever heard of a language called French, or a man called Rimbaud.' Pound seemed to feel Soutar's poems belonged in an age 'before railways, before steam boats, etc.' (He might not have meant this as a compliment, though Soutar could have taken it as one.) Still, he accepted Soutar's poem 'On a Mediocre Cellist' for *The Exile* – but the periodical folded before the poem appeared.[6]

Another contrast is in the way Scottish writers and thinkers began to consider their international context. They were not drawn primarily to African or Oriental forms (if we except for a moment the artists George Henry and E.A. Hornel – we will return to them later). An ideal of socialist republicanism seems implicitly to reside in the political internationalism implied in much of their work. The ideas they promoted seem more deeply politicised than the characteristic prioritisation of aesthetics by modernists such as Pound, Eliot, Stravinsky or Picasso.

On 4 December 1925, Grieve wrote:

A certain type of critic is apt to say that the movement so far has consisted only of propaganda – only 'of the posters' – that the actual work has still to be done. This is a mistake. The Scottish Renaissance has taken place. The fruits will appear in due course. Earlier or later – it does not alter the fact. For the Scottish Renaissance has been a propaganda of ideas and their enunciation has been all that was necessary.[7]

The 'ideas' were essentially to end the reliance upon sentimental, stereotypical representations of Scotland that had become common through the late nineteenth century and to bring modern Scottish culture into alignment with the most advanced European thought and avant-garde artistic techniques. Grieve attacked as many existing preconceptions responsible for the status quo as he could, in religious, political and social terms: on every front.

On 5 February 1926, he specified some of these ideas more closely:

> From the Renaissance point of view...it is utterly wrong to make the term 'Scottish' synonymous with any fixed literary forms or to attempt to confine it...The Scottish Renaissance movement...sets out to do all that it possibly can to increase the number of Scots who are vitally interested in literature and cultural issues; to counter the academic or merely professional tendencies which fossilise the intellectual interests of most well-educated people even; and, above all, to stimulate actual art-production to a maximum.[8]

As Grieve's notoriety spread, he began to be more widely read. His friend Helen Burness Cruickshank recalled being asked by a railway station bookshop manager why copies of *The Scottish Educational Journal* were selling out so quickly. 'People buy it to see who is being castigated by C.M. Grieve this week', she told him.[9]

Crucial in the development of the Scottish Renaissance movement was the role played by newspapers and little magazines: *The Scottish Chapbook* (1922–1923), *The Scottish Nation* (1923), *The Northern Review* (1924), *The Pictish Review* (1927–1928), *The Scots Independent* (1927–1933), *The Scots Observer* (1927–1934), *The Modern Scot* (1931–1934) and *The Free Man* (1932–1935). MacDiarmid and other Scottish writers also contributed to London-based intellectual journals like *The New Age* and *New Britain* and to the more widely distributed national press in Scotland.[10]

MacDiarmid also edited a series of three anthologies of Scottish poetry, *Northern Numbers*, in which older and established poets were published alongside their younger, more radical contemporaries. The sentimentalism of Donald A. Mackenzie (1873–1936) and Charles Murray (1864–1941), for example, was ruthlessly exposed by contrast with the modernity of new poets of the Scottish Renaissance – John Ferguson, William Jeffrey and Roderick Watson Kerr, for example. The proto-feminism of the younger generation is emphatic in the editorial policy of the third and most radical of the anthologies. Of twenty contributors, ten are women. No editor of Scottish poetry before or since has done as much as Grieve/MacDiarmid to insist that the voices of women should be heard to represent the nation. Moreover, the work of these women deserves further study: Jessie Annie Anderson, Marion Angus, Helen Cruickshank, May W. Fairlie, Mabel Christian Forbes, Muriel Graham, Christine Orr, Penuel G. Ross, Muriel Stuart and Mary Symon. Who were they? Four of them appear in Catherine Kerrigan's 1991 *Anthology of Scottish Women Poets*[11] but most have dropped from sight. In this instance, MacDiarmid's promotion of women's writing seems characteristically extreme but it was a well-reasoned part of his effort in the 1920s. He understood that the experience of women required literary and artistic expression, and that if he could help bring it about it might help change the nature of art altogether, and that was what he wanted to do.

The Scottish Renaissance should also be located in a broader historical context. It spurred cultural articulation in various forms: the literary and artistic production of Scotland throughout the twentieth century has been in advance of its political struggle towards national self-definition. The spirit of cultural independence from the aesthetic and economic 'centre' of south-east England was asserted in the 1920s and, as we have noted, found rich scholarly expression in the 1980s and 1990s. If the Scottish Renaissance movement has had an incalculable long-term effect, it arose in the aftermath of a distinct period of development in national artistic expression which began in the late nineteenth century.

Music

The history of Scottish classical music is a story of national self-definition drawing away from the heavy overburden of the Germanic orchestral tradition and the political structure of imperial Britain. For Scottish composers of classical music in the late nineteenth century, musical respectability was dependant upon a Germanic training in composition and concert music was overtly *British*.[12]

The settings of Scottish songs by Haydn and Beethoven transfer an idiom alive with ironic humour and sexual energy into a staged presentation of careful posturing. In the transfer, the songs become arch and potentially comic. The example we have already noted of the shift in emphasis from Burns's 'Now Westlin' Winds' to Scott's 'Jock o' Hazeldean' suggests the nature of the move from the outdoor world to that of the withdrawing room. Although there *were* continuities between the worlds and work of the prolific Scottish composer James Oswald (1710–1769) and the aristocratic bon viveur the Earl of Kelly, locally known as Fiddler Tam (1732–1781), whose compositions are rich in irony, wit, flair and enough good humour to rival Haydn, and the worlds and work of Burns, nevertheless the distinction between propriety and vulgarity is increasingly fraught from the eighteenth to nineteenth centuries.

With orchestral music, wonderful evocations of a Scottish idiom had been written by Max Bruch (1838–1920) and Felix Mendelssohn in highly colourful, virtuoso works. Bruch's 'Scottish Fantasia' for violin and orchestra, opus 46 (1880), uses traditional tunes and even attempts a bagpipe effect but is most famous for the highly charged last movement, where a lyrical melody is set against 'Scots wha ha'e' flaring up passionately. The Danish composer Niels Gade (1817–1890) achieved international recognition with his opus 1, the concert overture 'Echoes of Ossian' (1840), which begins with a Danish ballad melody, thus aligning his own national provenance with James Macpherson's European vogue. Mendelssohn's *Scottish Symphony* No. 3 (begun in 1829, completed and first performed in 1842) shows a similarly full-blown Romanticism, especially in its last movement, when the coda sweeps in with a new, hymn-like confidence in a melody derived from the introduction of the first movement. Above all, Mendelssohn's 'Overture: The Hebrides' (1832) succeeds in representing the ethos of water and rock, waves breaking and the basalt columns of Fingal's Cave – a natural spectacle and non-virtual reality approachable and comprehensible, with effort, in human terms. The scene is focussed beyond the Macpherson vogue for Ossian and Fingal, through the sharpest lenses that could have been made in Mendelssohn's time and while the overture richly exercises the orchestral resources of its era in its tone-painting, and is over-familiar in recordings and performance, it remains a unique musical evocation entirely appropriate to its subject.

But what was happening with Scottish composers? Victorian Scotland produced many composers whose work attempted to express distinctively Scottish qualities in both melody and idiom. John Thomson (1806–1841), in 'Three Lieder' (1838), sets poems by Byron (in German translation), Schiller and von Uhland in an exquisitely balanced triptych in a rich, moving and invigorating style, restoring virility to the withdrawing room while maintaining proprieties of form. He stayed with the Mendelssohn family in Germany and met Schumann but the songs are distinctive: the Byron all clean moonlit waters fragrant with summer love, the Schiller a wild description of a hunter's burial with distinctive Scottish motifs and the final song, 'The Serenade', filled with a proto-Straussian, unsentimental, adult sense of the mystery of mortality as a Mother listens to her sick child's song of farewell. Thomson's overture to his opera, *Hermann, or, The Broken Spear* (1834) is packed with robustness and colour, melodramatic gestures and spectacle, suggesting that the opera itself warrants revival. But all the Scottish composers noted here need much greater exposure and critical listening and have only recently been recorded after much scholarly research and investment.

Alexander Campbell Mackenzie (1847–1935), who knew Liszt, Greig and Paderewski and whose work was highly praised by Elgar, produced a *Burns Rhapsody* (1881), a *Pibroch Suite* for violin and orchestra (1889), a *Scottish Piano Concerto* (1897) and numerous other pieces with emphatic Scottish character (such as the piano pieces, 'Scenes in the Scottish Highlands' of 1880, with their use of folk-music, distinctly Scottish pentatonics and the 'Scotch Snap' – a quick rhythm of a short note on the beat immediately followed by a longer one). When the scholar, translator and poet J.S. Blackie dedicated his book *Scottish Song* to Mackenzie, the composer wrote to him in 1889: 'I do hope from time to time to add a little contribution to Scotch music, I mean in this popular way and apart from the more elaborate work to which I am devoted.' Mackenzie's affirmation of Scottish nationality had to be contained in his London-based role of Principal of the Royal Academy of Music, which he held for thirty-six years. His musical expression of national identity was therefore qualified by the necessities of professional rectitude and convention. Arguably, this underlies some of his most poignantly yearning music, the beautiful *Benedictus* or the great oratorio *The Rose of Sharon*. In such works, it is almost as if the passionate longing of Mahler, the sense of irrecoverable loss, were wedded to the enormous formal orchestral reassurances of Brahms. This is especially true of the central, slow movement of the *Scottish Concerto*, op. 55 (1897). The piano's lovely strengths and confident assurances are balanced against poignant, soberly restrained ideas of sorrow and unappeasable yearning. The traditional tune 'The Waulking of the Fold' (watching over the sheepfold) underlies the movement and its tenderness is uncloyingly sustained, especially as the oboe recollects pastoral pipes at its close. The longing is there as definitely as the comforting certainties of broad authority and the vigorously happy and brimful finale, but it is the memory of that yearning that makes the concerto heartbreaking as well as warm. This is music full of a refreshing sense of living presence. It never neglects liveliness.

But finally the gravity pulled towards London. Mackenzie's most famous concert overture runs spirited and sprightly variations on a sailor's hornpipe and 'Rule Britannia'. It is entitled 'Britannia' – not 'Caledonia' or 'Alba'. At one crucial level, imperial Britain is the focus of its celebration (though it is large-spirited and generous, not merely a piece of jingoistic chauvinism or bombast). Mackenzie's music may not be deeply searching, but neither is it merely superficial and there is a haunting, lyrical, introspective quality in its use of Scottish idioms in the great Victorian forms it inhabits so easefully: its achievement is real and distinguished.

A generation younger, Hamish MacCunn (1868–1916) was more radically devoted to finding forms for the orchestra to express Scottish identity. MacCunn saw himself as a composer for the new era, a musician of the future, combining the flair and flamboyance of Liszt with hard pragmatism, but he died in his forties, in the middle of the First World War. All his music is remarkable and all of it breathes with the energy of a young man. But his life's work seems unfinished. He remains best known for a high-spirited concert overture written at the age of 19, wonderfully evocative of the Highlands, 'Land of the Mountain and the Flood'. It was used as the theme tune for a fondly remembered 1970s television series starring Iain Cuthbertson, *Sutherland's Law*. But there is much more to him than that. Even the little piano piece 'In the Glen' suggests a subtlety and sensitivity of emotion and a strictness of structural design that balances the flamboyant lavish thundering of the setting for chorus and orchestra of Scott's 'Lay of the Last Minstrel' while dark colours and swirling narrative movement characterise the Border Ballad overture, 'The Dowie Dens o' Yarrow'.

His major work seems to have been the 'Grand Opera' of 1894, *Jeanie Deans*, an extremely tight composition (much compressed from its source, *The Heart of Midlothian*). Mainly set in eighteenth-century Edinburgh, arias and duets are fleeting and drama heightened by sharp turns of action. MacCunn learned much from Wagner but there is no Wagnerian expansiveness here. His work is resolutely quick-witted and sharp, though this is not to deny depths of feeling and insight in David Deans's moving expression of grief for his daughter's shame, or Effie's lullaby for her lost child. Sometimes, though, it does seem hastily written and perfunctory, as in Jeanie's plea to Queen Caroline – particularly disappointing, as it is such a vivid moment of demotic expressiveness in the novel.

In the Victorian era, 'serious' music was frequently indulgent of emotion and high drama to an extent that musical taste after Bartók, Schnittke and the Rolling Stones might find cloying or embarrassing. *Jeanie Deans* raises questions about religious fanaticism, child murder and the strength of women in a social order determined on oppression but it is ultimately a romantic celebration, with harvest dances and reels, laments from exiles, arias, madrigals and grand operatic choruses.

The music is gorgeous: sonorous as Schubert, bravura as Berlioz, through-composed as Wagner and at times there are hints of the haunting, unsettling tonalities of Debussy. But the melodies are Scots. No Italian or German composer could have created the idiom of this opera. Its nationality is palpable not only in the Scottish folk tunes, like the fiddler's reel 'Rantin', Roarin' Willie' which opens the work (the fiddler is on stage playing with the orchestra as the opera begins); it is also in the phrasing, movements that keep pushing the action of the music on. The 'Scotch Snap' is in evidence throughout, instantly recognisable. Key changes are frequent and quick. Arias are winning, but compared to Verdi's, they are brief. MacCunn simply refuses to linger. Again, this is emphatically the music of a young man, and its entire idiom is Scottish.

Born the same year as MacCunn, Frederic Lamond (1868–1948) lived till after the Second World War but his only symphony, in A major, op. 3 (1893) is very much contemporary with the late Romantic idiom of MacCunn, and since Lamond was merely twenty-one when he began sketching it, also shares with MacCunn a youthful dash and self-assurance. Its largesse and confidence place it in a line from Beethoven and Brahms but its unhesitating swerves to ironic lilting and a dark, slow march look forward to Mahler and troubles to come. As with Mackenzie, these worrying aspects are accommodated by the pleasures of the orchestral form itself. His overture 'From the Scottish Highlands' introduced his opera based on Walter Scott's *Quentin Durward*, about the adventures of a young Scot at the French court of Louis XI. As with the symphony, an air of high adventure, good spirits and mischief counterpoints the more sombre passages.

But sombre ideas of violence, sacrifice and heroism are deep and pervasive in the work of Cecil Coles (1888–1918), who was killed in the First World War and whose music survives through semi-miraculous recovery and the dedication of his family and musicologists who cared. Coles's music is sharp, bright and highly wrought, full of tensions and intensities. He did not have time for comfort: music was composed for army bands, small groups and orchestras assembled for the momentary concert. Yet there is a modern edge to it and a bite at the heart. This is music that points forward to more developed twentieth-century idioms and techniques. Ravel is nearby in scales of economy and it is the symphonic loneliness of Elgar rather than the central tradition-bearers of Beethoven and Brahms that come to mind with Coles's 'Scherzo'. Four song-settings of poems by Verlaine in English translations clearly suggest a proto-modernist inclination in their rejection of lush tonalities and spare balancing of enigmatic and mysterious simplicities. Two works suggest Coles's range: the setting of Robert Buchanan's poem 'Fra Giacomo' (scena for baritone and large orchestra) and 'Behind the Lines' (the two surviving movements of a suite for small orchestra). In Buchanan's poem, a Venetian merchant greets Fra Giacomo, the priest, who has arrived too late to administer the last rites to his newly deceased wife, but asks him to give her his blessing; Fra Giacomo agrees and then accepts a glass of wine from the merchant, who tells him how he courted and married his wife but grew to suspect her fidelity and one day in a priest's disguise, took the part of her confessor, discovering that her lover was in fact the very same Fra Giacomo. Too late, Fra Giacomo realises the merchant has poisoned his wife and with the wine he has already taken, poisoned him too. The poem has achieved its sinister turn but now becomes baroque in grand guignol: just in case the poison is not sufficient, the merchant stabs Fra Giacomo three times and instructs his faithful servant Pietro to throw the body into the deep canal below before bidding the monks pray for his dead wife's soul. For the late-Victorian Scottish poet, Catholicism and 'the fleshly school of poetry' embodied by the Pre-Raphaelites was anathema, and although he wrote memorably of Loch Coruisk in Skye, his dark vision has helped keep his poetry from the tastes of modern readers. He might be revalued alongside those other dark visionaries of proto-modern Scotland, James (B.V.) Thomson and John Davidson. Coles's setting perfectly matches and illuminates the spiralling drama of the poem, transforming the unremitting logic of the poem's unfolding (it is a dramatic monologue akin to Browning's 'My Last Duchess') into the almost ironic melodrama and pathos of its climax, from which no character emerges in a sympathetic light.

That quality of human complicity and the sense that mortality should be borne with dignity even in the worst of conditions, pervade the two short movements that survive from 'Behind the Lines', an orchestral suite at the end of which Coles wrote, 'Feb 4th 1918 In the Field'. The bloody and mud-stained manuscript of the first movement was sent to his friend Gustav Holst at Christmas 1917. 'Estaminet de Carrefour' evokes a northern French pastoral landscape and a coffee-house or inn at the crossroads, a refuge from the horrors of the front, a world in which, as Elgar said of his own Cello Concerto, 'Everything good and nice and clean and fresh and sweet is far away – never to return.' But the second movement, 'Cortege', only survived with indications for completion and was orchestrated by Martyn Brabbins, while the other two movements have never been found.

'Cortege' evokes the passing parade of death from the heart of the First World War. Its simplicity, melodic poise and restraint, its pace and pathos, are unforgettable. Like a very few other examples of music of this time, it marks an understanding of the utter finality the First World War signified in the human story, yet also conveys a feeling for the continuities by which something new might be made worthwhile. The military ethos (drums and horns) works against itself and seems a call to arms for a different way of seeing.

William Wallace (1860–1940) belonged to an earlier generation but his work extended more deeply into the twentieth century, carrying the then new form of the symphonic tone poem into a British musical context with a series of compositions in which Scottish subjects were placed alongside European ones with neither favour nor embarrassment. 'The Passing of Beatrice' (1892), 'William Wallace' (1905) and 'Villon' (1909) evoke Dante's Paradise and beloved, the Scottish freedom fighter and the medieval French poet with equally precise colouring and narrative skill.

It is worth noting the continuing contributions made by foreign composers imagining Scotland in their work. The most memorable of these include Sir Granville Bantock (1868–1946), the Australian Percy Grainger (1882–1961) and Sir Arnold Bax (1883–1953). Bantock's *Celtic Symphony* (1940) is written for string orchestra and six harps, makes use of traditional Hebridean folksongs, Highland reels and swirling, swooning intensities. The *Harp Quintet* (1918–1921) of Arnold Bax clearly utilises Celtic motifs, combining Ravel-like scrupulousness and economy of style with textures that suggest the west coast of Ireland or Scotland. Bax adopted the pen-name Dermot O'Byrne for his writings on Ireland and Irish themes and knew many of the patriots who were killed as a result of the Easter Rising of 1916. Later he re-invented himself in Morar, Inverness-shire, on the west coast of Scotland, where the white sands would have been grey and pock-marked with rain when he stayed in a freezing room at the Station Hotel making notes for what would become his *Third Symphony*, written between Autumn 1928 and February 1929. Its slow, beautifully melodic 'Epilogue' is imbued with a mystical air suggesting a relation between art and location irresistably in the quotation from Nietzsche with which Bax prefaced his score, but suppressed from publication: 'My wisdom became pregnant on lonely mountains; / upon barren stones she brought forth her young.'[13]

However, none of these composers can be located in a generic national cultural movement of integrated political purpose. Mackenzie remained a paragon of the British capital's establishment. MacCunn, radical as he was, took the arch-conservative Walter Scott and (arguably) Scott's most conservative novel for his finest operatic text. Wallace's orchestral mastery in the 1905 tone poem on his namesake has more in common with the late Romantic tone poems of Richard Strauss, such as *Ein Heldenleben* (*A Hero's Life*, 1889) or *Also Sprach Zarathustra* (1896) than with the expression of the ferocity of struggle and the primal scream in Stravinsky's *Rite of Spring* (1915); nevertheless, it was a far more sophisticated representation of national identity than the Victorian impulse to hero-worship which saw Lord Buchan's commissioning John Smith of Darnick to carve the red sandstone statue of Wallace erected overlooking the Tweed in 1814 or the Wallace monument at Stirling, of 1859–1869.

Perhaps most notable in this company is John Blackwood McEwan (1868–1948), whose 'Border Ballads', *Solway Symphony* and the landscape tone poem 'Hills o' Heather' create an impressionist or post-impressionist idiom with distinctively Scottish colours. McEwan is clearly attempting something in a line of descent from the landscape artists of Victorian Scotland, though he moves much further and much more clearly into a distinctly twentieth-century world, while also sharing the deepening sense of Scottish identity intrinsic to the song-settings of F.G. Scott. McEwan's piano works include delightful impressionist pieces like the *Vignettes from La Cote d'Argent* (number 5 is a brilliant depiction of a speedboat) and the spare, powerful second movement of the *Sonata* in E minor of 1903, 'Adagio – Grave', which commemorates General Sir Hector MacDonald (about whom Iain Crichton Smith wrote his 1992 novel, *An Honourable Death*). McEwan is close both to Ravel and to the Scottish Colourists in time and technique, bringing invigorating forms of modernity to Scottish music and basing his art on the conviction that sound is, as light was for the Colourists, a common property. His *Scottish Rhapsody for Violin and Piano, Prince Charlie* (1924) begins with an ironically funereal revision of the lively song 'Charlie is my Darling' before restoring its familiar high spirits, but an effervescent assertion of determination based on the tune of 'Johnnie Cope' leads to a closing reminder of the bitter darkness evoked in the opening, as if the fate of the failed Jacobite rebellion and Prince Charles's long exile foreshadowed Scotland's neglect of, not only his own music – including seventeen fascinating and thoughtful string quartets – but music more generally.

Indeed, much work is still to be done on F.G. Scott and his contemporaries. Scott's song-settings of Scottish poets are among the most inwardly precise interpretations, and active, illuminating readings of poets such as MacDiarmid, Burns and William Soutar and Scott's dynamic drive, authoritarian presence and wry humour were at the centre of that group of friends in the early 1920s that included, along with the artist William Johnstone, the key literary figures of MacDiarmid and Edwin Muir. Erik Chisholm was a champion and friend of Béla Bartók, bringing him to Glasgow and organising the Scottish premiere of *Bluebeard's Castle* and other works. Chisholm's later operatic work was produced in South Africa and his *Celtic Songbook* was published in the Soviet Union at the recommendation of Shostakovich, but Bartók remained the most intense influence. The scale of Chisholm's output was prodigious and has not yet been comprehensively gauged. In the *Scottish Airs* for piano, he achieves a unique blend of traditional sensibility and modernist technique, allowing familiar melodies to refresh themselves in the defamiliarised air of twentieth-century idiom. This is perfectly judged in the second *Air*, andante cantabile, and in the eighth, but can seem exaggerated and sometimes frantic, when the humour seems uneasy and the vigour of the traditional tune does not quite match that of the Bartókian mode. Is this 'MacBartók' (as he was termed, with, one suspects, a condescension worthy of tabloid journalism) affectionate and comfortable in his native idiom or trying to shock his listeners into a deeper recognition of its value? Both? Then perhaps, like MacDiarmid, he felt compelled to attempt too much in a difficult climate? Yet no-one would deny the need. When he presented Bartók's *String Quartets* at St Cuthbert's Church in Edinburgh, the undiscerning audience walked out. Chisholm's range, depth, ironic energies and deep seriousness are clear, however, in the *Night Song of the Bards* (*Six Nocturnes for Piano*) and the *Piano Concerto No. 1* (1937), which opens with another perfectly pitched evocation of a traditional bagpipe Pibroch tune: intimate, alien and unerringly scored for the new idiom.

Ronald Center (1913–1973) wrote a deeply moving cantata with settings of Walt Whitman, *Dona Nobis Pacem*. This brilliantly catches Whitman's ambiguous exhilaration in the face of war, horror at its price and tenderness at its human effects. There is also a remarkably gentle yet playful and occasionally vigorous piano piece, 'Children at Play' as well as an exciting piano *Sonata*. But Scott, Chisholm, Center and others were isolated from each other and often found themselves vying for what limited resources there were for performances, broadcasts and recordings. When Chisholm's ballet *The Forsaken Mermaid* was published in 1942 by William MacLellan in Glasgow, it used up so much of the funds available that publication of Scott's songs had to be postponed. No comprehensive overview and full critical evaluation of these composers has been attempted and no study describing their creative work in the context of other artistic production in Scotland in the first half of the twentieth century has yet been accomplished.

In the later twentieth century, there is an increasing self-confidence in works such as those by, for example, Peter Maxwell Davies, long resident in Orkney, prolific and well-known for a wide range of works, many of them large scale, but in the brief piano piece *Yesnaby Ground* he makes a beautiful and very simple melody seem endlessly haunting and plaintive; he played it himself at the funeral of the great Orkney-writer George Mackay Brown. The American-born, long-term Glasgow-resident Thomas Wilson (1927–2001) based his *St Kentigern Suite* (1986) on stories about the patron saint of Glasgow and his three-act opera of 1972–1975, *The Confessions of a Justified Sinner*, on James Hogg's 1824 novel, demonstrating a deep commitment to the Scottish context. Similarly, New Zealand-born Lyell Cresswell's mesmerically powerful *Salm* (1977) takes the form of Gaelic psalm-singing in the Outer Hebrides, where the precentor leads the congregation, each member of which contributes a separate vocal line, and applies it to orchestral resources with the cello leading the way. The same precedent is taken in William Sweeney's choral *salm an fhearainn*, where verses by Aonghas MacNeacail provide the first Gaelic text to be set in a modern classical idiom. In Sweeney's words,

> The plain psalm tunes, common to Scottish Presbyterian congregations, are decorated, stretched out of their original shape and interpreted individually by each member of the congregation, thus escaping the monotony of the lowland Scots act of worship. *salm an fhearainn* is an attempt to develop this tradition in a secular direction. The psychological and spiritual life of a people is expressed here in its material identification with the land on which its traditions have developed.[14]

Sweeney is also the composer of the orchestral tone poem *Sunset Song*, based on Lewis Grassic Gibbon's novel of 1932. Just as Gibbon prints the music of the old lament, 'The Flowers of the Forest' at the end of his book, Sweeney embeds the haunting melody in the dark, elegiac tones of his musical poem, remembering Gibbon's urging for a world that would be fit for those who died to make it better. These are only a few of the composers whose work might be discussed here: the adventurous inventiveness and imaginative tenacity of Sally Beamish or Judith Weir, the blend of the traditional and the experimental in Edward McGuire, John Maxwell Geddes or John Purser, and the radical work of Thea Musgrave and Iain Hamilton from a slightly older generation, and of Ian Whyte from the generation before that – the catalogue is rich.

Probably the most frequently recorded Scottish composer of the late twentieth and early twenty-first centuries is James MacMillan, whose first virtuoso orchestral tone poem, *The Confession of Isobel Gowdie*, established to a broad audience at the 1990 London Proms the strength of his orchestral command and the depth of his imagination, drawing from the Scots ballad tradition. MacMillan's percussion concerto *Veni, Veni Emmanuel* (1992) has had over 300 performances worldwide – phenomenal popularity in its own terms. MacMillan's commitment to melody and his religious faith combine in an expanding plenum of works which have found eager audiences internationally and in Scotland, although he has scorned the Scottish brands of philistinism and anti-intellectualism which can beset critical appraisal and creative effort.

Perhaps the most revealing developments in modern Scottish music can be heard in the work of Ronald Stevenson· in the early twenty-first century he was esteemed the senior figure among Scottish composers. His two piano concertos, violin concerto, song-settings (most piercingly beautiful when most simple, in the setting of four lines by MacDiarmid: 'Better a'e gowden lyric...'), his unendingly curious solo piano magnum compendium, the *Passacaglia*, as well as the shorter, deeply haunting and delicate elegy for Shostakovich: all his work contributes to a patient, expansive, intellectually demanding, coldly analytical but generous world-vision which self-consciously embraces internationalism from a national condition. Born in England, long resident in Scotland, there is no chauvinism about his stance: the nation is a key to other cultures, a mask by which expression can be formed. For example, 'A Wheen Tunes for Bairns tae Spiel' is a miniature equivalent of Bartók's *Mikrokosmos*. It is not traditional Scottish music but the 'Reel' (for example) would be completely unimaginable without the folk tradition. The same tune is transformed again in the 'Scots Suite' of 1984 (premiered 1987) where the violin utilises traditional Scottish dance forms – strathspey, reel and jig – but alters the folk idiom with its invocation of twelve-tone technique and rigorously defined shapes and musical trajectories. As Stevenson acknowledges, the whole remarkable work is activated by the example of Bartók.[15]

Bartók is crucial here – perhaps not primarily as a direct influence on individual composers so much as a key figure in modernity's comprehension of the individual, the local and the international political context. His example provides models of scrupulous attention to the details of one's native place, its popular idioms and non-human, elemental realities. These are conveyed with fierce, rebarbative energy, intuitive understanding, ironic distance and intense clarity of perception. There is charm and a core of generosity and Romantic individualism, but there is also a social sense of living traditions that inter-connect people and places, birds, animals and even insects. In Bartók's music, these natural things enter modernity hard-headedly and without sentimentality but with an underlying urgency about how they might be heard and where conditions might prevail that would allow and encourage the human response they need. Perhaps more than any other modern composer, Bartók addresses the perennial question of the unfinished business of home: the necessity of exile, the tension between location as a security for which we all yearn, and belonging as a distortion that might warp fulfilment, and we shall return to this question at the end of the book.

Painting

In Scottish painting, the late nineteenth century witnesses a split between romanticised landscapes of home and representations of the exoticism of foreign places. In the twentieth century there is a healing of this division. A reciprocal dialogue takes place. Home becomes exotic and the international becomes more familiar. By the beginning of the twenty-first century, there are a number of different ways of approaching a located identity. I would like to tell this story by looking at a few particular paintings and artists.[16]

'A Highland Funeral' (1882) by Sir James Guthrie (1859–1930) is a cinema-screen rectangular canvas: a framed, structured, outdoors scene. At first glance, it is all shades of white and grey and darker grey – austere, cold. Men are starkly grouped. Their flesh looks chilled beneath their thick black clothes. Their bones are imaginable. There is snow on the ground. Footprints have mushed it in a path to two wooden chairs on which a coffin is draped in black. On our side of it, a minister raises his hand in benediction. His face is pale, cheeks reddened, hair white, his gaze downturned. On the farther side of the coffin is a boy; his cheeks are also red, his stare is intense, questioning. He is supported on either side by two elders, one with hat in hand, the other bearded, at his side. The bearded man's fist is clenched with emotion, his head is bowed, helpless before mortality. Ten other men stand in a group beside them, some with hats in hands, some bearded – whiskered, senior men. All men. One has a sheepdog on a leash. The dog is facing away from us and away from the coffin, looking up at the man as if asking the question, 'Where is my master?' One man, younger than the rest, looks as though he has lost a friend. To the left, behind the minister, there is a whitewashed croft, from behind which a gleam of white light rays out horizontally into a slim band in the sky, under a big, dark, lowering cloud above. The colours in the painting are almost entirely chiaroscuro. The rosy cheeks of the minister and the boy and the hint of a dark red scarf at the neck of one of the mourners are the only brightnesses of colour.

Eight years later, 'The Druids – bringing in the mistletoe' (1890) is a massive, almost square painting of bright, glaring colour, a collaborative work by George Henry (1858–1943) and E.A. Hornel (1864–1933). A fantasy, or dream-like representation of a 'Celtic' ceremony, religious, sacral, festive, almost comic, certainly joyous, in its lavish use of colour. Next to 'A Highland Funeral' it seems immensely exotic. Another Hornel, 'The Fish Pool' (1894) and another Henry, 'Japanese Lady with Fan' (1894), both reek of exoticism: the colours of the Hornel are rich, enamel-like, unnatural and foreign. In the Henry, the Japanese lady has turned her face away into her fan: we can only see the pure curve of her cheek surrounded by the Eastern designs of her clothes, hair and the fan itself.

Come back to Scotland now: George Henry's 'A Galloway Landscape' (1889) depicts a Kirkcudbrightshire hillside and river flattened out of spectacular perspective until, from a distance, it looks like a patterned carpet. There are cows, trees, a hill. One cow looks out from behind a tree. But the cow seems enlarged and the tree diminished; they are strangely disproportionate. The trees seem to recede in conventional, normal perspective, as they go up the hill, but the river recedes as it comes into the foreground, turning more oily and dark, more enamelled and scarf-like, as it approaches us. Things seem to be out of kilter. This is, curiously, both unnerving and pleasing.

All three painters were grouped as 'The Glasgow Boys' but the contrast between Guthrie's 'Highland Funeral' and the work of Hornel and Henry suggests a way of sketching a history of Scottish painting into the Modern Movement that runs alongside contemporary histories in music and literature in inter-connected ways. Hornel and Henry were in Japan from 1893 to 1894, among the first European artists to visit the country and bring back the evidence of their lusty appetite for the exotic. Hornel is caricatured in Dorothy L. Sayers's Lord Peter Wimsey murder mystery of 1931, *Five Red Herrings*, in which the artists who colonised Kirkcudbright and Galloway are treated with delightful irreverence. But in terms of their attraction to the exotic and the exoticising of the local and familiar, Hornel and Henry point forward in the longer view of the traditions of Scottish painting.

The development of landscape painting tells a similar story of a movement from conventional and comfortable depictions whose appeal was predictable (for example, the work of Tom Faed or Horatio McCulloch) to more radical, austere and self-consciously European work by William McTaggart in the 1890s, and later, the Glasgow Boys and the Scottish Colourists (S.J. Peploe, F.C.B. Caddell, Leslie Hunter and J.D. Fergusson). It is not that Scottish painting before McTaggart or the Colourists was merely 'parochial' or had not been sufficiently 'European': both 'history' and landscape traditions developed in Scotland in the mid- to late nineteenth century in ways which had specific contemporary European counterparts. Most crucially, however, from the turn of the century to the outbreak of the First World War, the Colourists developed coherent and startling techniques evidently in the knowledge of work by Whistler, Cézanne, Van Gogh, Gaugain and Toulouse-Lautrec, and then Fauve and Cubist works by Matisse and Picasso. An international scope for a learning dialogue was self-determinedly extended by the artists themselves during this period. When the Colourists returned from Europe to Scotland with their own innovative work, they were among the first truly modern painters to be exhibited in Britain.[17]

The idea of Celtic identity entered Modernism proper at this point, particularly with the work of Fergusson. If the Colourists learned about light in France, they asserted its common property in Scotland. Nature, rhythm and structure or design were fused in their work and an ebullient sense of earthly, earthy pleasures runs through it all, from the bold flowers, rich clothes, polished coffee pots, wine bottles and fine furniture of the still-life paintings to the pulsing, luminous Iona landscapes and seascapes, to the figurative paintings of Fergusson, in which huge, heavy people seem to dance lightly in a buoyant air and laughter seems to be present everywhere.

Paris played a vital role in the development of the arts in Europe in the first decade of the twentieth century. Writers, musicians, performers and artists flocked to Paris from all over Europe and also from America to be part of an enormous melting pot of new ideas. On their first visits to Paris in the 1890s, Peploe and Fergusson were most taken with the work of the French Impressionists. The two friends and their families spent many summer holidays together painting in French beach resort towns as well as in the Scottish Islands and Highlands.

> One year we went together to Islay. In others it was to Etaples, Paris-Plage, Dunkirk, Verneval, Dieppe, Etretat and Le Tréport – all happy painting holidays. We worked all day, drawing and painting everything. And we thoroughly enjoyed the food and wine. We agreed on the importance of good food and drink, not fantastic food, but good peasant food in France and good Scots food in Scotland – what's better than good steaks and good Burgundy, good beef and good beer? We enjoyed and took time over our meals – time to eat and talk and draw the things on the table.[18]

Fergusson moved to Paris in 1907 and in between their summer painting forays the two artists continued their exchange of ideas with frequent letters until Peploe moved to Paris in 1910.

Fergusson, Cadell, Peploe and Hunter were largely forgotten outside Scotland until the later twentieth century, despite having exhibited widely in New York, Paris and London in their lifetimes. Theirs was the most radically modern painting in Britain and it marks a reintegration of the exotic and the local that was to characterise later twentieth-century work. It can be seen in terms of technique in the neo-cubist 'The Sensation of Crossing the Street, West End, Edinburgh' (1913) by Stanley Cursiter (1887–1976) or the independently developed quasi-pointillism of John Quinton Pringle (1864–1925), whose 'Two Figures at a Fence' (1904) and 'Poultry Yard, Gartcosh' (1906) invent unpredicted applications for recognisably modern idioms in local, city or domestic backyard scenes.

In William Johnstone's 'Border Landscape: The Eildon Hills' (1929) the dark colours and looming contours suggest a world of natural growth and unknown designs, with secrets, spiritual forces and shadowy colours. The precise landscape of Walter Scott's favourite place is somehow involved in modernist abstraction, in which place, with its shapes, colours and contours, is imbricated with the textures of machine-made fabric, man-made structures and movement. His most famous painting, 'A Point in Time' (1929), depicts a world of dark becoming, in which natural, biological and man-made forms seem to be taking unknowable shape: a painting saying and implying more about its time than anything merely literal could. Johnstone is the most radical and underrated of Scotland's major twentieth-century artists and his development of a unique, idiosyncratic, abstract idiom is as undervalued as it is accomplished.

More recognisabe figurative work is represented in Joan Eardley's 'Two Children' (1963), in which colours are intense. Red is predominant. There are bright silver sweetie-papers. One little girl wears a bright striped jacket, the other is in a radiant coat. A newspaper cutting advertises a 'winter sale' of bead necklets. Next to this figurative paintings, Eardley's seascapes, such as 'A Stormy Sea' (1960) or 'The Wave' present greens, greys, blues, sharp cuts of red, white spume and walls of water and sky. The elemental itself has acquired an exotic strangeness, an inhuman power. The element of abstraction in these works is never unconnected to elemental reality yet it is always prioritising and making evident its own media and means of construction. The lessons Johnstone learned, Eardley learned too.

She was born in 1923 at Warnham, Sussex, of English and Scottish parentage. In 1939 at the beginning of the war, her family decided to move to Glasgow. In 1948 she was finally able to take up her post-diploma year at the Glasgow School of Art. She won a travelling scholarship of £60 and went to Europe from 1948 to 1949 on her scholarships, spending most of her time in Italy and some time in Paris.

In Italy she found herself attracted not so much by the art as by the people, the peasants going about their everyday lives. Immediate relationships with the life about her nourished her art. She wrote home from Italy that she was troubled by the fact that she could not speak any Italian, so found it more difficult to form these necessary relationships.

> To become friends and, in this way, to partly understand these people, is the only way I feel I can paint them with truth ... otherwise as I am now, I only know what I see from outside. I suppose painting is only a visual reaction to things, in a way – but to me it must be more. The story part does matter.[19]

Drawings like 'Italian Peasant Sitting on the Ground' show Eardley not only learning from Van Gogh's technique but attempting, as he did, to convey sympathy without sentimentality. She brought this quality back with her to Glasgow.

She moved to the east-coast fishing village of Catterline, living in a cottage on the edge of a sea-cliff, open to all weathers. 'The Wave', painted in 1961, shows the cliff-face of a wave rushing towards the spectator. As your eye runs along the wave's crest, an eerily three-dimensional effect occurs: it is as if you momentarily encounter the wave *breaking*, at the precise moment *before* it breaks. Odd drops of colour are spotted on the painting, drips blown from her brush by the wind onto her work. She mixed her palette with the green emulsion used on the local fishing boats and pieces of earth and plant were applied with the paint as binding agents. Her fidelity to the exact authority of place, weather and sea literally depicts what John Berger has called 'the *address*' of the place, the way a landscape or seascape speaks to an observer: 'what a given landscape addresses to the indigenous imagination: the background of meaning which a landscape suggests to those familiar with it'.[20]

When she died of cancer, in 1963, in her forty-second year, her ashes were scattered on Catterline beach. A local anecdote repeated to me in 1995 told of a public discussion held at the time when American investment in North Sea Oil was escalating house prices (as was to be shown in *The Cheviot, the Stag and the Black, Black Oil* – which we will come to later). It was proposed that housing estates should be built near Catterline. But at the council meeting, a Catterline painting by Eardley was held up and described as representing the place as the people of that place would wish to have it remain. The housing estates were not built at Catterline.

Clearly, in musical and artistic terms, the cultural production of Scotland was rich and varied through the nineteenth and into the twentieth centuries. But it was unco-ordinated. The different fields of creative endeavour were related and overlapped, but without a corresponding or effective political dimension. The *rapprochement* between the exotic and the local took fifty years to come about effectively. However, in the twentieth century, after the Renaissance of the 1920s, the national expression of cultural diversity developed in connected ways that allow a coherent view of the entire culture.

The Scottish Renaissance initiated this vision of connectedness. We have noted F.G. Scott's centrality in the early days of the movement, and how MacDiarmid saw himself working closely in conjunction with Scott and Johnstone. Johnstone referred to them in his autobiography *Points in Time* as 'Three Borderers' setting out heroically, like three musketeers. Scott, Johnstone wrote, became greatly excited by the prospect of 'a Scottish Renaissance of the arts' and envisaged the three friends at the core of it, 'all having a revolutionary point of view', raising 'the standard of the arts right from the gutter into something that would be really important'. Johnstone pointed out that the music Scott composed as settings for MacDiarmid's poems 'broke entirely new ground... It was the birth of a twentieth-century Scottish Renaissance'.[21]

At the same time, a new writing of Scottish history was demanded, from a centre north of an Anglocentric perspective. Work in this direction was undertaken most notably by George Pratt Insh (1883–1956), in books such as *Scotland and the Modern World* (1932), which was structured in counter-pointed sections: 'The Scot at Home' followed by 'The Scot Abroad' and 'The

Eighteenth Century: Scotland' followed by 'The Eighteenth Century: Furth of Scotland'.[22] As an exercise in comparative history centred in native Scottish historiography but contextualising that in rigorous broad studies of other national and continental histories, this was an astonishing act of pioneering education, though one wonders how far it was taken in the schools. To twenty-first century eyes it might seem naïve: an attempt to replay imperial authority and so-called objectivity with a fair-play ethic. But what does such naïveté – if that is what it is – have to teach cynicism?

The whole matter of education was at the core of the effort of the Scottish Renaissance in a way quite different from international modernism, and Insh was championed by MacDiarmid in the 1920s.[23] If the ultimate ideal was a regeneration of the cultural life of the nation, the educational revolution that had to be effected to help bring this about was central to it. It has taken a long time. It was not until the 1990s that schoolchildren were officially encouraged to express themselves in the Scots tongue. The division between class-room English and playground Scots – dramatised by Lewis Grassic Gibbon in the novel *Sunset Song*, where the young heroine Chris Guthrie rejects Anglocentric education to hold on to her Scots character, and in his short story 'Clay', where Rachel Gault chooses to abandon the native community and go to university, trying to find a way through – was much more severe in the 1920s and 1930s.

Many of the Scottish poets who began writing seriously during or after the Second World War remained cautious about both MacDiarmid's extremism and the endless possibilities entertained by postmodernism's refusal of closure, which effectively endorsed statelessness. In a 'globalised' world increasingly unified by a single set of cultural ideals, the disabling sense of isolation any writer, composer or artist might experience could easily be crippling.

The story I have told, of the ideals and parameters of the Scottish Renaissance as described by its protagonists, of the context of that movement in terms of the traditions of music and painting in Scotland, of the increasing internationalism of the world in which the creative artists were working, leads us to a point of transition. We have traced the world from Burns and Scott to Doyle and Harris, through analyses of specific texts. After 1918 this could no longer be the same and the creative work of the 1920s and 1930s in Scotland made it possible to reimagine what this world might be for.

The international brigade

This section sets up a bagatelle of encounters with unpredicted characters, works and genres, but if a general trajectory can be traced it may be simply described. The various assertions of national identity in the late nineteenth century were complemented by an internationalist imagination in the 1920s and the dichotomy between the local and the exotic was reconfigured in the later twentieth century. There were numerous precedents for this in earlier eras, but in the twentieth century the reciprocal values of national self-determination and an international context for it came to be most fully articulated.

In the 1990 *Cencrastus* Hugh MacDiarmid Memorial Lecture, Edwin Morgan drew attention to a company of writers who immediately suggest the international provenance of modern Scottish writing.[24] R.B. Cunninghame Graham (1852–1936) was a meticulous writer of subtle and closely-observed stories and sketches which are set as frequently in Morocco or South America as in Scotland. John Henry Mackay (1864–1933) was a poet and novelist who lived most of his life in Germany, whose work was published in German and dealt with themes of homosexual love and anarchist politics. He was clearly attracted to the idea of being an outsider and insisted on his patronymic in rhyme: 'When they mangled his name he would cry: / "If you please just pronounce it Mackay!" '[25] He was republished in the first Scottish anthology of gay writing in 1989, *And Thus Will I Freely Sing* and deserves further research.[26] His 1926 novel *Der Puppenjunge* (*The Toy-Boy*, translated as *The Hustler*) remains moving and colourful, written in a style as lucid and quick as Jack London, vividly depicting Berlin subculture. His poems were set to music by Richard Strauss and the words of his poem 'Morgen!' ('Tomorrow!') suggest the prospect all these international Scots envision. It is Richard Strauss's single most popular song-setting, frequently performed, the melody perfectly balanced, the colours blissful, both tranquil and enraptured, full of the conviction of a new dawn coming and the prospect of the happiness it will bring.

> Und morgen wird die Sonne wieder scheinen,
> und auf dem Wege, den ich gehen werde,
> wird uns, die Glucklichen, sie weider einen
> inmitten dieser sonnenatmenden Erde ...
>
> Und zu dem Strand, dem weiten, wogenblauen,
> werden wir still und langsam niedersteigen,
> stumm werden wir uns in die Augen schauen,
> und auf uns sinkt des Gluckes stummes Schweigen ...
>
> And tomorrow the sun will be shining again,
> and all along the way that is chosen,
> it happily brings us together again,
> the centre of this sunshine-breathing earth ...
>
> And down to the strand, with its wide waves of blue,
> we'll slowly descend and be speaking no word,
> be wordlessly looking into each other's eyes
> and wordlessly happiness falling upon us ...[27]

John Buchan (1875–1940) is well-known as a thriller-writer, but his less familiar novels such as *The Half-Hearted* (1900), *Witch Wood* (1927), *The Courts of the Morning* (1929) and *A Prince of the Captivity* (1933) deal seriously with the complex morality of individual responsibility, social justice, imperial power and democracy. His most mature novel, *Sick Heart River* (posthumously published in 1941), might honourably feature in histories of Canadian as well as Scottish literature. Buchan is much closer to Kipling in his representation of the human cost of empire than the stigma of popular 'shocker'-writer allows. If there is little doubt about his political preference, there is a deep self-knowledge of loneliness in his main characters, Richard Hannay, Edward Leithen and Sandy Arbuthnot. Though in some of the novels they are grouped as friends, their solitariness speaks of their distance from societal identity. (As we shall see, it is inherited by their glamourised, commercialised successor, James Bond, in the 1950s and 1960s. His 'licence to kill' is a professional emblem of solitude but the trajectory of his written career decribes a man inescapably caught in a more poignant personal trap.)

Morgan takes this list further in his Edinburgh Book Festival Post Office Lecture, 'Scotland and the World' where he advises that we should remember 'the alternative exploratory possibility, not through physical action but through the translation of foreign texts'.[28] He cites Gavin Douglas's translation of Virgil's *Aeneid*, Thomas Urquhart's translation of Rabelais and notes that there is an important tradition of Scottish translators, but when he comes to the 'dusty-foot' travellers, he invites us to consider two important figures beside Cunninghame Graham: William Lithgow (c.1582–after 1645) and Helen Adam (1909–1993).

Lithgow, known as 'Lugless Will' because his ears were cut off by the brothers of a girl he was courting, was a tough, seasoned traveller who visited Italy, Greece, Turkey, Syria, Palestine, Egypt, Hungary, Poland, Germany, Ireland, Spain and Morocco. Morgan comments: 'This was Scotland and the world, not Scotland and Europe' and draws attention to what Lithgow calls 'the science of the world':

> this is it above all things that preferreth men to honours and the charges that make great houses and republics to flourish, and render the actions and words of them who possess it agreeable both to great and small. This science is only acquired by conversation and haunting the company of the most experimented; by divers discourses, reports, by writs, or by a lively voice, in communicating with strangers; and in the judicious consideration of the living with one another; and above all and principally by travellers and voyagers in divers regions and remote places, whose experience confirmeth the true science thereof and can best draw the anatomy of human condition.[29]

Lithgow's book, *The Totall Discourse of The Rare Adventures & Painefull Perergrinations of long Nineteene Yeares Travayles from Scotland to the most famous Kingdomes in Europe, Asia and Africa* (1632) culminates in his capture by the Spanish Inquisition, who tortured him viciously; when he finally made it home he was crippled for life.

> My destiny is such,
>> Which doth predestine me,
> To be a mirrour of mishaps,
>> A Mappe of misery.
> Extreamely do I live,
>> Extreames are all my joy,
> I find in deepe extreamities,
>> Extreames, extreame annoy.[30]

This foreshadows the verse from Hugh MacDiarmid's *A Drunk Man Looks at the Thistle* inscribed on MacDiarmid's tombstone in Langholm:

> I'll hae nae hauf-way hoose, but aye be whaur
> Extremes meet – it's the only way I ken
> To dodge the curst conceit o' bein' richt
> That damns the vast majority o' men.[31]

But it also adds depth to Lithgow's expression of fondness and love for his native land:

> Would God that I might live,
>> To see my native Soyle:
> Thrice happy in my happy wish,
>> To end this endless toyle:
> Yet still when I record,
>> The pleasant bankes of Clide:
> Where Orchards, Castles, Townes, and Woods,
>> Are planted by his side;
> And chiefly Lanerke thou,
>> Thy Countries Laureat Lampe:
> In which this bruised body now
>> Did first receive the stampe.
> Then doe I sigh and sweare,
>> Till death or my returne,
> Still for to weare the Willow wreath,
>> In sable weed to mourne.
> Since in this dying life,
>> A life in death I take,
> Ile sacrifice in spight of wrath,
>> These solemne vowes I make,

> To thee sweete Scotland first,
>   My birth and breath I leave:
> To Heaven my soule, my heart King James,
>   My corpse to lie in grave.
> My staffe to Pilgrimes I,
>   And Pen to Poets send;
> My haire-cloth roabe, and half-spent goods,
>   To wandering wights I lend.[32]

Morgan's list might be supplemented. The Jamaican poet Edward Kamau Brathwaite has described the mixture of tongues in his native place as 'nation language' and drawn attention to the fact that Scots was a significant component of creolisation. Yet the language of most of the Scottish poets in the early decades of the Caribbean literary tradition was not Scots, but English.

Scottish poets were among the earliest to describe the Caribbean in verse, working in a predominantly pastoral tradition. The work of James Grainger (1724–1767) and James Montgomery (1771–1854), for example, belongs to the literary tradition of the Caribbean, but it also must be understood in relation to eighteenth-century conventions of pastoral, radically established by James Thomson (1700–1748) in *The Seasons* (1726–1730). While these conventions were formulated in the context of the English literary tradition, they were initially brought about by Scots writers such as Allan Ramsay (1684–1758) and, indeed, Burns. It is arguable that a characteristic eighteenth-century distinction of Scottish writers was their ability to create and inhabit English literary models.

Grainger and Montgomery were writing at the beginning of the Caribbean literary tradition (just as Burns would have been, had he emigrated, though he may also have figured in the oral tradition as a writer of popular songs) and as such you will find their work in *The Penguin Book of Caribbean Verse* in the appropriate place. Let me quote a passage describing earthquakes, from James Grainger's 'The Sugar-Cane':

> Then earthquakes, nature's agonizing pangs,
> Oft shake the astonied isles: the solfaterre
> Or sends forth thick, blue, suffocating steams;
> Or shoots to temporary flame. A din,
> Wild, thro' the mountain's quivering rocky caves,
> Like the dread Crash of tumbling planets, roars.
> When tremble thus the pillars of the globe,
> Like the tall coco by the fierce North blown;
> Can the poor, brittle tenements of man
> Withstand the dread convulsion? Their dear homes,
> (Which shaking, tottering, crashing, bursting, fall)

The boldest fly; and, on the open plain
Appal'd, in agony the moment wait,
When, with disrupture vast, the waving earth
Shall whelm them in her sea-disgorging womb.[33]

And also this description of Spanish colonial invasion which appears as inhuman as the wildest natural forces, from James Montgomery's 'The West Indies':

Dreadful as hurricanes, athwart the main
Rush'd the fell legions of invading Spain;
With fraud and force, with false and fatal breath,
(Submission bondage, and resistance death,)
They swept the isles. In vain the simple race
Kneel'd to the iron sceptre of their grace,
Or with weak arms their fiery vengeance braved;
They came, they saw, they conquered, they enslaved,
And they destroy'd; – the generous heart they broke,
They crush'd the timid neck beneath the yoke;
Where'er to battle march'd their grim array,
The sword of conquest plough'd resistless way;
Where'er from cruel toil they sought repose,
Around, the fires of devastation rose.
The Indian, as he turn'd his head in flight,
Beheld his cottage flaming through the night,
And, amidst the shrieks of murder on the wind,
Heard the mute blood-hound's death-step close behind.[34]

It is only possible to suggest here that it would be a fascinating study to examine the kind of 'creative schizophrenia' which might connect these poets, on the one hand, through a tradition of Caribbean writing to the contemporary rhetorical magniloquence of Derek Walcott, and, on the other hand, back and across to James Thomson and *The Seasons* and to the pastoral poetry of Burns.

Of a younger generation than Grainger and Montgomery was Michael Scott (1789–1835), who, born in Cowlairs near Glasgow, after school and university, joined the office of a Kingston merchant whose business required Scott to travel extensively in the Caribbean. These travels resulted in the posthumous publication of *Tom Cringle's Log* in 1836, a 'rollicking, roystering rag-bag of a book and something of a literary curiosity'. Originally published as a series of anonymous articles in *Blackwood's Magazine* between 1829 and 1833, the book is a rambling adventure story with duels, pitched battles on land and sea, executions, escapades with guerillas in the jungles of Haiti, and high living with the planters of Jamaica ('the land of fun and fever'). Scott's book is a vastly entertaining representation of the rich and lusty life of Caribbean colonialism. It is also a seminal text in a marginalised tradition and seems in a sense to have been 'answered' by James Robertson's remarkable novel of 2003, *Joseph Knight*, which unsparingly describes the atrocities of Scottish slaveowners in the West Indies and the struggle of the eponymous freed slave to maintain his independence in defiance of his former master's authority.[35]

Of course, there is a long list of writers of Scots descent or connection in Australia, New Zealand, Canada and the United States. None of these authors are merely 'Scots abroad': each one is to a certain degree transgressing the security of national boundaries and risking a corresponding dissolution of identity. Yet the fact of their nationality and the national condition from which they arose is a qualification that is liberating as well as constricting – because with these authors, the essential struggle between articulation and position is singularly pertinent.

It is true that these modes of definition are formed in similar ways, by virtue of their national or territorial identity: that is, by a geographical idea. But all of these writers raise the question of transgression. The fact that Grainger, Montgomery and Michael Scott were Scottish opens up their position to a larger understanding of their cultural context and a sharper sense of their writing as something that takes place 'on the edge', on the margins of definition.

In the early twentieth century, a similar case might be made for Norman Douglas (1868–1952), whose travel book *Old Calabria* (1915) and novel *South Wind* (1917) established his reputation as a sophisticated, witty, strong writer, of tough moral engagement with the contradictory character of southern Italy and commitment to its enlightened hedonism and unrepentant paganism.

Another writer of this sort was Helen Adam (1909–1993), who belonged to the same generation as Sorley MacLean and Norman MacCaig, but who moved to America in 1939 and associated with the Beat poets. She became friendly with Allen Ginsberg and gained a reputation for stunning performances of her own poetry. She often wrote in Scots and, like MacDiarmid's, her work is related to the ballad tradition. Morgan notes: 'Her master subject was love in all its manifestations, but especially those that were not likely to lead to a happily lasting outcome. Jilting, two-timing, jealousy, adultery, idealised search, unrequited passion, over-requited passion, murderous revenge – these are her field of operations, and however bizarre the circumstances she at times would place her characters in, a deep psychological insight was at work.' In 'I Love My Love' a man in a suffocating marriage murders his wife but her hair grows out of the grave and smothers him: 'There was no sound but the joyful hiss of the sweet insatiable hair.' 'Miss Laura' is set in the deep south and its mixed race relationship is brutally, beautifully direct: 'My body's open, and I want you in. / Black,

black, black, black is the colour / Of my true love's skin.' What Morgan calls her 'number one phantasmagoria' is a ballad-opera, *San Francisco's Burning* (1963), performed in San Francisco and New York, with Adam herself in a leading part. Set just before the earthquake of 1906, it is full of foreboding, jazzy rhythms, black, nightmarish comedy and unforgettable characters: Mrs Mackie Rhodus, a dragon dowager, Spangler Jack, the King of the Gamblers, Mother Bronson's Babies and the Scotch Sailor (in tattered red kilt) who sings:

> Twa worlds o' life and death,
> Sae near, sae far apart,
> In between the twa worlds
> The crying o' the heart.

A daughter of the manse, born in Glasgow, brought up in the north-east of Scotland, Helen Adam might not have written if she had remained in Scotland. Morgan suggests that 'she needed the jolt of an entirely different environment to bring to the surface what was subterraneanly there'. She is referred to as an American poet but she is rather a Scottish poet 'who learned a new boldness and vivacity in California, but who never lost touch with the oral tradition she grew up with'.[36] The masks her new location provided afforded her new capacities for creative expression.

The republication in 2002 of the *Collected Works* of Lorna Moon (1886–1930) tells a similar story of an author deserving reappraisal.[37] Born in Strichen, a village in Aberdeenshire, Helen Nora Wilson Low was to change her name and become a Hollywood scriptwriter. She was also the author of a number of stories and a novel about her native place, with unsentimental, psychologically acute depictions of local life and mores. Whether the fiction could have been produced had she never left home remains an unanswerable question. Edwin Morgan sees the argument of 'stay-at-home versus dusty-foot' as irresolvable and perennial, noting that Emily Bronte did not need to leave Haworth to write *Wuthering Heights*. But to characterise such writers as 'Scots abroad' or 'wandering Scots', international travellers, prompts reflection on two other distinct kinds of writer: those who come from other parts of the world than Scotland but who have taken Scotland as the site and focus of their writing (like Wilson Harris in *Black Marsden*); and also those foreign writers Scots by descent, whose writing bears on Scotland.

A list of notable writers who have found a peculiar affinity with Scotland although they have come from other parts of the world could be very long. Visits by the Wordsworths, Coleridge and Keats are well documented but perhaps the key figure in it would be Queen Victoria herself. Her *Leaves from the Journal of Our Life in the Highlands* (1869) collects notes on various sojourns in Scotland, almost interchangeable in their over-use of words like 'picturesque', 'pretty', 'charming', 'beautiful', 'calm' and 'solitary'. 'Oh!

what can equal the beauties of nature!' she rhapsodises in 1844: 'What enjoyment there is in them! Albert enjoys it so much; he is in ecstasies here.' Her appreciation of the natives is appropriately definitive: describing John Brown (he was 40, the monarch 64), she says he is typical of 'the Highland race' – full of 'independence and elevated feelings... singularly straightforward, simple-minded, kind-hearted and disinterested; always ready to oblige; and of a discretion rarely to be met with'.[38]

Other visitors were more sensitive. Scotland made its impression in various ways upon J.D. Salinger, Beatrix Potter, George Orwell, Daniel Defoe, Charles Dickens, David Mamet, Washington Irving, Bret Harte, Gerard Manley Hopkins, Virginia Woolf and Louis MacNeice. Before writing *Frankenstein*, Mary Shelley watched whaling boats set out for the North Sea when she stayed on Tayside, where bloody fragments of whale blubber would litter the beach. Harriet Beecher Stowe's *Sunny Memories* recollecting time spent with the Duchess of Sutherland prompted Donald MacLeod to respond with *Gloomy Memories*, his classic account of the Highland Clearances that were happening on the Sutherland estates at the same time as Stowe's visit. And who could gainsay the influence of Scotland on the young Edgar Allan Poe, who, when he went to school in Irvine, was sent out to the local graveyard to copy the inscriptions on the headstones to improve his calligraphy?[39]

Among the most curious nineteenth-century visitors were Jules Verne and Bram Stoker. Verne, saturated in Scott, visited the country in 1859, writing a poem extolling the 'Lovely lakes with sleeping waters' and the 'charming legends' of Flora MacIvor, Diana Vernon and Rob Roy. However, he also wrote two novels set in Scotland: *The Green Ray* (1893) which depicts the Hebrides, and *Child of the Cavern* (1877) which picks up on the social degradation of the coal mines and offers an alternative vision of industrialism, located in a vast underground network of caves and tunnels beneath Loch Lomond. While following the conventions of formulaic popular fiction, the underground locations and focus on industrialisation and working communities make this a remarkable counterbalance to hackneyed representations of a picturesque Scotland.[40]

Bram Stoker's Scotland is coastal and scenic but equally strange, as Dracula's Castle seems at least partly modelled on Slains Castle, near Cruden Bay, Aberdeenshire, where Stoker frequently spent his summer months and where *Dracula* (1897) was written. In Chapter 6 of the novel, the ostensibly English fishermen of Whitby are speaking unmistakeable versions of Scots. Stoker also set short stories and another novel in Cruden Bay, describing the area's elemental inhumanity and mysteriousness, in 'Crooken Sands' and 'The Watter's Mou' and *The Mystery of the Sea* (1902).[41]

Two less-familiar writers are the Ghanaian Bernard Kojo Laing and the Nigerian Kole Omotoso. Bernard Kojo Laing was born in Kumasi, Ghana, in 1946 and went to schools in Ghana and Scotland, completing a degree at

Glasgow University in 1968, and returning to Ghana in the same year. His father was Scottish. In 1969, he published in the fourth collection of *Scottish Poetry* edited by George Bruce, Maurice Lindsay and Edwin Morgan, a strange, surreal poem entitled 'Jaw' which ran to a full ten pages.[42] This seems to have been written under the influence of Octavio Paz, Pablo Neruda and, perhaps most importantly, Aimé Césaire's *Return to My Native Land*. It contains little that is overtly Scottish in imagery or description but its inclusion in the anthology demonstrates a radical openness at editorial level, a desire to include such a text because, having been written in Scotland, it is inevitably part of the cultural bricolage of the country. The poem returns, with an absurd and dream-like sense of unwarranted concentration, to the poet's jaw: a symbol, perhaps, of the ego and egoistic determination, but also a symbol of the physical engagement required for the utterance of language. The poem begins: 'I do not belong to places where jaws are merely vanity, art or science. / After all I am here, trying to reach an inner world.' The poem mixes the sense of place and presence with abstract ideas, so that the poem's location remains ambivalent. Where is this poet taking us?

> Which path? I see a path, I see a path
> change direction and lose itself, and
> it rejects these feet that come to walk.
> A path lies dead and gardened by the sea.

Yet despite this, the poem is an affirmation. Laing spells out in capital letters his desire to 'BUILD A TOWN ON MY JAW' and to 'MAKE A BUILDING OF SURVIVAL':

> And I often place a hand on my rooted and bushy face,
> And I hear a wind of bushy screams,
> and the wall digests its chalk writing,
> in Cape Coast or the Vale of Leven,
> and I see a survival so narrow,
>   that I can hold it by the shoulders.

After returning to Ghana, Laing worked in central and local government and in 1985 he helped manage a private school established in 1962 by his mother. His first novel was published in 1986: *Search, Sweet Country*, an epic celebration of Ghana, in which an enthusiastic sense of Ghanaian national identity seems implicitly to counterpoint the condition of Scotland which Laing had experienced as a young man. Indeed, a reading of the novel might reveal Laing's kinship with Ivan T. Sanderson, as much of what he depicts in Ghana could well apply with an oblique accuracy to Scotland.

In his second novel, the links between the two countries are made explicitly. *Woman of the Aeroplanes* (first published in 1988, again by Heinemann) depicts the inhabitants of the town of Tukwan in the Asante region of Ghana, full of 'goats, elephants, ducks, lakes and lawyers'. It is twinned with 'Levensvale' in Scotland, from which two aeroplanes are procured in an unlikely exchange of palm nuts and cassava. In a narrative which owes something to South American magic realism, Scottish Gothic and Stevensonian phantasmogoria, the people of the twinned towns meet, and their profound relationship is marked by the invention of a 'stupidity machine'. The phenomena of 'twinning' is a recurrent theme in the novel, with occasional words having an alternative printed out below them in the text, under a horizontal line, as if readers might make their own choice of the most appropriate term. This is a wry and ironic comment on the doubling or schizophrenic aspect of Scottish culture, evident from the *Justified Sinner* through *Jekyll and Hyde* to R.D. Laing and so on. The novel is clearly drawing upon traditions, on the one hand, of Scottish humanism and reductive scepticism, and on the other, of the hallucinatory prose of Amos Tutuola or Ben Okri. The language of the book is peppered with a demotic vocabulary, and the 'Glossary of Ghanaian words and author's neologisms' includes the anomalous Scottish word 'oxter'!

By contrast, Kole Omotoso's beautifully understated first novel, *The Edifice* (1971), is set predominantly in Edinburgh.[43] It deals with the love affair of a Nigerian student with a Scots girl, their marriage and subsequent departure from Scotland to Africa. The final part of the book is told from the viewpoint of the woman as she becomes increasingly alienated from her husband and her social context, and increasingly distracted from her sense of her own identity when her husband takes a second wife. It is a tragic novel, all the more powerful for its balance and cool sense of observation, owing something to Chinua Achebe and something (perhaps) to the ironic detachment of Muriel Spark. The novel is, in an obvious sense, about the failure of a marriage, but it is also a shrewd comment both on racism and any anti-racist utopianism.

Inheritors

In an essay of 1980, published in a shortened version in the *New Edinburgh Review*, the Australian poet Les Murray wrote that the Scots, along with the Jews, have probably been the great ethnic success story in Australian history.

> Some Irish Australian friends of mine once demanded to know what the Scots, as compared with the Irish, had achieved in Australia. 'Well,' I replied, 'we own it.' The enormous number of Scots and Scottish descendants, in proportion to our share of the population, who have been leaders in commerce, in politics, in education, in military matters and in the pastoral industry is pretty well known . . . [One might add

philosophy, thinking of John Anderson.] ... [A]nother field in which we have been active and successful in a measure way out of proportion to our numbers is poetry.

Murray goes on to discuss why this should be so, and makes his point with reference to the differences between the Irish and the Scottish inheritance:

> Parts of the style of Irish Australia are attractive to Scots Australians, stirring ancestral chords, but other parts of the style irritate us; this is something enthusiasts for the Celtic cause need to face squarely. It may be that some of the dissonance merely reflects that our ancestral home-land is lost, while theirs is still a moral force to them, as it battles to save and restore itself. Their Jacobites won, in the end; ours lost. And this may be relevant to poetry, even among the descendants. Poetry has an enormous ancient prestige among both peoples, but in the Irish case, perhaps for the very reason that it was often the tough spine of an embattled civilization, Irish poetry even in English has never really developed the idiosyncratic, sometimes cross-grained venturesomeness of Scots, or the readiness to deal with new realities. For an Irish parallel to Hugh MacDiarmid, you would have to look to prose writers, perhaps pre-eminently to James Joyce. As descendants of a people which sold itself out, or was sold out, under pressure, we lack a Kathleen Ni Houlihan, the all-loving, all-demanding mother-muse who permits only endless variations on the one immemorial sad tune. If suffering narrowed and concentrated Irish poetry, grief and anger opened Scots poetry out.[44]

There are, of course, dangers in the decadent attractions of ethnic con-sciousness, and Murray is not unaware of them. However, his perceptive comments are linked to an autobiographical element which is typically humble. He has explored the culture of Scotland at a much deeper level than that of mere romantic or whimsical interest, feeling considerable distaste for the kitsch tartanry when he lived in the country following the Devolution referendum of 1979. 'And yet, when all has been said, Scotland is still the only overseas country in which I have never felt foreign.' But this attachment, he recognises, is a generational matter: 'I am probably one of the last of our lot to have felt, in a real way, some of the terrible gravity of the past; that won't persist beyond my generation at all, I suspect.' His children, and his children's children, he believes are 'unlikely to suffer possession by the spirits of the restless dead'.[45]

Murray's felicitous understanding of his inheritance is both historical and theoretical, in the sense that he can pin it down to particular generations, particular voyagers, his own ancestors, particular immigrants and families, yet he is also concerned to abstract from that into generalisations about the nature of cultural inheritance, and in his poetry these senses merge. For example, in 'Their Cities, Their Universities', the first stanza ends with the typically laconic, typically droll pronouncement, 'The past explains us and it gets our flesh.' The tone of that is both pontificatory and grudgingly admiring: a very Scottish emotional mix of distance and engagement. If the poem deals with Les Murray's own particular ancestors in specific historical moments, it rises to a philosophical generalisation in its closing lines which prompts reflection on a more theoretical level: 'we are going to the cause / not coming from it'.[46]

What this leads into is the post-colonial world, a world in which imperial centralities and authorial securities have been radically de-stabilised, if not altogether dissolved. Murray's admirably forthright manner is the direct expression of an anti-colonial, anti-imperial feeling. In an interview he has spoken of

> the dreadful tyranny where only certain privileged places are regarded as the centre and the rest are provincial and no good is expected to come out of them...I figure the centre is everywhere. It goes with the discovery that the planet is round, not flat. Every point on a sphere is the centre. It seems to be a corollary of the discovery of the roundness of the world that people haven't taken seriously yet.[47]

It is this conviction which brings Murray into the context of post-colonial literature. The contrast of Murray's sense of Australian identity with that of Patrick White, for example, makes this clear. For White sited himself very definitely in a high cultural tradition of the novel, and his despair owed a great deal to the hierarchical forms of definition involved in the sense of that tradition. For White, Australian literature was on the periphery of the European world, and in terms of Australia itself, literary civilisation consisted of another peripheral identity, scattered around the edge of an enormous, continental desert. His epic novel *Voss* recounts the story of an expedition to the heart of that continent through an inimical landscape profoundly associated with the absolute otherness of its indigenous and aboriginal inhabitants. The heart of this vision is a barren rock, its attitude to European culture so massively indifferent that it annihilates every member of the expedition.

For Murray, this set of multiple marginalisations and polarised 'centres' (European as against Australian) simply does not exist in the same way. Being of a later generation, opened to the cultural complexities of his own country as well as the country his people came from, the post-colonial world of continual displacements and perennial shifts of focus is the context for his wonderful and healthy logorrhoea. His recognition of generational evolution is a more hopeful one, even as it recognises the failure of all attempts to predict it. His poem, 'The Future' begins:

> We see, by convention, a small living distance into it
> but even that's a projection. And all our projections
> fail to curve where it curves.[48]

This is Murray at his most distinctive: vernacular, easeful, but serious and wise. But the theme is not Murray's alone. It is part of the legacy the inheritors of a Scottish history might be expected to bear. Another Australian poet, Chris Wallace-Crabbe, writes in similar fashion in his collection *For Crying Out Loud*. The Scottish element is seen here explicitly in 'The Last Ride', which describes the departure of 'The People of Peace', 'a motley cavalcade' riding on small shaggy horses, 'the riders crooked, wee, bizarre', passing by a cottage and disappearing from sight: 'The People of Peace shall never more / Be seen on the braes of Scotland.'[49]

But this Scottish element is also to be understood in the roaming but disciplined attention Wallace-Crabbe pays to other encounters in different parts of the world. *For Crying Out Loud* is most impressive in a series of poems where Wallace-Crabbe is struggling to come to terms with the death of his son. The first poem in the book, 'They', is a moving elegy whose roots go back to a Scottish literature rich in laments for all sorts of potentials that have been destroyed (the ghosts of all those projections which failed to curve into the future):

> They have passed through darkness into a radiance
> which we cannot know and they cannot comprehend
> but which does not remember the griefs of our world.

Wallace-Crabbe recognises a universal truth when he writes, 'Lamenting them, we weep for ourselves.'[50]

The Australian provenance of these poets is secure, and yet the evidence of the Scottish trace in their work is unmistakeable. The universality of the perceptions they make is akin to that in Christopher Okigbo's lines which we quoted at the beginning of the book: 'We carry in our worlds that flourish / our worlds that have failed.' However, the distinctive Scottish element in the work we have introduced in this chapter hopefully adds the value of particularity to the general truths their work embodies.

Two further contrasting examples define the lasting quality of such work, despite Les Murray's insistence on change across generations. Eric McCormack, born in Scotland in 1940, moved to Canada in 1966 and his novels *The Paradise Motel* (1989) and *The Mysterium* (1992) both cast oblique light back on the author's home territory. *The Paradise Motel* is a sinister comedy in which grotesque humour is wickedly deployed to emphasise the excesses of political fanaticism, Scottish nationalist extremism and the vicarious nature of human identity. It is as if the distance provided by his new location allowed McCormack the space to operate an irony that might otherwise have been cramped to extinction.[51] A very different writer was Carlos Drummond de Andrade (1902–1987), a major Brazilian modernist poet. Expelled from his Jesuit school for 'mental insubordination' he went on to work in the civil service, publishing his first book of poems in 1930 and living in Rio de Janeiro from 1934. Thomas Colchie describes him as a poet of quiet, lyrical intimacy, not the public, epic voice of Pablo Neruda but a more humble representative of 'the common man' in poems such as 'Song for That Man of the People Charlie Chaplin'. In 'Residue' he writes of the traces that remain in the world, of things that appear to have disappeared, as if speaking implicitly of the Scottish inheritance that survives in his own name:

> From everything a little remained.
> From my fear. From your disgust.
> From stifled cries. From the rose
> a little remained.

From emotions and images, from biological presence to spiritual substance, something stays present:

> So from everything a little remains.
> A little remains of your chin
> in the chin of your daughter.[52]

I have been arguing, at least implicitly, for a more comprehensive contextualisation of Scottish literature. Our critical reading of Scotland's cultural production, especially since the nineteenth century, might best be considered in the international context of the project of Empire. Reading Arthur Conan Doyle, Amos Tutuola and Wilson Harris opened up the field and this chapter, while noting the central significance of internationalism in the Scottish Renaissance has begun to extend that field and populate it.

Yet I hope that my argument clearly *opposes* the idea of 'internationalism' as something centred merely in the Anglo-American establishment. If my own limitations are marked by the imperium of the languages with which I am familiar, I should at least try to acknowledge those limitations. To explore the international references made in this chapter adequately – and I am keenly aware that this is no more than a sketchy beginning – it is vital to begin from the habitation of Scotland itself. The comprehensive contextualisation suggested here requires a reciprocal sense of the weighted or grounded reality that national identity provides.

We might therefore begin to review and re-evaluate not only those writers and texts hitherto consigned to the margins or peripheries, but to interrogate the processes which relegated them to such positions, and which have kept them there. For these processes are inevitably human constructions, and they operate across societies, nations and cultures. If we are to question and counter them, our practices must attend equally well to cross-cultural or trans-cultural texts, drawing strengths from conditions formerly considered debilitating. The next chapter will consider how these ideas apply in selected texts from Scotland after the Second World War.

8
Nobody's Children: Orphans and their Ancestors in Popular Scottish Fiction after 1945

The world is full of orphans: firstly, those
  Who are so in the strict sense of the phrase
(But many a lonely tree the loftier grows
  Than others crowded in the forest's maze);
The next are such as are not doomed to lose
  Their tender parents in their budding days,
But merely their parental tenderness,
Which leaves them orphans of the heart no less.

The first stanza of the last canto of Byron's *Don Juan* was written in 1823, in Genoa, and was followed by fourteen more, the last one scored out. Byron took them with him to Greece, but wrote no more. He died in April 1824. These, then, are poignant fragments: close to the last things the bad Lord ever wrote. The pathos is unavoidable. Byron continues: 'if examined, it might be admitted / The wealthiest orphans are more to be pitied. // Too soon they are parents to themselves'.[1]

Byron's ironic yet bitter brooding on the cost of what it means to be the wandering, outcast hero sets the tone for this chapter, for here I would like to consider some heroic, anti-heroic and mock-heroic characters in Scottish popular fiction since 1945. Byron, an exile from Scotland whose national identity has frequently been overlooked, sets a precedent for the character who was to evolve into the most popular Scottish hero of the 1960s: James Bond. When Ian Fleming introduced Bond to an international readership, he presented a distinctly Byronic character: 'The [baccarat] table was becoming wary of this dark Englishman who played so quietly, wary of the half-smile of certitude on his rather cruel mouth. Who was he? Where did he come from? What did he do?'[2]

Fleming's use of the term 'Englishman' here is patently a depiction of a political mask, not a description of ethnic identity but of ideological loyalty. We will come back to this in a moment. But first to consider Fleming's questions: when Kingsley Amis attempted to answer them, he too returned to the source: 'Well, he started life about 1818 as Childe Harold in the later cantos of Byron's poem, reappeared in the novels of the Brontë sisters and was around until fairly recently in such guises as that of Maxim de Winter in Miss Daphne du Maurier's *Rebecca*.'[3]

But Amis failed to mention the greatest absence in the background of these two 'rather cruel' characters, Byron and Bond: where did they come from? The answer deserves more comment than it has ever received: Scotland.[5]

Ancestors

When Byron died in Greece, his flag was pinned to the mast of Greek liberation. Byronic heroes are frequently found in the service of similar noble causes. But rarely (if ever) do they openly associate with Scotland's national history. Typical is the example of Thomas Carlyle, whose removal to London signalled another moment in a successive series of shifts towards Anglocentrism, of which only 1603 and 1707 are the most famous. Carlyle went to London in 1834. By 1841, in his lectures *On Heroes, Hero-Worship and the Heroic in History*, he can refer to Dr Johnson as 'by nature, one of our great English souls'.[4] Once again, this is a statement of ideological preference similar to that in the passage above, where Bond is referred to in passing as an 'Englishman'. Both Carlyle and Fleming establish their credentials and those of their literary inventions by affirming Anglocentric and cosmopolitan political and cultural authority.

Byron combines world-weariness with dash, youthful vigour with a mature authority. He is ruthlessly international in outlook and wisely derisive in pitch – but for all his multiple contradictions, his character is singular. He is a self-sufficient outcast (as the last extract from *Don Juan* quoted above laments). Byron's contemporary and peer, Sir Walter Scott, was the first writer to develop certain aspects of the singular hero significantly by dividing and defining two aspects of him.

Alexander Welsh delineates the main features of a Scott hero.[5] He is young. He is often unaware of the legacy he will come to inherit, but by its inheritance he will become eminently marriageable. He is passive, or at least distanced, in the context of massive social upheaval and action. But he is not alone; he has an active counterpart, a colourful and humorous character, apparently in command of his own destiny (but whose destiny is indissolubly linked with that of the hero: he is a complement to the hero's unplanned growth to maturity). The relationship between Waverley and Fergus Mac-Ivor is the classic example in *Waverley* (1814), and it provides an incipient formula which develops in the later Waverley novels, with Bailie Nicol Jarvie and Rob Roy, for example. But the formula evolves. Waverley's counterpart in *Rob Roy* is Fancis Osbaldistone and Nicol Jarvie is not a 'hero' himself but a rich, often comic 'character' who has a *national* complementary relationship with

Rob. *Redgauntlet* is made complex by the fact that the two young heroes are counterpoised to the 'dark' and violent man of action and *Old Mortality* by the extreme, covenanting darkness of its grim 'heroes'.

Stevenson inhabits this aspect of the legacy of Scott with David Balfour and Alan Breck, in *Kidnapped* (1886). If Breck is Rob Roy or Fergus Mac-Ivor, Balfour, the anti-hero, is a young Bailie Nicol Jarvie or Edward Waverley. Stevenson's development of the formula of double heroes highlights the double nature of their historical context, when one social order was accommodating itself to another. As we noted in the Introduction, the sub-title of *Waverley* (*'Tis Sixty Years Since*) draws attention to the historical changes in Scottish society after the Jacobite risings. Just as Washington Irving's Rip Van Winkle sleeps through America's Declaration of Independence, Scott's novel comes to light in a post-revolutionary period. It is retrospective and nostalgic from the start. So is *Kidnapped*: its full title specifies the year of its events as 1751 – so Breck's Jacobite world is firmly anachronistic.[6] This suggests an axis of doubleness. The twin heroes parallel each other, being contemporaries; but they are also in conflict with each other: one represents the past, the other the present and future. We have discussed a similar axis at work in *Treasure Island*.

The descendants of Fergus MacIvor and Alan Breck are James Bond's ethnic allies: West Indian (Quarrel) in *Dr No*, Turkish (Darko Kerim) in *From Russia with Love*, Corsican (Marc-Ange Draco) in *On Her Majesty's Secret Service*, and Australian (Dikko Henderson) and Japanese (Tiger Tanaka) in *You Only Live Twice* and so on. (Another pair of heroes, locked in a more subtle relationship, but still with their own Scottish background, would be Sherlock Holmes and Dr Watson.)

In the broad field of post-1945 Scottish cultural production, three significant shifts need to be kept in mind. The first is the phenomenal rise in mass-produced literature, pulp fiction, comic books, films, radio and television. Genre fiction becomes established: the genres of Romance, Western, Thriller (Crime, Detective, Spy Fiction, Police Procedural), Horror, Science Fiction and so on. The global phenomenon of popular mass-culture has become, perhaps, the most remarkable characteristic of the modern world.

The second is the way in which the Romantic movement developed in written fiction. The Romantic movement is crucial to our understanding of post-war popular fiction because the models formed then have inhabited popular texts ever since, from Byron to James Bond. Romance fiction is populated by descendants of the Byronic hero, available in bulk – not only in international airports but also in domestic supermarkets. Romanticism was an international but Eurocentric movement which involved all the arts, not only literature. Its impetus was inherited in America and retained in Scotland, and continued more generally in popular culture. But the high culture of England abandoned it. The strongest foundations of the period in each area were laid down by contemporaries: Sir Walter Scott (1771–1832),

Jane Austen (1775–1818) and James Fenimore Cooper (1789–1851). Scott and Cooper generated Romance; Austen did not. (Of course, the novel was not considered 'high culture' until quite late in the nineteenth century and although Austen continues to be deeply influential on formulaic romance genre fiction, she evidently also appealed to and influenced genteel social presumption in a history of self-legitimising class status. This is a different legacy from that of the Brontës, for example, who were disciples of Scott, but went beyond his effects to create new ones.)

The third crucial change in the cultural map is the rise to dominance of American power in the wake of the Second World War. Internationally, the United States became the most significant cultural authority both as a source and as an arbiter of cultural models (Romantic heroes and glamorous women are only the most obvious examples). The announcement that *From Russia With Love* was among President Kennedy's favourite books was crucial to James Bond's conquest of America in the 1960s and 1970s.[7]

It is in this new world that our heroes and the texts in which they figure are discovered.

Lobey Dosser (1949–1950s)

When Louis Dearborn L'Amour died in 1988, he was being advertised as an 'all-time bestselling author' and 'America's favourite frontier writer'. In 1983 he received a Congressional Medal of Honour and in 1984 President Ronald Reagan gave him the Presidential Medal of Freedom. He was the author of over one hundred novels and short-story collections, predominantly westerns, tried-and-true formula genre novels including a multi-volume dynastic saga about the Sackett family, tracing them from Europe through their arrival in America to their wild west escapades in the 1880s.

By the 1980s, L'Amour had so densely populated his imaginary west with fast-draw gunmen, iron guns, sons of wanted men, sky-liners and tall strangers that he was republishing material written and first printed a generation earlier for a new readership. *The Trail to Crazy Man* published in one book three short novellas written in the 1940s for pulp magazines, before his first novel appeared. It went through eight printings in 1988. The opening of 'Riders of the Dawn' gives a fair idea of the style: 'I rode down from the high blue hills and across the brush flats into Hattan's Point, a raw bit of spawning hell, scattered hit or miss along the rocky slope of a rust-topped mesa.'[8] When the hero comes to town, he sizes up the situation, meets the landowner-boss, his henchmen, the main villain, usually a hired, cold-bloodedly murderous gunfighter, and the heroine, often the boss's daughter. By the end of the story, he has ousted the boss, shot the villain in a fair fight, usually suffering a wound of some kind, and won the hand and procreational promise of the young woman.

Meeting the heroine for the first time is normally momentous: for example, 'She stood on the boardwalk straight before me, slim, tall, with a softly curved body and magnificent eyes and hair of deepest black. Her skin was lightly tanned, her eyes an amazing green, her lips full and rich.'[9] The hero is Byronic in his unworthiness:

> My black leather chaps were dusty, and my gray shirt was sweat-stained from the road. My jaws were lean and unshaven, and under my black, flat-crowned hat, my hair was black and rumpled. I was in no shape to meet a girl like that, but there she was, the woman I wanted, my woman.

The elisions in that last sentence are fast: the objectified 'girl' becomes the 'woman' at the same moment as she becomes imagined property. Stepping up to her, the hero introduces himself: ' "I realise," I said, as she turned to face me, "the time is inopportune. My presence scarcely inspires interest, let alone affection and love, but this seemed the best time for you to meet the man you are to marry. The name is Mathieu Sabre..." '[10]

This abrupt shift into baroque and stilted diction leads to the author's disclosure of the apparently rough hero's unsuspected pedigree. What he says, what she *hears*, is 'Matthew Saber' but what we *read* is French, European, Eastern. The east has arrived in the west: the dynastic succession promises a marriage between eastern cultural heritage (the ability to handle property and behave with propriety) and western practical experience. The formula insists that by the end of the story, the rough – sometimes outlaw – hero will have become the establishment patriarch. It was a formula most fully elaborated and laid down by Owen Wister (1860–1938) in *The Virginian*, in 1902, one of American literature's longest-term best-sellers. When the hero of that novel kills his former best friend – now an irredeemable outlaw – Trampas, it signals his own declaration of loyalty to the succession of civilisation. The hero settles on the civilised side of the frontier, and the frontier moves further west.

One other aspect of L'Amour's stories should be noted. In each of them there is usually a sidekick, a Sancho Panza, a figure of comic relief compared to the hero, but who is also reliable back-up if it comes to trouble. Generally in popular culture, this figure is different from the hero's friend, who is usually of the same physical stature and potential appeal (and who sometimes turns into an arch-enemy, like Trampas in Owen Wister's *The Virginian*). In different examples from popular culture, the sidekick is distinguished from the hero sometimes by race (the Lone Ranger and Tonto), sometimes by age (Batman and Robin, in other masks) and often by ethnicity. In two of L'Amour's stories in *The Trail to Crazy Man* this is painfully clear.

In 'Riders of the Dawn' Mathieu Sabre describes a man whose 'face was like that of an unhappy monkey...without a hair to the top of his head...broad in the shoulders...shorter than me by inches'. This man introduces himself: ' "I'm a handy all-round man ... gunsmith, hostler, blacksmith, an' carpenter, good with an ax. An' I shoot a bit, know Cornish-style wrestlin', an' am afraid of no man when I've my two hands before me...." ' When he gets to his feet, 'he could have been nothing over five feet four but weighed all of two hundred pounds, and his shirt at the neck showed a massive chest covered with black hair and a neck like a column of oak... "My name is Brian Mulvaney," he said. "Call me what you like." '[11]

He is a 'lad o' pairts' in the familiar Scottish tradition, able to turn his hand to anything, self-determined, so self-contained that he is unworried by what he might be called, familiar with his own physical abilities, combining a sense of Celtic 'otherness' in the Cornish-wrestling expertise and the Irish name. It would be pedantic to trouble over the inept repetition of the word 'neck' in one sentence, but note Mulvaney's height.

Now turn to the next story in the collection, 'Showdown on the Hogback' and meet its hero, Captain Tom Kedrick, 'a stranger in town' who, in need of a friend, answers a knock on the door of his hotel room.

> The man that stood with his back to it facing Kedrick was scarcely five feet four, yet almost as broad as he was tall. But all of it was sheer power of bone and muscle, with not an ounce of fat anywhere. His broad brown face might have been graved from stone, and the bristle of short-cropped hair above it was black as a crow's wing. The man's neck spread to broad, thick shoulders. On his right hip he packed a gun. In his hand he held a narrow-brimmed hard hat.

Kedrick recognises him and greets him enthusiastically as 'Dai Reid', asking what he is doing here. Dai Reid replies, ' "Ah? So it's that you ask, is it? Well, it's trouble there is, boy, much of trouble! An' you that's by way of bringin' it!" '[12] They team up, beat the opposition and the hero wins the day and a fair lady's hand as usual. But what I want to establish by quoting this material extensively here is how prevalent these stereotypes of Celtic ethnicity have been in the twentieth century. The Welsh name, 'Dai Reid' and the typical contortions of language characteristically distinguish mystically powerful characters in multi-million dollar franchises in the twenty-first century, such as the wizard Gandalf or the dwarf Gimli in the film version of *The Lord of the Rings* (2001–2003), or Yoda, the little green Jedi Knight in the *Star Wars* films. Yoda is even more massively compacted in height and power than Dai Reid or Brian Mulvaney, as he demonstrates when he leaps into athletic action against the villain embodied by the sinister-sounding, 'correctly-spoken', tall English actor Christopher Lee, in the fifth film to be released, *Attack of the Clones* (2001). The problem with clones, of course, is that it is impossible to tell them apart. Lee is also the wicked, sinister-sounding, 'correctly-spoken', tall English actor who plays the villain in

The Lord of the Rings. That Lee is the cousin of James Bond's creator, Ian Fleming, is worth noting, for his ostensibly 'English' propriety is surely another kind of mask. It is easy to overlook the connection between such texts as Louis L'Amour's stories or the *Star Wars* films with literary tradition but it is there, reminding us of a curious and essential continuity in the work of enchantment or entrancement in popular culture.

'Enchantments and Enchanters' is the title of Chapter 46 of Mark Twain's *Life on the Mississippi* (published in 1883, at the time when most of L'Amour's stories are set). It is here that Twain pronounces his famous judgement on Sir Walter Scott.[13] He says this:

> Against the crimes of the French Revolution and of Bonaparte may be set two compensating benefactions: the Revolution broke the chains of the ancien regime and of the Church, and made a nation of abject slaves a nation of freemen; and Bonaparte instituted the setting of merit above birth, and also so completely stripped the divinity from royalty, that whereas crowned heads in Europe were gods before, they are only men, since, and can never be gods again, but only figureheads, and answerable for their acts like common clay.

Twain might have noted that the Declaration of Arbroath had said it already. These, Twain says, are 'great and permanent services to liberty, humanity and progress'.

He goes on:

> Then comes Sir Walter Scott with his enchantments, and by his single might checks this wave of progress, and even turns it back; sets the world in love with drama and phantoms; with decayed and swinish forms of religion; with decayed and degraded systems of government; with the sillinesses and emptinesses, sham grandeurs, sham gauds, and sham chivalries of a brainless and worthless long-vanished society. He did measureless harm; more real and lasting harm, perhaps, than any other individual that ever wrote.

In the South, Twain says, progressive nineteenth-century civilisation is all mixed up with

> the Walter Scott Middle Age sham civilization ... the duel, the inflated speech, and the jejune romanticism of an absurd past ... It was Sir Walter who made every gentleman in the South a Major or a Colonel, or a General or a Judge, before the war; and it was he, also, who made these gentlemen value these bogus decorations. For it was he who created rank and caste down there, and also reverence for rank and caste, and pride and pleasure in them.

Twain's condemnation escalates savagely into monstrous proportions: 'Sir Walter had so large a hand in making Southern character, as it existed before the war, that he is in great measure responsible for the war.' Twain recognises the extremism of the statement himself but will not pull back from it. However personal the attack may be, it is founded upon a sense of Scott's popularity which Twain's readers in the 1880s would immediately acknowledge: 'It seems a little harsh toward a dead man to say that we never should have had any war but for Sir Walter; and yet something of a plausible argument might, perhaps, be made in support of that wild proposition.'

But perhaps the influence of Scott twisted in another way in a longer perspective, fostering popular constructions of chivalry and heroism, reflecting the sexist basis of gender-identification in handsome men and glamorous women, stretched into unconscious caricature in Louis L'Amour's fiction of a century later, endorsed by Presidential honours and the bodily deportment of millions of people. Characterisation becomes stereotype and caricature, simplification from Scott, to L'Amour, to the genre of western films of the 1940s. Then comes another war, and the 1950s, and then the 1960s, see different kinds of western hero.

Against this panoramic backdrop, Lobey Dosser is one of the earliest examples of colonisation-in-reverse, where the crossover from American popular culture to a Scottish idiom which reappropriates and redefines it is supremely effective. In cartoon cinerama, Lobey's story embodies a distinctively Scottish reductive idiom regenerating a healthy appetite for reappropriation of authority through native sharpness and wit.

When Lobey Dosser, the Sheriff of Calton Creek, rode across page 3 of Glasgow's *Evening Times* on 24 January 1949, and for six years or so thereafter, his phenomenal appeal was certainly as much literary as it was sociological. In the early 1950s, Bud Neill's *Lobey Dosser* cartoons represented a loving but ironic counter-appropriation of American popular culture, which lingered in the west of Scotland as a legacy of the Second World War. Some of his adventures were collected and printed in book form in the 1950s at the time of the strip's original popularity. But in 1992, five of the Lobey Dosser stories were collected for a different generation altogether, in *Lobey's the Wee Boy!* and these were followed in 1998 by *Lobey Dosser: Further Adventures of the Wee Boy!*[14] ('The Wee Boy' was an affectionate term of respect in the 1950s and 1960s. By the 1970s, the comparable term was more often tinged with irony: 'Big Man'.)

Lobey's creator, Bud Neill (1911–1970), a Glasgow man, had thrilled to the daring exploits in the westerns starring William S. Hart on the flickering screen of the Troon Playhouse. These westerns presented polite heroes. Their genealogy went back to the chivalrous knights and captive maidens of Walter Scott. It was only after the Second World War that the gentleman hero cowboy was superseded by the rougher character typified by John

Illustration 6 Bud Neill, 'Lobey Dosser' *c.* 1952 (*Lobey's the Wee Boy! Five Lobey Dosser Adventures* Mainstream Publications, 1992)

Wayne, and it is curious to note how that character was superseded by the cynical asocial western hero personified by Clint Eastwood. If westerns of the John Wayne era (1940s–1950s) gave way to Italian 'spaghetti westerns' of the 1960s, even within that succession anomalies persist and demonstrate the underlying tradition pulling against the fashions of the time. The export of Scots and Irish people to the United States underlies their influence on the western genre. It might be shown that Scott's novels and stories are prototype westerns but it is perhaps more challenging to consider the films of John Ford, Howard Hawks, George Stevens and others as products of distinctly Scottish or Scots–Irish heritage. The representation of community at the heart of Ford's *The Searchers* and Stevens's *Shane*, the struggle between the generations embodied by John Wayne and Montgomery Clift in *Red River*, the pervasive patriarchal family feudalism that was evident in television westerns of the 1950s, 1960s and 1970s – *Bonanza* (1959–1973), *Rawhide* (1959–1966), *The Big Valley* (1965–1969), *The High Chapparal* (1967–1971) – all speak of social and family structures made familiar by Scott. Ford's Irish background and disposition is well-known but at the heart of his interest and a recurring theme in his films is that of displacement and displaced peoples. The theme is universalised to apply internationally in America and indeed throughout Europe and elsewhere, but its source in Irish and Scottish history and myth is important. So many of the films and television series mentioned are essentially about lonely individuals or else the efforts of families to re-establish themselves in new and hostile environments. They are about orphans, wandering far from, and often in search of, a home.

The most notable Scottish writer who literally transferred to Hollywood is Alan Sharp, whose films, *The Hired Hand* (1971) and *Ulzana's Raid* (1972), are highly nuanced revisions of western mythology, the former addressing and subverting conventions of sexuality and heroism, the latter attacking racism. *Billy Two-Hats* (1973) is less successful, with Gregory Peck's earnest Scots accent weighing heavily on the action. *Night Moves* (1975), a pessimistic reworking of the themes of morality, integrity and fallibility pre-eminent in Raymond Chandler, Dashiell Hammett and James M. Cain is much keener, bleak, poignant and grim. Sharp, who began writing important novels, *A Green Tree in Gedde* (1965) and *The Wind Shifts* (1967), in the west of Scotland, went on to script *Rob Roy* (1995). The influence of Scott is explicit, but the plot is overtly that of a western transposed.

Early in the vogue of the classic spaghetti westerns of the 1960s – especially Sergio Leone's *A Fistful of Dollars* (1964), *For a Few Dollars More* (1965), *The Good, the Bad and the Ugly* (1966) and *Once Upon a Time in the West* (1968) – the director Franco Giraldi (Frank Grafield) made the extraordinary *7 Pistole per i Mac Gregors/7 Guns for the MacGregors* (1965). The script is credited to Fernand Lion, Vincent Eagle, David Moreno and Duccio Tessari and concerns four elderly Scots pioneers and the adventures of their seven sons against a gang of Mexican horse thieves. 'Ennio Morricone [Leone's composer, whose film scores usually sound like exploding alarm-clocks] wrote the music – trombones, blowing raspberries accompanied by electric organ, doubling for bagpipes.'[15]

Sexual relations in the film also play on the notion of Scottish identity. In the opening fight, when it looks as though the elder MacGregors might be killed, Alistair kisses his wife tenderly on the forehead. Towards the end of the film, the hero Gregor is arguing with the heroine Rosita. He tells her to go and get help.

Rosita: No. Even if it means being killed, I'm staying with you.
Gregor: Hmm. I've had enough of this nonsense. Anyway, I'm a Scotsman. Women aren't allowed to argue!

He knocks her unconscious with one punch. A tender love theme soars on the soundtrack. He kisses her forehead exactly as his father kissed his mother in the opening sequence, and whispers, 'Goodbye, my darling.'

It is as well that he leaves her for she then rounds up the old folks who arrive on the scene in the final gunfight just in time to rescue the boys, riding in, dressed in kilts and tartan bonnets, with bagpipes in full belligerent voice. Just before this final shootout, Gregor tells his brothers to count their bullets: 'Remember you're Scots! Be thrifty with the ammunition!' He is told in reply, 'Telling a Scot to be thrifty, that's an insult, Gregor.' He reconsiders and revises his phrasing to a much more terse western idiom: 'Mm. Hmm. I guess you're right. I meant to say, well, *don't waste bullets!*'

As they are running out of ammunition, still surrounded by the almost inexhaustible supply of Mexican outlaws, Peter MacGregor comments, 'It's not only thrift that makes a Scot... We MacGregors were always a fightin' clan and when they went into battle in the old days they always used to have a piper playing the bagpipes at their head.' Mark MacGregor, played by Julio Perez Tabernero, says it is a pity they do not have a piper with them now. Peter pulls out his harmonica: 'But I can play us a sort of makeshift on this.' Mark approves: 'I'll just close my eyes and imagine that I'm hearin' pipes...'

Gregor: You know right now it's as if I were listening to the real thing.
David: It's the real thing. Listen.

Of course, the pipes signal the arrival of the old folks to the rescue and the climactic fight in which 'gunpowder seems as plentiful as dust'.[16]

In *A Fistful of Dollars*, the hero, the Man with No Name, is accompanied by the town bartender, Silvanito, to a bluff overlooking a border river, where the villain, Ramon Rojo, and his gang, are about to slaughter a troop of soldiers and steal a gold shipment. As they crawl up the slope, the barman says to the Man with No Name, 'It's just like playing cowboys and

Indians, isn't it?' It is a key to the distance from the myth of authenticity which Italian westerns exploit and celebrate. Playfulness exploits verisimilitude not to authenticate myth but to play with it.

In *7 Guns for the MacGregors*, the outlaws roll around behind leather armchairs and domestic furniture in the MacGregor homestead in the opening battle and Gregor changes sides to dupe the bandits and outwit the villain, just like children at play. The dynamics of comedy drive most of the film and the violence is childlike in its speed of delivery and lurid excess. Spaghetti westerns did not replicate images of authenticity in the way of Hollywood westerns. In pacing, style, verbal and visual wit, their method was to maintain the quickness and eagerness of children. When adult issues enter them – and there are many of them, especially in Leone's films – seriousness does not push playfulness away but works with it, in that opened distance. This is why the references to Scottish meanness in *7 Guns for the MacGregors* are not simply trading on the cliché and exploiting it; it is rather that we encounter the cliché in a different light, a foreign dimension, and see it as the historically constructed, politically artificial thing it is. It is transformed into classic western idiom in Gregor's memorably succinct advice – *'don't waste bullets!'*

This is appropriate in a period where the letterbox-eyed hero cynically calculates how many 'dollars' he can get away with, within an ethos where the doubleness of reliable Good Guy versus Bad Guy of the John Wayne era has been complicated by the threeness in Leone's world (not just the good and the bad but also, equally, the ugly). The representation of Scots resuscitates the patriarchal structure and device of the chivalrous, benevolent, noble family, fighting in a feudal world. The success of *7 Guns for the MacGregors* prompted Giraldi to make a sequel, *7 Women for the MacGregors* (1966), released in America as *Up the MacGregors*, in which the brothers meet seven young Irish women. There are 'rumbustious punch-ups between the Scots and the Irish over who has the best Whisky'.[17] The MacGregors may have been brought up on chilli rather than oatmeal but they are, albeit at a long distance, orphans of Sir Walter Scott. They live in a Catholic world where Manichean morality is subverted. The trickster is also a god.

But the sexism of both MacGregors movies evidently derives from the chivalric idiom of Scott and the 1940s westerns which impressed Bud Neill in the Troon Playhouse. Lobey Dosser owed much more to them than to John Wayne. But Neill was a trickster himself, ingenious, transforming the wild west iconography into one that was unmistakably Caledonian. Gloriously incongruous, beyond the grasp of reason or realism, mounted on his two-legged horse, the trusty El Fideldo, Lobey and his cartoon companions became legendary, a part of Glasgow's verbal fabric and imaginary character. Neill's elevation of the ethnic 'sidekick' to the hero's role was an ironic comment on the glamour of chin-dimpled actors. Lobey Dosser himself looks more like a wizened dwarf or a Louis L'Amour 'sidekick' than a glamorous 'leading man'.

The villain of the series was named Rank Bajin (*anglice*, Extremely Bad One), 'a creep wi' a black hood an' teeth like a dozen chipped coffee cups'.[18] He had a public school education and spoke accordingly; there was Rank's wife, Ima Bajin (I am a Bad One); there were the Indians, Chief Toffy Teeth and Pawnee Mary o' Argyll (Bonny Mary o' Argyll was a popular song); there was Dunny Dosser, Lobey's brother (for Lobey, read Lobby, vestibule, close-mouth, or entranceway to a block of flats; for Dosser, read one who sleeps rough, in his clothes, maybe in the open air, a homeless person, perhaps; for Dunny, read outside toilet). Two of the regular characters were Fairy Nuff (who wore tackety boots and spoke only in verse – a tradition from pantomime), and Rid Skwerr, a Russian spy who had defected and was employed as the official ghost of the local cemetery.

The relation between the cartoon and Glasgow pantomime traditions was close. According to Ranald MacColl, the G.I. Bride, who appears from time to time with her thumb stuck out, hoping to hitch a ride back to Partick, carrying her baby, Little Ned, under one arm, was based on a stage character called Big Beenie, another G.I. Bride, made famous by the Glaswegian panto-mime artiste, Tommy Morgan.[19] The legacy of the American presence in the west of Scotland was appreciated in more than one way. The fantastic adventures recounted in Bud Neill's labyrinthine narratives are the product of a surrealist native Scottish genius and an arsenal of Americana. The G.I. Bride, a post-war phenomenon, is the butt of neither humour nor pathos: she is simply one of the characters. As such, while the racism and sexism which are so much the staples of working-class and popular humour may not be challenged overtly by the strip, they are placed at the mercy of Neill's sympathy, humour and wit.

In the first strip series, 'Lobey Dosser: His Life Story', we are introduced to Lobey's mother by two heavy-looking, overcoated women in a Glasgow street. One passes the news: 'Mrs Dosser's hud anither wan...A wee boy....' The other replies: 'Puir sowl...That's her 18th...'[20] The humour of this and its absurd pathos is too quick to allow us to dwell on its ambivalence. In the next frame we see Lobey (unmistakable even as a baby), held aloft by his mother, who says: 'We'll jist ca' ye "Lobey", son...I've rin oot o' names...An' ye'll hiv tae bide wi' yir Auntie Mabel for there's nae room for ye here...I'll pit yir peeny on an' gie ye a piece wi' ye...Cheerio, wee man – an' mind an' tak' yir gripe watter regular...sniff, sniff, sob....'[21]

The infant Lobey sets out to march the three miles to Auntie Mabel's with his gear slung on a stick held over his shoulder. At the age of six weeks, he runs away to sea and falls in with a band of pirates and a tribe of cannibals.

Visually, the cannibals are pantomime blacks and their depiction seems like racist stereotyping typical of the era. They come from a time when Golliwogs were common children's toys, like teddy bears. But their *language* is not that of comic blacks: Hannibal, their king, admits he comes from Clydebank, and their language as they prepare for an expedition to the

'Mountain o' the Deid' is a parody of Glasgow working-class speech: 'See's a haun' wi' ma shield, Cherlie...' or 'Haw Hughie – ye've forgot ye're piece!' [22] (The word 'piece' means 'sandwich'.) The effect of this is not to ridicule blacks but to exoticise the local. It is, arguably, an anti-racist strategy whose effectiveness works through persuasive humour and speed.

After encounters with a dinosaur, an octopus and a woolly mammoth, Lobey and his companions arrive at the City of Gold. They are guided to the Palace by a 'savage' who introduces himself as a 'Varsity' graduate, 'ectually'[23] and when they meet the Queen, she speaks with impeccable English locution. But Lobey elects not to stay there, and at his own request, goes hurling down a chute to Mexico, where his western adventures begin. No more is heard of Lobey's parents or the Glasgow from which he is in permanent exile. But the Scots idioms employed in the language of the characters, counterpointed against the stereotypes shown in their visual features, suggest that wherever Lobey goes, Glasgow goes with him. And whatever is happening in Glasgow, is happening in Lobey's world too. As Ranald MacColl says, 'Moon-rockets, "single-end" rockets powered by sherbet, plutonium plants, nuclear powered trams, G.P.O. telephones, Sherman tanks, two-legged horses, pirates, barra-boys and bun-hatted wee wimmen sporting six-shooters all co-existed seamlessly in and around the Caltonesque 1880 frontier Shangri-la known as Calton Creek, Arizona.' MacColl is right to suggest that the first readers of the strip turned the pages of the evening paper eagerly 'to catch up on the *real* news of the day at Calton Creek'.[24] But the character was popular well beyond Glasgow, and Scots all over the world kept up as best they could with Lobey's latest exploits.

There is one other precedent deserving recognition here, the D.C. Thomson character, Desperate Dan. Dan first appeared in the children's comic *The Beano* in 1938, where his home town of Cactusville, with its street-lamps, post boxes and steam rollers, was a recognisable small city such as Dundee, home of his publishers, though his adventures took him all over the world. Racist stereotypes characteristic of the period are evident enough: Chinese, Sikhs, Afro-Americans, Mexicans, Eskimos are all caricatured in the strips. The English artist Dudley D. Watkins, who drew the Desperate Dan strips, was also the most famous penman of 'The Broons' and 'Oor Wullie' – whom we encountered in the Introduction. When Watkins died in 1969, D.C. Thomson employed other artists to continue work on Watkins's other comic-strip characters, but from 1969 to 1982, Desperate Dan's adventures were reprints of earlier stories. He reappeared in new stories in the 1980s and 1990s, but he was then moved inside the comic and his former place on the cover taken over by a strip called 'Cuddles and Dimples'. In an age of 'political correctness', there was a problem with Dan's brazen appetites and overwhelming masculinity (he would typically wolf down a regular diet of cow-pie with horns and tail showing out of the pastry and exhibited chronic timidity in the company of Aunt Aggie). But there was also a need to keep the character in the mould of pastiche hero. What the contrast with Lobey Dosser makes clear though, is that the ironies evoked by the Desperate Dan strip were geared towards a children's comic, whereas Lobey's slippery playfulness in the major city's daily evening paper was read by adults at least as much as children.

Lobey Dosser acquired a following across all Glasgow's social boundaries through 1949 and the 1950s. The series was a unique example of cultural appropriation in the Scotland of its time. When mass cinema audiences queued regularly for Hollywood films, Bud Neill delivered a thorough over-haul to the influx of post-war American culture: he did not emulate, he transformed. But the final point to emphasise here is that he was almost alone in doing so. Part of his popularity rests on an affection for the singu-larity of his achievement and the uniqueness of the characters he created.

James Bond (1953–1965)

It was the poet George MacBeth who brought Ian Fleming and Raymond Chandler together in 1958 for an interview recorded for the BBC. Twenty-five years later, in fragment 13 of *My Scotland* – 'the nearest I shall come to writing an autobiography'.[25] MacBeth succinctly notes the genealogy of Fleming's character:

> As in Raeburn's portrait of The Two Archers, enigmatic, half-intrinsic to the arc suspended between the bow-string and the bent yews, they leap out, smiling, the two faces. Buchan's. Fleming's. If one is to drive, sur-mounting the other, into a frail lead, as horses, racing against the current of blocking air, towards fame, money, it might be Tweedsmuir's. Neck ahead by the edge of appropriate honours, anchoring the English empire as securely as Kipling. Later it flails, tail fluke in the squirm of dependent vassals, into the beached vortex of Southern Florida, the playfields of Bond, emergent over the shirred eggs and the waffles. Half-Scotsmen, androgynous heroes of mid-cult, they amaze, worry, and flicker, ghostly candles over the vault of fiction. Close behind them in the waxed air, I hear Byron chuckle, the cracked knuckles of the bad Lord.[26]

Bond is the commercialisation of Hannay. Fleming is moving into a market much expanded from the one to which Buchan appealed, and tickling appetites Buchan would have considered vulgar. He is beating the Americans at their own game, and the pathos of his aspiration to do so (as well as his success) parallel the career of his main character.

Although his national identity has rarely received comment, James Bond is the most important character in post-war Scottish fiction. Fleming's *ouevre* is a detailed guide to Cold War era fantasy, an inversion of imperial failure and collapse into an affirmation of suave assurance and confident self-assertion. But read carefully, Bond is a mask that reveals the anxieties and formulaic resources behind itself. As Tony Bennett and Janet Woollacott rightly observe, the Bond novels (especially the later ones), 'positively bristle with allusions . . . to Britain's declining power and status'.[27] The significance of the icon is inextricable from the *zeitgeist*. Bond's world is that of Suez, the Berlin Wall, the Cuban Missile Crisis and the Space Race. As British imperial authority declines, the imperial power of America grows, but Britain – and Bond – rises in mythic status as models of benign patriarchal protectiveness for the American cousins. Yet the whole cycle of novels describes a more complex and curious weave of involvement, disengagement and return to a world of mythic archetypes: the early books clearly come out of their political context and are rooted in the history of their times but the later ones exploit the dynamics of fantasy to a far greater degree. The enemy changes from the Union of Soviet Socialist Republics and their secret department, SMERSH (or Smiert Spionam – Death to Spies) to the monomaniacal individual, Ernst Stavro Blofeld and his much more geographically elusive organisation, SPECTRE (the Special Executive for Counterintelligence, Terrorism, Revenge and Extortion). The shift is also, of course, from imperialist nationalism in the Cold War (Britain and America versus Soviet Russia) to terrorist internationalism, a world of multi-national corporate identities where loyalty is emphatically *not* rooted in any particular piece of the planet. The ambivalence here is important. The figure of Bond requires a kind of nourishment from national imperial identity. Ethnic identity is essential in the imperialist environment, but republicanism would be as dangerous as multi-nationalism to the ideology that generated him.

According to his obituary, as published in *The Times* at the end of *You Only Live Twice* (1964),

> James Bond was born of a Scottish father, Andrew Bond of Glencoe, and a Swiss mother, Monique Delacroix, from the Canton de Vaud. His father [was] a foreign representative of the Vickers armaments firm. . . . When he was eleven years of age, both his parents were killed in a climbing accident in the Aiguilles Rouges above Chamonix. . . .'[28]

Bond grew up in Kent, went to Eton briefly, then Fettes, his father's old school, where the atmosphere was somewhat Calvinistic, and both academic and athletic standards were rigorous. He left school and entered the Special Branch of the RNVR in 1941. After the war he joined the Ministry of Defence, from which point his activities 'must remain confidential, nay secret'.[29]

In Bond's fictional biography by John Pearson, the gloomy, melancholic background of the Scottish legacy is emphasised. The early Bonds were:

tough, warlike people, who followed the MacDonalds and had lived in Glencoe for generations. Three Bonds, all brothers, were slaughtered at Glencoe during the massacre of 1692. Later Bonds preserved their sturdy independence; during the eighteenth century they had prospered, whilst by the nineteenth they had produced a missionary, several distinguished doctors, and an advocate...the Bonds clung to their identity as Scots...

While this underlines the obdurate independence of the character it also affirms his adherent loyalty. Bond's great-grandfather (and his namesake) 'won a V.C. with the Highland Infantry before Sebastopol'.[30] No clearer indication could be given of the peculiarly Scottish lineage James Bond embodies.

Fleming's own first biography, also by John Pearson, suggests a more ambivalent relationship. Fleming's Scots background is well documented. His grandfather's and his father's successes (both financial and personal) chart the movement of the Flemings from Scotland into English society circles, and Ian's introduction to Eton and Oxford was the result of their aspirations. Ian's experience of Scotland, though, was severely antipathetic. In John Pearson's words, 'He had a horror of family gatherings, especially at Christmas, and would do almost anything to avoid having to go near Scotland – "all those wet rhododendrons and people with hair on their cheeks sitting around peat fires wrapped in plaid blankets".'[31]

Despite this, of course, James Bond does have May, his treasured Scottish housekeeper (first introduced in *From Russia With Love*) and in Chapter 9 of *On Her Majesty's Secret Service*, when Irma Bunt (May's opposite number) asks him if he likes the Alps, Bond (acting the part of Sir Hilary Bray) replies 'I love them...Just like Scotland.'[32] Nevertheless, there are no Scottish locations in the Bond adventures, as there are in Buchan's Richard Hannay stories. Fleming never attempted to capture the landscape of Scotland as Buchan depicted it in *The Thirty-Nine Steps* (1915), *Mr Standfast* (1919) or *The Three Hostages* (1924). And in *Huntingtower* (1922), the Gorbals Diehards (like Barrie's Lost Boys, a golden-hearted pack of orphans) acting under the wing of Dickson McCunn (who is a mix of Peter Pan and Bailie Nicol Jarvie) enact their Empire-saving adventures in a Scotland that is beautifully evoked.[33] Fleming never loved Scotland as Buchan did. Like Buchan, however, Fleming's novels are steeped in sexist and racist attitudes and stereotypes. But Fleming's world was shifting quickly (more quickly than Buchan's), even as he wrote, and James Bond is the herald of post-colonialism in a way that Richard Hannay could never have imagined.

From *Othello* to *Prester John*, the connections between racism, sexism and the significance of otherness are profound. Fleming was steeped in the attitudes of his time and I am making no great claims for him as a literary artist. But I would like to emphasise the fact that he seems genuinely interested in the point of view of women. Why else would one of the Bond novels be written as if by a woman? Moreover, Vivienne Michel, the 'co-author' of *The Spy Who Loved Me*, is Canadian (a French Canadian Catholic and an orphan from an early age herself). Her accent is remarked upon and her nationality is a distinct mark of an identity outwith the Anglo-American hegemony. The desire to write *out of* an otherness is as marked in Fleming as it is in James Joyce, and as with Joyce, it betrays the significant otherness of a national identity for which the English language itself is a mask.

Just as Bond is an object of desire for the women Fleming invents, he is an object of hatred for the villains in the books, and the villains are usually based on racial stereotypes. It is tempting to make something of the fact that three of the most memorable are red-haired (a traditionally Scottish characteristic since Rob Roy): Red Grant, Hugo Drax and Goldfinger. (And Red Grant, like Medina in Buchan's *The Three Hostages*, is associated with the idea of an independent Ireland.)

The Bond villains are in a direct line of descent from the criminal masterminds who oppose Richard Hannay and Sherlock Holmes. But there is no need to elaborate here on the importance of repression in the formation of the identity of 'others'. The difficulty of creating villains was something to which Fleming himself drew attention in the 1958 radio conversation with Raymond Chandler. The difficulty of making Bond's relations with women credible was just as acute. If Fleming's writing is often reminiscent of a pre-war ethos in its affectation of imperial assurance, the sexual freedom which is associated with the women in the Bond books gives them a distinctly post-war flavour. Umberto Eco once drew up a scheme to chart Bond's formulaic relations with women in the novels:

1. The girl is beautiful and good.
2. She has been rendered frigid by severe adolescent trials.
3. She is thus conditioned to serve the villain.
4. Bond introduces her to an appreciation of human nature.
5. Bond possesses and liberates her but (with one exception) does not establish any lasting relationship.[34]

In fact, there is more than one exception. One, of course, is Tracy, to whom he is married at the end of *On Her Majesty's Secret Service* (1963), and who is killed within a few hours of their wedding. But the first was Vesper Lynd, who kills herself at the end of the first of the series, *Casino Royale*, ten years before Tracy, in 1953. Vesper's suicide happened soon after Bond felt tempted to ask her to marry him. The conventional preservation of the independence of the male hero is observed here, but in most of the Bond novels, this is not done at the expense of the women's lives. Usually, as Eco notes, the women Bond encounters are liberated by his intervention. When they part company (in the space between novels), one is meant to assume that the women continue leading independent lives of their own, and that Bond is merely a pleasing memory for them.

But the death of Vesper Lynd haunts Bond and ten years afterwards, at the beginning of *On Her Majesty's Secret Service*, he has been revisiting her grave near Royale-les-Eaux, when he meets the woman who will become his wife. Paradoxically (in terms of the conventions of series heroes), Tracy's death does not free Bond for further adventures: it virtually kills him. He starts a downward spiral from which he never recovers. He is a broken man at the opening of *You Only Live Twice*, and in the course of that book his appetites revive only momentarily: as soon as the villain is revealed as Tracy's murderer, Bond is turned into an avenging angel of death, whose success marks the dissolution of his own purpose. He begins as a neurotic, becomes obsessively (almost suicidally) dedicated to revenge, and ultimately falls victim to amnesia. The obituary towards the end of the book is well-placed.

The symmetry of the story is notable. In his first adventure, Bond becomes a Byronic hero, flawed by love for a woman who, it is revealed, has been working for the other side. He is toughened by the attitude he must take towards her death; he must cauterise his affections. He must develop cynicism, coldness and loneliness. Vesper's death projects Bond's opposition to Soviet Russia and its spy network SMERSH, and it sets a romance formula at the heart of Cold War political tensions. There is a dated, seedy, anti-romantic quality to *Casino Royale* which gives whiffs of British inadequacy. In the context of the Cold War, the Suez crisis confirms this and the development of American power is reflected in cosmopolitanism and fantasy. As is well-known, Fleming based SMERSH on the actual Soviet spy machine, but Bond's story curves away from that historical location into a mythic dimension. This is evident enough in the continuing Bond franchise but it is already present in the tragic relationship Bond develops with Tracy. She too is in trouble, like Vesper, and Bond inevitably tries to rescue her. The international world she moves in is, however, a fantasy-land of glamour and high fashion. The evil monster who takes the villain's role is no longer based in political structures but created in mythopoeic terms: Blofeld leads SPECTRE, and the different ethos of the organisation is clear in the name. The villains in the novels through to *Goldfinger* (1959) and *For Your Eyes Only* (1960) are employed by SMERSH and the USSR but in *Thunderball* (1961), *On Her Majesty's Secret Service* (1963) and *You Only Live Twice* (1964), the villain heads SPECTRE. In the final novel, *The Man With the Golden Gun* (1965), Fleming seems to return to earlier form, as Scaramanga's employers are Castro and the USSR – but, after losing Tracy and killing Blofeld, the mythic cycle is complete. This return is symptomatic rather than curative.

Despite the undeveloped Oedipal beginning of *The Man With the Golden Gun*, Bond is now a palimpsest: as a character, he has already been completely developed and written into fulfilment. Now, that character is written *over*. He is a cardboard figure going through the motions in a pastel Caribbean in the last book, sapped of the colour and tension of his earlier excursions in that part of the world (in *Live and Let Die* and *Doctor No*). Kingsley Amis suggested that the death of Tracy would turn Bond into the apotheosis of the Byronic hero: a man with a 'secret sorrow over a woman, aggravated by self-reproach'.[35] But he was wrong. When Bond meets Tracy, he is that already (as the reference to Vesper Lynd makes clear). When Tracy dies, Bond dies too. His last line in *On Her Majesty's Secret Service* – 'we've got all the time in the world'[36] – places them in a mythic dimension, tragic lovers. Fleming recognised the appropriateness of the Bond family motto: 'The world is not enough.'[37] It certainly suggests the final, cancelled stanza of Byron's *Don Juan*, which was scored out and not intended for publication:

> But oh that I were dead, for while alive,
> Would that I neer had loved! Oh woman, woman!
> All that I write or wrote can ne'er revive
> To paint a sole sensation – though quite common –
> Of those in which the body seemed to drive
> My soul from out me at thy single summon,
> Expiring in the hope of a sensation – [38]

Fleming himself referred to Bond as a 'cardboard booby'[39] and in the BBC archive interview between Fleming and Chandler, Fleming describes Bond as 'on the whole a rather unattractive man'. Subsequently, critics have seen him as either a template for fantasy (Kingsley Amis) or simply a stooge of Empire (Tony Bennett and Janet Woollacott). But he is more than merely pathetic. Fleming's Bond is a tragic figure. And the ending of the last novel in the series, *The Man With the Golden Gun*, reverts to Bond's Scottish origins in a wistful, strangely unsatisfying way. After his mission is accomplished, Bond receives an 'Eyes Only' telegram message from M: 'THE PRIME MINISTER PROPOSES TO RECOMMEND TO HER MAJESTY QUEEN ELIZABETH THE IMMEDIATE GRANT OF A KNIGHTHOOD.'

Bond responds at once. Like Sherlock Holmes before him, he refuses the knighthood earned for services rendered to his country: 'REQUEST THAT EYE MAY BE PERMITTED COMMA IN ALL HUMILITY COMMA TO DECLINE...MY PRINCIPAL REASON IS THAT EYE DONT WANT TO PAY MORE AT HOTELS AND RESTAURANTS.' Bond knows that this is too facetious (besides, it confuses humility with venality), so he offers a more poignant explanation: 'EYE AM A SCOTTISH PEASANT AND WILL ALWAYS FEEL AT HOME BEING A SCOTTISH PEASANT AND EYE KNOW COMMA SIR COMMA THAT YOU WILL UNDERSTAND MY PREFERENCE AND THAT EYE CAN COUNT ON YOUR INDULGENCE BRACKET LETTER CONFIRMING FOLLOWS IMMEDIATELY ENDIT OHOHSEVEN.'[40]

In 1965, Fleming was writing for people who were thinking of a Bond with Sean Connery's face and voice. Indeed, his most recent biographer Andrew Lycett records that Fleming, after an initial reaction against Connery, approved.[41] He wrote the later novels with the actor in mind. Fleming saw the first two Bond films, *Dr No* (1962) and *From Russia With Love* (1963), and with his approval Sean Connery brought out the Scottish aspect of the character in memorable, momentary asides in the films.

The crucial turning point in this version of the story of cultural counter-appropriation, or colonisation-in-reverse, comes near the end of *Goldfinger*, as Bond/Connery is walking across the runway towards the small plane which is to take him to a congratulatory lunch at the White House. Bond/Connery, without breaking pace, remarks, pointing, 'I suppose I'll be able to get a drink here.' He is advised, 'I told the stewardess, liquor for three.' He asks, 'Who are the other two?' and is answered, 'Oh, there are no other two.' Connery's tone, facial expression and body language all bespeak the actor's nationality and play ironically with popular conceptions of it. It is a signal moment that marks the beginning of a recovery of confident self-determination in late twentieth-century representations of Scotland.

It is worth pausing on the coincidence of dates here, the overlap between the arc of the story in Fleming's books, and the development of the image of Bond in the person of Connery in the films and the franchise they were to lead to.

Books	Date	Films
The Spy Who Loved Me	1962	*Dr No*
On Her Majesty's Secret Service	1963	*From Russia With Love*
You Only Live Twice	1964	*Goldfinger*
The Man With the Golden Gun	1965	*Thunderball* (death of Ian Fleming)
Octopussy (posthumous)	1966	
	1967	*You Only Live Twice*

This chart makes clear how pivotal 1964 was in the saga: the trajectory of Fleming's Bond had been almost completely drawn while two things happened simultaneously in the Bond films. The first was a determining factor in all subsequent Bond movies: the escalation in gadgetry. The Aston Martin's 'ejector seat' is the first indication in the films of the excesses of techno-fantasy that were to come. But more subversively, Connery's infiltration of a Scots identity – self-ironising, comically reductive yet self-determined and independently minded – off-set the excesses of sordid violence and pornographic exploitation which, however occasionally they are explicitly present, always remain the hinterland of the James Bond story. A different reading from the conventional one of Bond as imperialist metaphor was possible – indeed, an anti-imperialist reading was now imaginable.

But that happy thought does not cancel the story's pathos. For Fleming, after 1964, in *The Man With the Golden Gun*, there is something too personal in the frailty of Bond's final telegram for it to be explained away by mere opportunism. It is self-indulgent, yet unexpectedly moving and valedictory. The last chapter of the last novel is called 'ENDIT': there is something sad and valedictory about that, too.

The post-colonial world which was coming into being through the 1950s and 1960s was to historicise Bond and M and their viewpoints of imperial stability. As Michael Denning has suggested, Bond's licence to look (as a British subject, a tourist, a man, a superior white) would be revoked.[42] In a sense this is the equivalent of the lucky escapades of Young Jim Hawkins turning into the measurements and balances of his adult narrative prose. Fleming's Bond does not live to see that happen.

In the 1970s, the British film industry turned him into a comic figure. Attempts to revivify the deeper character have failed, although the icon continued to embody the character of Britishness as only an imperial Scot could do. Tony Bennett and Janet Woollacott are surely wrong to describe him as 'first and foremost an English hero'.[43] An Englishman could neither speak nor act so honestly on behalf of all of Her Majesty's British subjects (nor embody them so well), as a Scot in Her Majesty's Service. Still, Michael Denning is right to describe 'the Bond image' as an effacing of its own origins: 'Bond is a character of the present, not one with a particular history, or regional rootedness.'[44] My point is that it is only and exactly by providing him with a Scottish background that such rooted identity could be transcended in his 'image' or mask – because, in the history of the British Empire, the Scottish nation had 'transcended' itself. Bond's only functional identity in that context is one of service.

This quality of anonymity suggests that the Bond image has a life beyond Fleming's novels, and of course this is true. It is not only an icon, it is an industry. But although occasionally recognisable atmospheric qualities were evoked in the post-Fleming films and the novels by Robert Markham (Amis again), John Gardner and others, and although more recent critical readings of Bond have further elaborated sometimes tiresomely arch theoretical approaches, the saga of James Bond as Fleming presented it is beautifully and tragically shaped, from *Casino Royale* to *On Her Majesty's Secret Service* and its aftermath, and it is complete.[45]

The Player of Games: Iain Banks (from 1984)

Iain Banks made an astonishing literary debut with his first novel, *The Wasp Factory*, in 1984. His publishers were astute to open the paperback edition of 1985 with three pages of extracts from reviews – both good and bad. Some critics hailed him as the great white hope of English literature but he is irretrievably Scottish. (He was born in Dunfermline in 1954, and brought up in the east, in North Queensferry; in 1964, the family moved to Gourock, in the west.) Other critics considered his work the uttermost expression of perverse depravity, both savage and puerile. Most of the English reviewers failed to notice a sense of humour in the book, but *The Times* said: 'Perhaps it is all a joke, meant to fool literary London into respect for rubbish.' *The Financial Times* seemed to fall for it: 'A Gothic horror story of quite exceptional quality.'[46] Banks followed *The Wasp Factory* with six further novels in rapid succession, each building bridges from dream-worlds into contemporary reality.

These novels frequently depend upon or obliquely comment on trad-itional genre fiction. Science fantasy is folded into *Walking On Glass* (1985), as three distinct but echoing stories are told parallel to each other. In each of them, wierd, mundane or fantastic, the main character seems trapped and struggling to break out from the limits of its world. *The Bridge* (1986) takes the same theme further, and is Banks's most accomplished achieve-ment. A comatose young man reviews his life up to the point of his disas-trous car crash, while struggling to get out of his frightening dream-world. It is Kafkaesque, and also reminiscent of William Golding's *Pincher Martin*, but it is primarily an adventure story, belonging to a kind of 'great escape' genre. The happy ending twists the sense of despair in Kafka or Golding into a welcome, triumphant tone.

The relation between dream and actuality becomes the source of the book's tension. For Banks, the condition of Scotland is a basal reality, but the real world in *The Bridge* is that of a crushed man in a hospital ward. The dream-Scotlands are tied down to the cramped and broken body: recovery is a possibility, but pain is inevitable. Towards the end of the book, with lovely irony, the character tells himself: 'Take it easy. Lie back and think of Scotland. Just calm down, laddie. Breathe, feel your blood pump, feel the tucked-in weight of the blanket and the sheets, feel the tickle where the tube goes in through your nose....'[47]

Espedair Street (1987) focuses on the world of rock music and a reclusive musician in Glasgow. Urban realist comedy (familiar from Billy Connolly, naturalist theatre and earlier Music Hall traditions) collides with the biography of a rock star at the end of his musical career, and at the start of another kind of life. *Canal Dreams* (1989) is an eerie mixture of exotic espionage thriller and hallucinatory horror fiction. *The Wasp Factory* itself was thought of by some critics as belonging to the Horror genre, although Banks distances himself from that genre, and in an interview published in 1990 claimed that he had read hardly any Stephen King, for example.[48]

Banks's sense of humour delivers him from the Horror genre. His most ambitious novel, *The Crow Road* (1992) begins: 'It was the day my grand-mother exploded...'[49] – and goes on to portray a broad range of eccentric characters over two generations of the McHoan family. The novel is centred on Prentice McHoan, a Glasgow University student whose investigations into his family's past lead him to the solution of one of its darkest secrets. As Prentice unearths a number of unsuspected truths, he comes to terms with himself, his father and his world. The novel deliberately exploits a fluent and journalistic idiom, from the sensational first line on. While *The Crow Road* is a murder mystery, a very black comedy, an infuriating love story, a tale of a young man growing up, a dynastic family saga and an exploration of the relations between dream and actuality, its central concern is the tension and support that exist simultaneously between the world we are given and the worlds we imagine. The bridges formed thereby are affirmations of the world that imagination helps us shape.

Complicity (1993) brings the brutally competitive aspect of modern Britain into focus and opens with an apparently ruthless main character obsessed with fashionable drugs, high-speed cars, and sadomasochistic sex. Banks's *ouevre* is entirely of the era of Margaret Thatcher and John Major: Conservative Party rule in the United Kingdom.

Banks was veering into fantasy while writing these novels, folding graphic accounts of imaginary acts into vivid depictions of a mundane world, populated by trapped, lonely or puzzled people. His main characters are often adolescent, or full of adolescent concerns. Developing the fantasy more exclusively, he counterpointed the output listed above with a series of science fiction short stories, collected in *The State of the Art* (1991: the stories date from 1987 to 1989), and a series of vast science fiction novels, which he described in the 1990 interview as 'space operas'. *Consider Phlebas* (1987), *The Player of Games* (1988), *Use of Weapons* (1990) and *Against A Dark Background* (1993) certainly conform to Banks's description of 'space opera': 'Space opera works on a broad canvas, it gives an impression of the operatic where some science fiction might feel like a small ensemble. Space opera is going for the big effect, with lots of characters, gigantic space ships, and is usually set in a context of conflict. Yet in a way I am just trying to tell a yarn. There's all this space paraphernalia, but you can paraphrase the story as just being about a ship-wrecked sailor who falls in with a gang of pirates and goes off in search of buried treasure....' Banks agreed with the interviewer's description: 'Robert Louis Stevenson "somewhere out there".'[50]

What unifies this large and various corpus is a consistently immediate and arresting pitch. Although there are longeurs in the space operas where some of the arias seem to extend to infinity, the opening of *The Crow Road* is not untypical of the kind of imaginative velocity at which Banks is most comfortable. The dramatic (indeed, melodramatic) moments are sometimes formulaic, but often the formulae themselves are of interest. Banks writes with the fluency of a good journalist (as Fleming did), and the popular mass-appeal of his style has been rewarded by an international readership, both for his 'mainstream' novels and in the science fiction genre. *Whit* (1995) followed a Candide-like innocent on an exploration of the modern city and her family past, a female Prentice uncovering hypocrisy and maturing

184 The Theatre of Infinity

her own worldly wisdom. But it was in *A Song of Stone* that Banks entered dark territory again.

In 1939, the great artist Jack Butler Yeats remarked, 'War has its charm. It feeds something that all men and women long for – excitement. Indeed I have thought that if the range of guns could have been limited by the League of Nations...the tourist companies could have continued for their customers. "Travel round the world and see the wars from a swivel chair."' [51] And of course, every night on television, every day in newspapers, millions of us do.

A Song of Stone (1997) is a dark, pessimistic anti-war parable. While contemporary popular media seems complicit in making meaningful expression of grief increasingly difficult, and people seem increasingly reluctant to attempt any deep understanding of the causes of barbarism, here, in the form of popular fiction, Banks offers a frightening story about our capacities for self-destruction. It gives no relief.

No state is named as a location for the novel's events; but if refugees and the ruined castle suggest contemporary or near-future Europe, the sense that savagery is anyone's potential condition is universal. In a sense, despite the jeeps, guns and shrapnel, the story feels as if it might have taken place in an unknown past, or that we are doomed to repeat it in an unknowable future.

The plot is skeletal: Abel, a landowner, with his lover/sister, abandons his ancestral home, attempting retreat with a directionless stream of displaced humanity, only to be taken back by an army lieutenant and her small band of soldiers. In the castle and in skirmishes around it, the soldiers attempt to regroup and Abel witnesses the final destructions of the symbols of permanence his inheritance has given him. The mortal end of the main characters is unreservedly appalling, both liquifyingly brutal and irredeemably tragic.

But perhaps the most stunning creation in the novel is the character of the lieutenant. The abundance of her authority, strength, speed and intelligence makes her entirely memorable and, undoubtedly, frighteningly attractive. If the events described occur in a 'contrarily minor eddy of creation in these fiercely corrosive times' then the lieutenant 'is a spirit freed by the re-ordering implicit in this general disorder'. Abel observes, 'That which has dragged us down has buoyed her up.' She is 'one of those for whom such troubles are in truth a liberation, providing the making of the individual character within the theatre of this greater destruction'. As Margaret Thatcher once said, 'How thin is the crust of order over the fires of human appetite and the lust for naked power.'

Despite the doom that falls in *A Song of Stone*, Banks remains one of the last defiantly unreconstructed optimists. At the tail-end of the managerially over-populated 1990s, he wrote *The Business* (1999), a thoroughly refreshing satire on the whole stale matter of multi-national corporate power. The glossy vacuity of the jargon which sounded throughout the decade, counterpoints the real work of *The Business*. The Business is a long-term high-level global corporation whose effectiveness depends on acuity, insight, organisation, probity, imagination, speed and balance. Always ahead of the contemporary, it is opposed to dullness, ignorance, dysfunction, indifference and procrastination. After all, action is more fun.

Kate Telman, a senior executive with fast knowledge of technological developments, uncovers a well-hidden plot at the highest levels of the organisation, and has to determine her own position and the deepest needs of her own desires before she can act – for, or against, the benefit of others.

From Silicon Valley (USA) to Silicon Glen (Scotland), from ski-slopes to ranch-house, from Swiss chateau to a marvellously labyrinthine, Gothic English mansion, from luxury yacht to Himalayan principality (of which Kate may – or may not – become princess), the story's rapidly changing locations keep you on the move. It is a risky book, with a first-person female narrator whose first clue is an early hour phone-call from a friend who has just woken up to find he has had most of his teeth mysteriously extracted. But then, risk is business.

I want to go back and focus briefly on *The Wasp Factory*, because I think it presents a handful of key images and ideas which Banks has elaborated and developed in his later fiction, but which underlie all of it. *The Wasp Factory* sets out to be sensational and nasty. It is a deliberate excavation of an adolescent world written by an archaeologist of that world close enough to remember its pains as clearly as its pleasures, and distanced enough to ironise them. The ironies come at the reader's expense, as well as the author's. The first chapter opens with the heads of mice, seagulls, two dragonflies and a rat, looking out blindly from the 'Sacrifice Poles' surrounding an east-coast island connected to the mainland by a footbridge. The main character, Frank, an adolescent boy, keeps the heads fresh, and thinks of them as a protective warning system. When the local policeman arrives to tell his father that his brother Eric has just escaped from an asylum and is on his way back to the island, the tension in the book begins to work. As Eric comes closer, burning dogs and phoning Frank to threaten his imminent arrival, a circling sense of destiny forecloses on the novel's options.

Island life with Frank is an anti-pastoral, an inverted idyll. He introduces us to his arsenal of weapons and takes us on a number of adventures, including his vengeful destruction of a rabbit warren, and fills in the details of his past. As a child, his genitals were torn off by a savage dog. Developing an attitude of whimsical cruelty, he murdered an irritating cousin by dropping an adder into his hollow wooden leg. He encouraged his baby brother to beat an unexploded mine with a wooden stick, and effectively murdered him. And he sent another young cousin on a fatal flight, across the North Sea attached to a home-made kite.

Frank's cruelty is puerile but the ironic tone of Banks's writing should be emphasised. The breathless pace at which horrific events are recounted is set against the cool and unflustered character of the narrator. Told in the first person, the confessional becomes conspiratorial as the reader is introduced to Frank's imagination at its most febrile. He retains the appeal of a gentleman mass murderer (think of the film, *Kind Hearts and Coronets*), while behaving like a hooligan. This is clear from his drunken loquacity going home after a night at the local pub:

> I saw the sign for Union Street where it was fixed to a low wall. I turned to Jamie and then the girl, cleared my throat and said quite clearly: I didn't know if you two ever shared – or, indeed, still do share, for that matter...the misconception I once perchanced to place upon the words contained in yonder sign, but it is a fact that I thought the 'union' referred to in said nomenclature delineated an association of working people, and it did seem to me at the time to be quite a socialist thing for the town fathers to call a street...but...I was disabused of this sadly over-optimistic notion when my father – God rest his sense of humour – informed me that it was the then recently confirmed union of the English and Scottish parliaments the local worthies – in common with hundreds of other town councils throughout what had until that point been an independent realm – were celebrating...
>
> The girl looked at Jamie. 'Dud he say sumhin er?'[52]

The ellipses here cover a fair amount of eloquently garbled circumlocution which exacerbates the ponderous humour and the preposterous situation. This loquacity is soon followed by a bout of vomiting, leaving Frank with a head 'like a ripe tomato, ready to burst'.[53]

The diametric opposite to Frank's liveliness provides the most nightmarish image in the book. To explain why his brother broke down and was locked away, Frank gives us Chapter 9: 'What happened to Eric'. This recounts Eric's work as a young man in a ghoulish ward for babies and children so badly deformed they would die outside of hospital. Finding a child lying on the floor smiling inanely, Eric approaches, only to discover, suddenly and sickeningly, that the boy is dead, his brain-pan teeming with maggots.

The force of the image in context is straight out of the worst horror films, but its *grand guignol* should not obscure its symbolic weight. The child's brain-dead smile and Frank's lively and profligate nastiness are the opposite sides of a teeming, vital universe. As with the absurd peroration on 'Union Street' the symbolism of images, words and casual actions is heavily underscored. As Frank tells us in Chapter 7: 'All our lives are symbols. Everything we do is part of a pattern we have at least some say in. The strong make their own patterns and influence other people's, the weak have their courses mapped out for them. The weak and the unlucky, and the stupid. The Wasp Factory is part of the pattern....'[54]

At the heart of the book is the Wasp Factory itself, and over half of the novel is spent working up to the moment when it is put into action. When it comes, it is something of an anti-climax unless one acknowledges the symbolic significance attached to it. The Wasp Factory is an enormous clock-face, placed flat in the attic and redesigned as a maze for live wasps. Once introduced, a wasp has to follow any one of a series of options, all of which lead to its death (by drowning, electrocution, a carnivorous plant or other means), but all of which are variable and open to the insect's momentary preference. Like Tarot cards, the mode of death foretells by its imagery imminent events. Symbolically, it is a platform upon which mortality plays itself out. But the clock-face itself comes from an old Royal Bank of Scotland building; Frank discovered it in the town dump. While it is a universal sign for time, it also suggests the idea of Scotland as a failed economic unit, a lapsed state.

The attempt to find out the truth of his own lapsed state leads Frank to the discovery of what he takes to be his own genitalia, tiny and pickled in a jar in his father's study, along with a quantity of hormone pills. Frank thinks of his parents as children of the 1960s and he suspects that his father's domesticity and his mother's wayward independence (she makes a brief appearance as a wandering biker) might signify their reversal of gender-roles. When Frank confronts his father at knife-point, he discovers his father's genitalia to be intact. His father reveals that he has been feeding the hormone pills to Frank in a bizarre attempt to conceal his female identity. Eric's return is indeed an anti-climax after this revelation. The novel concludes: 'Poor Eric came home to see his brother, only to find (Zap! Pow! Dams burst! Bombs go off! Wasps fry: *ttsss!*) he's got a sister.'[55]

As the language here suggests, *The Wasp Factory* might be thought of as an 'underground' or 'adult comic' like *Maus* (which effectively deals with the horrors of the Holocaust by employing the form of the graphic novel). The lurid sensationalism of the novel enhances its comic book qualities, yet far from diminishing its seriousness, the result is a diabolically truthful mini-ature. Chapter 4, 'The Bomb Circle', can thus be read as a critique of power and its abuses. And the novel as a whole can be read as a critique of values associated with the 1960s, from the point of view of the late 1970s or early 1980s. When Frank's father gives him copies of *The Tin Drum* and *Myra Breckenridge*, the implications are clear.

This accounts for the opposition between punks and hippies, embodied in the relationship between Frank and his father. It would also account for the deeper resonance of the book as a satirical reading of J.D. Salinger's *The Catcher in the Rye*, another *livre de cachet* in its own time. Frank Cauldhame is a version of Holden Caulfield (who ends up in a sanatorium), updated to the age of Space Invaders and the Sex Pistols. Instead of a sister, Phoebe, 'out there', he has a brother, who, on his return, discovers that he has a sister still at home. Banks offers a ruthless critique of American sentimen-talism and the idealism of the 1960s, playing the expectations of his readers (which differ according to their own age and background) off against that of his characters. In this respect his writing is exceptionally adroit.

The Bogie Man (1989–1993)

The graphic novel or comic book reaches full maturity in the Scottish idiom with *The Bogie Man*. It is an essential text of late twentieth-century Scottish literary culture.

Illustration 7   John Wagner, Alan Grant and Robin Smith, 'The Bogey Man' 1989–1990

In the first series (issued as four comic books from 1989 to 1990), Francis Forbes Clunie, an inmate of a Scottish asylum for the mentally ill, escapes one New Year's Eve, to exercise his fantasy by taking on the persona of Humphrey Bogart in a bizarre series of adventures set in the Glasgow of 1990, when the city carried the title of 'European Capital of Culture'. By 1993 an American adventure (*The Manhattan Project*) and another series (*Chinatoon*) carried the saga forward and a self-contained film version was broadcast on BBC Scotland in December 1992. The titles of each of the four issues of the first series reflect their sources: 'Farewell, My Loonie' and 'The Wrong Goodbye' refer to Chandler, of course, and B. Traven and Ernest Hemingway provide the titles of 'The Treasure of the Ford Sierra' and 'To Huv and Huvnae'.

The Bogie Man is a singularly Scottish phenomenon (the title itself is an idiomatic Scottish pun – a 'bogie man' is a nocturnal figure of threat); but (like Lobey Dosser) it is unimaginable without American sources. The television film version, written by Paul Pender, produced by Andy Park and directed by Charles Gormley, is poised between festive humour (it was a Christmas show) and film noir macabre – it transgresses the genres. Clunie is a kind of hero – but he might also be a kind of villain. In one scene, 'Lauren MacCall' (who manages a soup kitchen for down-and-outs) introduces herself to Clunie. (In the comic book series, the corresponding character bears the equally idiomatic name 'Yvonne Skelly'.) Clunie gives his own name as Riley, because Lauren has an Irish voice. But when he asks, she tells him she was born in Glasgow, and continues: 'I came back here to look for my roots.' Clunie approves. 'Good idea, kid. Everyone in the world should know who they are.'[56]

The traditional Romance-formula love story enacted by Francis and Lauren is a counterpoint to the blossoming relationship between Sergeant Ure and Dr Branch. Meanwhile, the plot is revolving around Gus McCurdie's plan to take over the soup kitchen and turn it into a fast-food joint. McCurdie is also the villainous criminal ringleader Mr Happy of the Happy Gang, fortuitously uncovered by Clunie's schizoid antics. 'Mr Happy' is a reference to a character from a series of children's books, *Mr Men*, by Roger Hargreaves. The otherwise blank but smiling face was used widely in a promotional campaign through the 1980s and early 1990s with the banner catch-phrase 'GLASGOW'S MILES BETTER' (or, 'GLASGOW SMILES BETTER'). But behind the topical reference, there is a perhaps unconscious recollection of Hamlet's observation that a man 'may smile, and smile, and be a villain'.

In the television film version, the soup-kitchen for the homeless (where the walls are dingy and even the heroine, Lauren MacCall, smokes cigarettes) presents the antithesis to the new Glasgow of fast-food, nicotine-free drinking parlours and boutiques, the chic, svelte 'European City of Culture' in which McCurdie thrives, an arbitrageur in new money and designer drugs. The function of the soup-kitchen is to provide another exact counterpoint – against the new, the nostalgic. The tone was not uncommon at the time. The recalcitrant eponymous hero of the internationally popular Scottish televison thriller series *Taggart* memorably commented in one episode, 'I remember Glasgow when culture was something that grew on walls.' But in *The Bogie Man*, the inhabitants of the soup kitchen (unlike Taggart) have adapted to the new conditions. Poor Joe the Tramp, instead of asking for some small change for a drink, complains that he needs at least '200 quid' for a season ticket for the opera.

In a variation on the graphic book version, the TV film allows for Clunie's personality (as played by Robbie Coltrane) to accommodate those of Arnold Schwarzenegger and Sean Connery (as James Bond) as well as Humphrey Bogart. Clunie's ability to mimic multiple personalities from popular culture and not only inhabit their stories but weave them in new and elaborate ways into his own is the counterpoint to his sense of himself as an abandoned waif, alone in the world. When he goes into 'Tommy Trotter's', the bar owned by Gus McCurdie, the jukebox country and western background music (crooning 'High in the saddle...') gives way to the heroine's live rendition of 'Nobody's Child'. The song is credited to Mel Foree and Cy Coben and was popularised in a recording by Hank Snow in 1949, then recorded by the Beatles in 1961 in Hamburg in an arrangement by Tony Sheridan and released as a B-side on a single in 1964, and recorded again by the Travelling Wilburys for the Romanian Angel Appeal in 1990. That is, it was first released in straight-faced, sentimental style as a plea from the heart for compassion and care, but our text comes to us through the renewed popularity it was given when Billy Connolly recorded it in the 1970s and it became ironically, critically and comically referred to as Scotland's national anthem. In the context of the folk-song revival and the popularity of country and western music, especially in the west of Scotland, Connolly's version played havoc with the song's earnestness but also exploited the potency of its appeal. This change of interpretive attitude and its popular reception, eagerly approving the irony, suggests a development away from self-pity towards self-consciousness and a healthy derision of the sham and pretentious. It is this that lies behind the tender, nostalgic version of it heard in *The Bogey Man*:

> As I was slowly passing
> An orphanage one day
> I stopped there for a moment
> Just to watch the children play
>
> Alone a boy was standing
> And when I asked him why
> He turned with eyes that could not see
> And he began to cry:

> I'm nobody's child
> I'm nobody's child
> Just like a flower
> I'm growing wild
>
> No Mummy's kisses
> And no Daddy's smiles
> Nobody wants me
> I'm nobody's child

In the television film, the final confrontation between McCurdie and the Bogie Man takes place at 2.00 am in the Glasgow Necropolis. When Clunie tells McCurdie that he cannot be bought off, McCurdie asks him what he wants. 'I want you to give yourself up. I want you to confess to your crimes. I want you to make reparations to your victims. And I want you to stop poisoning this city.'

'And I want', McCurdie replies, 'a return to the old values ... you know, when men were men and joined razor gangs and lived up closes and only the strong survived – you know, the real Glasgow, before all this "culture" crap ....'

McCurdie places himself in another fictional (or semi-fictional) tradition from popular culture: he presents himself as a direct descendent of the world of Alexander McArthur and H. Kingsley Long's novel *No Mean City* (1935): the Glasgow of the hard men, tenement slums, violence and villains. (The mainstream literary inheritance of this world in Scottish fiction is to be found in the work of William MacIlvanney, especially in the 'Laidlaw' novels, which also exploit American hard-boiled detective and police procedural conventions.) By citing the conventions of that world, McCurdie provides a satisfactory way of concluding the film. When Clunie shoots him in the climactic gun-battle, the conventions are being observed.

Clunie's dreams come true in the end. He falls, wounded, on the tombstone of his mother – suddenly, traumatically realising the truth of his own personality and history – and as Lauren, Dr Branch, Sergeant Ure and a nasty English sharpshooter look on, he returns to being simply Francis Clunie – the Bogie Man no longer. Dr Branch, however, quietly hints at the possibility of a relapse at some future time. ('Yes, the Bogie Man's gone – barring regressive trauma, of course.') But the graphic novel ends with Francis in full flight. The literary conventions exquisitely parodied in the book are different in effect from the filmic conventions parodied in the television version.

Unlike Lobey Dosser, *The Bogie Man* comic books were deliberately aimed at an international readership. The 'European City of Culture' label attached to Glasgow in 1990 allowed the city to present itself in a different image from the one which had prevailed internationally since the 1930s, and which McCurdie calls down upon himself in the climax described above. Clever, allusive, self-controlled, linguistically witty and quick, festive, celebrative, generous in spirit and above all funny, the comic books present a Glasgow that is characteristically *expressive* – precisely the opposite of its oppressive 1930s image. Wordplay and linguistic inventiveness abound. Language is shown to be a more subtle manoeuvre than physical violence.

When McCurdie encounters a flatulent henchman, topicality (in 1990, in the US Navy base in the Holy Loch, missiles were stockpiled just outside Glasgow, near the Erskine Bridge) combines with ribald wit: 'It's well seein' your name's Erskine. Your erse can do more damage than a Polaris missile!' In the TV film, Clunie is able to evoke a range of different celluloid heroes, but in the comic book, he is obsessed exclusively with Humphrey Bogart. In the comic book, the verbal brio of the writing is conveyed by the climactic dialogue between Clunie and Yvonne, which takes place in Glasgow Central Station. It glitters with misunderstanding, as the Bogie Man elaborates his fantasy with various references to the film *Casablanca*, while for Yvonne, on board a train about to leave for Carstairs (where a well-known 'secure' mental hospital is located) the comprehension slowly starts to dawn.

Bogie: Have you any idea what you've got to look forward to if you stay here? Nine chances out of ten we'd both wind up in a concentration camp.
Yvonne: Concentration camp?
Bogie: Inside of us we both know you belong with Victor. You're part of his work – the thing that keeps him going.
Yvonne: Victor? Who the hell is *Victor*? . . . Whit are ye haverin' aboot noo? Victor? Concentration camp? Carstairs? Phoney Fat Man – Big Birds! Nothin' you say makes any *sense*, Bogie! I'm rapidly comin' tae the conclusion the polis wuz *right* aboot you! You are roond the *twist* – aff yer *chump* – yer heid is fulla broken *bottles*! Ye ken whit Ah mean? You are totally *radio rental*!
Bogie: The world's crazy, sweetheart – but it doesn't take much to see that the problems of three little people don't amount to a hill of beans.
Yvonne: Three?[57]

The comic books' sophisticated humour, playing self-consciously on the exaggerated language and postures and *look* of familiar Hollywood gangster, adventure and film noir conventions, was intended to appeal to American and international readers as well as to Scottish ones and was successful in the United States and internationally. The latest issues were eagerly anticipated in New Zealand. The comic book Clunie actually *resembles* Bogart a little more closely than the actor who played him, Robbie Coltrane. The success of the ploy is attested by Clunie's second outing, *Chinatoon*, in which Spinbinnie hospital burns down, releasing him to new adventures.

In surprising contrast to the television film, which takes off from the premise that the violent death of Clunie's mother triggered his insane quest, Mrs Clunie actually appears in the comic book series, alive and well. A reporter tracks her down (his father is never mentioned). Her optimism reaches the heights. Asked whether she ever considered seeking professional help for the child, she replies 'It was just a *childhood fantasy*. I knew he'd soon grow out of it.' The reporter exclaims, 'Mrs Clunie – Francis is *forty*!' She answers: 'There's time yet, son!'

There was also an American adventure timed for US release in July 1992 as an 'Election Special'. In *The Manhattan Project*, Clunie finds his way to New York and kidnaps Dan Quayle (then Vice-President of the United States). Pursued by the FBI, he foils their attempts to trap him while rescuing the Vice-President from what he takes to be an assassination attempt. As he says at the end of the first series, 'The story ain't over till the Fat Lady sings . . .'

Scotland: an orphan of statehood

The line I have drawn in this chapter takes us through four sets of texts from the popular fiction of post-war Scotland, from 1949 to 1993. It reveals significant historical change specifically in the increasingly self-confident use of cultural models and in the increasingly international appeal made by the 'Scottishness' of these texts, in whatever degree of self-conscious deployment.

In the early 1950s, Bud Neill's loving but ironic appropriation of American popular culture in *Lobey Dosser* was a fairly lonely example. The appeal of Lobey Dosser was to a satirical intelligence. Critical readings of contemporary films like *Whisky Galore!* (1949) or *The Maggie* (1954) – in the latter film an American businessman is outwitted and upstaged by the crew of a West Coast puffer – have interpreted them as sentimental compensation-fantasies, in which native wit and wiliness outsmart and outlast American money and bravado; more sympathetic analysis suggests that these films offered a deeper critique. Certainly, both respond to the moment of quasi-colonial imposition with intelligent engagement, rather than defeatism or passive retreat and this is carried further in Bill Forsyth's refashioning of the convention in ·*Local Hero* (1983). We will return to screen media in the next chapter, but here we should note that along with *Lobey Dosser*, the 1940s and 1950s films are relatively rare examples of self-assertion. By the time of *The Bogie Man*, however, in the late 1980s and early 1990s, the American models and cultural icons could be deployed to more general effect (even to the extent of exporting the Glasgow Bogart back to America for the 1992 election). As we shall see, this reappropriation extends to Scottish writers taking up the Batman saga and bringing the 'caped crusader' to Scotland. The pleasure of such deployment is evident enough in the popularity of the texts, but here I want to emphasise the nature of the cultural shift that has taken place.

In our era, we are familiar with the condition in which texts talk to each other. Novels beget films which in turn beget novels. Comic books, films and television programmes beget each other. The culture of America bleeds into Scotland, but this can bring a strange transfusion of health, with an enhancement of sharp wit and caustic, derisive laughter. If the character of our epoch is one of intertextuality, a mixing and mingling of genres, then cultural distinction is not to be found in isolation but in confident modes of dialogue and counter-appropriation, a more assured use of the masks made newly available after 1945. This can be seen happening in the *Lobey Dosser* series and in the James Bond saga, as the character reverts to his ancestry and the actor insinuates his accent and pattern. But the tendency increases noticeably through the 1980s and early 1990s, as in Iain Banks's novels and the *The Bogie Man* series. The process is part of a general cultural condition. These texts of popular Scottish fiction represent a developing confidence. If we began this chapter with Byron, wandering and outcast, we end with the Bogie Man, a stray, certainly, but very much at home in a world of multi-valent media.

Just as Raymond Chandler required a mythic world of chivalry and honour to validate and valorise Philip Marlow's world of mean streets and shady dives, Scotland provides a mythical, sub-textual identity for the fictional worlds of these 'heroes'. But for Scotland, the long-term effect of the unions of 1603 and 1707 was to create a stateless nation in both actual political and imaginary space. The flourishing of a distinct national culture in late twentieth-century Scotland co-existed with the widely felt absence of any vital political entity. Scotland was in search of its own statehood, a nation orphaned from itself.

The texts we have looked at might be complemented by numerous others. We started this book with Burns and Walter Scott but we might suggest that further work remains to be done on the nineteenth- and early twentieth-century works of R.M. Ballantyne, S.R. Crockett, J.M. Barrie, Fiona MacLeod, Neil Munro, Annie S. Swan, Compton Mackenzie, John Buchan and Eric Linklater, and in the later twentieth century, the crime genre fiction of Hugh C. Rae, William McIlvanney, Gordon Williams and Terry Venables, Glenn Chandler, Ian Rankin, Quentin Jardine, Denise Mina and Robbie Coltrane's ground-breaking television series *Cracker*, massively opposed to political correctness, or the historical romance fiction of Jessica Stirling, Dorothy Dunnett and others. The list is open. These texts are very much of their own time – as any texts of popular culture are, by definition. Therefore, necessarily, their individual historical contexts show that as they bequeathe their legacies, their own historical moments will pass. Of course, the period in which Scotland made such orphans as these and remained estranged from statehood is itself historical. So if change comes surely for 'Nobody's Children' then someday 'Nobody' might be 'Somebody' once more.

9

It Happened Fast and it was Dark: Cinema, Theatre and Television, Comic Books[1]

Cinema

The history of the representation of Scotland and Scottishness in television and film presents innumerable examples of the crass cliché but it also reveals unexpected complexities. It is not defined by its medium. Film is not only film. Both the complexities and the clichés were developed from literary forms and work alongside and in dialogue with them. Film is literature.

Scotland is the oldest of European nations and in the media made possible by modern technology, the nation remains a central question. From the country's foundations vivaciously depicted in the saga of William Wallace to the physical and linguistic energy abounding among the 1990s drug-addicts of Irvine Welsh's Leith, nationality in 1990s Scottish cinema was a continuing concern. How much did Mel Gibson understand about what he was tapping into with *Braveheart* and what he was giving to the Scottish National Party? Was there actual moral conviction in all the Hollywood neon and glitz? Whose conviction? Alex Salmond, leader of the Scottish National Party between 1990 and 2000, commented,

> In 1995, *Braveheart* mania broke out, and it had a pretty powerful political impact. The SNP campaigned on the back of the film, and surged to 30 per cent in the polls. I well remember 20th Century Fox sending the SNP a lawyer's letter demanding that we 'cease and desist' from distributing *Braveheart* leaflets outside cinemas. They changed their minds when I gently pointed out that while we may have appropriated the stills from their film, they had appropriated the story of our hero![2]

The Conservative Scottish Secretary Michael Forsyth was roundly booed at the *Braveheart* premiere. The road was opening up to the 1997 referendum when the people of Scotland voted overwhelmingly in favour of a resumed parliament, devolved from Westminster to Edinburgh.

But to understand how the rising tide of national self-confidence in Scotland in the 1990s altered the country's political identity, *Braveheart* would have to be held alongside its contemporary post-punk version, *Trainspotting* (directed by Danny Boyle, 1996). They are two sides of the same coin, for what is Gibson's Wallace if not Hollywood's wode version of Mark Renton, and what is Ewan McGregor's Renton if not the defiant hero in extremity, taking drugs, as his author puts it, 'in psychic defence'?[3] There is a complex hinterland to these strange and unpredicted sibling film successes.

The assertion of national identity traditionally associates individual and landscape and remains politically ambivalent. The unionist argument is that national identity can be incorporated by the British state and express itself through patriotic unionism. In 1805, in Canto 6, stanza 1, lines 1–3 of *The Lay of the Last Minstrel*, Walter Scott made the ultimate Romantic identification of self and land:

> Breathes there the man, with soul so dead,
> Who never to himself hath said,
> This is my own my native land![4]

One of the most memorable scenes in the film version of Irvine Welsh's *Trainspotting* shows the four main characters arriving by train in the middle of a typically Romantic Scottish landscape. Their response to Scotland's natural beauty is rejection. One of them asks, 'Doesn't it make you proud to be Scottish?' and is answered with stunning invective by the central character, Renton, who says he hates being Scottish, because the Scots are 'the scum of the earth, the most wretched, servile, miserable, pathetic trash [...] we can't even pick a decent culture to be colonised by' – and all the fresh air in the world will not make any difference.[5]

This is not an escape from national identity, it is the curse of it. Fresh air and natural beauty magnify the frustrations of the stateless nation. If 'Scotland takes drugs in psychic defence' then the nationalism of Walter Scott has not been abandoned at all, but its tendency towards complacency has been shattered. It is nationalism of a kind, reintroduced in a different mask: Renton's speech *depends upon* a national distinction in being Scottish (as opposed to English – 'we can't even pick a decent culture to be colonised by'). In a text so blatantly concerned with operations of the body and bodily functions as *Trainspotting* this negative identification of self and land distorts and reinterprets Scott's conservative affirmation. Indeed, such juxtaposition throws light back on the ambivalence of Scott's position: while he appears to endorse patriotic unionism his poem is after all, the lay of the *last* minstrel, signifying the final representative of a kind of Scot and Scottish song that cannot be incorporated into a new world and may well die in it. Yet the minstrel and his song might be surplus to the requirements of nascent imperialism (as was the Whistler), but their values resurface and are asserted once again in the late nineteenth century and then irreversibly in the 1920s. In any event, it would be too simple to describe Victorian imperialism simply as the villain in the story: Victoria herself supported and fostered particular aspects of Scottish music-making and thus kept the material in some form of currency, even as the pragmatic politics of the situation changed.

As with these changing pragmatic politics, screening Scotland is a phenomenon that works in a varied spectrum, from blatant literalism to subtle gradation. Hollywood constructions, the Grierson-led documentary tradition, the significant development of television versions of Scotland, new Scottish 'art' cinema, the institutions which have fostered production and the themes and ideas which preoccupied producers, and finally the nouveau-chic and nouveau-kitsch in popular representations of Scottishness are all part of the story.[6] They lead to a cautious but affirmative positioning at the outset of the twenty-first century, where the liabilities, embarrassments and clichés of the past can be seen in a critical but sympathetic light, and the potential for a more comprehensive understanding suggests a ground of unprecedented possibility.

This comprehensiveness distinguishes Duncan Petrie's book *Screening Scotland* (published in 2000) from its most important predecessors: Forsyth Hardy's *Scotland in Film* (1990) and *From Limelight to Satellite: A Scottish Film Book* (1990), edited by Eddie Dick.[7] Petrie's pitch is much more inclusive of television screening as well as film, and complemented by discussion of the economic and industrial modes of production in the whole political context of cultural change in the twentieth century.

The most damning indictment of representations of Scotland within the field of British and American film and TV came in the slim 1982 volume, *Scotch Reels*, edited by Colin McArthur. McArthur judged that cinematic representation of Scotland and the Scots had been characterised by a total inadequacy in addressing 'historical and contemporary reality'. He called for film-makers to search for 'a path through the myths to reality'. Petrie offers a critique of McArthur's study while acknowledging that 'it provides an invaluable starting point to thinking systematically and critically about the dominant cinematic representations that have defined a certain national image'.[8]

The antidote to the belittling image inherent in the clichés can be found not only in film but also in literary sources. The dark visions in the novels of George Douglas Brown and John MacDougall Hay were contemporary demolition-jobs on the benevolent 'Kailyard' fiction where the focus was the small town looked after by a benevolent minister, a world of 'light romance', 'boy's-own adventures' and 'harmless escapism'. In Douglas Brown's novel *The House with the Green Shutters*, nascent capitalism in a village community leads to a Greek extremity of tragic devastation, absolute and horrifying. Similarly, films like Bill Douglas's *Trilogy* (*My Childhood*,

1971; *My Ain Folk*, 1973; *My Way Home*, 1979), David Macdonald's *The Brothers* (1947), or even parts of Hitchcock's *The Thirty-Nine Steps* (1935), might reveal their own interrogations of acceptable realism and comfortingly familiar tropes of Scottishness. The myths of Scottishness are not merely the masks which divert attention from underlying conditions of economic and class oppression. They are masks which might actually speak of those conditions.

Crucial to this way of reading is the proposition that Scotland has traditionally been seen as 'an imaginary space' where fantasies, desires and anxieties have been projected. Perhaps the epitome of this is the Hollywood producer Arthur Freed's declaration after he had been taken around the country, that he had to go back to America to produce a conspicuously studio-bound set for *Brigadoon* (Vincente Minelli, 1954): 'I went to Scotland but I could find nothing that looked like Scotland.'[9] Yet in this light, the delightful absurdities of *Brigadoon* are not unrelated to the nightmarish foreclosures of *The Wicker Man* (Robin Hardy, 1973), where 'the blond trio' of Britt Ekland, Diane Cilento and Ingrid Pitt help make 'one of the most bizarre depictions of a peripheral Scottish community in cinema history'.[10] Indeed, Duncan Petrie rather mischievously suggests that *The Wicker Man* can be seen as a refashioning of *Whisky Galore!* (Alexander Mackendrick, 1949) – the principled, arrogant, authority-figure is outwitted and out-manipulated by wily locals. Variations in this tradition might run from *The Maggie* (Alexander Mackendrick, 1954) to *Local Hero* (Bill Forsyth, 1983).

The potential value of the country's 'imaginary space' was more often surrendered to pre-formulated imagery, however. There is 'The Jacobite Legacy' – from silent cinema to David Niven as *Bonnie Prince Charlie* (Anthony Kimmins, 1948), Walt Disney's version of *Rob Roy – The Highland Rogue* (Harold French, 1953) and Errol Flynn as *The Master of Ballantrae* (William Keighley, 1953). The latter turns to the pleasure of swashbuckle Stevenson's most completely tragic story, while in *Bonnie Prince Charlie*, the tone of the entire film seems predestined as the Jacobite rising is inevitably depicted with a foreordained outcome. There is little sense of the real threat of the Jacobite march on London. Here again, the literary influence is close: Scott's post-Culloden Highlands of lost causes and tragic survivors and Stevenson's David Balfour, on the run from the redcoats in *Kidnapped*, are pervasive paradigms. Balfour's breathless chase in Stevenson's novel of 1886 prefigures Richard Hannay's in Buchan's *The Thirty-Nine Steps* of 1915. Petrie's summation is that 'the cinematic projection of Scottish history is dominated by the romance, the images, tropes and symbols of eighteenth-century Jacobitism'.[11]

There is an urban alternative. The rate of urbanisation in Scotland, the rising numbers of emigrants leaving the country and the increasing concentration of the population in the cities, particularly in Glasgow through the late nineteenth century, had a deep legacy in terms of modern national self-representation. While most Scots were urbanised by the early twentieth century, Scotland's transformation from a rural and agricultural ethos to a city-centred one happened more quickly than was generally represented in most modes of cultural production, partly because the rate of change meant that a rurally-grounded sense of community could be maintained, albeit in evolving forms, in the alienating world of late-Victorian capitalism. Thus, ideals of communal morality might confront amoral economic imperatives and the excesses of individualism in fiction, from John Galt to Robert Louis Stevenson. The city sharply focused these confrontations.

In cinema, Edinburgh provided a deeply shadowed image of an ancient capital, a medieval city of body-snatchers, duplicitous lawyers, demonic doctors, needy students and necessary victims in an urban jungle of the well-to-do and desperately poor. From *Dr Jekyll and Mr Hyde* (Reuben Mamoulian, 1932; Victor Fleming, 1941) to *The Prime of Miss Jean Brodie* (Ronald Neame, 1969) the ambivalence of high principles and good intentions in the unrequitable human world of appetites, desires and vanities seems to have been Edinburgh's prerogative. Glasgow, by contrast, became much more familiar as a post-Victorian, modern industrial city, progressive with industry and social consensus, home of shipbuilding, heroic with the huge ambition of capitalist enterprise and the pathos of the socialist effort. 'Clydesidism' – John Caughie wrote in 1990 – is 'the mythology of the Scottish twentieth century, the discourse which seems currently most potent, and not yet universally acknowledged as mythology'.[12] But such 'mythological histories' are both mythologies and enormously potent ways by which people make sense of their own reality. Familiar films might be re-read in this light. For example, *I Know Where I'm Going* (Michael Powell and Emeric Pressburger, 1945) is a formulaic romance story yet it also contains elements of Gothic chiaroscuro cinematography, baroquely self-conscious narrative and surreal characterisations.

Having considered these major areas – the Highlands and Islands as metaphorical space, the Metropolitan projection of 'Scottishness' into that space, the Jacobite films and the City films – Petrie's study begins the story again, firmly repositioning himself within the country. The second part of his book is entitled 'The Making of a National Cinema'. He quotes Jean-Luc Godard's provocative remarks from 1991:

> there have been very few national cinemas. In my opinion there is no Swedish cinema but there are Swedish movie-makers – some very good ones such as Stiller and Bergman. There have been only a handful of [national] cinemas: Italian, German, American and Russian. This is because when countries were inventing and using motion pictures, they needed an image of themselves.[13]

These comments indicate the dangers of complacency in trying to establish grounds for national self-representation on screen. Yet the external construction of various 'Scotlands' has in some ways helped to create a multiple sense of possible developments. This parallels the representation of Scotland in other media (such as literature, painting, music) and underlies our sense of the positive possibilities made visible by the late twentieth-century re-readings of Scottish cultural production. The constraints of caricature do not necessarily lead to straightjacket categories in which crea-tive energies are frustrated. Considered in a context of national change in self-perception, self-definition and representation to both national and international audiences and readerships, Scotland on screen is an essential part of a larger story.

Hugh MacDiarmid's speculations on the possible relationship between film and poetry and his insistence on the reciprocity of particular local actu-alities and universal significance are pertinent.[14] This is a characteristic of MacDiarmid's championship of the short Orkney and Edinburgh films of Margaret Tait in the early 1960s, but it also links the writers with the documentary innovations of John Grierson in the 1930s.[15] The fact that these documentaries were specifically crafted, edited and shaped – not by any means unprocessed footage of 'verité' – connects them to the writing of Lewis Grassic Gibbon. In his great trilogy of novels, *Sunset Song*, *Cloud Howe* and *Grey Granite*, Gibbon created a linguistic idiom deliberately representative of the speech-idiom of Aberdeenshire, beautifully cadenced and vocal, but never so reeking of verisimilitude that it became incomprehensible to outsiders. It was an artistic balance, a compromise between authentic tones and rhythms of native speech and the capacities of an international reader-ship to comprehend both the local and the universal in the characters. Something similar was going on in Grierson's work, from *Drifters* (1929) right up to the 1960s. On this basis, a nascent 'native' film industry was developing, with Bill Forsyth's *That Sinking Feeling* (1979) and *Gregory's Girl* (1981) and in the pioneering moments of a new relationship between TV and cinema in Britain with the advent of Channel 4, which began broad-casting on 2 November 1982.

Considering Scotland and the Television Play, the connections between film and literary culture are vital. Adaptations of literary classics – including *The House with the Green Shutters* and the Gibbon trilogy – alongside television versions of theatre-plays like Roddy McMillan's *The Bevellers* and John Byrne's *The Slab Boys* – led towards the radical television reinterpret-ation of John McGrath and the 7:84 Theatre Company's *The Cheviot, the Stag and the Black, Black Oil*. The effectiveness of its adaptation to the medium of television was reflected in its splicing of contemporary documentary film from the North Sea oil-rigs about working conditions and the economic effects of the oil-boom in Aberdeenshire. This hammered out the message about the continuing, current relevance of the story of subjuga-tion and exploitation which the play traced from the eighteenth and nineteenth centuries.

However, in 1970s Scotland, the influence of Eastern-European theatre and especially Brechtian technique was giving way to the influence of the naturalism of American popular culture. Certainly these influences found unusual companionship in later years (in *Trainspotting*, for example – unavoidably glamorised yet alienating and morally deeply unresolved), but in the 1970s, American popular culture was coming through powerfully in the work of Peter McDougall. Of McDougall's TV plays, *Just Another Saturday* (1975) presents a version of Holden Caulfield as a young stick-thrower in a Protestant flute band taking part in his first city-parade, having to pass through 'Fenian Alley' as if he were the scout at the head of a cavalry regiment riding through 'Indian Territory'. John Ford's Monument Valley was urbanised to Glasgow. *Just a Boy's Game* (1979) had rock-star Frankie Miller as a Glasgow hardman forced to face up to a younger generation of toughs much as the gunfighter wanting to hang up his guns is forced 'out of retirement' in countless westerns. In both texts, the *geist* of drink, rising unemployment, night-time wandering, comradeship and family betrayals also drew on the world of noir film and fiction from the 1920s on.

The excitement of the influence of American popular culture was a source of strength and sustenance. It might be traced back to the James Bond movie *Goldfinger* (Guy Hamilton, 1964), as we have noted in the previous chapter. The appropriation of American popular culture was most fruitful in Scottish television drama in the 1980s and 1990s in John Byrne's bitterly ironic and unpredicted genre-shifting serials *Tutti Frutti* and *Your Cheatin' Heart* (which highlighted rock and roll, and country and western music as crucial components of west-of-Scotland working-class culture). It is also evident in the international popularity of the police series *Taggart* which even survived its principle character's death in 1994. Work like this established a new image of Glasgow (and by extension, Scotland), trading on the caricatures to subvert them.[16]

Alongside these developments in TV, a Scottish Art Cinema was growing. In the work of Bill Forsyth, for example, as well as the popular qualities of charm and humour, there are serious and repeated themes to do with loss, loneliness and isolation. Lynne Ramsay's *Ratcatcher* (1999) and *Morvern Callar* (2002), like Forsyth's films, treat serious issues but address a popular audience with sympathetic humour and no condescension. Moreover, the English director Ken Loach, in *My Name Is Joe* (1998) and the Danish director Lone Scherfig, in *Wilbur Wants to Kill Himself* (2002), take the Scottish characters and locations, and pursue the themes of their narratives keeping a deliberate balance and distance from the siren-calls of cliché or the greased tracks to caricature. Their distance from the location their films depict actively helps to renew familiarity with it and offers new ways of entering it.

The story of Scotland on screen charts a successful journey away from the homogenised, platitudinous comforts of the small-town 'Kailyard' version of Scottishness, a journey out of the ineptitude and infantilism of fantasies unconnected to reality, a movement towards a tougher sense of what myths like 'Clydesidism' are, how they are made and why they are needed. This movement need not seek to destroy or reject such myths but to reveal their purposes and principles of construction, and ultimately to redirect their potential and force. This is a journey towards a position which might, as Petrie says, 'demonstrate the expression of cultural specificity in terms that are both resolutely national and international in their relevance and appeal'.[17]

Theatre and television

This book has had little enough to say about Scottish theatre and although the subject is in the title of this chapter I want only to look briefly at a play which is most famous for its anti-theatricality. John McGrath and the 7:84 Theatre Company's production of *The Cheviot, the Stag and the Black, Black Oil* achieved historical distinction in 1973 for being toured around Scotland and performed in town halls and community centres, at non-theatrical locations, outside the parameters of bourgeois theatre, far beyond the cities. Its audience was intended to be – and found among – people who would not normally go to city theatres, whose interest was less in the comfort and spectacle of such theatres and rather in the stories being told and the entertainment of the songs and history being performed.

This has been recognised as a breakthrough in British dramatic tradition, a watershed in what might be done in the medium of drama. Introducing the collection of talks McGrath gave at the University of Cambridge in 1979, *A Good Night Out*, Raymond Williams said that McGrath's

> main drive ... is a contemporary case for theatre, of a kind which can only happen by deliberate distancing from what is conventionally established as Theatre. What interests me about this is its connection with the quite different work I and some others have been doing about the 'audience' – in that significant way of describing it – and its active or passive role in the actual creation of dramatic forms.[18]

Marshall Walker described the play as 'Scotland's most vital theatrical event since Lyndsay's *Ane Pleasant Satyre of the Three Estaitis* spoke out some 400 years earlier for the rights of the folk against corruption in Church and state.'[19] There may be 'no sign of a "Wullie Shakespeare"' so far but Scottish theatre since *The Cheviot* has been 'back on track with Sir David Lyndsay'.[20]

The play's success was achieved through a number of things happening together. Its composition, performances and impact are described by McGrath in the introduction to the 1981 edition, in which he comments on the extent to which knowledge of the events depicted in the play was still extremely obscure in popular terms through the early 1970s: 'it was a source of amazement that so little was known of it [the Highland Clearances] outside, even inside, Scotland'.[21] 'The theatre can never cause a social change' he writes, but 'it can articulate the pressures towards one...it can be the way a people can find their voice, their solidarity and their collective determination'.[22] The company's name derived from a statistic in *The Economist*, that 7 per cent of the country owned 84 per cent of the country's wealth.

The play was built upon a number of interacting dynamics: a fidelity to the lived experience of the audience it was intended for and an unembarrassed use of music hall and traditional song and ceilidh forms. This involved a deliberate comprehensive deployment of what some critics have separated as 'phony' and 'authentic' aspects of Scottishness. This deployment was tactical and dramatic. Superficial songs, apparently catchy and singalong, were used to get the audience to join in with characters who were then revealed as leading the singing in the direction best suited to their own profit. Their greed is exposed as they go on singing after the cast and audience have woken up to their exploitative charm. This is most evident when Texas Jim sings 'For these are my mountains' with a sinister shudder on the last line: 'And I – have come home.' Then he fires a pistol in the air, oil rigs appear and Jim gets into his stride: 'Pipe that oil in from the sea, / Pipe those profits – home to me...//...Screw your landscape, screw your bays / I'll screw you in a hundred ways...'[23]

The traditional songs and music appeal differently. Both idioms – infectious dance song and plaintive lament – are made to work self-consciously. They are raised to a level at which their performance is self-consciously enacted, not merely accepted as given. And this self-consciousness itself becomes a depth of pleasure. They both serve as warning. They both link what has happened to what is present and perhaps to come. Their very use suggests that the future depends upon acts of choice. Fishing crews refused to leave for the tide until a song was sung for them by a singer and actress whose seven brothers, father and grandfather were fishermen themselves.[24] Popular idioms combined stand-up joke routines and political satire, sometimes polarising the company to some extent, though McGrath said he never knew a company 'with as much respect for one another'.[25] The entire company 'had worked in many different situations, from Ibsen via panto to spieling on strip-shows'.[26] That is, pointed topicality and a repertoire of familiar jokes were in a new alliance. So the appeal of storytelling and daily news-reviewing internationally popularised in extended anecdotes over the last thirty years of the twentieth century by Billy Connolly was a technique explored foundationally and locally in *The Cheviot*.

However, what the 7:84 company were self-consciously emphasising (and which Connolly normally does not) was the recognition of the duplicity of pleasure. It can serve any political end. The storytelling was clearly structured through specific historical episodes. One might disagree with interpretation or standpoint, but the interpretation and standpoint of the play were explicit. This made the production fast: it had speed, but not psychological depth. Its sweep of historical vision and panoramic sense of economics had both political and social relevance to its audiences. And the political moment was right.

As a televised 'Play for Today' in 1974, it included documentary footage from Aberdeenshire, artfully edited but evidently showing actual young people looking for a home when the market had raised house prices to impossible levels after the oil boom. Scottish oil-rig workers and American representatives of the oil companies were filmed without explicit comment, clearly showing how far apart their interests were and how closely they were tied to the economic history the play had represented. Press reaction at the time acknowledged the value of the play but criticised its use of documentary footage on aesthetic grounds.

It is dispiriting to follow the career of the company after the success of *The Cheviot*, as political opposition to the essential qualities that made it successful became entrenched after the election of Margaret Thatcher as Prime Minister of Great Britain in 1979. The struggles they faced, courageously and with increasing desperation, were evident when McGrath visited New Zealand in 1988. In a panel discussion at the Wellington International Arts Festival, he used the word 'capitalism' and was greeted with a ripple of laughter as if the new right were sniggering at the very idea of political engagement and denying as ridiculous possible representations of alternative economic structures. Others in that audience did not laugh. Simon Wilson, in the *New Zealand Listener* (4–10 June 1988), patronisingly reported that McGrath 'doesn't know how to behave. Resorts to literary one-upmanship... Lets the "Hour with John McGrath" session get sidetracked from his prepared material.' Wilson commented, 'Partly it's a difficulty with his role... this is his first invitation to simply be a writer among writers.' But Wilson did recognise some political context: 'Nine years of Thatcherism have hurt badly. They have, says McGrath, "annihilated the prospect of politics on stage, unless they are right-wing". Now, "there's a terrific temptation to become strident, to be very, very shrill".' Wilson pronounced judgement: 'It doesn't work.' And quoted McGrath again: '"Ten years ago, after seeing a play like *The Little Red Hen* [about Scottish nationalism and the Red Clyde], audiences really would have stormed the barricades if we'd called for it. Not now. You have to be more thoughtful, not so rhetorical. You've got to talk to people in a talking voice."' McGrath's account of these years, *The Bone Won't Break*, carries on its back cover a 1988 *New Zealand Herald* photograph of its author talking with striking workers from the Nissan car company.[27]

Further details about that period and what followed it, the changes in the company and McGrath's work, are in McGrath's posthumous collection of essays and reflections, *Naked Thoughts that Roam About*[28], but here I want to pick up on that last comment, that in 1988 it seemed to McGrath that in the changed political circumstances of the mid- to late-eighties, a more persuasive, talking voice had to be used. And I want to turn to the most persuasive, talking medium yet invented: television.

The turn is not difficult. Indeed, it is a simple step to go from *The Cheviot*'s seminal exposition of economic history with reference to the Highland Clearances and sheep farming, land-exploitation for sport by landowners and absentee interests and the development of the North Sea oil industry, to the fictional representation of the nuclear industry in Troy Kennedy Martin's 1985 television series *Edge of Darkness*. Here is *The Cheviot*'s true successor: popular, addressing an audience uncertain at first of what it was getting, quickly applauded and internationally broadcast after a number of prizes had made it honourable, safer television. Both texts seem to emphasise that, as McGrath puts it in *The Cheviot*, 'Nationalism is not enough.'[29] But both have specific things to say about the international context of Scotland and Scottish people, about the local impact of global dynamics, about how individuals live and die. The turn from theatre to television, then, is not a juxtaposition of media so much as a continuity in the recognition of an observation made by McGrath in 1992. In a lecture delivered on 13 October 1992, Colin MacCabe argued that great art might be produced by a collective authorship, whether through film or television, and that it is not dependent on the individual author. It is 'in terms of groups, both of producers and audiences, that we need to think, if we are to understand questions of value in relation to television and film'.[30] He notes, however, that 'after the lecture John McGrath convinced me that the group simply reproduced the problems of the category of the author and needs to be replaced with a much more difficult and complex concept of social experience'. MacCabe suggests that we might start with a case history of *Z Cars*.

Troy Kennedy Martin worked with John McGrath on the early episodes of *Z Cars* and on the final one. The parallels and divergences in their careers led into fascinating territory: McGrath, moving from England to Scotland, working in film as well as theatre and TV; Martin, moving from Scotland where he was born (and after service with the Gordon Highlanders) to London via Hollywood, where he scripted films such as *The Italian Job* (1969), pretty much a paradigm of the English cult movie with Michael Caine, Noël Coward and the 'Self-Preservation Society' theme song and *Kelly's Heroes* (1970), a war-movie in which Clint Eastwood offers knowing pastiche of his Spaghetti western persona. He returned to Britain to work on the twelve-part series *Reilly – Ace of Spies* (1983), which foreshadows his later work in a number of scenes and underlying themes. But here I want to concentrate briefly on Martin's finest work in writing and television production, a central text of the 1980s, *Edge of Darkness*.

John Caughie decribes the generic importance of the form *Edge of Darkness* takes: while 'the drama series was becoming uneconomic, there was still an audience for "serious" drama and an obligation within public service broadcasting to satisfy it... Much of the best, and most "serious" drama of the 1980s and 1990s appeared in serial or series form' and he cites *Edge of Darkness* along with John Byrne's *Tutti Frutti* (1987), the work of Dennis Potter and others.[31] Caughie is right to claim literary status for such texts: 'Whatever generic form it takes, the extension in time of an interrupted dramatic narrative seems to me to be one of television's specific contributions to the long history of the novelistic. Bakhtin's biographical narrative in which characters are taken on a spiritual or intellectual journey through time and space – whether it be through the historical environment of *Our Friends in the North* or the paranoid environment of *Edge of Darkness* – reaches a particularly developed form in the television dramatic serial.'[32] Martin himself agrees with this view of the genealogy: 'While the modern novel has developed on mainly personal lines [he seems to be referring to the English rather than the Scottish tradition], the television mini-series has inherited many of the characteristics of the nineteenth-century public novel, particularly its strong narrative and characters; *Edge of Darkness* was consciously written to reflect this.'[33] Television is literature.

Martin describes the work as 'a product of the years 1982 to 1985... when born-again Christians and cold-war warriors seemed to be running the United States... Mrs Thatcher began to outdo the White House when it came to talk about the "Evil Empire" and the need to replace ("modernize") one nuclear system with another'. The scripts were written at a time of political pessimism, but a moral optimism seemed to be gaining strength underground, so that a mythic dimension of earthly rootedness and the authority of the earth itself might legitimately be called up.

Given the literary credentials of the text and the published script, and assuming the author's national origins can allow us to claim him as one of the 'unpredicted voices of our kind', I would like to point out the few specific references to Scottish and Celtic identity and consider their place in the trajectory of the work as a whole, and then offer a few observations about the serial in its entirety.

The larger context is emphatically Britain and America, the main characters from Yorkshire and Texas, but the *international* provenance of capitalism and the nuclear industry sets the dynamics of the scene. In Episode 1, Michael Meacher, a Labour MP of the time, plays himself, addressing students at the college where Craven is meeting his daughter. His speech is undercut by action and humour – Craven is waiting to meet Emma and we want to know what will happen to them – Emma brings the meeting to an end with a joke – so we hardly pay attention to Meacher's words. Yet they echo forward ironically through the story to come: 'Education and welfare, which were once the great equalizers of our society, are being cut down at their roots...And schools and colleges such as this one, which do not contribute directly to the technological future of the nuclear state, face closure.'[34] 'Your future, the country's future, is at stake. You may save the nation yet.'[35]

When Craven and Emma arrive home, Emma is killed by a hooded man with a shotgun firing both barrels into her chest. Much of the first episode is then taken up with establishing the conventions of a police procedural thriller but there is a slow, moving, extended scene in which Craven, finally left alone in his house, starts to go through his daughter's things. There is shock as we see him find a vibrator, which he kisses tenderly; there is reassurance as he finds her old teddy bear; there is the pleasure of recognising narrative conventions when he finds a handgun – Emma has been involved in something potentially murderous. What we pay little attention to, though we notice it on the soundtrack, is the song playing from an LP record Craven picks up from Emma's collection and places on the turntable.

The script emphasises that among her things, there is a picture of Billy Connolly, and, over the bed, a big NASA poster of the earth as seen from the moon. (This is reminiscent of the opening of the televised version of *The Cheviot*, with its overview of Scotland seen from outer space.) Her records are all predictable – 'soul/reggae, rhythm and blues, UB40, etc.'. But the country and western singer Willie Nelson is the one on top, and Craven puts it on. It is a ballad, 'The Time of the Preacher', and it comes up again, curiously, twice in the series.

In Episode 2, Craven is taken to the office of Pendleton and Harcourt, two Whitehall snoops who tell him a little more about Emma's activities. As Pendleton leads Craven up a staircase, he remarks, 'I myself favour an Irish education. Anyone who has examined the Book of Kells cannot but be impressed by the labyrinthine coils of the Celtic imagination. Are you a Celt by any chance, Craven?' Craven's reply suggests a complete impatience with the fatuous irrelevance of the question: 'No'.[36]

It is a small exchange, but layered with irony. The series itself is labyrinthine, literally and metaphorically, and Craven becomes increasingly caught up in the tunnels and underground passages of the plot. On a literal narrative level, he is already well-acquainted with 'the Celtic imagination' through his policework in Northern Ireland. On a mythical level, he is a green man – a man of the country, not the city – whose identification with Celtic nature gods does not survive very clearly in the programmes but was a major component in his author's imagining of him. The curt answer belies the complex ironies behind it.

Later, Craven meets Jedburgh in the Tiberio restaurant late at night and Jedburgh steers Craven towards the subject of country music, Willie Nelson and 'that song that Willie had out about a year ago?... "The Time of the Preacher". Something about the year of 01. You familiar with the words at all?' They recognise mutually some significance in the ballad and, piecing it together, begin to sing it. This signals a shared mystery: Jedburgh seems to know something about the ballad's significance, but we do not, and neither does Craven. The whole scene hovers between sinister threat and comic ebullience as Jedburgh looms large and Falstaffian and his two colleagues, returned from South America, are drunk after a celebration dinner. The implication of what they have been doing in South America is balanced against their post-festive repletion, which is cut through when one of them sobers up utterly for a moment and tells Craven, 'I just want to say ... I was damned sorry to hear about your daughter.'[37] Seriousness shifts through the comedy and the securities of comic characterisation are destabilised by shady mystery.

When Jedburgh and Craven take them home, the conversation turns to golf:

Jedburgh: When I think of St Andrews and Carnoustie and Leith, I begin to realise that it is more than a coincidence that divine providence has brought forth oil from the depth of the North Sea. That oil will help to save the golf courses of Scotland.

Craven: From what?

Jedburgh: From the Communists, Craven. Can you imagine what would happen to the golf courses of this country if a Communist government ever got in power? God may not be a Communist Craven, he may not even be a Republican, but I know damned well he's not a member of the Socialist Advance.[38]

This is full of prolepsis. While it establishes Jedburgh's attractively outrageous eccentricity, it also foreshadows the political tensions that will become increasingly fierce. If it seems to pick up from *The Cheviot* it points forward to a world in which Emma's boyfriend's party, the Socialist Advance, is negligible in the larger power-play.

Danger goes with depth and knowledge. 'To know is to die,' Jedburgh says twice in the serial.[39] In Episode 3, Craven tells Emma's ghost, 'You took on some of the toughest men in the most dangerous business on this earth ...' and in Episode 4, in a flashback, he is shown telling her about the nuclear industry, 'It's the most dangerous business in Britain.'[40] After he decides that he must get into the nuclear plant at Northmoor himself, Emma's ghost returns and asks him what he is going to do. 'I'm going to go in,' he says. She approves, but ironically cautions him: 'I thought you said it was the most dangerous business in England run by the most dangerous men.' Relieved that his mind is made up, Craven jokes, 'You're exaggerating again.'[41] But the elisions between 'on this earth', 'Britain' and 'England' quietly suggest that nuclear power has nothing to do with national boundaries or status. Even the vexed relation between Westminster and Northern Ireland is presented as background to the central concerns. Emma's killer is discovered to be an ex-Provisional IRA man, McCroon, who introduces Craven's unsavoury previous work as a special police agent recruiting Irish informers. When Craven visits his friend Mac, in hospital, we are told that they knew each other from that time in his life. 'Lesson Number One, when fighting terrorism, is – be ordinary...That put Mac at a disadvantage, he had red hair. From Portadown to Ballymena he was known as Carrot Top. It was only a matter of time before they got him.'[42] The name and hair suggest that he is Scottish, and the relationship emblematises Scottish complicity in British state power. The power structures thus sketched add a deeply ironic humour to the enigmatic dialogue at the end of Episode 4:

Jedburgh: Still in one piece, I see.
Craven: What's that supposed to mean?
Jedburgh: People have a habit of dissolving into their constituent parts these
  days. The political climate does not favour homogeneity...[43]

By Episode 5, the global and mythic themes begin to dominate, and what started out within the conventions of a police procedural thriller (a *Z Cars* for the 1980s) has turned into something much more potent. It begins at Craven's house, in rolling Yorkshire countryside, where at dawn, in the garden,

Jedburgh *walks over to the tree near where* Emma *had been shot. Below it a*
  spring now trickles. Around it are some wild marsh flowers. Here Craven *sits*...
Jedburgh: Is this where she died?
Craven: He was over there...We were standing here...
Jedburgh: Is this stream a permanent feature?
Craven: No. (*He turns back towards the house.*) It's new.[44]

The impact Episode 5 delivers is remarkable, as Craven and Jedburgh descend through caverns and tunnels to a nuclear bunker, neglected since 1964, when it was set up during the Cuban missile crisis. This Jedburgh describes as 'the floor of Plato's cave' referring to the discussion about illusion and reality in Book VII of *The Republic*. Martin notes: 'Like his prisoners held in a cave who mistake the shadows on the wall for reality, in this nuclear world it is hard to tell what is real and what is an illusion.'[45] But the mythic framework affords some security:

Craven: Why do you hate Grogan so much?
Jedburgh: Because of who he is.
Craven: And who is he?
Jedburgh: He's part of the Dark Forces who would rule this planet.
Craven: You believe in all that stuff?
Jedburgh: Yeah, sure. Why not? Look at yourself. You think of yourself as an
  English provincial detective...whose daughter died in tragic circum-
  stances. Yet where she fell a well sprang, flowers grew. Now what kind of
  power is that?
(Craven *is silenced for a moment.*)
Craven: I don't know.[46]

As they leave, Jedburgh adds with Texan flair, 'Mind you, I do have a personal grudge against Grogan – his great, great great-grandfather killed my great, great, great great-grandfather. We Jedburghs never forget...' But the humour of the moment is countered as the camera zooms up to an open-palmed statue of Christ, the clay in close-up foreshadowing the appearance of the decaying flesh that will be seen on Jedburgh's and Craven's faces in Episode 6, after their fatal exposure to radiation.

That happens in the most conventionally thriller-like climax to the series, when masked and suited armed men at the power plant shoot it out with Craven and Jedburgh. Jedburgh steals the plutonium and they manage to escape. As they are about to split up, the dialogue points forward to the final programme:

Jedburgh: Craven, if we make it, I'll see you in Scotland.
Craven: Where?
Jedburgh: You're the detective, find me.[47]

Episode 6 is largely set in Scotland. Martin notes: 'The Scottish locations were originally included as a homage to John Buchan.'[48] Craven has been caught but is in the custody of the Westminster snoops, Pendleton and Harcourt. Pendleton tells him when he wakes up that he is 'in an American Air Force hospital' and the radiation sickness in him is 'bad'.[49] From this point on the tension increases as the days – later, hours – of the two principal characters are literally numbered. Pendleton reports to Harcourt.

Harcourt: Has Craven got any idea where Jedburgh went?
Pendleton: He says his last words were something about 'meeting Moriarty at the Falls'!
Harcourt: If there is an Irish component to this, I shall retire.[50]

The reference, of course, is to Sherlock Holmes, and the last story Conan Doyle hoped to write about him, in which he sends the detective plunging over the Reichenbach Falls locked in a fatal embrace with his arch-enemy Moriarty. The allusion is appropriately apocalyptic, though it does not refer to anything in the dialogue in the previous episode and Harcourt, Martin notes, 'deliberately misunderstands', playing on the thought that the reference is to the Falls Road in Belfast, and that the IRA might be directly involved. What it does clearly, however, is to link *Edge of Darkness* back through John Buchan to Conan Doyle in a generic tradition of popular Scottish detective stories.

We finally meet Jedburgh again, at last on a golf course in Scotland, sporting a tartan cap.[51] When his golf partner Jemima tells him, 'You're in with a chance, my dear' the line resonates into the script. After a 'Bloody good shot' she drives him to his guest house, dropping him off with a sprightly, 'Home again, home again, jiggedy jig.' And again, while Jedburgh's obvious physical decay counterpoints Jemima's brightness, the line haunts the memory: Jedburgh is very far away from any sense of 'home'. Jemima asks him if he is all right: 'You're not looking too good.' He gestures at the guest house behind him. 'I think that old lady in there is trying to poison me.'[52] As he goes in, he is greeted by the austere owner of the guest house, Mrs Girvan, who accosts him: 'Mr Jedburgh. [She pronounces it "Jedborough" as in the Borders town.] You forgot your sandwich again today, Mr Jedburgh.' She gets a good answer:

Jedburgh: Mrs Girvan, mince between two slices of white bread is not my idea of lunch. [On screen, Joe Don Baker, the actor playing Jedburgh, adds an angry 'Hell,' here, further offending the old woman.] I'd rather eat the damned Bible.
Mrs Girvan: Mr Jedborough!
(*Jedburgh corrects her.*)
Jedburgh: Jedburgh.[53]

The comic beat of this exchange runs quickly along with the anger in the scene. We noted previously that Mrs Girvan is cousin to Holmes's Mrs Hudson, Dr Finlay's Janet, James Bond's Mae and other matriarchal housekeepers. Played to perfection by Irene Sunters, she jumps at the shock of Jedburgh's blasphemy, her eyes starting open as her Calvinist domineering is rebuffed by a man who has no time for it. Seriousness and comedy continue as, now in his room, Jedburgh phones a South American terrorist to invite him to come and get him in a final showdown.

Jedburgh: Listen to me, Hernandez, I'm taking a vacation in Scotland – [the pause on screen is perfectly held] – it's in Great Britian. Yeah. Kilmichael. Kil, as in the word, death, murder; Michael, as in St Michael – the patron saint of the CIA . . . I know he is your patron saint, Hernandez, but haven't you wised up yet? Every time you pray to him he sends a copy to the Agency . . .[54]

The international ignorance about Scotland's location is marked unobtrusively, with a perfectly realised combination of comic and serious effect.

Harcourt advises Craven to try to track Jedburgh down in Scotland, because 'Grogan's there. He's at a conference at the Gleneagles Hotel.' As if picking up on the mythic theme of a final confrontation, Jedburgh explains his presence at Gleneagles as 'fulfilling a long-standing engagement . . .' Pendleton gets wind of this: 'Jedburgh's at Gleneagles and he's not playing golf.' Craven drives north, talking to Emma's guiding spirit: 'I feel so much is left undone.' But she assures him, 'Other people will continue the job.'

After Jedburgh has exposed Grogan to a fatal dose of radiation, he escapes once again with the stolen plutonium. A Westminster minister arrives:

Minister: Are twenty kilos enough?
Grogan: To dispose of the the east coast of Scotland? . . . Yes.[55]

But Craven is getting closer. At Gleneagles golf club, a Porter takes him to Jedburgh's locker:

Porter: He was a good loser, which is just as well. We have a lot of strong players...
>   (...*At the bottom of Jedburgh's locker is...a plastic container with a con-gealed mince sandwich inside. On the bottom of the container is a sticker proclaiming that it belongs to Mrs Girvan, Girvan Guest House, Crieff.*)[56]

The black comedy is there in small touches throughout the script. When Harcourt is told that the 'state executioner' is on the prowl and may be looking for him, as the Minister did not approve of Harcourt's report on Northmoor, a waiter delivers a room service tea tray. Harcourt looks utterly discomfited: 'I thought I ordered oatcakes.'[57]

When Craven finally catches up with Jedburgh, an electric guitar version of the Willie Nelson ballad is on the soundtrack and 'There is the sound of a rushing stream', as there was at the spring where Emma died, which Jedburgh noted at the beginning of Episode 5. They are glad to see each other, but wary. Jedburgh tells Craven what he has done: the plutonium is packed in chalk with a pound of plastic explosive at its core, and he has a plutonium bullet, which 'just might' work.

Craven: A nuclear explosion?
Jedburgh: It'd be one hell of a way to go, huh?
Craven: It seems rather hard on the rest of Scotland.
Jedburgh: Yeah, that's what I thought, too. Especially the golf courses. So, I decided against it.[58]

Craven phones to tell Pendleton and Harcourt where the plutonium is. They trace the call. The state armed forces are sent to get Jedburgh, thus taking the role Jedburgh would have assigned to the South American terrorist Hernandez. In the penultimate scene, Craven and Jedburgh sit across from each other at a table, raggedly singing the ballad, 'The Time of the Preacher'. The conflict we mentioned above, between human authority and that of the earth, or between political power and 'nature' features memorably in the final discussion between Jedburgh and Craven in the last episode, resolving itself on a question. By this time, both are dying of radiation sickness and about to be attacked by government troops, but, guns at the ready, sipping Macallan malt whisky, they sit waiting, having a quiet conversation as time passes. Craven asks Jedburgh whether he believes in the idea of Gaia, the mythic notion of a living, regenerative earth, or biosphere, on the surface of which mankind might seem only a guest. Jedburgh says that he places his faith in mankind always winning against nature (in this he resem-bles his arch-enemy Grogan, though Grogan's ambitions to place man 'in charge' imply an authoritative position for himself, while Jedburgh will always be 'with the company' and 'on the side of the angels'). Craven tells Jedburgh that if there is a battle between the planet and mankind, the planet will win. Jedburgh asks him, 'Where's that going to leave you?' It's a question Craven answers with mild, almost indifferent certainty: 'On the side of the planet.' And then the subject is changed by impending action.

The last scene is on a Scottish hillside overlooking Loch Lednock. Harcourt's voiceover explains: '... within hours of Jedburgh's death and in conditions of great secrecy, the plutonium was recovered from Loch Lednock... Grogan was there, watching the proceedings like some twentieth-century vampire, although after his exposure to Jedburgh's plutonium at the conference I don't hold out much for his chances'.[59] Craven 'was up on the hill overlooking the loch, staring down at us like a wild animal. Neither myself nor Pendleton felt it appropriate to wave. Besides, by my reckoning he was not long for this world. When we left he was still on the hill.... As we drove down the valley, I thought I heard a cry, but it was lost in the noise of the helicopter. When I looked back he was gone.'[60] The hillside is bare, but as the shot dissolves to winter, we see rising through the snow, the black flowers Emma promised Craven would come in time to preserve the planet against mankind. They are *'beginning to grow'* as the end titles roll.

Sketches of selected scenes like this hardly do justice to the careful pacing, gathering momentum and depth of the series. From its opening scenes, concealment is the key. What is hidden? What is the mystery? The series begins with an alleged union cover-up (which remains unexplained until much later on) but it quickly seems to become a murder-mystery. And the questions multiply. Who killed Emma? What had she been hiding? Who was behind her murder? As it unfolds, we realise that the series is exploring ideas about forms of knowledge and action. What would one do if one knew certain things? How would one act?

There is, also, the relationship between the personal and the social worlds. Individual and family life are seen in a social and international context, perspectives constantly moving from dramatic consequences to familiar motivations. Structurally and aesthetically, episodes relate to each other: lines are repeated, echoed in different settings; camera angles repeat perspectives ironically (when Craven goes to Jedburgh's locker the movement and dialogue recollect his earlier visit to retrieve Emma's things from the hospital; the proximity of death and ironic understatement chime). But the shocking effect of literally taking the main characters underground, into an actual 'underworld' in Episode 5 heralds the climactic thrust of the series. In the end, its depiction of the ecological world in danger from the human motives valorised in the Anglo-American ideology of the 1980s is more convincing than could have been predicted, given the normal ambitions of the genre and medium and the constraints set on them. It might be an unrepeatable achievement – like *The Cheviot*, perhaps – but that it happened at all is astonishing.

Is it Scottish literature? The references to Scotland are sufficiently knowing to suggest they were made with intentional self-consciousness. In *Edge of Darkness*, the relation between physicality, materialism and spirituality is central to the themes of nuclear power and weaponry, the dissolution of the body and the guidance offered by spiritual presence (specifically, the ghost of the central character's daughter). Moreover, the key characteristic of black, reductive humour working along with serious commitment seems traditional in many texts of Scottish literature and is everywhere in *Edge of Darkness*. Martin, born in Scotland, nowhere makes claims one could easily call nationalist, but the political critique of the British state in the Thatcher era and the Anglo-American alliances which underpinned it recall us to a point of view that is decidedly outwith the Anglo-American establishment and much closer to McGrath's in *The Cheviot*. Indeed, it is clear that the main character, Craven, approaches that establishment from the outside. (In the first episode, he recollects that for his young daughter, London was associated with Buckingham Palace, when the Queen gave him a medal, whereas, because he visited his dying wife in hospital there, he always associated the city with cancer.)[61] He is ill-at-ease in London (he seems more at home in Scotland, in fact), while the Falstaffian CIA agent Darius Jedburgh deliberately caricatures the perspective from the United States capitol. Rising to address the delegates at the nuclear conference at Gleneagles, he begins by saying, '500,000 million dollars for a defence system for Washington DC seems a bit pricey to me. But then, I don't live there.'[62] Again, the quality of humour underpins and sustains the serious implications of the statement.

Martin's seminal 1964 attack on television naturalism, 'Nats Go Home' ('Nats' signifying those who believed in theatrical naturalism for the medium of television drama, rather than nationalists) suggests the struggle that was to come for his work.[63] He opened his McTaggart lecture of 1986 with a reference to John McGrath, a decade earlier, making 'a swingeing attack on naturalism' and charted his own progress 'on a mission' to change the possibilities of television as a medium. He began with the premise that 'television did not belong to the theatre' so it followed that 'naturalism (the language of the proscenium-arch theatre) did not belong on television. We were not sure what did, but we pinned our faith on Story as the best way forward and Narration as the best way of telling a story.' The problem was that 'almost the entire Establishment of Britain was led by people who believed in naturalism'. Many of the techniques he was trying to establish, he noted, 'are now commonplace in commercials and videos'. But it is hard to believe they could be better used than in *Edge of Darkness*, to bring about a profoundly ethical critique of the politics of the nuclear state.[64]

Directed by Martin Campbell and produced by Michael Wearing, when first broadcast in six episodes from November to December 1985 on BBC2 it attracted four million viewers. Within ten days it was repeated and viewing figures doubled. In 1986 it received six BAFTA awards, for Best Drama Series, Best Actor (Bob Peck as Craven), Best Music (by Eric Clapton and Michael Kamen), Best Photography (Andrew Dunn), Best Editor (Andrew Fisher and others) and Best Sound (Dickie Bird and others). By December 1986 it had been sold to nineteen countries.

The awards helped objectify the exported commodity but the impact of viewing the series in Scotland in 1985 remains memorable. It was the only television I have ever seen that literally had me on the edge of my seat. This, I fear, was not only to do with its aesthetic merit and political message, but its historical moment. Its verisimilitude worked within its mythic and symbolic design, bringing real people, places and things into its fiction: not only Michael Meacher, but also Margaret Thatcher herself asserting government nuclear policy on a television programme Craven is watching; there was Ronald Reagan in the White House, El Salvador, Nicaragua, the Falklands, Northern Ireland, a news report about the House of Commons enquiry into the fictional nuclear takeover bid, and a BBC presenter playing herself. As Lez Cooke puts it,

> might not then the fictional world of *Edge of Darkness* take place in the real world inhabited by the viewers?...In the context of a reactionary conjuncture, the act of confirming half-formed beliefs and suspicions which viewers might hold can be considered progressive, especially if it serves to make those viewers question the ideology of 'the dark forces that [would] rule our planet'.[65]

Comic books

The endpapers of *The Amazing Spider-Man: Spirits of the Earth* by Charles Vess (1990)[66] depict the (fictional) small Scottish village of Lochalsh. This is evidently a neo-feudal community, with the castle looming from the top of the mountain on the right, the houses low down in the valley and, on the left, perched pensively on what looks like a large cairn or memorial, the superhero Spider-Man.

The book opens with 'your friendly neighbourhood Spider-Man' swinging through his own 'friendly neighbourhood' New York. When Spider-Man's civilian alter-ego Peter Parker returns home he discovers that his wife, Mary Jane, has inherited a croft in the Scottish Highlands from a recently deceased relation. They set off together to claim Mary Jane's inheritance but it is not long before the Spider-Man costume is out of the suitcase. The anomalous aspect is played up gently with the superhero leaping athletically over the roofs of the sleeping villagers, leaving the adoring Mary Jane in their hotel room. Spider-Man is next seen clumping through the heather, a long way from New York, quipping, 'There's never an upstate bus when you want one' and 'This heather is for the birds.'

He climbs the castle walls only to find a whole set of clichés and caricatures: bagpipes, exiled chieftains, claymores, ghosts of dispossessed Highlanders marching through the night in a great procession. But of course, these are not ghosts at all but hologram projections, hi-tech images perpetrated by the ultra-modern sophisticated villain of the piece who is intent on keeping the villagers in thrall, and whose ultimate aim is to destroy the community entirely and plunder the area's natural resources. Spider-Man foils his plan, but not on his own, for, by the end of the story, he has been battered about pretty thoroughly, seems to have broken an arm and needs all the help he can get from Mary Jane and her ancient, ghostly new friend 'Dark Mairi'. This semi-supernatural figure is derived from the ancient wise woman of Neil Gunn's novel, *Butcher's Broom* (1934). Charles Vess, the author of *Spirits of the Earth*, explicitly acknowledges both Gunn and Gunn's friend the Irish author Maurice Walsh, another novelist of the Scottish Highlands. Indeed, *Spirits of the Earth* is dedicated to them both with the acknowledgement that their works 'brought the people and landscapes of Scotland alive for me'. The association of people and land is characteristically close. Spider-Man's final victory, in fact, depends most of all on the assistance he gets from the spirits of the earth themselves – inexplicable energies that boil up from the ground below. It is significant that Spider-Man does not physically vanquish the villain, who takes his own life. Recognising the futility of his vain desires, he leaps into a desolate tarn. Spider-Man is not only in charge here; his authority as hero is superseded by that of the land itself.

Through the 1980s and 1990s, Scottish writers were employed by DC Comics in what was clearly a self-conscious attempt to re-vitalise the canon of the comic-book world. Grant Morrison, a Glasgow man, worked on such minority-interest comics as *Animal Man* and *The Doom Patrol*, introducing animal rights philosophy. He also worked with one of the best Batman artists, Frank Quitely, on new X-Men comics. Eddie Campbell worked with Alan Moore to produce *From Hell*, a revisioning of the Jack the Ripper story, later filmed starring Johnny Depp.[67] But the central figure here is Alan Grant, the writer of *The Bogey Man*, which we discussed in the previous chapter. I would like to consider three further examples of his work.

Veterans of the publishing world of D.C. Thomson, Alan Grant and John Wagner became better known for their work on the punk-era comic series *2000AD* (which began in 1977), with its main character the ferocious Judge Dredd. The film version starring Sylvester Stallone, directed by Danny Cannon and released in 1995 was much softer than the comic-book character. Stallone as the Judge is actually seen smiling. Yet it captured an aspect of the comic character in the undeniable attractiveness of asserting absolute order over the complexities of chaos: 'I AM duh law!' exclaims Judge Dredd, in case there was any doubt. Using incontrovertible weaponry he blasts away anybody offering anything like an alternative point of view. He stalks out of a room he has destroyed, self-righteously proclaiming, 'This room has been pacified!' The satiric edge of the writing is not entirely lost in the film although the humour of the line may blur the fact that Grant intended Judge Dredd as an ambivalent hero or anti-hero. He was a character born in the era of Margaret Thatcher and Ronald Reagan, a champion not of freedom but of order, a hero of a Fascist state where chaos is the enemy, threatening total inundation. For Judge Dredd, to make a desert really is to bring about peace.[68]

The *Judge Dredd Megazine* spawned another Scottish comic series for which Grant was to write regularly, *Strontium Dog*, about a post-nuclear Britain in which mutant bounty-hunters led by Johnny Alpha take on jobs no one else would consider. Among the mutants from the Highlands and Islands division are The Alexander Brothers, a two-headed Siamese twin. Middenface McNulty represents the Scotland division, who features in a series of his own. In 2002, Grant was working on Middenface's boyhood

> and the events which led to a wee Scottish boy becoming the country's number 1 outlaw ('He Ate His Own Granny!' as the tagline puts it). It's *Oor Wullie* with guns and mutations, with a modicum of the 'Mutie Clearances' thrown in. There's a wide range of Scottish mutants, from Arbroath Smokie to Wally Dug to Ironbroo and Bonnie Charlie Prince. Middenface doesn't have the same *gravitas* as Batman, but he's a real hoot to write.[69]

In 1990, Grant was the guest writer and Cam Kennedy the guest artist for a one-off issue of *Nick Fury, Agent of S.H.I.E.L.D.* (it stood for Supreme Headquarters International Espionage Law Enforcement Division from 1963–1988, then after 1991 and a major plot reshuffle, Strategic Hazard Intervention Espionage, and Logistics Directorate).[70] Nick Fury had in fact already visited Scotland in 1968 in *Dark Moon Rise, Hell Hound Kill*, the third issue of the original comic-book series written and illustrated with magnificent flamboyance by Jim Steranko. The story is a variation on Conan Doyle's Sherlock Holmes classic, *The Hound of the Baskervilles* (it even includes reference to Holmes and a character named after Holmes's brother Mycroft). Fury is visiting a Scottish castle after its owner, an old friend from Fury's war years, has been found dead in mysterious circumstances on the moors. Ancient legends of devil-worship, Black Hugh Ravenlock, fratricide and a 'giant hound' provide Fury with clues and lead him to the discovery of an underground chamber and a Nazi U-Boat running as a modern pirate ship, raiding ocean-going ships and sinking them while masquerading as the Loch Ness Monster. Fury manages to foil the plot, blow up the sub, destroy the hound and see the villain killed (Mycroft turns out to be Miles Von Croff, ex-Nazi U-Boat Commander). Thus Fury ends the curse of Castle Ravenlock.[71] It is a magnificently arch and lavish homage to Doyle and the relocation of the legend from Dartmoor to Scotland is tellingly appropriate.

The ironic edge prevalent in the *Judge Dredd* stories is deployed more slyly in Grant's Nick Fury story, however. The cover presents the muscular eyepatched secret agent tied to a cross as two enormous eagles descend on him, talons extended. The caption reads, 'Just a typical relaxing vacation in Scotland?' The story, entitled 'Greetings from Scotland', opens with Fury climbing up the Old Man of Hoy in Orkney, under fire from two villains in microlight planes. The first words take the form of a postcard home: 'Hey Kate: Remember when I told ya I'd be visitin' the Orkney Islands, ya said to be sure an' take in the Old Man of Hoy on my tourist map? Well, babe, I went one better. I CLIMBED the sucker! An' that's not even ta mention the gun-totin' maniacs in microlights who were tryin' ta show me the fastest way down!'

Grant explained that in the story, 'the eyepatched one visits Orkney and uncovers a truckload of extremely spurious events. The story was inspired by Cam [Kennedy, the artist]'s and my visit to Isbister, the so-called Tomb of the Eagles, not far from Cam's home on Mainland [in Orkney].'[72] The story shows Fury bemused by Scots speech. As he leaps onto one of the microlights, his weight brings it, and him, down from the top of the Old Man of Hoy. The pilot calls out, 'Ya crazy eejit! Ye're draggin' us doon! Let go, ye bampot, or I'll slice ye like a damp clootie!' Fury replies with characteristic laconic wit, 'Come again, Jock? On second thought, don't bother. I'll catch the translation later...' before dropping safely to the water as the microlight and pilot are smashed against the cliff-face. Picked up by Murdo Mackay and drying on his boat, Fury concludes that he can now rule out the Old Man as a possible base for terrorists – unless, he wonders, it is hollow. Mackay gives Fury 'a wee taste o' that hospitality ye were expectin', an Orkney malt...' and the back-story unfolds.

Readers of the Nick Fury saga will recall that he began life in a comic series set in the Second World War, *Sergeant Fury and His Howling Commandos*. Murdo reminds him that they first met during the war, in occupied France, when, facing imminent capture, Murdo rescued Fury and his men and introduced himself as a Chaplain: 'One thing war's taught me, sojer – kill them first an' pray for their souls efter!' Murdo's call for Fury's help has brought the secret agent to Orkney, but by the end of the story, Murdo himself is revealed as the villain and Fury, after defeating his old friend, is left Byronic in his loneliness. The final panels show Fury alone in the ring of standing stones as the eagles swoop across the face of the moon. Now the letter home which has provided the story's narrative continuity concludes: 'For just a second, I couldn't tell if it was now or a long, long time ago. Then I remembered a man once saved my buddies' lives. Debt cancelled. See ya soonest.'

Despite its spectacular locations, the story is rueful and dark, coloured in shadowy blues, greys, browns and greens. Scots words and humour are used sparingly but with effective understatement, such as the magnificently absurd suspicion that a terrorist camp might be based either in the Old Man of Hoy (if it was hollow!) or on top of it (that's why Fury is climbing it in the first place, and all he finds is a small table of 'tuft-grass and seagulls'). The evocation of the original Sea Eagle tribe recollects images associated more closely with native American tribes than Scots – the huts, travois, stone-age garb and clubs are as likely to appeal to an American readership as to a Scottish one. But as Murdo says, in the Orkney Islands, 'Ye're thirty miles north o' Scotland . . . wi' a clear sea all the way frae America . . .'

The clear sea brought a more famous visitor to Scotland six years later. In *Shadow of the Bat*, with the artist Dave Taylor and colourist Stan Woch, Alan Grant contributed a self-contained episode in the series *Batman: Legacy*, which itself followed on from *Knightfall*, *Prodigal* and *Contagion*.[73] The long-running plot of the series was set in motion by a man-made viral disease, the Apocalypse Plague, which is unleashed in Batman's home town, Gotham City, where it reduces the population by hundreds of thousands. The *Legacy* series propels Batman away from Gotham City to various different parts of the world in the attempt to stop the spread of contagion. The villain's airline tickets suggest possible destinations: Paris, Edinburgh and Gotham. Robin goes to Paris. Batman heads for Edinburgh.

The cover of *Shadow of the Bat* shows Batman standing next to an ancient standing stone, on which are carved various indecipherable Pictish runes and Celtic designs, and above them, the sign of the Bat. The story begins 'On a bleak Scottish hillside, an ancient cottage continues its long, slow decline into oblivion . . .' Crops fail, rain falls, promise is unfulfilled and dreams are crushed and 'an old man wheezes away the final days of a life that went wrong . . .'. He is pictured in tartan shawl, bonnet and plaid. Then we move to Edinburgh, where a tourist guide is showing a group around an exhibition of Pictish Culture in Edinburgh Castle. Among them is Bruce Wayne, checking on anything imported from the Sudan. The guide tells him: 'There's many who believe that the stones have power – that they were erected across the land to heal it, the way needles are inserted into acupuncture points.' He replies: 'Mm'. On watch later that night, Batman sees three men in Highland dress furtively entering the Castle. When he stops them, they explain that they are dressed as Picts to mislead people – they have come 'to take back our stone'. Batman queries: 'You mean stealing?' They deny it, explaining they will return the money they were paid for it but they need the stone back. Suddenly a bunch of professional criminals appear. While Batman is fighting, two of these thieves slip away with two phials of the deadly virus. With the 'Picts' in support, Batman surfs down the steep stairs of Edinburgh's wynds and alleyways on a menu-board snatched from outside a restaurant, advertising 'Ye Olde Bathgate Haggis 'n Neeps'. He catches one villain and gets the phial but the other has escaped. The 'Picts' return and introduce themselves – Ranald, Lorne and Euan Tasker – and advise Batman that if the other villain is planning to release the virus from a high, windy location, the Scott monument in Princes Street could only be bettered by Salisbury Crags. On the way there, Batman is asked if he is not, in fact, the Bogey Man – in reference to the comic books that had appeared in the early 1990s, and Ranald speculates whether the villain is a Malthusian: 'They believe that a finite earth can't sustain mankind's indefinite expansion, so they want to wipe out most of humanity and start again – with the future made in their own image, of course! The same misguided nonsense that sustained Hitler!' Batman is impressed: 'First time I've come across a philosopher stealing stones from a castle.' Ranald corrects him: he is a university lecturer, 'actually'. His brothers run a decorating firm. They want the stone back for the sake of their father, who, we understand, was the old man at the opening of the story.

They catch up with villain number two, who kills himself as he tosses the phial towards the rocks, crying, 'Tonight Edinburgh – Tomorrow the woorrrlld!' Batman throws himself off the cliff, catches the phial unbroken, and dives straight into the handy little loch at the base of Salisbury Crags.

Batman is persuaded by the brothers of the virtue of their case and reckons that returning their stone to its rightful place would not be stealing. 'We helped you save a city, Batman,' Ranald pleads, 'Help us save an old man's spirit.' And in the closing pages, the standing stone is returned to the landscape depicted in the opening scene. There is the same view of the crumbling cottage but now there are shafts of bright sunlight on the land, and we note that what looked like broken ground in the first picture was the cavity from which the stone had been removed, and into which it is now replaced. A gravestone reads: 'Lachlan / Tasker / At rest / At last' – suggesting that the return of the stone may have eased the old man's final days even if it has not prevented his dying.

Further episodes in the series take Batman to Calcutta then back to Gotham, where he finally saves the day but cannot prevent the deaths of many more innocent people. He and Robin are left at the end remorseful, rather than triumphant.

The increasing darkness of the whole series was characteristic of the Batman universe in the 1990s. In 1999, an earthquake hits Gotham and the authorities seal the city off. The survivors are the criminal underworld and their helpless victims, only protected by what is left of the police force and Batman. As John Newsinger puts it, 'This is a dark reactionary vision of a predatory world where ordinary people are portrayed as weak and helpless' and the only protection comes from 'authorised vigilantes'. Meanwhile, in May 1999, Alan Grant began writing another monthly series for DC comics, *Anarky*, in which a teenage libertarian idealist calls into question 'the ideological underpinnings of the Batman universe. Why was it that Batman only ever went after the small fry, leaving the real criminals, the politicians, the businessmen, the bankers and the generals free?' Anarky plans 'to set the people free, to overthrow tyranny and to create a just society'. In one episode, he lectures Batman:

> where administration bigwigs view the world from stretch limos, while families sleep in cardboard boxes; corrupt businessmen flourish, while honest men beg in the gutter... The world is collapsing, Batman... The religious slaughterers, the inter-tribal massacres, the wars for oil have turned our planet into a charnel pit. Grinding poverty affects half mankind. 20 million people die each year because they're hungry... The élite have always won. The common man has always lost. Until tonight.

Batman accuses him of trying to brainwash people, Anarky replies that he intends to 'de-brainwash them'.[74] The political thrust of the message seems characteristically stern. But I want to end this brief look at comic books and their Scottish connections with a more positive, subtle and ambiguous case.

The cover of *Batman: Scottish Connection* (see frontispiece) shows the Caped Crusader doing battle with the villain, the last of the Sliths.[75] But the complex background of the story carefully decodes the clichés of tartan kilt and broadsword represented in the cover picture. The villain, Fergus Slith, is, like Batman, a visitor to Scotland from the USA, a bitterly vengeful descendant of Scots who were brutally sent into exile during the Highland Clearances.

Fergus Slith returns to Scotland to wreak vengeance on the Clan MacDubh, the landowners who originally sent his ancestors to New England's shores. Batman, as it turns out, is in fact related to the culpable Clan MacDubh. This compromises any sense of the 'purely' heroic in his character and underscores his role as 'the dark knight' (dubh is Gaelic for black). Batman's family connection is explicit. On the third page he says, 'Some of my more recent ancestors were actually Scots.' It is an important statement, offering the Batman franchise a new alliance with Scottish identity, touching on the idea that America is an immigrant nation and traditionally holds forth the ideal of tolerance of difference and variousness within its federated states. If we interpret this Batman, as written by Alan Grant, in this way, is he not worth having as an ally? The healthily ambivalent question of Grant's irony and our own ironic reading of it, as well as our knowledge of the commercial structures in which comic books operate, need not compromise this sense of the value of the dark knight's example.

So Batman is in fact fighting against entrenched sectarianism and villainously fixed and determined notions of identity, cross-generational resentments and the futile hatreds of the self-righteous deprived. He is fighting for tolerance, sympathy and a more progressive understanding of contemporary possibilities. He even wears the kilt himself, at the Clan MacDubh family reunion in Edinburgh Castle.

At this gathering, when Fergus launches his final attack, Bruce Wayne slips into a handy castle-turret to change out of his dress kilt and into the Batman costume. Like Spider-Man, he requires the assistance of the heroine, Fergus's good sister, Sheona, to bring the story to its happy resolution. In fact it is Sheona who sacrifices herself to stop her brother when Batman is helpless, his right arm almost chopped off in the climactic fight.

With the previous visits to Scotland made by Nick Fury and Batman, the country seems to have been used primarily as exotic locale, co-opted for colour and novelty. In *Batman: Scottish Connection*, such comedy is present while something different seems to be happening as well. As Alfred the Butler is driving Bruce Wayne through the Highlands, dodging murderous villains on the twisting roads, he comments: 'You might care to note, sir, that the area through which we're now passing is reputed to be some of the most beautiful scenery in western Europe.' Belying the calm tone, the panel shows the car in mid-air going over a humpback bridge in Glencoe as if it were a San Francisco movie set. Alfred reflects: 'A pity we're having to view it at eighty miles an hour!' This humour exploits the locale as exotic but it also displays a sympathetic irony. In the story as a whole, it is not simply that Batman is in a foreign location. It is rather that he has been co-opted into a place whose history and popular mythologies are connected to the American superhero. He has a stake in them and, for a time, his strangeness is appropriate to them. 'You may have seen Scotland from angles no-one else ever has, sir,' Alfred the butler tells Bruce Wayne as the story closes: '... but I enjoyed it immensely!'

The cover of the book is vivid: muscular and powerful, Batman is over-bearing in battle with wee Fergus Slith, yet Slith's tense posture, sinewy legs dynamic in kilt, the ferocity with which he is wielding a Wallace-sized broadsword, suggest that he is the aggressor. Batman's mask is as we would expect. But Slith's face is also masked, strangely, with a rectangular visor covered in large pustules – it is a plague-pockmarked mask and therefore a paradox. The mask of the Phantom of the Opera, for example, was intended to conceal the disfigured face beneath it. Fergus's mask is intended to bring forward the plague-scars his ancestors suffered when they were being transported to America after the Clearances. Although Fergus is smaller, thinner and lower in the picture than Batman, his raised sword, the angular, energetic posture and the viciousness of the pose suggest that Batman is in the weaker position, under threat, defending himself.

Behind both figures, there is an enormous blue and silver Saltire fluttering. The question is: who's fighting for the flag?

Conclusion: The Magnetic North

Tuesday, 6th. [Samoa, June 1893, aet. 42] – I am exulting to do nothing. It pours with rain from the westward, very unusual kind of weather; I was standing out on the little verandah in front of my room this morning, and there went through me or over me a wave of extraordinary and apparently baseless emotion. I literally staggered. And then the explanation came, and I knew I had found a frame of mind and body that belonged to Scotland. . . . . Very odd these identities of sensation, and the world of connotations implied; highland huts, and peat smoke, and the brown swirling rivers, and wet clothes, and whisky, and the romance of the past, and that indescribable bite of the whole thing at a man's heart . . .

– Robert Louis Stevenson, *The Letters*

'The Magnetic North' was the promotional slogan devised by the publishers Jonathan Cape and Vintage in the 1990s to advertise new Scottish writing – primarily fiction – by Janice Galloway, A.L. Kennedy, Duncan McLean, Tom Leonard, Alan Warner, Irvine Welsh, Alasdair Gray, James Kelman and Agnes Owens. It was the title given to a small, free anthology of their writing in 1995 and I would like to look briefly at some of this work and try to relate it to matters of language, voice and social identity in this final chapter.[1]

The conclusions I will come to, about the need to understand and experience home and belonging in different, sometimes difficult, but finally, I hope, affirming ways, might be more firmly made if we begin with a sense of the connection between the ethos of these writers, alongside their contemporaries in late twentieth-and early twenty-first century Scotland, with the politics of the left.

The politically progressive thrust of their work is varied but interconnected. It stands at a radical distance from the politics of the extreme right associated with the major poets of the Modern Movement, Ezra Pound and T.S. Eliot. Eliot's political vision is 'narrower, more dated, and far less accessible to imaginative assent than the vision of the verse' as Michael Long says; and Pound's political writing is

> aggressively suggestive of belts and toe-caps. Some of it, in prose and verse, seems to have been written with a knuckle-duster. His language often smells of the gang and the gutter. When he disagreed with someone he was not above simply dismissing his opponent as a Jew, yid, or kike...The vulgarity of the poet's human and political content is in stark, hardly believable contrast with the sophistication of rhythm and melody of which the accomplished verse in still capable.[2]

The Scottish writers of the 'magnetic north' are at the other end of the spectrum in the ethos of their work and the consistency of their commitment. Underlying their writing, as it underlies the writing of Eliot and Pound despite the grinding, opposing pull of their politics, is a locatable sense of desire. Location provides ground for balance and perspective to generate irony and compassion as well as difference and distinction. Specificity of place or history and the dynamics of social change in which these Scottish writers articulate their designs do not reject but endorse a politically forceful, leftist energy, which moves across time and place. In John Berger's words, 'The means used by each art at different periods for giving form to "what is held" are often historically determined. To analyse these determinants helps us to understand better the conditions under which people were living or were trying to live, and this is to understand better the form of their hopes.' But, he reminds us helpfully, 'What is *ahistorical* is the need to hope. And the act of hoping is inseparable from the energy of love, from that which "holds," from that which is art's constant example.'[3]

This sense of the *constant* value of art underlies the discussions we have engaged with, whether in terms of a recognised hope (say, for an achieved nation state with full powers of political and artistic self-determination) or in terms of an inarticulate yearning (as in so many examples of popular culture). In Chapter 7 we suggested that the Modern Movement was about exile as much as it was about art as an alternative home – or an alternative to home – in the modern world, and that the Scottish Renaissance of the 1920s was less about abandoning the home of one's native place than about re-inhabiting it with longer and more complex perspectives. The aestheticism in which the forms of modernist art become the model of a home that no individual can actually inhabit – because it can exist only in art – is one of the things that our focus on popular art helps both to define and to undermine. It defines it by clearly highlighting the aesthetic priorities of modernist art, whether in Joyce, Eliot or Pound, yet it undermines it by emphasising both the history of popular culture which was crucially transformed from the eighteenth to the nineteenth century (and vitally infused the work of Joyce, Eliot and Pound – despite the latter's political judgements) and by recognising the post-1940s world as one of mass media technology in which the aesthetics of modernism are recontextualised and altered.

In this conclusion, I would like to briefly look at some of the writers of the 'magnetic north' whose work proceeds in this latter context, clearly in contrast with the political bias of the modernist poets noted above; then I would like to consider some aspects of the familiar iconography of Scotland from the Victorian era through to ways in which it can be reconfigured in that more contemporary context; and then finally to approach a way of reading the idea of home as something both grounded and metaphoric, that distorts as well as heals, that needs to be rejected as well as inhabited. These conflicts and contradictions have been underlying all the arguments of this book and are reflected in the notion of masks as signals of *both* dissimulation *and* expressivity.

If nations themselves have to be masks, then they may intervene effectively in the world of international capitalism, both the capitalism of imperial struggle of the sixteenth century and the multi-national capitalism of the modern world. They are therefore part of, and may be resistant to, that international system. For example, New Zealand's resistence to nuclear power and weaponry in the 1980s was made possible by its national self-determination as a state. The virtues of that strength may have been belied by the nation's status in the hierarchy of global economic or military authority but were no less real for its inhabitants. Equally, Scotland's subjection to Westminster authority in the 1980s may have been dictated by British democratic process but it allowed for no such act of intervention beyond the protest of its citizens. In the twenty-first century, the climate of fear generated by the threat of terrorism coming from those who claim no necessary allegiance to nation or state seems a more frightening reaction to ambitions of comprehensively 'globalising'. This opens up questions for theoretical debate as well as pragmatic politics which must be deferred for the sake of the focus I intend to maintain on matters of literature and cultural production. However, it would be wise to register the fact that not all of Scotland's masks may be available for benign use. It is arguable that even George Davie's key-work *The Democratic Intellect*, with reference to which we began this book and which has supplied a running theme of egalitarian idealism recognised in the Preface as a distinctive Scottish myth, offers a version of Scotland in which intellect is precisely the preserve of a meritocracy that has no designs on democratising its power. There are always systems that protect vested interests just as there are always spanners to throw in them.

So, to what extent is the work of the writers of the 'magnetic north' democratising Scotland? I would like to suggest a context of precedents and continuities for the work of such fiction writers as Kennedy, Kelman and

Leonard. I will begin by considering them briefly and individually, then sketch in one immediate forebear. Then I will go back to the larger context with which we began this book and the notions of change, the canon and 'home'.[4]

I would like to complement these separate sub-chapters with a consideration of visual representations of Scots or 'Scottishness' in images which repeat, but vary, an immediately recognisable stance. If there are identifiable masks in all these images we might consider their function in enabling expression, rather than inhibiting or constricting it. Such familiar masks or postures may be comforting but if they are to be used creatively, we cannot be complacent about them. They must keep their 'unpredicted' aspect. They might be as intimate as languages, forms of speech with which we are familiar, idioms of sound in which we feel at home.

But one of the great lessons of the Modern Movement was that if all its major writers were, in some sense, exiles, then each of them fashioned their writing in a language they had to reapproach or reappropriate, in order to occupy it as comprehensively as they did. In the art that mediates between a geographical location and linguistic communication, there is another kind of home. Aesthetics is vitally important in the work of art that mediates in this way, but the work of art is also a practice, and can be a daily engagement with reality in all its forms, changing whatever home might be, or might be made into. Finally, therefore, I would like to consider the idea of home more closely and more universally, to approach the idea of inhabiting Scotland's masks in ways that can make the best use of them.

A.L. Kennedy's first collection of short stories *Night Geometry and the Garscadden Trains* suggests these capacities of familiarity and unpredictedness. The nocturnal transports named in the title – Garscadden is a railway station near Glasgow where an uncanny number of trains 'terminate' after midnight – apply not only to her tracing the lives of the curiously unexceptional people who are her characters and narrators, but also to the strange meaninglessness in their lives: 'contrary to popular belief', she writes in the title-story, 'people, many people, almost all the people, live their lives in the best way they can with generally good intentions and still leave nothing behind'.[5] An Olympic skier or a chat show host will get some proof of their own existence, but the silent majority have only one memorial, 'The Disaster': 'We have small lives, easily lost in foreign droughts, or famines; the occasional incendiary incident, or a wall of pale faces, crushed against grill work, one Saturday afternoon in Spring. This is not enough.'[6]

Kennedy's second novel, *So I Am Glad*, boldly departed from naturalist conventions, introducing Cyrano de Bergerac into modern Glasgow and making of him a very tangible, lonely and bewildered present-day lover at the same time as he is a ghostly figure from a half-remembered past, a foreign country he is haunted by. Kennedy's unstrained use of the conventional science fiction trope of time-travel initiates a metaphorical understanding, as the narrator, who becomes Cyrano's lover, poignantly realises how distant she is from him as their intimate selves draw closer.

Kennedy's deployment of emotional states is matched by her unemphatic use of the exotic: she can write alarmingly lucid prose about terribly volatile conditions with almost no recourse to sentimentalism. If sentimentalism entails a claim to be exempt – when a special case is made for a particular character or relationship the risk is always that it will seem sentimental – then Kennedy keeps free of that tendency by insisting on the commonality of the experiences she evokes. This is a rare skill, not just in modern Scottish fiction but generally. Kennedy is, perhaps, of all contemporary English-language novelists, the one who has been dwelling most thoughtfully on all the resonant meanings in the words with which George Eliot closed *Middlemarch*: 'for the growing good of the world is partly dependent on unhistoric acts; and that things are not so ill with you and me as they might have been, is half owing to the number who lived faithfully a hidden life, and rest in unvisited tombs'.[7]

Beside Kennedy stand her contemporaries and seniors: Janice Galloway, Liz Lochhead, Iain Banks, James Kelman, Alasdair Gray, Agnes Owens, Jeff Torrington, Tom Leonard, and behind these, Alexander Trocchi and Catherine Carswell and others. Behind them all, there is the argument of 1936 which we discussed in Chapter 1, when Edwin Muir declared that Scottish literature could only be advanced through writing in English and Hugh MacDiarmid rejected Muir's proposition on the grounds that, since there are lots of different voices, the work of literature should be to represent their full range. MacDiarmid's counter-proposition was that anyone who denies any voice its validity is not simply a literary critic but a political enemy, and he set out to oppose Muir from that point on. While the writers of the 'magnetic north' are attentive to the complexities of their own time, their work is an affirmation of MacDiarmid's stand for a plurality of voices and political self-consciousness. As Seamus Heaney has said, 'There is a demonstrable link between MacDiarmid's act of cultural resistance in the Scotland of the 1920s and the literary self-possession of writers such as Alasdair Gray, Tom Leonard, Liz Lochhead and James Kelman in the 1980s and 1990s. He prepared the ground for a Scottish literature that would be self-critical and experimental in relation to its own inherited forms and idioms, but one that would also be stimulated by developments elsewhere in world literature.'[8]

Related to this generation of writers are three elders and a fourth. Alasdair Gray, James Kelman and Tom Leonard were often linked before their joint appointment to the Chair of Creative Writing at the University of Glasgow in 2001 gave their association a formal academic status. It was a courageous proposition for the three writers to make, to job-share the appointment, and if controversial, it was equally brave of the institution to make it happen. Their association was based in friendship, respect for each other's work and political affinities, and the connections between their writings are deeper than a shared position of paid employment. (The position dissolved in 2003 with Gray's retirement and Kelman's resignation.) Here, I would like to emphasise the significance of the publication of Gray's novel *Lanark* in 1982, and recollect the way in which it shifted attention crucially and permanently to the social position of artistic vision in urban Scotland in an affirmation of both the strengths of that world and the value of that vision. The social location of citizenship, Gray reminds us persistently, is where such arts must function as best they can.

Most of James Kelman's work is insistently committed to the meticulous exposition of the condition of disempowered, working-class men. The extent of his attention is exhaustive. His rigorous rejection of middle-class hope, with its susceptibility to the attendant privileges of benevolent values and a glib sense of possibility, makes humour in his work a rare thing since his first novel in 1984, *The Bus Conductor Hines*. The presence of laughter in *The Good Times* (1998) signals an elaboration on the sense of absurdity which was central to his earliest writing. In 'Comic Cuts' – a long, rambling account of a small group's drink-fuelled late-night conversation as they wait for one of their number to deliver bowls of soup (which, like Godot, reliably fail to arrive) – the comedy is both hilarious and bitter. The penultimate line – 'the door creaked open, or seemed to' – hints at the 'imperceptibly open door' in the stage directions of one of Samuel Beckett's plays. When a director asked him what on earth this meant, Beckett is said to have replied, 'The door's shut.' Kelman keeps stylistic balance by never giving way to cliché or facile humour. The ancestors of his characters are K, in Kafka's *The Trial*, Melville's 'Bartleby the Scrivener' with his repeated line, 'I would prefer not to' and Beckett's *Molloy*, discovering even when he falls, 'Christ there's crawling, I never thought of that.'[9] Humour is a clue to the strength of these characters, but not in any easy way. The men in Kelman's fictions are intelligent, strong, resourceful, and painfully delimited by a class structure that, again and again, denies them any possibility of further expression. They need all the words Kelman gives them.

Tom Leonard also has much to say about language, class and the structures of power, hierarchies of authority and the actual, living voices of women and men. No map of modern Britain can be true without taking account of him. That his writing is true to those voices and responsible both to the accuracy of his reports and the lives he is speaking for is to his credit as an artist as much as it is a register of his tenacity, determination and faith in a culture to resist the normality of a world where the doors between compartments are usually kept bolted. He tells us (and the complicity of deadly serious statement with immediately accessible comic effect is typical, and characteristically Scottish) in 'Unrelated Incidents 2':

fyi stull
huvny
thoata lang-
wij izza
sound-system;
fyi huvny
hudda thingk
aboot thi dif-
frince tween
sound
n object n
symbol;
well,
ma innocent
wee
friend – iz
god said ti
adam:

a doant kerr
fyi caw it
an apple
ur
an aippl –
jist leeit
alane![10]

In the poignant, searching essay 'Poetry, Schools, Place', Leonard reflects on the best way to present poetry to pupils in schools. He ends with an auto-biographical picture of a boy walking by a stream, thinking of the library at Pollok House, the people who were allowed to visit it and those who would have been kept out. Leonard's prose weaves narrative, immediate visual imagery and abstract contemplation. The essay ends with a memorable reading of the climactic scene of *The Winter's Tale* which demonstrates the connection between fundamental human truths and the value of art: for it is only in art that an object can 'come to have human life in your presence'.[11]

Christ and the Demon

The fourth figure, a little older than Leonard, Kelman and Gray, but standing beside and behind all the writers mentioned in the conclusion, is Edwin Morgan.

Greatest living poets are frequently unknown to the professoriat, the reviewers, the custodians of laurels and the general populace. Edwin Morgan, however, increasingly towards the end of the twentieth century and in the early twenty-first was taught in schools and universities, was widely read and gave sell-out public readings, gained awards and recognitions such as the Queen's Award for Poetry and was appointed Poet Laureate of Glasgow. On 16 February 2004, the First Minister for Scotland appointed him 'Poet for Scotland' or 'Scots Makar' – effectively, Scotland's first national Poet Laureate. This was done with unanimous cross-party support. As far as it was possible to be a popular poet, Morgan was it.

At the turn of the century, Morgan published two books that dovetail into each other perfectly. In 1999, a slim sequence appeared from the small Glasgow press Mariscat, wrapped in a red cover with black endpapers (red and black being the traditional colours of the Devil) entitled *Demon*. The poems are mischievous, bitter, hard reminders of an underworld, narrated in the first person by the Demon himself. Who is the Demon? He is singular but he is not the Devil, not an embodiment or symbol defined within any given orthodoxy. He is rather something any human being has, potentially or actually, to whatever degree, a kind of ferocious soul. He is the corrective to tranquillity, when serenity becomes complacent. He begins by telling us, 'My job is to rattle the bars. It's a battle.' He drags an iron shaft along the iron gate and drives the guard-dog berserk, 'not trying / To get out; nor ... trying to get in'. The point I would like to emphasise here is that the Demon is related to Christ, in Morgan's trilogy of plays on the life of Jesus, *A.D.* (published in 2000). Here we have Jesus tell us, 'Nothing is due to Caesar / Who is an oppressor all over the world' and that we should 'Take a crossbow to the bloated belly of convention.'[12] There is nothing compromised in this judgement. As we noted in Chapter 2, Morgan's Jesus rejects the morbid and speaks invigorating truth: 'In the midst of life I find myself in art. / In the midst of art I find myself in life.'[13]

In the pavement at Candleriggs, in Glasgow's Merchant City, outside the Glasgow Concert Hall, near the former Victorian Market, now Merchant Square, four poems are set in concrete. You walk around them, turning 90 degrees for each as they are set against each other. They commemorate the tradesmen, market wares, the City Motto and the industrial workers. Above, on the wall, a plaque memorialises John MacLean, 1879–1923: 'socialist pioneer who spoke here frequently to unemployed workers...'. But the poems do not prioritise their subjects. The tradesfolk are attractively varied, sometimes unexpected – not only 'heavy hammermen' and 'sinewy sawyers' but also 'well-read weavers', 'toty tailors' and 'aroculous maltsters' and a 'bonny barber'. The fruits of the old market are vividly present: the apples piled high, the tangerines tingling, the grapefruit eyes up the bellying melon basket, and we hear the voices of older generations: 'have you a – / Pumpkin, is that big enough' and there are cherries by the thousand, 'earthy mushrooms', crisp, cool lettuces, 'crated pineapples, fierce / as lobsters, watch them!' And the tomatoes 'pour and settle / in the great red / flood in the sun'. But the most haunting of them is the four-line poem you read facing north:

> Ghostly workers sleep below
> They hear no rain or heel and toe
> Think of them where the forges glow
> In the Glasgow of long ago

No author is named. There is no signature on the concrete pavement slabs, but there is a mark: six marks, small straight lines, three horizontal (a capital 'E' without the vertical) three vertical (a capital 'M' without the leaning). Reading them in the knowledge of Morgan's work, their author is unmistakeable, even without the mark. But the anonymity says something about the way they work: their commemoration is of the people they name and suggest, more than their author. The representation of these people is there to help the living – who notice and read – to celebrate, feel fond, attracted, strengthened, hungry, haunted, perhaps fearful, perhaps empowered.

Art makes long conversations possible with those who have gone. And popular art – popular culture in the most general sense now – can help bring such living possibilities closer. This is its attraction and danger. The sound-systems that are languages are omnipresent, essential to being human. If this is a banal observation to those of us privileged by the sophistication of the experience of higher forms of education, it should always keep us in mind of the offence we perpetuate if we are complacent about the currency of operating sound-systems. Dr Johnson and Robert Fergusson, Edwin Morgan's anonymous concrete poems and a multitude of other texts are, to paraphrase Morgan, art in the midst of life. They remind us of popular culture – what music, painting, television, what radio, cinema, comic books, can do. They remind us of the spectrum of that currency, its promise and its debasement and the longing within it. And they ask us to take seriously the ways the means of production and distribution of sounds and attitudes, confidence and embarrassment, the manufacture of cool and hard, fashion and irony, the generation of comfort and wit, engagement and apathy affect us all.

Canons and change

To draw towards a conclusion, we need to keep the value and danger of this potential in all art keenly in mind. Elitist disdain of ephemeral, populist, mass-produced work, or philistine disregard of high art and difficult work are equally inappropriate here. The point is, they are connected. I would like to elaborate this point briefly through a simple observation about Scottish cultural history and a popular, iconic image. The image is that of the damned but defiant figure of self-determined opposition. Unpersuadable and permanently resistent, this image is there from the very beginnings of our constructions of Scottish literature and cultural history. And the simple observation I want to make about this is that historical events are very quickly entered into cultural representation. The canon quickly accommodates change. I wish to make a further point also: it is possible to restructure the image itself so that the tendency to defuse its political charge is blocked and a defiant potential retained. This will become clear as we look at some examples.

The first example is the well-known passage in Tacitus, in *Agricola*, where the Roman writer describes his uncle's campaign in Scotland and the military conflict with the tribes of Calgacus. Tacitus lived 55–120 AD and *Agricola* was written 97–98 AD, twenty years after he had married Agricola's daughter and about thirteen years after the battle of Mons Graupius, in 83 AD, in the Grampians (in Perthshire or Aberdeenshire). The speech Calgacus makes to the men in his army before the battle seems to define a position and describe a commitment that has entered the mythos of popular culture. It may have been reported to Tacitus by Agricola himself, who may have actually heard it (though if he did it is doubtful whether he could have understood it). Whatever its accuracy as history, though, its literary art is outstanding. Calgacus reminds his men that their backs are to the wall: 'There are no lands behind us and even the sea is menaced by the Roman fleet.'

> We, the last men on earth, the last of the free, have been shielded till to-day by the very remoteness and the seclusion for which we are famed. We have enjoyed the impressiveness of the unknown. But to-day the boundary of Britain is exposed; beyond us lies no nation, nothing but waves and rocks and the Romans... Brigands of the world, they have exhausted the land by their indiscriminate plunder, and now they ransack the sea. The wealth of an enemy excites their cupidity, his poverty their lust of power. East and West have failed to glut their maw. They are unique in being as violently tempted to attack the poor as the wealthy. Robbery, butchery, rapine, the liars call Empire; they create a desolation and they call it peace.[14]

Of course, this is Tacitus's writing. Calgacus would have to have been educated in Rome himself to be able to see the world in this way. It is as fictional a refashioning of a story and a posture as that accomplished by Mel Gibson in *Braveheart*. It seems likely that Tacitus made up Calgacus's speech as a literary device, probably derived from conventions of epic. Tacitus then has Calgacus urge his men not to fear 'the outward show that means nothing, the glitter of gold and silver' and he commands, 'On, then, into action and, as you go, think of those that went before you and of those that shall come after.'

Tacitus reports 10,000 deaths among the Britons and 360 among the Romans. 'A grim silence reigned on every hand, the hills were deserted....' Tacitus ends his account of Agricola's life by saying that his 'story has been told to posterity and by that he will live'. But the name of Calgacus and the stance by which Tacitus defined him and his army resonates beyond the specific story and its historical moment.

A similar quality is there in *The Gododdin*, the sixth-century poem on the battle of Catraeth, whose author, Aneirin, may have been one of the few who survived it. The land of the Gododdin lay between the Forth and the Tyne, and Edinburgh was its capital. No single hero emerges in the poem, but a prevalent sense of the universal end of heroic idealism surrounds it: 'Golden this brave's band./Half the wolf in him./Half the temple too... He ended in bloodshed./Blood belongs everywhere.'[15] Here it is not a David-and-Goliath scenario but a fatalism and dark purposefulness that drives the action while a heavy sense of mortality pervades the poem's terse lines.

But Calgacus's affirmation of individual freedom, social liberty and national self-determination is as vividly present in Robert Burns's 'Scots wha hae' as Bruce addresses his troops before Bannockburn, just as we have seen the scorn for the show of silver and gold in 'Is there, for honest poverty...' ('A Man's a Man...'). The same affirmation is passionate in Burns's patriotic letter to Dr Moore of 2 August 1787, in which he declares that reading the history of William Wallace 'poured a Scottish prejudice into my veins which will boil along there, till the flood-gates of life shut in eternal rest'.[16]

It is there in a whole catalogue of references to Celtic gods and heroes from Macpherson's Ossian to Lady Gregory's Cuchulainn of Muirthemne, who dies with his back to a standing stone, sword in his hand: 'He drank a drink, he washed himself, and he turned back again to his death, and he called to his enemies to come and meet him.' Seeing a pillar-stone by the lake, he ties himself to it, 'the way he would not meet his death lying down, but would meet it standing up'. [17]

It is there in the resonant climactic phrase of the *Declaration of Arbroath* in 1320: 'We fight not for glory nor for wealth nor for honours: but only and alone we fight for FREEDOM, which no good man surrenders but with his life.' And this is confirmed in the famous lines from Barbour's *Bruce* (1375):

> A! fredome is a noble thing!
> Fredome mays man to haiff liking:
> Fredome all solace to man giffis:
> He lyvs at es that frely levys.[18]

It is there in Blind Harry's *The Actes and Deidis of the Illustre and Vallyeant Campioun Schir William Wallace*, written around 1477 and described by Elspeth King as 'one of the most popular works of literature and history in Scotland of all time' – particularly after its revisions in the version by William Hamilton of Gilbertfield in 1722 (the version Burns read), then in Jane Porter's novelised version of 1810, *The Scottish Chiefs* (a best-seller translated into Russian, German and French), and then in Randall Wallace's script for Mel Gibson's film *Braveheart* in 1994.[19] It is evoked by the moral certainty in the image of Bruce in retreat in his cave, watching the spider returning to weave its web and resolving proverbially, in the face of seemingly insuperable odds, 'If at first you don't succeed, try, try again.' It is part of the myth of defeat which surrounds the imagery of the Jacobite risings, doomed at a time when the whole imperial weight of the United Kingdom was moving away from the reactionary ideals of Prince Charles Edward Stewart.

The literary appropriation of the mythic stature of this quality of affirmation presents the Celtic hero defiant even in the face of destruction, the Dying Gaul, hounded by empire to the edges of Europe, then finding on the other side of the Atlantic a regenerated myth of the furthering frontier in America. We recognise its universal relevance in the closing sequence of Sam Peckinpah's film *The Wild Bunch* (1969), when the outlaw leader Pike Bishop offers an abbreviated version of Calgacus's speech in the words, 'Let's go . . .' before he and his men walk through the town to try to help one of their own, knowing that death is inevitable. In Scotland, though, the tone of damned defiance links back to where we began, with Edward MacGuire's tone poem *Calgacus* (1976), this time depicted in an orchestral composition where, anachronistically but to brilliant effect, a solitary pipe-tune breaks out over the gathering orchestral masses and its courageous, independent, self-determined note continues as the orchestra gathers, rises and crushes it.[20] The myth might seem over-familiar but here it is intensely expressed.

Edna Longley has written closely on the myths of Celt and Saxon in modern poetry, wondering whether, for a time, Seamus Heaney and Ted Hughes were subscribing to a kind of Celt/Saxon 'double act'.[21] It is well-known that the idea of the Celtic character comes through Matthew Arnold's 'On the Study of Celtic Literature' of 1867 and Ernest Renan's 'The Poetry of the Celtic Races' and is a familiar nineteenth-century trope. It is worth noting that Arnold's support of Saxon hegemony and simultaneous attraction to the Celtic spirit has its own roots in the dichotomy between Highlander and Lowlander founded in Scott's *Waverley* – another key text appropriating recent history to literary myth. Political Union meant the fusion of Anglo-Celtic identity and economic progress for Scott as for Arnold. The myth could serve in the furtherance of political design. Yet if it feeds kitsch, we might remind ourselves of Ben Okri's perception that kitsch might also serve *progressive* political ends. When George MacDonald, in Chapter 28 of *The Marquis of Lossie*, includes reference to 'The ancient fury of the Celt' it may be an unconscious drawing up of a sense of innate capacity that links back to Shakespeare's Douglas and a composite figure made from Caliban and Ariel, flaring, earthy, gutteral, but also flighty and quick.[22] The origins of

Illustration 8   Sir Edwin Landseer, 'The Monarch of the Glen' 1851

the idea might be deeper than nineteenth-century racial theory, and they might yet have more to do than can be predicted.

Edwin Landseer (1803–1873), in *The Monarch of the Glen* (1851), produced the most famous image of what has been termed the 'Stag at bay/Lord of all I survey' genre.[23] The two aspects of this 'genre' are clearly seen in the texts we have been discussing: both the nobility of the solitary creature, mortal, proud, self-possessed and self-determined, yet there to be hunted, cornered, doomed, damned but defiant. The painting was originally intended to adorn the House of Lords refreshment rooms yet the patrician element in that image is tainted with bitterness, irony and pathos when T.S. Eliot alludes to it in 'Rannoch, by Glencoe' when he writes of a place where 'the crow starves' and 'the patient stag/Breeds for the rifle'.[24]

Illustration 9   Cynicus, 'Thistleman' nineteenth century

As we have seen in his photograph of John Brown and Queen Victoria, George Washington Wilson seems to capture some of the same spirit in the attitude of the kilted Scot, sternly staring at the cameraman, reconfirming the hierarchical status of Victorian authority. Derived from this stance, if not literally then by a descent of affinity, is the memorable representation of the *praefervidum ingenium Scotorum* in the postcard 'Wha Daur Meddle Wi' Me' by the cartoonist Cynicus (Martin Anderson, 1854–1932). His biographers describe it as 'a tiny furious scarlet-faced creature...its Balmoral bonnet rammed down, in its hand a pennant bearing the national motto. On a closer look we discover that the imp is not human at all but vegetable. It is the Scotch thistle.'[25] The personality depicted is curiously infantile, spiky and brist-lingly hostile and unfriendly yet the eyes seem beseeching, frustrated, trapped in the caricature the creature has become, flat-footedly rooted under the banner and the bonnet. The downcurved mouth is as grim as John Brown's. The expression seems both comic and pathetic. The boast seems feeble. A good pair of secateurs or a gloved hand's swift wrench could decapitate this thistle easily. Cynicus, it appears, was both sympathetic and ruthlessly scathing in his postcard caricatures of contemporary Scotland.

There is surely a resemblance between Cynicus's Thistleman and the kilted, toorie-bunneted Elmer Fudd character in the Bugs Bunny cartoon which pits Elmer against Bugs in a golfing match on the prairie. Fudd – or MacFudd, as he is in the cartoon – has the same tightly drawn down bon-net and veers between anger and frustrated rage when Bugs repeatedly and laconically outwits him. He makes an emblem of his costume in his actions. Meanness catches him out as Bugs conducts a mock-auction in which he brings the numbers *down*, leading MacFudd deeper into ridicu-lousness. With snatches of Scottish popular song on the soundtrack ('Ye'll take the high road and I'll take the low road...' and 'Wi' a hundred pipers an' a', an' a'...') their battle culminates in MacFudd's desperate cry of, 'Well, at least ye canny beat me at the pipes!' He pulls out a set of bagpipes and gives an impressive performance for three seconds, only to be bested by Bugs, walking on with a set of bagpipes, to which are attached kettle drums, trumpets and various other instruments, so that for a few seconds longer we see the traditional instrument of Scotland jazzed up into some-thing cool, at the centre of an orchestral rag-bag all controlled by Bugs's dexterity.

MacFudd is fuming. Bugs winks at the camera. '"That's all folks!"' The best – or worst – example of this stereotyping is perhaps Scrooge MacDuck, in the Donald Duck cartoons. But does not Bugs Bunny hold forth a more flexible image, one that might be appropriated? For MacFudd, the playing of the pipes is an equaliser similar to the contest in Chapter XXV of Steven-son's *Kidnapped*, between Alan Breck Stewart and Robin Oig Macgregor. MacFudd plays in frustration at being unable to win otherwise. For him, the bagpipes are an expression of guilt. But if Stevenson resolves the situ-ation in *Kidnapped* happily within the historical context of his narrative, no such rules need apply to cartoon fantasy. The travelling one-man-band bagpipes Bugs walks on playing at the end need not be rejected *tout court*. They might afford an example of adaptability. Bugs uses them with guile, but without guilt. Elmer could not learn from that because he exists within the dictatorship of the constraints of formulaic cartoon characters. But we might.

Illustration 10   Peter Howson, 'Heroic Dosser' 1987 (National Galleries of Scotland)

In Peter Howson's painting *Heroic Dosser* (1987), the posture has been redeployed to intensely powerful, subversive and serious effect. The strength of the image, the power in the fingers, the set of the shoulders and forehead tilted up, the hands on the rail and the boots, all advertise self-determination. This is a lastingly emphatic reassertion of Burns's sentiments of human worth residing in the individual beyond constraints of class, financial means or social privilege. Homeless he may be, but the heroic stance rejects condescension or pity and more than that, it effects a valiant judgement upon those who helped drive distance between privilege and ruin in the 1980s. In 'Proclamation / 15 May 88', in his book *Abhorrences*, the American poet Edward Dorn described the ethos of the era:

> Where there is wealth
> let us create excess . . .

where there is need,
let us create hardship,
where there is poverty,
let us create downright misery.[26]

At the height of the 1980s Conservative Government rule in Britain, when what
Liz Lochhead called 'the Thatcher monster' seemed unstoppable, Howson's
painting inhabits and exhibits a world of 'honest poverty' in which a kind of
tenderness prevails. There is human sympathy in this painting: it is emphatically not a caricature. The man himself is big but not insensitive. He did not
create his own condition and he is standing against it, a permanent reminder of
things we might rather forget. All the writers of the 'magnetic north' evoke this
figure, in different masks or stories. As Edwin Morgan puts it in 'Day's End':

The night wind rises, and the rain is bold.
The homeless in their doorways clutch the cold,
still real, still waiting for the tale to be told.[27]

The unfinished business of home

In the Introduction to this book I referred to images reliably associated with
Scotland and reassuringly familiar to students I taught through fourteen
years in New Zealand: tartan, haggis, whisky, heather, wild mountain scenery and bad weather. I said that these images might be contextualised with
purpose, not to deny the pleasures they afford, but to see deeper into where
they come from. I would like to draw to a close by suggesting the major
themes noted when I pursued the question with students in Glasgow in the
early years of the twenty-first century. The same images came up but then
we began to ask about how Scottish literature, music and art, television programmes, films and the whole paraphernalia of recognisable iconography
had been presented in schools. It had not been discussed very frequently
as an object for serious consideration. Beyond the clichés, key themes in
Scottish literature emerged. These might be itemised.

1. The matter of *voice*, voices, sound-systems in speech, hierarchies of power
   encoded in these systems of sound, articulation and approach. A recognition of different voices in a conversation whose first principle is not to
   drown out or overwhelm each other, nor to competitively persuade each
   other into speaking in the same way and uniformly, but to speak or sing
   in order to engage in acts of listening, to pay attention to the differences
   between voices and what they mean. This is not to endorse acquiescence
   but to heighten understanding and empower voices, and it recollects not
   only Tom Leonard's 'Unrelated Incidents' quoted above but also, as we
   noted, the conflict between Muir and MacDiarmid after 1936.

2. The importance of *place*, location, where the voices come from and how they relate to the geography, or even the geology, of such locations. Few other literatures at any time have so closely related themselves to particular landscapes or specific terrain. Wordsworth's lakes, Dickens's London, Joyce's Dublin, arguably, are exceptions that prove the rule. Consider the case in Scotland: the Glasgow of Morgan, Lochhead, Gray, Kelman, the Skye and Raasay of MacLean, Crichton Smith's Lewis, the Orkney islands of Muir and Mackay Brown, MacDiarmid's Borders and Shetlands, the Edinburgh of Irvine Welsh, Walter Scott, Stevenson, Spark, Ramsay and Dunbar, Burns's Ayrshire and Duncan Ban MacIntyre's Ben Dorain. Students regularly notice how the naming of familiar places enhances their sense of what it is to live there. This is true of cities as much as of moors and mountains. The list could go on much further but the essential point is that Scottish writers and artists are gravitationally concerned with 'the background of meaning which a landscape suggests to those familiar with it'. John Berger describes this: 'It begins with what the eye sees every dawn, with the degree to which it is blinded at noon, with how it feels assuaged at sunset. All this has a geographical or topographical basis.' And here 'the geographic' means 'a representation which is constant yet always ambiguous and unclear because what it represents is about the beginning and end of everything. What we actually see (mountains, coastlines, hills, clouds, vegetation) are the temporal consequences of a nameless, unimaginable event. We are still living that event, and geography . . . offers us signs to read concerning its nature.'[28]

3. The matter of *the nation*, Scotland itself, the value of national identity that occurs again and again, not in the form of banal nationalism but as a curious, unanswered question, the unfinished business of home. It exists between the particular localities and the international context, recognising the internal complexities and global relationships but still negotiating, questioning, sometimes with intense urgency, sometimes exhaustedly, sometimes almost contemptuously, the status of a describable national character which might work in a comity of nations and states. In a world of globalised interest, self-determined nationality may be the only viable opposition to imperial power.

4. The things that can be done with *language* – the idea that language is only partly natural, a given thing, innate in being human, but that it is also not to be taken for granted – it is constructed. Alongside a recognition of variations in voices, there is this recognition of language as something which might ground you, but from which you must depart and to which you must return as a foreigner, to see it fresh and build into its potential. We have noted that this is one of the great lessons of the Modern Movement, that the major writers of that movement were all exiles, often in geographical terms but more closely in terms of their language. Consider Conrad's credo in the Preface to *The Nigger of the 'Narcissus'*: 'My task

which I am trying to achieve . . .' (that phrasing already slows you down enough to grasp the struggle behind it) '. . . is, by the power of the written word to make you hear, to make you feel – it is, before all to make you *see*. That – and no more, and it is everything.'[29] This *seeing* is to do with more than the picturable. It is about comprehension, understanding, contemplation and critical engagement in the processes and mechanisms available for such activities – in the language itself. And here language might be understood metaphorically too, to mean media – any form of communication from words to pigments, musical tones in the air, moving images, cartoons, operas, comic books.

5. A sense of *people* as various and capable of more than any life can give them. Consequently a sense of education as a birthright, an egalitarian principle by which art and creativity are given access to people and people to their own potential. A democratic intellect alongside a rigorously reductive sense of what makes common our humanity. Animal facts as well as the capacities of mind. Perhaps this links back to the variousness of the terrain – the sense of place – in the context of the radical egalitarianism each north European winter reminds us of annually.

6. And with that, a sense of darkly sustaining *humour*. It is possible to imagine Muriel Spark's world written by someone else without a sense of humour but it is, most essentially, that combining of deadly seriousness with murderous laughter that is so entirely characteristic of that world. It is the most unmistakeable quality in *The Prime of Miss Jean Brodie* or *The Ballad of Peckham Rye*.

These themes run deep. Voice, place, the nation, language, people, education, humour – these are all things individuals leave behind them, and then make again, or remake in new ways, or return to with new knowledge and experience.

This book has approached Scotland in various texts written within or beyond the country's borders, and explored forms in which aspects of the nation's identity have found expression. These texts and forms – masks that reveal various kinds of depth and capacity – are always figured in terms of the technology (narratology, literary fashion, cultural transport) of their historical moment, but the best of them are always returning us to essential truths, which, luckily, every generation rediscovers. It is, then, finally a matter of how to approach them.

The two slogans MacDiarmid devised in the 1920s, which we discussed in Chapter 1, may remind us now of two ways of approaching the texts and authors we have been considering. Each is different but they overlap or interpenetrate each other, apparently contradictory, but at best, effectively complementary. One, as we noted, implies the investigation and thorough revaluing of cultural traditions, the other the abandoning of traditional definitions or constraints and the seizing of initiatives that can be put to creative use. One represents an impulse towards categorical knowledge, comprehensive understanding, codification and securities, the other represents a drive towards spontaneity – not in the total abandonment of form, but in a different, unpredicted kind of inhabitation of it. One might be embodied by scholarship, the other by artistry.

Scotland, like anywhere else, may be cursed and possessed by the worst exaggerations of either in extremes: the mortmain of weighted pedantry or the emptiness of mere gesture, the tedium of solemnity and the tiresomeness of vandalism are equally dangerous forms of delusion in the modern world. Yet the closure canonicity may seem to threaten is always open to revision when the impulse to subversion remains as essential as the recognition of the authority of co-ordinates. It would be a mistake to be locked into one or the other posture: either active in the constant subversion of canonicity or fixed in support of a perpetually unchanging canon. Both positions are false promises of stability. They offer, not securities, but predictable reflexes: iconography at its worst. Perhaps, because of its unfinished business of self-determination, its diversity and contradictions, its linguistic heterogeneity, its curiously evolving forms of representation, modern Scotland is well qualified to address the complementarity of these two forms of the practice of imaginative thought and the masks of the modern nation. But perhaps, becoming inured to such unfinished business, the nation may sometimes seem prone to inertia, a cultural nouveau-kitsch. There is no inevitability about this. If anything truly worthwhile emerges from such conditions, it will not be foreclosed. And this returns us to the epigraph with which the book began: the 'unpredicted voices of our kind' – recognisably ours, but unpredicted, and approached on unpredicted roads.

This kind of approaching is vividly presented in the three quotations with which I will close. The first, from Joseph Conrad's *Lord Jim*, is part of a speech by the character Marlow, and so, carefully distanced from total authorial sanction. Conrad's editors make a critical point by annotating this speech: 'At his narratorial best, Marlow is shrewdly observant, wise and incisive; at his worst, as in parts of this long paragraph, he can be facile, prolix and near-sentimental.'[30] However, to select a few sentences from a four-page paragraph may effectively extract a compact statement with which Marlow's creator might have concurred:

> We wander in our thousands over the face of the earth, the illustrious and the obscure, earning beyond the seas our fame, our money, or only a crust of bread; but it seems to me that for each of us going home must be like going to render an account. We return to face our superiors, our kindred, our friends – those whom we obey, and those whom we love.... Say what you like, to get its joy, to breathe its peace, to face its truth, one must return with a clear conscience.... [F]ew of us understand, but we all feel it though, and I say *all* without exception, because those who do not

feel do not count. Each blade of grass has its spot on earth whence it draws its life, its strength; and so is man rooted to the land from which he draws his faith together with his life.[31]

But Conrad's editors are right to caution us against agreeing too quickly with Marlow's sentiments. There is another aspect to this truth that is equally important, that helps to explain why we must *leave* home, before we can ever think of how to approach it again. It is magnificently articulated in Béla Bartók's *Cantata Profana*, here described by Marshall Walker:

> The opening music refers to Bach's *St Matthew Passion*, implying that what may seem to be profane in Bartók's celebration of nature is for him the equivalent of a religious position.... He prepared the text from a Rumanian ballad, 'The Hunting Boys Turned into Stags', which he recorded and notated in 1914. A father raises nine sons, not to farm but to hunt. When the sons cross a magical bridge in a forest, they are turned into stags....
>
> The father enters the forest to look for his sons. When he crosses the same bridge, he sees the nine stags and aims his rifle at the biggest. The stag speaks and warns his father that he will be torn to pieces by his son's antlers if he tries to shoot. The father entreats his sons to come home but they can't – their antlers wouldn't pass through the doorway. They must live in the valleys and forests now, and they must drink, not from silver goblets but from cool mountain springs...
>
> It's a rich parable, about the need to forsake the securities and distortions of home if we are to achieve ourselves, the need to be outsiders, like Bartók, and about the sacrifices that must be made if we wish to live naturally and truly.[32]

To go home, to face its truth and render the account, to recognise its uniqueness and its distortions, requires the sacrifice involved in forsaking its securities. Conrad knew it as keenly as Bartók. And Stevenson, in the epigraph to this Conclusion, is clearly in their company.

In that epigraph, from a letter written from Samoa in the South Pacific, near the end of his life (although he did not know that), it is possible to see the suggestions of tendencies that could easily be exaggerated, and by lesser writers, were: the sentimental nostalgia, the 'baseless' (both profound and irrationally excessive) emotion and the list of connotations running into 'wet clothes, and whisky'. But Stevenson pulls his sentence in tight and sharp with the last phrase, 'that indescribable bite of the whole thing...'. This is not to reject the emotional power of the idea of home nor to exaggerate it beyond recognisable reality but to face the hard truths of its capacity to distort, alongside its authority. And in varying degrees, all the authors and artists we have encountered in this book are concerned with this too.

Their work is a continuing articulation of the masks which present human expressivity and recognise human potential, in a nation's story character-ised by its own unfinished business.

The word *home*, in this sense, brings into play both geographical location and intellectual apprehension. It is not only place but also the expression of people, the representation of the people, in relation to that place and to each other. Such representation finds form in masks that allow us to disclose what homes we have, whether comfortable or unjust, festive or damnable, happy or intolerable. Art in its various forms is a kind of home too, but never one to feel complacent about. We might occupy *this* home more naturally and truly, only by making the same necessary sacrifices, and understanding their value. That is perhaps the only way to reach the point from which we might begin to render the account in full, to begin to offer our partial repayment on a debt we will never want to close.

Notes

1 Introduction: the terms of the question

1. T.J. Cribb, 'Transformations in the Fiction of Ben Okri', in *From Commonwealth to Post-colonial*, ed. Anna Rutherford (Sydney, Mundelstrup and Earlsdon: Dangaroo Press, 1992), pp. 145–150 (p. 149).
2. Theodor W. Adorno, *Mahler: A Musical Physiognomy*, trans. Edmund Jephcott (Chicago: The University of Chicago Press, 1996), p. 39.
3. Edith Hall, 'Introduction', in Euripedes, *Bacchai: A New Translation by Colin Teevan* (London: Oberon Books, 2002), pp. 9–14.
4. William Black, *Macleod of Dare* (London: Macmillan, 1879).
5. George MacDonald, *The Marquis of Lossie* (London: Everett & Co. [n.d.] 1877).
6. Sir Alexander Campbell Mackenzie, 'Early Years and Recollections', *A Musician's Narrative* (London: Cassell, 1927), Chapter 1, pp. 14–15.
7. Ibid., p. 16.
8. Ibid., p. 6.
9. Hugh MacDiarmid, *Selected Prose*, ed. Alan Riach (Manchester: Carcanet Press, 1992), p. 3.
10. Ibid.
11. Peter Arnott, 'Connections with the Audience: Writing for a Scottish Theatre [Peter Arnott interviewed by Greg Giesekam], *New Theatre Quarterly*, Vol. 6, No. 24 (November 1990), pp. 318–334.
12. Charles Olson, 'Projective Verse', in *Poetics of the New American Poetry*, eds Donald Allen and Warren Tallman (New York: Grove Press, 1973), pp. 147–158.
13. Stephen Rodefer, 'Plastic Sutures', in *Four Lectures* (Berkeley: The Figures, 1982), p. 53.
14. I am indebted to Professor Douglas Gifford, Honorary Librarian of Abbotsford and the Director of the Abbotsford Library Research Project for this information.
15. Hugh MacDiarmid, *Selected Prose*, pp. 7–8. 'Thrums' is the name of one of the small towns of Scotland made popular in sentimental novels of the period.
16. Mark Twain, *The Adventures of Huckleberry Finn* (1885; Harmondsworth: Puffin, 1967), p. 6.
17. James Kelman, *Some Recent Attacks: Essays Cultural & Political* (Stirling: AK Press, 1992), p. 81.
18. John Pilger, *The New Rulers of the World* (London: Verso, 2002), pp. 1–2.
19. Hugh MacDiarmid, 'Glasgow', *Complete Poems*, Vol. 1, pp. 1048–1052 (pp. 1050–1051).
20. George Bruce, quoted in John Purser, *Scotland's Music: A History of the Traditional and Classical Music of Scotland from Early Times to the Present Day* (BBC Radio Scotland, programme 26 'The Tartan Scarf'. First broadcast 1992).
21. Jacqueline Rose, *States of Fantasy* (Oxford: Clarendon Press, 1996), p. 3. See also Benedict Anderson, *Imagined Communities: Reflections on the Origin and Spread of Nationalism* (London: Verso, 1983); Homi K. Bhabha, ed., *Nation and Narration* (London and New York: Routledge, 1990); and Homi K. Bhabha, *The Location of Culture* (London and New York: Routledge, 1994).
22. Rose, *States of Fantasy*, pp. 4–5.

23. *Dream State: The New Scottish Poets*, ed. Daniel O'Rourke (Edinburgh: Polygon, 1994). *Dream State: The New Scottish Poets Second Edition*, ed. Donny O'Rourke (Edinburgh: Polygon, 2002). The Alasdair Gray motto can be found, for example, under the dustjacket, on the front and back covers of the hardback edition of *Unlikely Stories, Mostly* (Edinburgh: Canongate, 1984).
24. John Prebble, *The King's Jaunt: George IV in Scotland, 1822 'One and Twenty Daft Days'* (London: Collins, 1988).
25. Angus Calder, 'Tartanry', in *Revolving Culture: Notes from the Scottish Republic* (London and New York: I.B. Tauris, 1994), pp. 95–103 (p. 103).
26. Cited in Hugh MacDiarmid, *The Raucle Tongue: Hitherto Uncollected Prose*, 3 vols, ed. Angus Calder, Glen Murray and Alan Riach (Manchester: Carcanet Press, 1996, 1997, 1998), Vol. 3 (1998), pp. 119–120.
27. Cited in *Radical Scotland*, February/March 1983, p. 2.
28. Cited in Alan Bold, *MacDiarmid: Christopher Murray Grieve. A Critical Biography* (London: Paladin, 1990), p. 204 and p. 157, respectively.
29. Edwin Muir, *Scott and Scotland: The Predicament of the Scottish Writer* (London: Routledge, 1936), p. 178.
30. *The Broons and Oor Wullie, 1936–1996 (60 Years in The Sunday Post)* (London: DC Thomson & Co. Ltd, 1996). *The Broons and Oor Wullie, At War, 1939–1945 (The Lighter Side of World War Two)* (1997); *The Broons and Oor Wullie, The Fabulous Fifties* (1998); *The Broons and Oor Wullie, The Swinging Sixties* (1999); *The Broons and Oor Wullie, The Nation's Favourites* (2000). See also *The D.C. Thomson Bumper Fun Book* (Edinburgh: Paul Harris, 1976).
31. Hugh MacDiarmid, *Selected Prose*, p. 291.
32. Cited in *Fiosraich: Scottish National Party Newsletter*, Spring 1995, p. 4.
33. Iain Crichton Smith, 'The Beginning of a New Song', published as a postcard by The Scottish Arts Council (Edinburgh, n.d.)
34. I am indebted to Dorian Grieve for this quotation.
35. Hugh MacDiarmid, 'The Little White Rose', in MacDiarmid, *Selected Poems*, eds Alan Riach and Michael Grieve (Harmondsworth: Penguin Books, 1994), p. 190. In MacDiarmid's poem, the first line ends with a full stop and the last two lines as printed on the card form a single long line connected by a long dash.
36. T.J. Cribb, *From Commonwealth to Post-colonial*, p. 149.

2   Shakespeare and Scotland

1. Declan Kiberd, *Inventing Ireland: The Literature of the Modern Nation* (London: Jonathan Cape, 1995), pp. 12–13. Quotations from Shakespeare are normally identified by Act, Scene and line numbers.
2. Aimé Césaire, *A Tempest: An Adaptation for Black Theatre*, trans. Philip Crispin (London: Oberon Books, 2000).
3. Mary Floyd-Wilson, 'Delving to the Root: *Cymbeline*, Scotland and the English Race', in David J. Baker and Willy Maley, eds, *British Identities and English Renaissance Literature* (Cambridge: Cambridge University Press, 2002), pp. 101–115 (p. 102).
4. Colin MacCabe, ed., 'The Voice of Esau: Stephen in the Library', in *James Joyce: New Perspectives* (Sussex: The Harvester Press, 1982), pp. 111–128.
5. MacDiarmid, *Selected Poems*, pp. 130–131.
6. Edwin Morgan, *Sonnets from Scotland* (Glasgow: Mariscat Press, 1984).

7. Willy Maley, ' "Another Britain"?: Bacon's *Certain Considerations Touching the Plantation in Ireland* (1609)', *Prose Studies*, Vol. 18, No. 1, April 1995, pp. 1–18 (p. 7).

8. Helen Ostovich, 'Introduction', in Ben Jonson, John Marston and George Chapman, *Eastward Ho!* (London: Nick Hern Books, 2002), p. x.

9. Ibid., p. 40.

10. Rainer Maria Rilke, 'The Spirit Ariel (After reading Shakespeare's *Tempest*)', in *Selected Poems*, trans. J.B. Leishman (Harmondsworth: Penguin Books, 1972), pp. 73–74. According to the *historisch-kritische Ausgabe* of Rilke, the poem was written in early 1913 and first published in *Das Inselschiff*, No. 2 (1922) (which was actually published in December 1921); it was later collected in *Gesammelte Werke*, Vol. 3 (1927). I am indebted to Dr Paul Bishop of Glasgow University for this information.

11. Lilian Winstanley, *"Hamlet" and the Scottish Succession* (Cambridge: Cambridge University Press, 1921).

12. Stuart M. Kurland, '*Hamlet* and the Scottish Succession?', *Studies in English Literature 1500–1900*, Vol. 34 (1994), pp. 279–300 (p. 279).

13. Ibid., p. 293.

14. Stuart M. Kurland, ' "The care . . . of subjects' good": *Pericles*, James I, and the Neglect of Government' *Shakespearian Criticism Yearbook 1996* (Detroit, New York, Toronto, London: Gale, 1996), pp. 360–372.

15. Ibid., p. 361.

16. Ibid., p. 368.

17. Norman MacCaig, 'Go Away, Ariel', in *A World of Difference* (London: Chatto & Windus, 1983), p. 46.

18. Norman MacCaig, 'Helpless Collector', in *A World of Difference* (London: Chatto & Windus, 1983), p. 7.

19. Norman MacCaig, 'Journeys', in *The Equal Skies* (London: Chatto & Windus, 1980), p. 64.

20. Edwin Morgan, 'Caliban Falls Asleep in the Isle Full of Noises', *Hibernia*, Vol. 43, No. 37 (20 September 1979), p. 20 (for this information I am grateful to Hamish Whyte); also in *Collected Poems* (Manchester: Carcanet, 1990), p. 420.

21. Edwin Morgan, 'Ariel Freed', in *Virtual and Other Realities* (Manchester: Carcanet Press, 1997), p. 101.

22. Edwin Morgan, 'Memories of Earth', in *The New Divan* (Manchester: Carcanet Press, 1977), pp. 57–69.

23. Edwin Morgan, 'Jack London in Heaven', from the 'Uncollected Poems 1976–1981' section of *Poems of Thirty Years* (Manchester: Carcanet New Press, 1982), pp. 438–440.

24. Edwin Morgan, *A.D.: A Trilogy on the Life of Christ* (Manchester: Carcanet Press, 2000), p. 54.

25. Edwin Morgan, 'A Home in Space', in *Star Gate: Science Fiction Poems* (1979), in *Poems of Thirty Years* (Manchester: Carcanet New Press, 1982), p. 390.

3   Foundational texts of modern Scottish literature

1. See also Thomas Crawford, *Boswell, Burns and the French Revolution* (Edinburgh: The Saltire Society, 1990).

2. Adrian Poole, *Tragedy: Shakespeare and the Greek Example* (Oxford: Basil Blackwell, 1987), pp. 209–210.

3. Ibid., pp. 227–228.

4. Michael Long, *The Unnatural Scene: A Study in Shakespearian Tragedy* (London: Methuen & Co., 1976), pp. 11–12.

5. Robert Burns, 'Now Westlin Winds', in James Kinsley, ed., *Poems and Songs* (London: Oxford University Press, 1969), pp. 2–3. Dick Gaughan, *Handful of Earth* (Topic Records, 1989: TSCD419).

6. Walter Scott, 'Jock of Hazeldean', in David McCordick, ed., *Scottish Literature: An Anthology*, Vol. II (New York, Washington, DC/Baltimore, Bern, Frankfurt am Main, Berlin, Vienna, Paris: Peter Lang, 1996), pp. 405–406. Dick Gaughan, *No More Forever* (Leader, 1972: CD2072). Jo Miller, *the Whistlebinkies 5* (Claddagh Records Ltd, 4 CC 50).

7. Malcolm MacLean and Christopher Carrell, eds, *As an Fhearann / From the Land* (Edinburgh, Stornoway, Glasgow: Mainstream, an Lanntair, Third Eye Centre, 1986), p. 36.

8. James Boswell, *The Life of Samuel Johnson* (London: J.M. Dent Everyman's Library, 1914), p. 459.

9. Robert Fergusson, 'To Dr Samuel Johnson. Food for a New Edition of his Dictionary', in *The Works* (London: S.A. & H. Oddy, 1807; repr. Edinburgh: James Thin The Mercat Press, 1970), pp. 203–206.

10. Henry Mackenzie, *The Man of Feeling*, ed. Brian Vickers (Oxford: Oxford University Press, 1970), p. 103.

11. Robert Fergusson, 'The Sow of Feeling', in *The Works* (London: S.A. & H. Oddy, 1807; repr. Edinburgh: James Thin The Mercat Press, 1970), pp. 181–184.

12. Robert Burns, 'Epistle to a Young Friend', in *Poems, Chiefly in the Scottish Dialect*, with a note on the text by Michael Schmidt (Harmondsworth: Penguin Books, 1999), pp. 115–118 (p. 116).

13. See also Alasdair Gray, 'On Neglect of Burns by Schools and His Disparagement by Moralists and Whitewashers With Some Critical Remarks', in G. Ross Roy, ed. and Lucie Roy, assoc. ed., *Studies in Scottish Literature*, Vol. xxx (1998), pp. 175–180 (p. 179).

14. Robert Burns, 'The Cottar's Saturday Night', in *Poems, Chiefly in the Scottish Dialect*, pp. 83–90 (p. 89).

15. Ibid.

16. Sir Walter Scott, *The Lay of the Last Minstrel*, Introduction, in *The Poetical Works of Sir Walter Scott* (London: Macmillan, 1906), p. 11.

17. Celtic legend has Ossian returning to Ireland from Tir-nan-Og, the afterworld, land of the ever young, because of his love for his country, only to find his former companions have departed. The phrase 'Ossian after the Fianna' signals the pathos of the conjunction of that yearning for home and the loss of loved companions.

18. David Daiches, 'Chapter One: The Scottish Literary Tradition', in *Robert Burns* (London: G. Bell & Sons, Ltd, 1952), pp. 1–33 (pp. 28–29). See also David Daiches, *The Paradox of Scottish Culture: The Eighteenth Century Experience* (Oxford: Oxford University Press, 1964), pp. 84–86.

19. Marshall Walker, *Scottish Literature since 1707* (London and New York: Longman, 1996), p. 38.

20. Norman MacCaig, *Collected Poems New Edition* (London: Chatto & Windus, 1993), 'An Ordinary Day', pp. 154–155; 'No Consolation', p. 163; 'Helpless Collector', p. 369.

21. Ibid., 'Praise of a Collie', p. 318; 'Praise of a Boat', p. 319; 'Praise of a Thorn Bush', pp. 319–320; 'Praise of a Road', p. 320; 'Praise of a Man', p. 336.

22. Simon Schama, *Landscape and Memory* (London: HarperCollins, 1995), pp. 466–469.

4 Walter Scott and the Whistler: tragedy and the Enlightenment imagination

1. David Daiches, 'Scott's Achievement as a Novelist', in A. Norman Jeffares, ed., *Scott's Mind and Art* (Edinburgh: Oliver & Boyd, 1969), pp. 21–52 (p. 45).
2. Thomas Crawford, *Scott* (Edinburgh and London: Oliver & Boyd, 1965); *Scott* (Edinburgh: Scottish Academic Press, 1982).
3. Marshall Walker, *Scottish Literature since 1707* (Harlow: Longman, 1996).
4. Ludovic Kennedy, '12', in Allan Frazer, ed., *Sir Walter Scott, 1771–1832: An Edinburgh Keepsake* (Edinburgh: Edinburgh University Press, 1971), pp. 162–173 (p. 167). Though when I checked in 2004 only two copies were marked out 'On loan' on the City Library's online catalogue.
5. Daiches, op. cit., Georg Lukács, *The Historical Novel*, trans. Hannah and Stanley Mitchell (Harmondsworth: Penguin Books, 1969).
6. Graham McMaster, *Scott and Society* (Cambridge: Cambridge University Press, 1981), p. 49.
7. Sir Walter Scott, *The Heart of Midlothian*, ed. Claire Lamont (Oxford and New York: Oxford University Press, 1982), p. 42, Chapter IV.
8. Hamish MacCunn, *Land of the Mountain and the Flood and Other Music*, BBC Scottish Symphony Orchestra/Martyn Brabbins (Hyperion CDA66818).
9. Crawford, *Scott* (1965), p. 91.
10. Walker, *Scottish Literature since 1707*, p. 125.
11. John O. Hayden, ed., *Scott: The Critical Heritage* (London: Routledge & Kegan Paul, 1970), p. 169.
12. Ibid., p. 224.
13. Crawford, *Scott* (1965), pp. 89, 96–97; (1982), pp. 93, 103.
14. James Kerr, *Fiction Against History: Scott as Storyteller* (Cambridge: Cambridge University Press, 1989), p. 84.
15. Scott, *The Heart of Midlothian*, p. 479, Chapter L.
16. David Richards, *Masks of Difference* (Cambridge: Cambridge University Press, 1994), p. 135.
17. Scott, *The Heart of Midlothian*, pp. 479–480, Chapter L.
18. Cf. Ernest Renan, 'In most ancient languages, the words used to designate foreign peoples are drawn from two sources: either words that signify "to stammer" "to mumble" or words that signify "mute".' Cited in Richards, *Marks of Difference*, p. 1. Compare the decision of Dr Johnson to reject Boswell's offer to teach him Scots, described in Chapter 3. Johnson's repudiation effectively renders him deaf to Scots, but to Johnson's Anglocentric establishment, the effect is the opposite: it renders the Scots mute.
19. Scott, *The Heart of Midlothian*, p. 480, Chapter L.
20. Ibid.
21. Ibid., pp. 501, 502, 504, Chapter LII.
22. Ibid., p. 506, Chapter LII.
23. John Sutherland, *The Life of Walter Scott* (Oxford: Blackwell, 1995), p. 217. The point, of course, is that Scott could not have written 'volumes of romance' about this story: two sentences are all he can give it.
24. Scott, *The Heart of Midlothian*, p. 506, Chapter LII.
25. Alexander Welsh, *The Hero of the Waverley Novels* (New York: Atheneum, 1968), p. 90.
26. Ibid., p. 90.
27. Cited in ibid., p. 90.

28. Cited in Richards, *Marks of Difference*, p. 74.
29. Ibid., pp. 122, 126–127.
30. Louise K. Barnett, *The Ignoble Savage* (Westport and London: Greenwood Press, 1975), p. 65.
31. Edgar Johnson, 'Scott and the Corners of Time', in Alan Bell, ed., *Scott Bicentenary Essays* (Edinburgh and London: Scottish Academic Press, 1973), pp. 18–37 (p. 37).
32. Richards, *Marks of Difference*, p. 133.
33. Ibid., p. 127.
34. Ben Okri, 'Diary', *New Statesman*, Vol. 112, No. 2889 (8 August 1986), p. 16.
35. David Daiches, 'Scott and Scotland', in Alan Bell, ed., *Scott Bicentenary Essays*, pp. 38–60 (p. 40).
36. Hugh Trevor-Roper, '13', in Allan Frazer, ed., *Sir Walter Scott 1711–1832: An Edinburgh Keepsake*, pp. 174–191 (p. 181).
37. Archie Turnbull, 'Scotland and America', in David Daiches, Peter Jones and Jean Jones, eds, *The Scottish Enlightenment 1730–1790: A Hotbed of Genius* (Edinburgh: The Saltire Society, 1996), pp. 136–152 (pp. 138, 143).
38. Mary Shelley, *Frankenstein*, ed. J. Paul Hunter (New York and London: W.W. Norton & Co., 1996), pp. 191–196.
39. Sutherland, op. cit., p. 218.
40. Shelley, *Frankenstain*, p. 81.
41. Ibid., pp. 194–195.
42. Ibid., p. 86.
43. Ibid., p. 87.
44. Ibid., p. 99.
45. Ibid., p. 195.
46. Ibid., p. 156.

5   *Treasure Island* and time: childhood, quickness and Robert Louis Stevenson

1. Quotations from *Treasure Island* are cited in the text by chapter number.
2. Jacqueline Rose, *The Case of Peter Pan or The Impossibility of Children's Fiction* (London: Macmillan, 1984; revised edition, 1994), pp. 1–2.
3. Ibid., p. 2.
4. Ibid., p. 78.
5. Angus Calder, 'A Descriptive Model of Scottish Culture', *Scotlands*, 2.1, 1995, pp. 1–14 (p. 2).
6. Daniel O'Rourke, ed., *Dream State: The New Scottish Poets* (Edinburgh: Polygon, 1994).
7. Robert Louis Stevenson, 'A Fable, *The Persons of the Tale*', in *Treasure Island* (London: Tusitala Edition, William Heinemann, 1927), pp. 223–226 (pp. 223–224).
8. Louis MacNeice, 'To Posterity', in *Collected Poems* (London: Faber & Faber, 1979), p. 443.
9. John Berger, *Ways of Seeing* (London: BBC; Harmondsworth: Penguin Books, 1972), p. 7.
10. Ibid., p. 7.
11. Quotations from *The Mill on the Floss* are cited in the text by chapter number.
12. Another exiled Scot and writer of children's fiction suggests a parallel for Jekyll and Hyde: Sir Arthur Conan Doyle's Sherlock Holmes and his arch-enemy and haunting alter ego, Professor Moriarty. As for a different configuration of the

geography of childhood, one might compare the guiltless wonder of Pablo Neruda, writing in Chapter 11, 'Poetry is an Occupation', of his *Memoirs* (Harmondsworth: Penguin, 1978), pp. 253–328 (p. 269): 'In my house I have put together a collection of small and large toys I can't live without. The child who doesn't play is not a child, but the man who doesn't play has lost forever the child who lived in him and he will certainly miss him. I have also built my house like a toy house and I play in it from morning till night.' Stevenson's most fearful patriarch, Weir of Hermiston, would seem an appropriate example of 'the man who doesn't play' (except for his adherence to the Scots language). His self-righteousness and cruelty are in a wicked compact. Neruda suggests a more liberating configuration of adulthood and play. See also the reference from Sir Alexander Campbell Mackenzie, in chapter 1, the Introduction.

6   In pursuit of lost worlds: Arthur Conan Doyle, Amos Tutuola and Wilson Harris

1. Robert Louis Stevenson, 'To A. Conan Doyle' from Vailima, Apia, Samoa, 5 April 1893, in *The Letters of Robert Louis Stevenson*, Vol. 5 (London: Tusitala Edition, William Heinemann, 1924), p. 22.
2. Hugh MacDiarmid, 'Sea-Serpent', in Michael Grieve and W.R. Aitken, eds, *The Complete Poems of Hugh MacDiarmid*, Vol. 1 (Manchester: Carcanet Press, 1993), pp. 48–51 (p. 50).
3. Arthur Conan Doyle, *The Lost World* (1912; Oxford and New York: Oxford University Press, 1998). Page references are to this Oxford World's Classics edition.
4. Michael Swan, *The Marches of El Dorado* (1958; Harmondsworth: Penguin, 1961), p. 205.
5. Doyle, *The Lost World*, p. 117.
6. Ibid., p. 65.
7. Ibid., pp. 65–66.
8. Ibid., p. 67.
9. Amos Tutuola, *The Palm-Wine Drinkard* (1952; London: Faber & Faber, 1977), pp. 7–8.
10. Ibid., p. 9.
11. Doyle, *The Lost World*, p. 66.
12. Hesketh Pearson, *Conan Doyle* (1943; London: Guild Books, 1946), p. 176.
13. Adam Phillips, *The Beast in the Nursery* (London: Faber & Faber, 1998), p. 6.
14. Ibid., p. 108.
15. Paul Edwards, 'The Farm and the Wilderness in Tutuola's *The Palm-Wine Drinkard*', in Bernth Lindfors, ed., *Critical Perspectives on Amos Tutuola* (Washington, DC: Three Continents Press, 1975), pp. 255–263.
16. Dylan Thomas, 'From *The Observer*, July 6, 1952: "Blithe Spirits"', in Bernth Lindfors, ed., *Critical Perspectives on Amos Tutuola* (Washington, DC: Three Continents Press, 1975), pp. 7–8.
17. Hugh MacDiarmid, in Michael Grieve and W.R. Aitken, eds, *The Complete Poems of Hugh MacDiarmid*, Vol. 2 (Manchester: Carcanet Press, 1994), p. 793.
18. Arthur Hugh Clough, 'Blank Misgivings of a Creature moving about in Worlds not realised', in *Collected Poems* (London: Oxford University Press, 1974), pp. 28–34 (p. 30).
19. Robert Louis Stevenson, *Kidnapped* (1886).
20. Wilson Harris, *Black Marsden* (London: Faber & Faber, 1972), p. 11.

21. Ibid., p. 11.
22. 'Wilson Harris Interviewed by Alan Riach', in Alan Riach and Mark Williams, eds, *The Radical Imagination: Lectures and Talks* (Liège: L3 – Liège, Literature, Language, 1992), pp. 33–65 (p. 64).
23. Harris, *Black Marsden*, p. 11.
24. Ibid., p. 51.
25. Ibid., p. 72.
26. Frantz Fanon, *Black Skin White Masks*, trans. Charles Lam Markmann (London: MacGibbon & Kee, 1968). The implications of Fanon's work have been applied to Scotland by Craig Beveridge and Ronald Turnbull in *The Eclipse of Scottish Culture: Inferiorism and the Intellectuals* (Edinburgh: Polygon, 1989).
27. Michael Gilkes, *Creative Schizophrenia: The Caribbean Cultural Challenge* (Coventry: Centre for Caribbean Studies, University of Warwick, 1986).
28. Harris, *Black Manden*, p. 62.

7 The international brigade: modernism and the Scottish Renaissance

1. Hugh MacDiarmid, *Lucky Poet: A Self-Study in Literature and Political Ideas* (London: Methuen & Co., 1943; repr. ed. Alan Riach, Manchester: Carcanet Press, 1994), p. 352.
2. Marshall Walker, *The Literature of the United States of America* (London: Macmillan, 1983), p. 132.
3. Stephen Rodefer, 'Plastic Sutures', in *Four Lectures* (Berkeley: The Figures, 1982), p. 53.
4. Tom Normand, *The Modern Scot: Modernism and Nationalism in Scottish Art 1928–1955* (Aldershot and Brookfield, Vermont: Ashgate Publishing, 2000), p. 1.
5. Cited in Walker, *The Literature of the United States of America*, p. 129.
6. Ezra Pound, letter to William Soutar, *Chapman 53*, Vol. 10, No. 4 (Summer 1988), p. 30.
7. Hugh MacDiarmid, *Contemporary Scottish Studies*, ed. Alan Riach (Manchester: Carcanet Press, 1995), p. 210.
8. Ibid., pp. 264–265.
9. Ibid., p. xii.
10. Many of MacDiarmid's articles from these periodicals are collected in *The Raucle Tongue: Hitherto Uncollected Prose*, 3 vols, ed. Angus Calder, Glen Murray and Alan Riach (Manchester: Carcanet Press, 1996, 1997, 1998).
11. Catherine Kerrigan, ed., *An Anthology of Scottish Women Poets* (Edinburgh University Press, 1991). Muriel Stuart was Scottish only by name – her birth, background and upbringing were English and her poetry was fairly typical of good English women's poetry of her day, and not particularly 'modernist' at all.
12. The major source for this section is John Purser, *Scotland's Music: A History of the Traditional and Classical Music of Scotland from Earliest Times to the Present Day* (Edinburgh: Mainstream, 1992). I have also made use of booklet notes from a number of CDs, many new performances having been recorded in the fertile wake of Purser's work: these are listed in the Discography.
13. For some of my comments of Bax, I am indebted to Marshall Walker's radio programme, *Composer of the Week: Arnold Bax* (Radio New Zealand, Concert FM, 2001). The Nietzsche quotation is taken from the Booklet notes by Lewis Foreman for the CD of Bax's *Symphony No.3*, *Dance of Wild Irravel* and *Paen*

performed by the London Philharmonic Orchestra conducted by Bryden Thomson (CHAN 8454, 1986).

14. William Sweeney, in Booklet notes for CD *Cappella Nova: Twentieth Century Scottish Choral Music* (Glasgow: Linn Products, 1994), p. 10.

15. See also Cedric Thorpe Davie, *Scotland's Music* (Edinburgh: William Blackwood, 1980); Maurice Lindsay, *Francis George Scott and the Scottish Renaissance* (Edinburgh: Paul Harris, 1980); Malcolm MacDonald, *Ronald Stevenson: A Musical Biography* (Edinburgh: National Library of Scotland, 1989); Sir Arnold Bax, *Farewell, My Youth: An Autobiography* (London: Longmans, Green & Co., 1943).

16. The major source here is Duncan MacMillan, *Scottish Art 1460–1990* (Edinburgh: Mainstream, 1990). But Tom Normand's study of Scottish culture and the Modern Movement focuses more closely on MacDiarmid's relationship with William MacCance and J.D. Fergusson, the importance of the idea of Celtic identity in Scottish art and the general thrust of political, literary and artistic work in the period 1928–1955. Tom Normand, *The Modern Scot: Modernism and Nationalism in Scottish Art 1928–1955* (Aldershot and Brookfield, Vermont: Ashgate Publishing, 2000).

17. Important sources are T.J. Honeyman, *Three Scottish Colourists: S.J. Peploe, F.C.B. Cadell, Leslie Hunter* (first published 1950; Edinburgh: Paul Harris Publishing, 1977); T.J. Honeyman, *Art and Audacity* (London: Collins, 1971); Roger Bilcliffe, *The Glasgow Boys* (London: John Murray, 1987); Roger Bilcliffe, *The Scottish Colourists* (London: John Murray, 1989); Jude Burkhauser, ed., *'Glasgow Girls': Women in Art and Design 1880–1920* (Edinburgh: Canongate, 1990).

18. Margaret Morris, *The Art of J.D. Fergusson* (Glasgow and London: Blackie, 1974), p. 44.

19. Cordelia Oliver, *Joan Eardley, RSA* (Edinburgh: Mainstream, 1988), p. 32.

20. Iain Gale, 'Artist's Brief Life Lived in the Moment', *Scotland on Sunday*, 13 October 2002, p. 8. John Berger, 'A Story for Aesop', in *Keeping a Rendezvous* (New York: Vintage Books, 1991), pp. 53–81 (p. 68).

21. William Johnstone, *Points in Time: An Autobiography* (London: Barrie & Jenkins, 1980), p. 72.

22. G.P. Insh, *Scotland and the Modern World* (Edinburgh and London: W. & A.K. Johnston, 1932).

23. Hugh MacDiarmid, *Contemporary Scottish Studies*, pp. 218–225.

24. Edwin Morgan, 'Some Figures Behind MacDiarmid', *Cencrastus*, 40 (Summer 1991), pp. 14–19.

25. Cited in Hubert Kennedy, 'Introduction', in John Henry Mackay, ed., *The Hustler: The Story of a Nameless Love from Friedrich Street*, trans. Hubert Kennedy (Boston: Alyson Publications, 1985), p. 9.

26. Toni Davidson, ed., *And Thus Will I Freely Sing: An Anthology of Gay and Lesbian Writing from Scotland* (Edinburgh: Polygon, 1989).

27. Richard Strauss, *Orchestral Songs*. Felicity Lott, Scottish National Orchestra, Neeme Jarvi (Chandos CHAN 9054, 1992). The English version here is by Alan Riach.

28. Edwin Morgan, 'Scotland and the World', *Chapman*, No. 95 (2000), pp. 2–15. (Also published in *PN Review*.)

29. Ibid., p. 6.

30. William Lithgow, *The Totall Discourse of The Rare Adventures & Painefull Peregrinations of long Nineteene Yeares Travayles from Scotland to the most famous Kingdomes in Europe, Asia and Africa* (Glasgow: James MacLehose & Sons, 1906), p. 100.

31. Hugh MacDiarmid, *A Drunk Man Looks at the Thistle*, ll.141–144, in *Selected Poems*, ed. Alan Riach and Michael Grieve (Harmondsworth: Penguin Books, 1994), p. 30.
32. Lithgow, *The Totall Discourse of The Rare Adventures & Painefull Perergrinations of Long Nineteene Yeares Travayles from Scotland to the most famous Kingdomes in Europe, Asia and Africa*, pp. 100–101.
33. Paula Burnett, ed., *The Penguin Book of Caribbean Verse in English* (Harmondsworth: Penguin Books, 1986), p. 104.
34. Ibid., p. 113.
35. Michael Scott, *Tom Cringle's Log* (London: J.M. Dent, Everyman's Library, 1969), introduction by Richard Armstrong, P.V. James Robertson, *Joseph Knight* (London: Fourth Estate, 2003).
36. Morgan, op. cit., pp. 10–14. Helen & Pat Adam, *San Francisco's Burning* (Berkeley, California: Oannes, 1963).
37. Lorna Moon, *The Collected Works*, ed. Glenda Norquay (Edinburgh: Black & White Publishing, 2002).
38. Queen Victoria, *Leaves from the Journal of Our Life in the Highlands* (London: Smith, Elder & Co., 1869), p. 87.
39. See Chris Dolan, 'Plots on the Landscape' (an article about his BBC Radio Scotland series, *The Edge of the World*), *The Sunday Herald*, 25 February 2001, p. 7.
40. Jules Verne, *The Underground City or The Black Indies (Sometimes Called The Child of the Cavern) [or, Strange Doings Underground]*, trans. W.H.G. Kingston (London: S. Low, Marston, Searle and Rivington, 1877. Available online from Project Gutenberg, website http://promo.net/pg/). See also Peter Haining, *The Jules Verne Companion* (New York: Baronet Publishing Company, 1978), pp. 14, 25.
41. Bram Stoker, *Dracula*, ed. Glennis Byron (Peterborough, Ontario: Broadview Press, 1997); *The Bram Stoker Bedside Companion: 10 Stories by the Author of Dracula*, ed. Charles Osborne (London: Victor Gollancz, 1973); *The Mystery of the Sea* (Guernsey, Channel Islands: Sutton Publishing, 1997). See also Barbara Belford, *Bram Stoker: A Biography of the Author of Dracula* (London: Weidenfield & Nicolson, 1996).
42. Bernard Kodjo [sic] Laing, 'Jaw', in *Scottish Poetry 4*, ed. George Bruce, Maurice Lindsay and Edwin Morgan (Edinburgh: Edinburgh University Press, 1969), pp. 59–69. And *Woman of the Aeroplanes* (London: Heinemann, 1988). Both this and *Search, Sweet Country* were published by Picador.
43. Kole Omotoso, *The Edifice* (London: Heinemann, 1971; repr. 1978).
44. Les A. Murray, 'The Bonnie Disproportion', in *Persistence in Folly: Selected Prose Writings* (London, Sydney and Melbourne: Angus & Robertson, Sirius Books, 1984), pp. 61–85 (p. 82).
45. Ibid., pp. 84–85.
46. Les. A. Murray, 'Their Cities, Their Universities', in *Collected Poems* (Port Melbourne, Victoria, Australia: William Heinemann, 1997), pp. 94–97.
47. Les A. Murray interviewed by Iain Sharp, *Landfall*, 42, 2 (June 1988), p. 160.
48. Les. A. Murray, 'The Future', in *Selected Poetry*, pp. 64–65.
49. Chris Wallace-Crabbe, 'The Last Ride', in *For Crying Out Loud* (Oxford: Oxford University Press, 1990), pp. 48–49.
50. Ibid., p. 1.
51. Eric McCormack, *The Paradise Motel* (London: Bloomsbury, 1989); *The Mysterium* (London: Viking Penguin, 1992).
52. Carlos Drummond de Andrade, 'Residue', in *Travelling in the Family: Selected Poems*, ed. and trans. Thomas Colchie and Mark Strand with Elizabeth Bishop and Gregory Rabassa (Hopewell, New Jersey: The Ecco Press, 1986), pp. 58–60 (p. 58).

8 Nobody's children: orphans and their ancestors in popular Scottish fiction after 1945

1. Byron, *Don Juan*, ed. T.G. Steffan, E. Steffan and W.W. Pratt (Harmondsworth: Penguin, 1986), pp. 555–556.
2. Ian Fleming, cited in Kingsley Amis, *The James Bond Dossier* (London: Jonathan Cape, 1965), p. 35.
3. Ibid., p. 36.
4. Thomas Carlyle, *On Heroes, Hero-Worship and the Heroic in History* (London: Chapman & Hall, 1897 [1841]), p. 178.
5. Alexander Welsh, *The Hero of the Waverley Novels* (New York: Atheneum, 1968).
6. *KIDNAPPED being the memoirs of the adventures of DAVID BALFOUR in the Year MDCCLI. How he was kidnapped and cast away; his sufferings in a desert isle; his journey in the wild Highlands; his acquaintance with Alan Breck Stewart and other notorious Highland Jacobites; with all that he suffered at the hands of his Uncle, Ebenezer Balfour of Shaws, falsely so-called; written by himself, and now set forth by ROBERT LOUIS STEVENSON.* It is worth pausing to consider how many genres the title sets up as fair game for the novel's subversive de-romanticising: desert island fables of self-reliance and adventure such as Defoe's *Robinson Crusoe* (itself based on the life of the Scot Alexander Selkirk) and Stevenson's own *Treasure Island*; and 'South Seas' pastoralism, already ironic in Melville's *Typee*; travel journals, Jacobite romances and family sagas (Fielding's *Tom Jones*) are a few examples.
7. John Pearson, *The Life of Ian Fleming* (London: Jonathan Cape, 1966), p. 327.
8. Louis L'Amour, *The Trail to Crazy Man* (New York: Bantam Books, 1988), p. 127.
9. Ibid., p. 128.
10. Ibid., p. 128.
11. Ibid., pp. 157–158.
12. Ibid., p. 238.
13. Mark Twain, *Life on the Mississippi*, ed. James M. Cox (Harmondsworth: Penguin Books, 1984), pp. 326–329.
14. Bud Neill, *Lobey's the Wee Boy! Five Lobey Dosser Adventures*, compiled and introduced by Ranald MacColl (Edinburgh: Mainstream, 1992) and *Lobey Dosser: Further Adventures of the Wee Boy!* Foreword by Tom Shields, introduced by Ranald MacColl (Glasgow: ZIPO Publishing Ltd, 1998).
15. Christopher Frayling, *Spaghetti Westerns: Cowboys and Europeans from Karl May to Sergio Leone* (London: Routledge & Kegan Paul, 1981), p. 95.
16. Ibid., p. 88.
17. Howard Hughes, *Spaghetti Westerns* (Harpenden, Herts & North Pomfret, Vermont, 2001), pp. 29–30.
18. Bud Neill, *Lobey's the Wee Boy! Five Lobey Dosser Adventures*, compiled and introduced by Ranald MacColl (Edinburgh: Mainstream, 1992), p. 6.
19. MacColl, in ibid., p. 7.
20. Ibid., p. 14.
21. Ibid., p. 23.
22. Ibid., p. 29.
23. Ibid., pp. 7–8.
24. Ibid., p. 8.
25. George MacBeth, *My Scotland* (London: Macmillan, 1973), p. v.
26. Ibid. pp. 9–10.

256   Notes

27. Tony Bennett and Janet Woollacott, *Bond and Beyond: The Political Career of a Popular Hero*. (London: Macmillan, 1987), p. 110.
28. Ian Fleming, *You Only Live Twice* (London: Jonathan Cape, 1964. Paperback edition: London: Pan Books, 1966), p. 178.
29. Ibid., p. 179.
30. John Pearson, *James Bond: The Authorized Biography of 007* (London: Sidgwick & Jackson, 1973), pp. 21–22.
31. Pearson, *The Life of Ian Fleming* (London: Jonathan Cape, 1966), p. 18.
32. Fleming, *On Her Majesty's Secret Service* (London: Jonathan Cape, 1963. Paperback edition: London: Pan Books, 1965), p. 81.
33. John Buchan, *Prester John* (London: Hodder & Stoughton, 1910); *The Thirty-Nine Steps* (London: Blackwood, 1915); *Mr Standfast* (London: Hodder & Stoughton, 1918); *Huntingtower* (London: Hodder & Stoughton, 1922); *The Three Hostages* (London: Hodder & Stoughton, 1924).
34. Umberto Eco, *Ian Fleming*, Bruce A. Rosenberg and Ann Harleman Stewart, eds (Boston: Twayne Publishers, 1989), p. 95.
35. Amis, *The James Bond Wossier*, p. 42.
36. Fleming, *On Her Majesty's Secret Service* (London: Jonathan Cape, 1963. Paperback edition: London: Pan Books, 1965), p. 238.
37. John Pearson, *The Life of Ian Fleming* (London: Jonathan Cape, 1966), p. 335.
38. Byron, *Don Juan*, p. 756.
39. Pearson, *The Life of Ian Fleming*, p. 258.
40. Ian Fleming, *The Man With the Golden Gun* (London: Jonathan Cape, 1965. Paperback edition: London: Pan Books, 1967), pp. 186–189.
41. Andrew Lycett, *Ian Fleming* (London: Phoenix, 1996), p. 393.
42. Michael Denning, 'Licensed to Look: James Bond and the Heroism of Consumption', *Contemporary Marxist Criticism*, ed. and introd. Francis Mulhern (London and New York: Longman, 1992), pp. 211–229 (p. 223).
43. Bennett and Woollacott, *Bond and Beyond: The Political Career of a Popular Hero*, p. 99.
44. Denning, *Contemporary Marxist Criticism*, p. 214.
45. See Ian Fleming, *Casino Royale* (London: Jonathan Cape, 1953); *Live and Let Die* (London: Jonathan Cape, 1954); *Moonraker* (London: Jonathan Cape, 1955); *Diamonds Are Forever* (London: Jonathan Cape, 1956); *From Russia With Love* (London: Jonathan Cape, 1957); *Doctor No* (London: Jonathan Cape, 1958); *Goldfinger* (London: Jonathan Cape, 1959); *For Your Eyes Only* (London: Jonathan Cape, 1960); *Thunderball* (London: Jonathan Cape, 1961); *The Spy Who Loved Me* (London: Jonathan Cape, 1962); *Octopussy* (London: Jonathan Cape, 1966). See also Christoph Lindner, ed., *The James Bond Phenomenon: A Critical Reader* (Manchester University Press, 2003).
46. Iain Banks, *The Wasp Factory* (London: Macmillan, 1984. Paperback edition: London: Futura Publications, 1985), pp. i, iii.
47. Iain Banks, *The Bridge* (London: Macmillan, 1986. Paperback edition: London: Pan Books, 1987), p. 285.
48. James Robertson, 'Bridging Styles: A Conversation with Iain Banks', *Radical Scotland*, No. 42. (December/January 1990), pp. 26–27 (p. 26).
49. Iain Banks, *The Crow Road* (London: Scribners, 1992. Paperback edition: London: Abacus, 1993), p. 3.
50. Robertson, *Radical Scotland*, pp. 26–27 (p. 27).
51. Jack B. Yeats, cited in John W. Purser, *The Literary Works of Jack B. Yeats* (Gerrards Cross: Colin Smythe, 1991), p. 27.

52. Iain Banks, *The Wasp Factory* (London: Macmillan, 1984. Paperback edition: London: Futura Publications, 1985), p. 81.
53. Ibid., p. 84.
54. Ibid., p. 117.
55. Ibid., p. 184. See also Iain Banks, *Walking On Glass* (London: Macmillan, 1985); *Espedair Street* (London: Macmillan, 1987); *Consider Phlebas* (London: Macmillan, 1987); *The Player of Games* (London: Macmillan, 1988); *Canal Dreams* (London: Macmillan, 1989); *Use of Weapons* (London: Macmillan, 1990); *The State of the Art* (London: Orbit, 1991); *Against A Dark Background* (London: Orbit, 1993); *Complicity* (London: Little, Brown & Co., 1993); *Whit* (London: Abacus, 1995); *A Song of Stone* (London: Abacus, 1997); *The Business* (London: Little, Brown & Co., 1999).
56. It will be clear from the context whether a quotation comes from the television film version or one of the comic books listed in the bibliography. No page references are given for the comic books because they are not paginated.
57. John Wagner, Alan Grant and Robin Smith, *The Bogie Man* (Glasgow: Fat Man Press, 1989–1990), n.p. See also *The Bogie Man: The Manhattan Project* (London: Tundra Publishing, 1992) and *The Bogie Man: Chinatoon* (London: Tundra Publishing, 1993).

9   It happened fast and it was dark: cinema, theatre and television, comic books

1. 'It happened fast and it was dark' is the opening line of John Wagner, Alan Grant and Robin Smith, *The Bogie Man: The Wrong Goodbye*, Vol. 1, No. 4 (Glasgow: Fat Man Press, 1990).
2. Alex Salmond, 'Devolution and a Scottish Renaissance', *The Herald*, colour supplement, 2 October 2001, *Decades: A Pictorial Series Celebrating Scottish Life, Culture and Events. Part 4. The 90s*, pp. 12–13 (p. 13).
3. Irvine Welsh, *Trainspotting* (London: Minerva, 1994), p. 71.
4. Sir Walter Scott, *The Lay of the Last Minstrel* Canto 6, in *The Poetical Works of Sir Walter Scott* (London: Macmillan, 1906), p. 42.
5. John Hodge, *Trainspotting & Shallow Grave* (London: Faber & Faber, 1996), p. 46.
6. See Duncan Petrie, *Screening Scotland* (London: British Film Institute, 2000).
7. Forsyth Hardy, *Scotland in Film* (Edinburgh University Press, 1990). Eddie Dick, ed., *From Limelight to Satellite: A Scottish Film Book* (British Film Institute, 1990). Colin MacArthur, *Scotch Reels: Scotland in Cinema and Television* (London: BFI, 1982).
8. Petrie, *Screening Scotland*, pp. 4–5.
9. Forsyth Hardy, *Scotland in Film*, p. 1.
10. Petrie, *Screening Scotland*, p. 49.
11. Ibid., p. 69.
12. John Caughie, cited in Petrie, *Screening Scotland*, p. 80.
13. Jean-Luc Godard, cited in Petrie, *Screening Scotland*, p. 148.
14. Hugh MacDiarmid, 'Films and the Scottish Novelist', in *The Raucle Tongue: Hitherto Uncollected Prose*, Vol. III, ed. Angus Calder, Glen Murray and Alan Riach (Manchester: Carcanet Press, 1998), pp. 107–109.
15. Hugh MacDiarmid, 'Intimate Film Making in Scotland', in *The Raucle Tongue: Hitherto Uncollected Prose*, pp. 415–416.

16. See Petrie, *Screening Scotland*, p. 142.
17. Ibid., p. 226.
18. Raymond Williams, 'Foreword', in John McGrath, ed., *A Good Night Out: Popular Theatre: Audience, Class and Form* (London: Methuen, 1981), p. x.
19. Marshall Walker, *Scottish Literature since 1707* (London: Longman, p. 267).
20. Ibid., pp. 272–273.
21. John McGrath, *The Cheviot, the Stag and the Black, Black Oil* (London: Methuen, 1981), p. vi.
22. Ibid., p. xxvii.
23. Ibid., p. 59.
24. Ibid., p. xviii.
25. Ibid., p. xxvi.
26. Ibid., p. xi.
27. John McGrath, *The Bone Won't Break: On Theatre and Hope in Hard Times* (London: Methuen, 1990).
28. John McGrath, *Naked Thoughts that Roam About: Reflections on Theatre*, ed. Nadine Holdsworth (London: Nick Hern, 2002).
29. McGrath, *The Cheviot*, p. xxvi.
30. Colin MacCabe, *On the Eloquence of the Vulgar: A Justification of the Study of Film and Television* (London: British Film Institute, 1993), pp. 18, 25–26.
31. John Caughie, *Television Drama: Realism, Modernism and British Culture* (Oxford: Oxford University Press, 2000), p. 204.
32. Ibid., pp. 205–206.
33. Troy Kennedy Martin, *Edge of Darkness* (London: Faber & Faber, 1990), p. vii.
34. Ibid., pp. 7–8.
35. Ibid., p. 8.
36. Ibid., p. 45.
37. Ibid., p. 55.
38. Ibid., p. 57.
39. Ibid., in episode 3, p. 88 and episode 5, p. 145.
40. Ibid., p. 103.
41. Ibid., pp. 104–105.
42. Ibid., p. 78.
43. Ibid., p. 125.
44. Ibid., p. 128.
45. Ibid., p. 141.
46. Ibid.
47. Ibid., p. 149.
48. Ibid., p. 156.
49. Ibid., p. 153.
50. Ibid., p. 154.
51. Ibid., p. 156.
52. Ibid.
53. Ibid., p. 157.
54. Ibid.
55. Ibid., p. 168.
56. Ibid., p. 169.
57. Ibid., p. 170.
58. Ibid., p. 172.
59. Ibid., pp. 177–178.

60. Ibid., p. 178.
61. Ibid., pp. 26–28.
62. Ibid., p. 166.
63. Troy Kennedy Martin, 'nats go home', *Encore*, Vol. 11/12 (March–April 1964), pp. 21–33.
64. Troy Kennedy Martin, 'The McTaggart Lecture: Sharpening the Edge of TV Drama', *The Listener*, 28 August 1986 (pp. 9–12).
65. Lez Cooke, '*Edge of Darkness*', *Movie*, Vol. 33 (Winter 1989), pp. 41–45 (p. 45).
66. Charles Vess, *The Amazing Spider-Man: Spirits of the Earth* (New York: Marvel Comics, 1990).
67. Teddy Jamieson, 'Scotland's Comic Book Heroes', *The Herald Magazine* (Glasgow) 19 May 2001, p. 13.
68. See John Newsinger, *The Dredd Phenomenon: Comics and Contemporary Society* (Bristol: Libertarian Education, 1999).
69. Alan Grant, John Wagner, Carlos Ezquerra, *Strontium Dog: Portrait of a Mutant* (London: Titan Books, in association with *2000 AD*, 2002). The quotation is from a personal letter from Alan Grant to Alan Riach, 24 December 2002.
70. Alan Grant and Cam Kennedy, *Greetings from Scotland* (*Nick Fury, Agent of S.H.I.E.L.D.*), Vol. 2, No. 11 (New York: Marvel Comics, May 1990).
71. Jim Steranko, *Nick Fury Who is Scorpio?* (New York: Marvel Comics, 2000). This edition collects issues 1–3 and 5, originally published as individual comics from June to October, 1968. *Dark Moon Rise, Hell Hound Kill* was number 3, published in August 1968.
72. Personal letter from Alan Grant to Alan Riach, 13 September 2002.
73. Alan Grant, Dave Taylor and Stan Woch, *Batman: Shadow of the Bat*, in *Batman: Legacy* (London: Titan Books [DC Comics], 1997), pp. 141–162.
74. John Newsinger, *The Dredd Phenomenon: Comics and Contemporary Society* (Bristol: Libertarian Education, 1999), pp. 85–86.
75. Alan Grant and Frank Quitely with Matt Hollingsworth and Brad Matthew, *Batman: Scottish Connection* (London: Titan Books [DC Comics], 1998).

Conclusion: the magnetic north

1. Janice Galloway, A.L. Kennedy, Duncan McLean, Tom Leonard, Alan Warner, Irvine Welsh, Alasdair Gray, James Kelman and Agnes Owens, *The Magnetic North* (Jonathan Cape/Vintage, n.d. [1990s]).
2. Michael Long, 'The Politics of English Modernism: Eliot, Pound, Joyce', in *Visions and Blueprints: Avant-garde Culture and Radical Politics in Early Twentieth-century Europe*, ed. Edward Timms and Peter Collier (Manchester: Manchester University Press, 1988), p. 108.
3. John Berger, 'That Which Is Held', in *Keeping a Rendezvous* (New York: Vintage International, 1992), pp. 25–35 (p. 34).
4. Full details of the books by Kelman, Kennedy and Leonard are given in the bibliography.
5. A.L. Kennedy, *Night Geometry and the Garscadden Trains* (London: Phoenix, 1993), p. 34.
6. Ibid., p. 64.
7. George Eliot, *Middlemarch* (Harmondsworth: Penguin Books, 1979), p. 896.
8. Seamus Heaney, 'A Torchlight Procession of One: On Hugh MacDiarmid', in *The Redress of Poetry: Oxford Lectures* (London: Faber & Faber, 1996), p. 104.

9. Samuel Beckett, *Molloy* (New York: Grove Press, 1955), p. 120.
10. Tom Leonard, 'Unrelated Incidents 2' collected in *Intimate Voices: Selected Work 1965–1983* (Newcastle: Galloping Dog Press, 1984), p. 87.
11. Tom Leonard, *Reports from the Present: Selected Work 1982–1994* (London: Jonathan Cape, 1995).
12. Edwin Morgan, *Demon* (Glasgow: Mariscat Press, 1999), p. 5. *Demon* is collected in *Cathures: New Poems 1997–2001* (Manchester: Carcanet Press/Mariscat Press, 2002), pp. 91–115 (p. 93). Edwin Morgan, *A.D. A Trilogy of Plays on the Life of Christ* (Manchester: Carcanet Press, 2000), pp. 50, 163.
13. Edwin Morgan, *A.D. A Trilogy of Plays on the Life of Christ* (Manchester: Carcanet Press, 2000), p. 54.
14. Tacitus, *On Britain and Germany*, trans. H. Mattingly (Harmondsworth: Penguin, 1965), p. 80.
15. Aneirin, *The Gododdin*, a version by Desmond O'Grady (Dublin: Dolmen Press, 1977), p. 19.
16. Robert Burns, *The Letters*, selected and arranged by J. Logie Robertson (London: Walter Scott, The Camelot Series, 1887), p. 68.
17. Lady Gregory, *Cuchulain of Muirthemne. The Story of the Red Branch of Ulster Arranged and Put into English*, with a preface by W.B. Yeats (Gerrards Cross: Colin Smythe, 1976), p. 256.
18. John Barbour, *The Bruce*, ed. W.M. Mackenzie (London: Adam and Charles Black, 1909), p. 7. Book 1, II. 225–228.
19. Elspeth King, 'Introduction', in William Hamilton of Gilbertfield, *Blind Harry's Wallace* (Edinburgh: Luath Press, 2000), p. xi.
20. Edward McGuire, *Calcagus*, in *Scotland's Music* (2 CD set: Linn CKD 008, 1992).
21. Edna Longley, 'The Poetics of Celt and Saxon', in *Poetry & Posterity* (Tarset, Northumberland: Bloodaxe Books, 2000), pp. 52–89.
22. George MacDonald, *The Marquis of Lossie* (London: Everett & Co. [n.d.] 1877), Chapter 28, p. 110.
23. Malcolm MacLean and Christopher Carrell, eds, *As an Fhearann/from the land: Clearances, Conflict and Crofting: A Century of Images of the Scottish Highlands* (Edinburgh: Mainstream; Stornoway: an Lanntair; Glasgow: Third Eye Centre, 1986), p. 72.
24. T.S. Eliot, *The Complete Poems and Plays* (London: Faber & Faber, 1977), p. 141.
25. Elspeth Reid and Flora Davidson, *The Fortunes of Cynicus* (Kirriemuir: Forest Lodge, 1995), p. 98.
26. Edward Dorn, 'Proclamation/15 May 88', in *Abhorrences* (Santa Rosa: Black Sparrow Press, 1990), p. 144.
27. Edwin Morgan, 'Day's End', in *Virtual and Other Realities* (Manchester: Carcanet Press, 1997), p. 98.
28. John Berger, 'A Story for Aesop', in *Keeping a Rendezvous* (New York: Vintage International, 1992), pp. 53–81 (p. 68).
29. Joseph Conrad, 'Preface to *The Nigger of the "Narcissus"*', in *The Norton Anthology of English Literature. Sixth Edition. Volume 2*, Gen. Ed. M.H. Abrams (New York and London: W.W. Norton & Co., 1993), pp. 1756–1758 (p. 1757).
30. Joseph Conrad, *Lord Jim*, ed. Cedric Watts and Robert Hampson (Harmondsworth: Penguin, 1989), p. 362.
31. Ibid., Chapter 21, pp. 206–207.
32. In the *Cantata Profana*, the father fails to teach his sons to earn a living at home. He teaches them to hunt, not to farm. For Bartók, whose very homeland

disappeared under new and different maps or masks of nationality, the necessity of separation was acute. He was 'one of Hungary's greatest sons' but the knowledge that he was born in 1881 'in Nagyszentmiklos, Torontal county, is of limited help, since no such place is to be found on any modern map of the country'. See Hamish Milne, *Bartók* (London: Omnibus Press, 1982), p. 7. Later in his life, too, exile was a forced choice. Marshall Walker's text notes: 'There's also the irony of accidental prophecy in the *Cantata*. In 1940, Bartók became a refugee from a Europe poisoned by hunting and killing. "I'd so much like to go home," he said. But he was never to pass again through a doorway in his own country . . .' Marshall Walker, *Béla Bartók* (Radio New Zealand, Concert FM, 2001).

Select Bibliography

Adorno, Theodor, *Mahler: A Musical Physiognomy*, trans. Edmund Jephcott (Chicago: The University of Chicago Press, 1996).

Amis, Kingsley, *The James Bond Dossier* (London: Jonathan Cape, 1965).

Anderson, Benedict, *Imagined Communities: Reflections on the Origin and Spread of Nationalism* (London: Verso, 1983).

Andrade, Carlos Drummond de, *Travelling in the Family: Selected Poems*, ed. and trans. Thomas Colchie and Mark Strand with Elizabeth Bishop and Gregory Rabassa (Hopewell, New Jersey: The Ecco Press, 1986).

Aneirin, *The Gododdin, a Version by Desmond O'Grady* (Dublin: Dolmen Press, 1977).

Baker, David J. and Maley, Willy (eds), *British Identities and English Renaissance Literature* (Cambridge: Cambridge University Press, 2002).

Barbour, John, *The Bruce*, ed. W.M. Mackenzie (1377; London: Adam and Charles Black, 1909).

Barnett, Louise K., *The Ignoble Savage* (Westport and London: Greenwood Press, 1975).

Bax, Sir Arnold, *Farewell, My Youth: An Autobiography* (London: Longmans, Green & Co., 1943).

Beckett, Samuel, *Molloy* (New York: Grove Press, 1955).

Belford, Barbara, *Bram Stoker: A Biography of the Author of Dracula* (London: Weidenfield & Nicolson, 1996).

Bell, Alan (ed.), *Scott Bicentenary Essays* (Edinburgh and London: Scottish Academic Press, 1973).

Bennett, Tony and Woollacott, Janet, *Bond and Beyond: The Political Career of a Popular Hero* (London: Macmillan, 1987).

Berger, John, *Ways of Seeing* (London: BBC, and Harmondsworth: Penguin Books, 1972).

———, *Keeping a Rendezvous* (New York: Vintage Books, 1991).

Beveridge, Craig and Turnbull, Ronald, *The Eclipse of Scottish Culture: Inferiorism and the Intellectuals* (Edinburgh: Polygon, 1989).

Bhabha, Homi K. (ed.), *Nation and Narration* (London and New York: Routledge, 1990).

———, *The Location of Culture* (London and New York: Routledge, 1994).

Bilcliffe, Roger, *The Glasgow Boys* (London: John Murray, 1987).

———, *The Scottish Colourists* (London: John Murray, 1989).

Black, William, *Macleod of Dare* (London: Macmillan, 1879).

Boswell, James, *The Life of Samuel Johnson* (1791; London: J.M. Dent Everyman's Library, 1914).

The Broons and Oor Wullie, 1936–1996 (60 Years in The Sunday Post) (London: DC Thomson & Co. Ltd, 1996).

The Broons and Oor Wullie, At War, 1939–1945 (The Lighter Side of World War Two) (London: DC Thomson & Co. Ltd, 1997).

The Broons and Oor Wullie, The Fabulous Fifties (London: DC Thomson & Co. Ltd, 1998).

The Broons and Oor Wullie, The Swinging Sixties (London: DC Thomson & Co. Ltd, 1999).

The Broons and Oor Wullie, The Nation's Favourites (London: DC Thomson & Co. Ltd, 2000).

Brown, George Douglas, *The House with the Green Shutters* (1901; Edinburgh: Canongate, 1996).

Bruce, George, Lindsay, Maurice and Morgan, Edwin (eds), *Scottish Poetry 4* (Edinburgh: Edinburgh University Press, 1969).

Buchan, John, *Prester John* (London: Hodder & Stoughton, 1910).

——, *The Thirty-Nine Steps* (London: Blackwood, 1915).

——, *Mr Standfast* (London: Hodder & Stoughton, 1918).

——, *The Half-Hearted* (1900; London: Nelson, 1922).

——, *Huntingtower* (London: Hodder & Stoughton, 1922).

——, *The Three Hostages* (London: Hodder & Stoughton, 1924).

——, *The Courts of the Morning* (London: Hodder & Stoughton, 1929).

——, *Witch Wood* (1927; Oxford: Oxford University Press, 1993).

——, *Sick Heart River* (1941; Oxford: Oxford University Press, 1994).

——, *A Prince of the Captivity* (1933; Edinburgh: B & W Publishing, 1996).

Burkhauser, Jude (ed.), *'Glasgow Girls': Women in Art and Design 1880–1920* (Edinburgh: Canongate, 1990).

Burnett, Paula (ed.), *The Penguin Book of Caribbean Verse in English* (Harmondsworth: Penguin Books, 1986).

Burns, Robert, *The Letters*, selected and arranged by J. Logie Robertson (London: Walter Scott, The Camelot Series, 1887).

——, *The Poems and Songs of Robert Burns*, ed. James Kinsley (London: Oxford University Press, 1969).

——, *Poems, Chiefly in the Scottish Dialect*, with a note on the text by Michael Schmidt (1786; Harmondsworth: Penguin Books, 1999).

Byron, *Don Juan*, ed. T.G. Steffan, E. Steffan and W.W. Pratt (Harmondsworth: Penguin, 1986).

Calder, Angus, *Revolving Culture: Notes from the Scottish Republic* (London and New York: I.B. Tauris, 1994).

——, 'A Descriptive Model of Scottish Culture', *Scotlands*, 2, 1, 1995, pp. 1–14.

Carlyle, Thomas, *On Heroes, Hero-Worship and the Heroic in History* (London: Chapman & Hall, 1897 [1841]).

Caughie, John, *Television Drama: Realism, Modernism and British Culture* (Oxford: Oxford University Press, 2000).

Césaire, Aimé, *Return to My Native Land* (Harmondsworth: Penguin, 1969).

——, *A Tempest: An Adaptation for Black Theatre*, trans. Philip Crispin (London: Oberon Books, 2000).

Clough, Arthur Hugh, *Collected Poems* (London: Oxford University Press, 1974).

Conrad, Joseph, *The Nigger of the "Narcissus"* (1897; Harmondsworth: Penguin, 1988).

——, *Lord Jim*, ed. Cedric Watts and Robert Hampson (1900; Harmondsworth: Penguin, 1989).

Craig, Cairns (ed.), *A History of Scottish Literature*, 4 vols (Aberdeen: Aberdeen University Press, 1986–1987).

——, *The Modern Scottish Novel* (Edinburgh: Edinburgh University Press, 1999).

Crawford, Thomas, *Scott* (Edinburgh and London: Oliver & Boyd, 1965; Scottish Academic Press, 1982).

——, *Boswell, Burns and the French Revolution* (Edinburgh: The Saltire Society, 1990).

Crichton Smith, Iain, *Collected Poems* (Manchester: Carcanet, 1992).

——, 'The Beginning of a New Song', published as a postcard by The Scottish Arts Council (Edinburgh, n.d.).

Daiches, David, *Robert Burns* (London: G. Bell & Sons, Ltd, 1952).

——, *The Paradox of Scottish Culture: The Eighteenth Century Experience* (Oxford: Oxford University Press, 1964).

Daiches, David, Jones, Peter and Jones, Jean (eds), *The Scottish Enlightenment 1730–1790: A Hotbed of Genius* (Edinburgh: The Saltire Society, 1996).

Davidson, Toni (ed.), *And Thus Will I Freely Sing: An Anthology of Gay and Lesbian Writing from Scotland* (Edinburgh: Polygon, 1989).

Davie, Cedric Thorpe, *Scotland's Music* (Edinburgh: William Blackwood, 1980).

Davie, George, *The Democratic Intellect* (Edinburgh: Edinburgh University Press, 1961).

——, *The Crisis of the Democratic Intellect* (Edinburgh: Polygon, 1986).

D.C. Thomson Bumper Fun Book (Edinburgh: Paul Harris, 1976).

Dick, Eddie (ed.), *From Limelight to Satellite: A Scottish Film Book* (London: British Film Institute, 1990).

Dorn, Edward, *Abhorrences* (Santa Rosa: Black Sparrow Press, 1990).

Douglas, Gavin, *Virgil's Aeneid Translated into Scottish Verse*, ed. D.F.C. Caldwell (Edinburgh and London: STS, 1957).

Douglas, Norman, *South Wind* (1917; London: Secker & Warburg, 1946).

——, *Old Calabria* (1915; Harmondsworth: Penguin, 1962).

Doyle, Sir Arthur Conan, *The Lost World* (1912; Oxford and New York: Oxford University Press, 1998).

Eliot, George, *Middlemarch* (1871–1872; Harmondsworth: Penguin Books, 1979).

——, *The Mill on the Floss* (Edinburgh: William Blackwood & Sons, 1860).

Eliot, T.S., *The Waste Land* (1922; Buckingham: Open University Press, 1994).

Euripedes, *Bacchai: A New Translation by Colin Teevan* (London: Oberon Books, 2002).

Fanon, Frantz, *Black Skin White Masks*, trans. Charles Lam Markmann (New York: Grove Press, 1967).

Fergusson, Robert, *The Works* (London: S.A. & H. Oddy, 1807; repr. Edinburgh: James Thin The Mercat Press, 1970).

Fleming, Ian, *Casino Royale* (London: Jonathan Cape, 1953).

——, *Live and Let Die* (London: Jonathan Cape, 1954).

——, *Diamonds Are Forever* (London: Jonathan Cape, 1956).

——, *From Russia With Love* (London: Jonathan Cape, 1957).

——, *Doctor No* (London: Jonathan Cape, 1958).

——, *Goldfinger* (London: Jonathan Cape, 1959).

——, *For Your Eyes Only* (London: Jonathan Cape, 1960).

——, *Thunderball* (London: Jonathan Cape, 1961).

——, *The Spy Who Loved Me* (London: Jonathan Cape, 1962).

——, *On Her Majesty's Secret Service* (London: Jonathan Cape, 1963. Paperback edition, London: Pan Books, 1965).

——, *You Only Live Twice* (London: Jonathan Cape, 1964. Paperback edition, London: Pan Books, 1966).

——, *The Man With the Golden Gun* (London: Jonathan Cape, 1965. Paperback edition, London: Pan Books, 1967).

——, *Octopussy* (London: Jonathan Cape, 1966).

Frayling, Christopher, *Spaghetti Westerns: Cowboys and Europeans from Karl May to Sergio Leone* (London: Routledge & Kegan Paul, 1981).

Frazer, Allan (ed.), *Sir Walter Scott, 1771–1832: An Edinburgh Keepsake* (Edinburgh: Edinburgh University Press, 1971).

Gibbon, Lewis Grassic, *A Scots Quair* (1946; Edinburgh: Canongate, 1995).

Gifford, D. and McMillan, D. (eds), *A History of Scottish Women's Writing* (Edinburgh: Edinburgh University Press, 1997).

Gifford, D. *et al.* (eds), *Scottish Literature in English and Scots* (Edinburgh: Edinburgh University Press, 2002).

Gilbertfield, William Hamilton of, *Blind Harry's Wallace*, Introduction by Elspeth King (Edinburgh: Luath Press, 2000).

Gilkes, Michael, *Creative Schizophrenia: The Caribbean Cultural Challenge* (University of Warwick: Centre for Caribbean Studies, 1986).

Glen, Duncan, *Hugh MacDiarmid and the Scottish Renaissance* (Edinburgh: W. & R. Chambers, 1964).

Grant, Alan and Kennedy, Cam, *Greetings from Scotland* (Nick Fury, Agent of S.H.I.E.L.D.), Vol. 2, No. 11 (New York: Marvel Comics, May 1990).

Grant, Alan, Taylor, Dave and Woch, Stan, 'Batman: Shadow of the Bat', *Batman: Legacy* (London: Titan Books [DC Comics], 1997).

Grant, Alan and Quitely, Frank with Hollingsworth, Matt and Matthew, Brad, *Batman: Scottish Connection* (London: Titan Books [DC Comics], 1998).

Grant, Alan, Wagner, John and Ezquerra, Carlos, *Strontium Dog: Portrait of a Mutant* (London: Titan Books, in association with 2000 AD, 2002).

Gray, Alasdair, *Lanark* (Edinburgh: Canongate, 1981).

——, 'On Neglect of Burns by Schools and His Disparagement by Moralists and Whitewashers With Some Critical Remarks', G. Ross Roy, ed. and Lucie Roy, assoc. ed., *Studies in Scottish Literature*, Vol. xxx (1998).

Gregory, Isabella Augusta, Lady, *Cuchulain of Muirthemne. The Story of the Red Branch of Ulster Arranged and Put into English*, with a preface by W.B. Yeats (Gerrards Cross: Colin Smythe, 1976).

Gunn, Neil, *Butcher's Broom* (Edinburgh: The Porpoise Press, 1934).

Haining, Peter, *The Jules Verne Companion* (New York: Baronet Publishing Company, 1978).

Hardy, Forsyth, *Scotland in Film* (Edinburgh: Edinburgh University Press, 1990).

Harris, Wilson, *Black Marsden: A Tabula Rasa Comedy* (London: Faber & Faber, 1972).

——, *Companions of the Day and Night* (London: Faber, 1975).

——, *The Radical Imagination: Lectures and Talks*, ed. Alan Riach and Mark Williams (Liège: L3 – Liège, Literature, Language, 1992).

Hay MacDougall, J., *Gillespie* (1914; Edinburgh: Canongate Press, 1993).

Hayden, John O. (ed.), *Scott: The Critical Heritage* (London: Routledge & Kegan Paul, 1970).

Herdman, John, *Pagan's Pilgrimage* (London: Akros, 1978).

Hodge, John, *Trainspotting & Shallow Grave* (London: Faber & Faber, 1996).

Hogg, James, *The Brownie of Bodsbeck* (1818; Edinburgh: Scottish Academic Press, 1976).

——, *The Private Memoirs and Confessions of a Justified Sinner* (1824; Edinburgh: Edinburgh University Press, 2001).

Home, John, *Douglas* (1756; Edinburgh: Oliver & Boyd, 1972).

Honeyman, T.J., *Art and Audacity* (London: Collins, 1971).

——, *Three Scottish Colourists: S.J. Peploe, F.C.B. Cadell, Leslie Hunter* (1950; Edinburgh: Paul Harris Publishing, 1977).

Hughes, Howard, *Spaghetti Westerns* (Vermont: Harpenden, Herts & North Pomfret, 2001).

Hume, David, *Treatise of Human Nature* (1739; Oxford: Clarendon Press, 1968, ed. L.A. Selby-Bigge).

Insh, G.P., *Scotland and the Modern World* (Edinburgh and London: W. & A.K. Johnston, 1932).

Jeffares, A. Norman (ed.), *Scott's Mind and Art* (Edinburgh: Oliver & Boyd, 1969).

Johnstone, William, *Points in Time: An Autobiography* (London: Barrie & Jenkins, 1980).

Joyce, James, *Ulysses* (1922; London: Picador, 1997).

Kelman, James, *The Busconductor Hines* (Edinburgh: Polygon, 1984).

——, *Some Recent Attacks: Essays Cultural & Political* (Stirling: AK Press, 1992).

——, *The Good Times* (London: Secker & Warburg, 1998).

Kennedy, A.L., *Night Geometry and the Garscadden Trains* (London: Phoenix, 1993).

——, *So I am Glad* (London: J. Cape, 1995).

Kerr, James, *Fiction Against History: Scott as Storyteller* (Cambridge: Cambridge University Press, 1989).

Kerrigan, Catherine (ed.), *An Anthology of Scottish Women Poets* (Edinburgh: Edinburgh University Press, 1991).

Kiberd, Declan, *Inventing Ireland: The Literature of the Modern Nation* (London: Jonathan Cape, 1995).

Kurland, Stuart M., 'Hamlet and the Scottish Succession?', *Studies in English Literature 1500–1900*, Vol. 34 (Houston, Texas: Rice University, 1994).

——, ' "The care ... of subjects' good": Pericles, James I, and the Neglect of Government', *Shakespearian Criticism Yearbook 1996* (Detroit, New York, Toronto, London: Gale, 1996).

Laing, Bernard Kodjo [sic], 'Jaw', in George Bruce, Maurice Lindsay and Edwin Morgan (eds), *Scottish Poetry Number 4* (Edinburgh: Edinburgh University Press, 1969), pp. 59–69.

——, *Search Sweet Country* (London: Heinemann, 1986).

——, *Woman of the Aeroplanes* (London: Heinemann, 1988).

L'Amour, Louis, *The Trail to Crazy Man* (New York: Bantam Books, 1988).

Leonard, Tom, *Intimate Voices: Selected Work 1965–1983* (Newcastle: Galloping Dog Press, 1984).

——, *Radical Renfrew* (Edinburgh: Polygon, 1990).

——, *Reports from the Present: Selected Work 1982–1994* (London: Jonathan Cape, 1995).

Lindfors, Bernth (ed.), *Critical Perspectives on Amos Tutuola* (Washington, DC: Three Continents Press, 1975).

Lindsay, Maurice (ed.), *Modern Scottish Poetry: An Anthology of the Scottish Renaissance 1920–1945* (London: Faber & Faber, 1946).

——, *A Pocket Guide to Scottish Culture* (Glasgow: William Maclellan, 1947).

——, *Francis George Scott and the Scottish Renaissance* (Edinburgh: Paul Harris, 1980).

Lithgow, William, *The Totall Discourse of The Rare Adventures & Painefull Perergrinations of long Nineteene Yeares Travayles from Scotland to the most famous Kingdomes in Europe, Asia and Africa* (1632; Glasgow: James MacLehose & Sons, 1906).

Locke, John, *Two Treatises of Government*, ed. Peter Laslett (Cambridge: Cambridge University Press, 1690).

Long, H. Kingsley, *No Mean City* (London: Longmans, 1935).

Long, Michael, *The Unnatural Scene: A Study in Shakespearian Tragedy* (London: Methuen & Co., 1976).

Longley, Edna, *Poetry & Posterity* (Tarset, Northumberland: Bloodaxe Books, 2000).

Lukács, Georg, *The Historical Novel*, trans. Hannah and Stanley Mitchell (Harmondsworth: Penguin Books, 1969).

Lyndsay, Sir David, *Ane Pleasant Satyre of the Three Estaitis* (1602; Edinburgh: Canongate, 1989).

Lysett, Andrew, *Ian Fleming* (London: Phoenix, 1996).

MacArthur, Colin, *Scotch Reels: Scotland in Cinema and Television* (London: BFI, 1982).

MacBeth, George, *My Scotland* (London: Macmillan, 1973).

MacCabe, Colin (ed.), *James Joyce: New Perspectives* (Sussex: The Harvester Press, 1982).

MacCaig, Norman, *The Equal Skies* (London: Chatto & Windus, 1980).

——, *A World of Difference* (London: Chatto & Windus, 1983).

——, *Collected Poems*, New Edition (London: Chatto & Windus, 1993).

MacDiarmid, Hugh, *Stony Limits and Other Poems* (London: Victor Gollancz, 1934).

——, *Golden Treasury of Scottish Poetry* (New York: Macmillan, 1941).

——, *Selected Poems*, ed. Riach and Grieve (Harmondsworth: Penguin, 1992).

——, *Selected Prose*, ed. Alan Riach (Manchester: Carcanet, 1992).

——, *The Complete Poems of Hugh MacDiarmid*, 2 vols, ed. Michael Grieve and W.R. Aitken (Manchester: Carcanet Press, 1993–1994).

——, *Lucky Poet: A Self-Study in Literature and Political Ideas* (London: Methuen & Co., 1943; repr. ed. Alan Riach, Manchester: Carcanet Press, 1994).

——, *Contemporary Scottish Studies*, ed. Alan Riach (Manchester: Carcanet Press, 1995).

——, *The Raucle Tongue: Hitherto Uncollected Prose*, 3 vols, ed. Angus Calder, Glen Murray and Alan Riach (Manchester: Carcanet Press, 1996, 1997, 1998).

MacDonald, George, *Malcolm* (first published as *The Fisherman's Lady*, London: George Routledge & Sons, 1875 and *The Marquis' Secret*, London: J.B. Lippincott & Co., 1877; published in one volume as Malcolm, Minneapolis, MN: Bethany House Publishers, 2001).

——, *The Marquis of Lossie* (London: Everett & Co., 1877).

MacDonald, Malcolm, *Ronald Stevenson: A Musical Biography* (Edinburgh: National Library of Scotland, 1989).

Mackay, John Henry, *The Hustler: The Story of a Nameless Love from Friedrich Street*, trans. Hubert Kennedy (Boston: Alyson Publications, 1985).

Mackenzie, Henry, *The Man of Feeling*, ed. Brian Vickers (1771; Oxford: Oxford University Press, 1970).

Mackenzie, Sir Alexander Campbell, *A Musician's Narrative* (London: Cassell, 1927).

MacLean, Malcolm and Carrell, Christopher (eds), *As an Fhearann/from the land: Clearances, Conflict and Crofting: A Century of Images of the Scottish Highlands* (Edinburgh: Mainstream; Stornoway: an Lanntair; Glasgow: Third Eye Centre, 1986).

MacLeod, Donald, *Gloomy Memories in the Highlands of Scotland: Versus Mrs. Harriet Beecher Stowe's Sunny Memories in (England) a Foreign Land: or a Faithful Picture of the Extirpation of the Celtic Race from the Highlands of Scotland* (Glasgow: Sinclair, 1892).

Macmillan, Duncan, *Scottish Art 1460–1990* (Edinburgh: Mainstream Pub., 1990).

Macpherson, James, *The Works of Ossian* (1765; Edinburgh: Edinburgh University Press, 1996).

Maley, Willy, '"Another Britain"?: Bacon's Certain Considerations Touching the Plantation in Ireland (1609)', *Prose Studies*, Vol. 18, No. 1, April 1995, pp. 1–18 (p. 7).

Martin, Troy Kennedy, *Edge of Darkness* (London: Faber & Faber, 1990).

McCordick, David (ed.), *Scottish Literature: An Anthology*, Vol. II (New York, Washington, DC/Baltimore, Bern, Frankfurt am Main, Berlin, Vienna, Paris: Peter Lang, 1996).

McCormack, Eric, *The Paradise Motel* (London: Bloomsbury, 1989).

——, *The Mysterium* (London: Viking Penguin, 1992).

McGrath, John, *The Cheviot, The Stag and the Black, Black Oil* (Kyleakin: West Highland Pub. Co., 1974).

——, *A Good Night Out: Popular Theatre: Audience, Class and Form* (London: Methuen, 1981).

——, *The Bone Won't Break: On Theatre and Hope in Hard Times* (London: Methuen, 1990).

——, *Naked Thoughts that Roam About: Reflections on Theatre*, ed. Nadine Holdsworth (London: Nick Hern, 2002).

McMaster, Graham, *Scott and Society* (Cambridge: Cambridge University Press, 1981).

Miller, J.H., *A Literary History of Scotland* (London: T. Fisher Unwin, 1903).

Milne, Hamish, *Bartók* (London: Omnibus Press, 1982).

Moon, Lorna, *The Collected Works*, ed. Glenda Norquay (Edinburgh: Black & White Publishing, 2002).

Morgan, Edwin, *The New Divan* (Manchester: Carcanet Press, 1977).

——, *Complete Poems* (Manchester: Carcanet, 1990).

——, *Virtual and Other Realities* (Manchester: Carcanet Press, 1997).

——, *Demon* (Glasgow: Mariscat Press, 1999).

——, *A.D. A Trilogy of Plays on the Life of Jesus Christ* (Manchester: Carcanet Press, 2000).

Morris, Margaret, *The Art of J.D. Fergusson* (Glasgow and London: Blackie, 1974).

Muir, Edwin, *Scott and Scotland* (London: Routledge, 1936).

Murray, Les A., *Persistence in Folly: Selected Prose Writings* (London, Sydney and Melbourne: Angus & Robertson, Sirius Books, 1984).

——, *Collected Poems* (Port Melbourne, Victoria, Australia: William Heinemann, 1997).

Neill, Bud, *Lobey's the Wee Boy! Five Lobey Dosser Adventures*, compiled and introduced by Ranald MacColl (Edinburgh: Mainstream, 1992).

——, *Lobey Dosser: Further Adventures of the Wee Boy!* Foreword by Tom Shields, introduced by Ranald MacColl (Glasgow: ZIPO Publishing Ltd, 1998).

Neruda, Pablo, *Memoirs* (Harmondsworth: Penguin, 1978).

New Theatre Quarterly, Vol. 6, No. 24 (November 1990).

Newsinger, John, *The Dredd Phenomenon: Comics and Contemporary Society* (Bristol: Libertarian Education, 1999).

Normand, Tom, *The Modern Scot: Modernism and Nationalism in Scottish Art 1928–1955* (Aldershot and Brookfield, Vermont: Ashgate Publishing, 2000).

Okigbo, Christopher, *Labyrinths with Path of Thunder* (London: Heinemann, 1977).

Okri, Ben, *Stars of the New Curfew* (Harmondsworth: Penguin Books, 1988).

Oliver, Cordelia, *Joan Eardley, RSA* (Edinburgh: Mainstream, 1988).

Omotoso, Kole, *The Edifice* (London: Heinemann, 1971; repr. 1978).

O'Rourke, Daniel (ed.), *Dream State: The New Scottish Poets* (Edinburgh: Polygon, 1994).

O'Rourke, Donny (ed.), *Dream State: The New Scottish Poets 2nd Edition* (Edinburgh: Polygon, 2001).

Ostovich, Helen, 'Introduction', in *Ben Jonson, John Marston and George Chapman, Eastward Ho!* (London: Nick Hern Books, 2002).

Pearson, Hesketh, *Conan Doyle* (1943; London: Guild Books, 1946).

Pearson, John, *The Life of Ian Fleming* (London: Jonathan Cape, 1966).

——, *James Bond: The Authorized Biography of 007* (London: Sidgwick & Jackson, 1973).

Petrie, Duncan, *Screening Scotland* (London: British Film Institute, 2000).

Phillips, Adam, *The Beast in the Nursery* (London: Faber & Faber, 1998).

Pilger, John, *The New Rulers of the World* (London: Verso, 2002).

Poole, Adrian, *Tragedy: Shakespeare and the Greek Example* (Oxford: Basil Blackwell, 1987).

Porter, Jane, *The Scottish Chiefs* (London: Ward, Lock & Co. Limited, 1810).

Prebble, John, *The King's Jaunt: George IV in Scotland, 1822 'One and Twenty Daft Days'* (London: Collins, 1988).

Purser, John, *Scotland's Music: A History of the Traditional and Classical Music of Scotland from Early Times to the Present Day* (Edinburgh: Mainstream, 1992).

Reid, Elspeth and Davidson, Flora, *The Fortunes of Cynicus* (Kirriemuir: Forest Lodge, 1995).

Richards, David, *Masks of Difference* (Cambridge: Cambridge University Press, 1994).

Rilke, Rainer Maria, 'The Spirit Ariel (After reading Shakespeare's Tempest)', *Selected Poems*, trans. J.B. Leishman (Harmodsworth: Penguin Books, 1972).

Rodefer, Stephen, *Four Lectures* (Berkeley: The Figures, 1982).

Rose, Jacqueline, *The Case of Peter Pan or The Impossibility of Children's Fiction* (London: Macmillan, 1984; revised edition, 1994).

——, *States of Fantasy* (Oxford: Clarendon Press, 1996).

Rosenberg, Bruce A. and Stewart, Ann Harleman, *Ian Fleming* (Boston: Twayne Publishers, 1989).

Sayers, Dorothy L., *Five Red Herrings* (London: Gollancz, 1931).

Schama, Simon, *Landscape and Memory* (London: HarperCollins, 1995).

Scott, Alexander, *The Collected Poems*, ed. David S. Robb (Edinburgh: Mercat Press, 1994).

Scott, Michael, *Tom Cringle's Log*, introduction by Richard Armstrong (London: J.M. Dent, Everyman's Library, 1969).

Scott, Sir Walter, *Minstrelsy of the Scottish Border* (Kelso: James Ballantyne, 1802–1803).

——, *Peveril of the Peak* (1822; in the Border Edition [24 vols, Vol. 15], with introductory essay and notes by Andrew Lang, London: Macmillan & Co., 1901).

——, *The Lay of the Last Minstrel* Canto 6, in *The Poetical Works of Sir Walter Scott* (London: Macmillan, 1906).

——, *The Heart of Midlothian*, ed. Claire Lamont (1818; Oxford and New York: Oxford University Press, 1982).

——, *The Bride of Lammermoor* (1819; Edinburgh: Edinburgh University Press; New York: Columbia University Press, 1995).

——, *Redgauntlet* (1824; Edinburgh: Edinburgh University Press, 1997).

——, *Rob Roy* (1817; Oxford: Oxford University Press, 1998).

——, *Waverley or ' 'Tis Sixty Years Since'* (1814; Oxford: Oxford University Press, 1998).

Shakespeare, W., *The Complete Works*, ed. Peter Alexander (London; Glasgow: Collins, 1954).

Sharp, Alan, *The Green Tree in Gedde* (Glasgow: Drew, 1965).

——, *The Wind Shifts* (London: New England Library, 1967).

Shelley, Mary, *Frankenstein* (1818; Oxford; New York: Oxford University Press, 1998).

Smith, G. Gregory, *Scottish Literature: Character and Influence* (London: Macmillan, 1919).

Smith, Sydney Goodsir, *A Short Introduction to Scottish Literature* (Edinburgh: Serif Books, 1951).

Spark, Muriel, *The Ballad of Peckham Rye* (London: Macmillan, 1960).

——, *The Prime of Miss Jean Brodie* (London: Macmillan, 1961).

Steranko, Jim, *Nick Fury Who is Scorpio?* (New York: Marvel Comics, 2000).

Stevenson, Robert Louis, *Travels with a Donkey in the Cervennes* (London: Kegan Paul, 1879).

——, *Kidnapped* (1886; London: Penguin, 1994).

——, *Dracula*, ed. Glennis Byron (1897; Peterborough, Ontario: Broadview Press, 1997).

——, *Treasure Island* (1883; London: Penguin, 1999).

——, *The Strange Tale of Dr Jekyll and Mr Hyde* (1886; London: Penguin, 2002).

Stoker, Bram, *Dracula*, ed. Glennis Byron (1897; Peterborough, Ontario: Broadview Press, 1997).

——, *The Bram Stoker Bedside Companion: 10 Stories by the Author of Dracula*, ed. Charles Osborne (London: Victor Gollancz, 1973).

——, *The Mystery of the Sea* (1902; Guernsey, Channel Islands: Sutton Publishing, 1997).

Stowe, Harriet Beecher, *Sunny Memories* (Boston: Phillips, Sampson and Company, 1854).

Sutherland, John, *The Life of Walter Scott* (Oxford: Blackwell, 1995).

Swan, Michael, *The Marches of El Dorado* (1958; Harmondsworth: Penguin, 1961).

Tacitus, *On Britain and Germany*, trans. H. Mattingly (Harmondsworth: Penguin, 1965).

Thomson, James, *The Seasons* (1730; Oxford: Clarendon Press, 1972).

Timms, Edward and Collier, Peter (eds), *Visions and Blueprints: Avant-garde Culture and Radical Politics in Early Twentieth-century Europe* (Manchester: Manchester University Press, 1988).

Tutuola, Amos, *The Palm-Wine Drinkard* (1952; London: Faber & Faber, 1977).

Twain, Mark, *The Adventures of Huckleberry Finn* (1855; Harmondsworth: Puffin, 1967).

——, *Life on the Mississippi*, ed. James M. Cox (Harmondsworth: Penguin Books, 1984).

Verne, Jules, *The Underground City or The Black Indies (Sometimes Called The Child of the Cavern) [or, Strange Doings Underground]*, trans. W.H.G. Kingston (London: S. Low, Marston, Searle and Rivington, 1877) [available online from Project Gutenberg, website http://promo.net/pg/].

Vess, Charles, *The Amazing Spider-man: Spirits of the Earth* (New York: Marvel Comics, 1990).

Victoria, Queen of Great Britain, *Leaves from the Journal of Our Life in the Highlands* (London: Smith, Elder & Co., 1869).

Wagner, John and Grant, Alan, *The Bogie Man: The Manhattan Project* (London: Tundra Publishing, 1992).

Wagner, John, Grant, Alan, and Smith, Robin, *The Bogie Man* (Glasgow: Fat Man Press, 1989–1990).

——, *The Bogie Man: Chinatoon* (London: Tundra Publishing, 1993).

Walker, Marshall, *Scottish Literature since 1707* (London and New York: Longman, 1996).

Wallace-Crabbe, Chris, *For Crying Out Loud* (Oxford: Oxford University Press, 1990).

Watson, Roderick, *The Literature of Scotland* (Basingstoke: Macmillan, 1984).

Welsh, Alexander, *The Hero of the Waverley Novels* (New York: Atheneum, 1968).

Welsh, Irvine, *Trainspotting* (London: Minerva, 1994).

Winstanley, Lilian, *"Hamlet" and the Scottish Succession* (Cambridge: Cambridge University Press, 1921).

Wittig, Kurt, *The Scottish Tradition in Literature* (Edinburgh: Oliver & Boyd, 1958).

Select Discography

Composers

Bantock, Sir Granville, *Celtic Symphony*, Hyperion CDA66450.
Bartók, Béla, *Cantata Profana*, Deutsche Gramophon 457 756-2.
Bax, Arnold, *Symphony No. 3*, CHANDOS CHAN8454.
——, *Harp Quintet*, CHANDOS CHAN8391.
Beamish, Sally, *River*, BIS-CD-971.
——, *Bridging the Day*, BIS-CD-1171.
——, *The Imagined Sound of Sun on Stone*, BI-CD-1161.
Bruch, Max, *Scottish Fantasia*, Decca 425 035-2.
Chisholm, Erik, *Piano Concerto No. 1; Eight Piano Works*, DRD0174.
——, *Piano Music*, Olympia CD 639.
Coles, Cecil, *Music from Behind the Lines*, Hyperion CDA67293.
Cresswell, Lyell, *Orchestral Music 2*, Continuum CCD 1034.
Davies, Peter Mawell, *A Celebration of Scotland*, Unicorn-Kanchana DKP(CD)9070.
Gade, Niels, *Overture: Echoes of Ossian*, CHANDOS CHAN9075.
Grainger, Percy, *Salute to Scotland*, Altarus AIR-CD-9040.
Lamond, Frederic, *Symphony in A major* (includes *Overture: From the Scottish Highlands*), Hyperion CDA67387.
MacCunn, Hamish, *Land of the Mountain and the Flood and Other Music* (includes extracts from *Jeanie Deans*), Hyperion CDA66815.
Mackenzie, Sir Alexander Campbell, *Scottish Concerto*, on *The Romantic Piano Concerto – 19*, Hyperion CDA67023.
——, *Violin Concerto / Pibroch Suite*, Hyperion CDA66975.
——, *Alexander Mackenzie* (includes *Burns–Second Scottish Rhapsody*), Hyperion CDA66764.
——, *Concert Overture: Britannia*, on *Victorian Concert Overtures*, Hyperion CDA66515.
MacMillan, James, *Veni, Veni, Emmanuel* Catalyst 09026-61916-2.
——, *Seven Last words from the cross*, catalyst 09026-68125-2.
McEwan, Sir John Blackwood, *Three Border Ballads*, CHANDOS CHAN9241.
——, *A Solway Symphony*, CHANDOS CHAN9345.
——, *Hymn on the Morning of Christ's Nativity*, CHANDOS CHAN9669.
——, *Violin Sonatas Nos 2, 5 & Etc.* (includes *Prince Charlie*), CHANDOS CHAN9880.
——, *Piano Works*, CHANDOS CHAN9933.
——, *String Quartely*, 3 vols, CHANDOS CHAN9926, CHAN10084, CHAN10182.
Mendelssohn, *Symphony No. 3 'Scottish'*, CAMERATA SCOTLAND NYOS 003.
Stevenson, Ronald, *Passacaglia on DSCH*, Altarus AIR-CD-9091 (2).
——, *Piano Music*, Altarus AIR-CD-9089.
——, *Piano Concertos 1 & 2*, Olympia CD 429.
——, *Sing a Song of Seasons! Song Cycles*, Musaeus MZCD100.
——, *Scots Suite*, on *Petr Maceček – Violin/Slavický-Stevenson-Fišer-Hanuš*, Waldman JW 014.
——, *A Wheen Tunes for Bairns tae Spiel* is on the collection *Essentially Scottish* – see below.

Thomson, John, *Three Lieder* and *Overture to 'Hermann – The Broken Spear'*, CAMERATA SCOTLAND NYOS 003.
Wallace, William, *Creation Symphony* (includes *Pelléas and Mélisande* and *Prelude to The Eumenides*), Hyperion CDA66987.
——, *Symphonic Poems: The Passing of Beatrice, Sir William Wallace, Villon, Sister Helen*, Hyperion CDA66848.
Weir, Judith, *Three Operas*, Novello Records NVLCD109.
Wilson, Thomas, *St Kentigern Suite*, VC 7 91112-2.

Collections

Essentially Scottish (includes piano music by Mackenzie, MacCunn, Ronald Stevenson and others), KOCH/SCHWANN 3-1590-2H1.
Piano Music from Scotland (includes F.G. Scott song-settings transcribed for solo piano by Ronald Stevenson and Ronald Center's Piano Sonata), Olympia OCD 263.
The Scottish Romantics (piano music by MacCunn, McEwan and Mackenzie) DDD2-5003.
300 Years of Music from Scotland, MMSCD951.
Twentieth Century Scottish Choral Music (includes Sweeney, *salm an fhearrain*) LINN CKD 014.
Scotland's Music (2 CDs), LINN CKD 008.

The booklet notes for many of these CDs are vitally informative and many were written by John Purser (see his book *Scotland's Music*, listed above). As of 2004, no CD exists of the music of the foremost composer of the Scottish Renaissance, F.G. Scott.

Index